Social Psychology
SYP 3000

Compiled by Christina Partin

WITHDRAWN

Taken from:
Social Psychology: Sociological Perspectives, Second Edition
by David E. Rohall, Melissa A. Milkie, and Jeffrey W. Lucas

Psychology: The Science of Behavior, Seventh Edition
by Neil R. Carlson, Harold Miller, C. Donald Heth,
John W. Donahoe, and G. Neil Martin

Sociology: A Down-to-Earth Approach, 2010 Census Update,
Tenth Edition by James M. Henslin

Think Sociology 2010
by John D. Carl

Cover Art: Illustration by Eric Tamlin.

Taken from:

Social Psychology: Sociological Perspectives, Second Edition
by David E. Rohall, Melissa A. Milkie, and Jeffrey W. Lucas
Copyright © 2011, 2007 by Pearson Education, Inc.
Published by Prentice Hall
Upper Saddle River, NJ 07458

Psychology: The Science of Behavior, Seventh Edition
by Neil R. Carlson, Harold Miller, C. Donald Heth, John W. Donahoe, and G. Neil Martin
Copyright © 2010, 2007, 1997, 1993, 1990, 1987, 1984 by Pearson Education, Inc.
Published by Allyn & Bacon
Boston, Massachusetts 02116

Sociology: A Down-to-Earth Approach, 2010 Census Update, Tenth Edition
by James M. Henslin
Copyright © 2012, 2010, 2008 by James M. Henslin.
Published by Allyn & Bacon

Think Sociology 2010
by John D. Carl
Copyright © 2010 by Pearson Education, Inc.
Published by Prentice Hall

Pearson Learning Solutions, 501 Boylston Street, Suite 900, Boston, MA 02116
A Pearson Education Company
www.pearsoned.com

Printed in the United States of America

4 5 6 7 8 9 10 V0ZN 17 16 15 14 13

000200010271685273

CT/MM

ISBN 10: 1-256-83440-8
ISBN 13: 978-1-256-83440-3

Contents

Chapter 1

Introduction to Social Psychology

I guess you could say that I became obsessed with figuring the man out. He was so rude to me in the classroom that day, basically telling me that I had no business in college. I had to know what this guy was about. Was he just a jerk? Did he have a bad day? I wanted to know why he was so hurtful to me. I started asking around and everyone said that he was a great guy. Then I wondered if I might have been the problem—maybe I said something to set him off. I tried to ask him but he did not want to talk about it. The professor later told me that the guy was going through some hard times. Maybe that was it....

—Krystal, sophomore English major

Trying to understand the behaviors of other people can be puzzling. Although social psychologists take numerous approaches to looking at the social world, we all have an interest in understanding the thoughts, feelings, and behaviors of the people around us. You are probably reading this book because you also share this desire to learn about people. You may even have developed some personal theories about human behaviors. Some of these views may focus on a particular person—for example, a "theory" about why one of your friends has difficulty in dating relationships. But you may also have come up with larger-scale explanations to account for the behaviors of many people in various situations—for example, explaining behavior by saying, "It's all about the money," reflecting a belief that most actions are driven by material interests.

Although these personal opinions do not meet a social scientist's criteria for "theory," the general idea is the same: Social scientists seek to develop explanations for the often-complex ways that people act.

In the vignette that opens this chapter, we see a student trying to make sense of another student's behavior. Apparently the second student has done something to her that makes her wonder what might have caused the behavior. At first she relies on the nature or personality of the other person: "Is he just a jerk?" Because the man will not tell her why he was rude, she has to rely on information from

From: *Social Psychology: Sociological Perspectives*, Second Edition by David E. Rohall, Melissa A. Milkie, and Jeffrey W. Lucas

other people. She discovers that other people think highly of him and realizes that she probably does not have the whole picture. Gradually, she begins to put together a story about the man and how his current life circumstances may have contributed to his poor behavior.

Most of us engage in similar efforts to gather and use available information about people to have enough data to reach conclusions about them. In this way, we are all social scientists, searching the world around us for clues as to how and why people act the ways they do. But two crucial things separate social science from personal theories of human behavior. First, social scientists do not rely on speculation. They systematically test theories and often revise them based on what they learn by testing. Second, social scientists do not develop theories about the behavior of a single individual. Rather, social scientists seek to develop theories that explain how and why very different people will tend to behave in similar ways when facing similar situations or when placed in similar roles. Social psychologists develop theories and then test them by using observations, surveys, experiments, and other forms of research. Unlocking these social forces can be very powerful because seeing them helps us predict others' behavior.

Social psychology is the systematic study of people's thoughts, feelings, and behavior in social contexts. Social psychologists approach the study of human behavior in different ways. Some social psychologists focus on the impact of our

Social psychologists study individuals in social contexts.

immediate social environments on our thoughts, feelings, and behavior. But they soon find that even these immediate contexts are influenced by larger social forces and conditions. In the opening vignette, for example, Krystal could continue her social investigation by incorporating additional levels of analysis. She might investigate the larger social conditions that may be exacerbating this person's immediate social problems. Maybe he recently lost his job in a recession, as part of a large-scale downsizing at his workplace, causing additional stresses in his life that led him to be more irritable on a day-to-day basis.

When sociologists study social psychology, they emphasize the ways in which society shapes the meanings of social interactions, while also assessing the effects of broad social conditions on our thoughts, feelings, and behaviors. Sociological social psychologists study many of the same topics as psychological social psychologists— for example, emotions, identity, and attitudes—but they use theories and perspectives that tend to place emphasis on the role of society in social processes.

Sociology, Psychology, and Social Psychology

Sociology first came alive to me after watching the film Fahrenheit 9/11. *I didn't agree with everything Michael Moore had to say about former President Bush, but his film made me wonder how much power other people had over me. It's amazing that the president can send a bunch of troops to war, but I can't even get the local government to fix the potholes down the street! I can't even get the restaurant owner I work for to give me more time off when I want it. It just doesn't seem right. Those people are not necessarily smarter than I am!*

—Steve, junior Political Science major

Sociology is the systematic study of society. Society is a broad term that includes many levels of social interaction, from interactions among individuals to relationships among nations. Sociologists analyze social life across these levels of analysis (Aron 1965; Collins 1985). We usually think of society as a larger entity that exists above and beyond its individual members. Until something bad happens to us, we may not think much about the impact of society on our lives. If a downturn in the economy leads to a job loss, for instance, we may blame the government or get angry at "the direction society is going." But what do we mean by "society" beyond government rules and regulations? In what other ways can society affect our lives? Sociologists try to elaborate the specific ways that societal processes work to influence people's lives.

In the previous vignette, we see "society" come alive for a student after he watches a controversial film about the American presidency. Steve notices that some people in our country have more power than others, and he questions whether those with power are actually any better than him. He seems to think that he is not different from the people in power: He believes he has the same abilities as politicians or business owners, so he should have some of the same control over others and over the way things work. Finally, Steve begins to question where that power comes from and who has the right to exercise power.

Steve's experience helps him realize that some people in society have power over other people through the positions they hold. When sociologists study social life, their goals often include examining how people's positions—for example, being married, being a woman, or being wealthy—affect their thoughts, feelings, behaviors, and their power over others. This section will review the different levels of analysis found in sociology, including macrosociology and microsociology. It will also discuss differences in how psychologists and sociologists approach the study of social psychology. Finally, we will review the history of sociological social psychology.

Macrosociology and Microsociology

Our society and culture affect us in many ways; to understand these influences, sociologists study social phenomena in different ways. Suppose you are interested in studying racial discrimination. One way to explore this interest would be to conduct a field experiment in which employers are presented with resumes from fictitious pairs who differ only in race and to assess the number of callbacks from employers for African American versus white applicants. You also might study discrimination by examining how people experience racial stratification on a day-to-day basis; more specifically, in the lives and interactions of people from different racial and ethnic backgrounds (May 2001; Nash 2000). For example, you might find that minority group members, on average, are treated with more suspicion in retail stores than are members of the majority group. Both of these examples demonstrate the same basic social phenomena—discrimination that favors majority group members and disfavors minority group members. The studies, however, approach the issue in different ways.

Macrosociology focuses on the analysis of large-scale social processes. Instead of researching individual thoughts, feelings, and behavior, macrosociology looks at larger groups and social institutions (Nolan and Lenski 2004). Macrosociologists use societal-level data to examine phenomena such as poverty rates, incidence of violence, or large-scale social change. For instance, C. Wright Mills (2002, originally 1951) traced patterns of change in the American economy from the late nineteenth century into the early twentieth century, showing the fall of independent farming and concurrent rise of white-collar professions. He went on to explain the long-term effects of the early American economy on the society and culture of the United States in the 1950s. Mills showed that companies in the bureaucratic age of the 1950s exerted a great deal of control over people's lives, despite the emphasis that U.S. culture placed on independence and freedom. In Mills's view, this converted the American middle classes from independent entrepreneurs to a group alienated from their own labor.

Macro-Level Sources of Information

Social psychological information is all around us. Macrosociologists, who use information that applies to whole societies, rely on a number of sources of data in particular. For example, the U.S. Census Bureau (www.census.gov) is the hub of a great deal of demographic information about the United States today. In addition to conducting a count of the U.S. population every 10 years, the Census Bureau maintains current population estimates for the United States and the world. Census Bureau data is a valuable resource for sociologists interested in studying the U.S. population. It includes detailed information about Americans' income levels, health, education, and housing, among many other topics. Sociologists regularly use census data to track important social issues such as poverty or segregation and to examine broad societal conditions associated with those issues—for example, comparing poverty rates by region, race, or gender.

The United Nations (www.un.org) and the World Bank (www.worldbank.org) provide extensive sets of data on nations across the world. Like the Census Bureau, these organizations allow researchers to examine basic demographic information for all the countries on the planet. Researchers can also use these data to study poverty, conflicts, and other important social issues. Macrosociologists use these and other sources of data to track large-scale social processes.

Although macro-level data may not directly relate to our day-to-day lives, it provides a context for understanding individuals' thoughts, feelings, and behavior. Macro-level data, including population size and literacy and unemployment rates, provide an understanding of the social and economic context of people's lives and the types of problems people face in their daily lives.

Macrosociologists also conduct studies across societies and cultures. There are currently 191 members of the United Nations (www.un.org), representing almost all countries in the world. Sociologists, especially demographers, examine differences in such parameters as fertility, mortality, and immigration rates across the world. For example, when researchers study how resource levels relate to trends in fertility and mortality, they find that some of the richest nations in the world—those with the most resources to raise children—have the lowest fertility and mortality rates (Pampel 2001).

The subject of this book is **microsociology** (the domain, in part, of sociological social psychology), the study of the effects of larger society on social psychological processes. In addition to studying the impact of larger social factors on individuals and their interactions, microsociologists are concerned with the role of the individual in the creation and maintenance of society.

As you can see, both macrosociologists and microsociologists study society, but they do it at different levels and in different ways. Consider divorce as a social phenomenon. Macrosociologists are typically interested in rates of divorce and in how changing divorce rates affect the institution of the family. They may also compare divorce rates by region or across nations in an effort to understand the conditions that affect the rate of divorce in each country (Diekmann and Schmidheiny 2004; Wilde 2001; Yi and Deqing 2000). In contrast, microsociologists would be more interested in the perceived causes and outcomes of divorces than in the divorce rates. A microsociologist might conduct a study in which a number of divorced men and women talk about the factors that influenced their decisions to divorce their spouses. Or, a microsociologist might study the mental health consequences of going through a divorce and whether these consequences are different for women than for men. Both macrosociological and microsociological approaches contribute to our understanding of the social aspects of divorce. One involves societal-level factors, and the other involves the connection of society to the individual and individual-level perceptions—the senses people make of their divorces.

Both the macrosociological and microsociological levels of analysis require some understanding of the effects of the larger society on divorce. Social conditions provide a context for understanding interactions between individuals. In one study, a researcher examined divorce rates across 22 countries, finding that the rates are associated with marital equality (Yodanis 2005). That is, countries in which divorce is more common (represented by rates of divorce) also have a more equal distribution of work between men and women in the household. Hence, a "divorce culture" may affect men's and women's personal relationships in a direct way, giving women more leverage in their marriages. However, individuals may not be aware of how larger social conditions affect their decision-making processes, making it challenging to understand links between macro- and micro-level processes.

Sociological and Psychological Social Psychology

We have defined microsociology as the study of how the larger society influences basic social psychological processes. Some social psychologists come from the field of **psychology,** the study of human thought processes and behavior. There is some overlap between sociology and psychology. Scholars in sociology, particularly microsociology, like those in psychology, look at how the behaviors, thoughts, and emotions of individuals are created and modified by the social conditions in which they live. However, sociological social psychology, as we discussed earlier, is an extension of the larger field of sociology that emphasizes the impact of societal forces—in addition to immediate social contexts—on individuals' lives.

Social contexts can range from a small group of people to the larger culture and social conditions manifested in a society as a whole. In a sense, social psychology

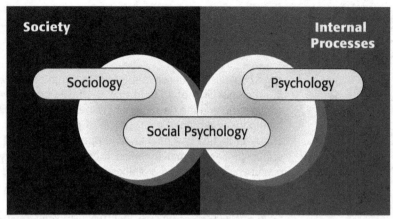

Social Psychology Merges Elements of Two Fields

serves as a natural bridge between the fields of sociology (which focuses on the social aspect) and psychology (which studies the individual). However, sociologists are more likely than psychologists to take into account the effects of larger structural forces on individual thoughts, feelings, and behavior. For instance, sociologists are more likely than psychologists to compare the self-esteem levels of different racial and ethnic groups (Rosenberg 1986; Schieman, Pudrovska, and Milkie 2005). Conversely, psychologists are more likely than sociologists to study the thinking processes associated with self-esteem (Crocker and Park 2003).

As a subfield of sociology, sociological social psychology brings sociological perspectives to the study of social psychology. Early scholars, such as William James (1842–1910), George Herbert Mead (1863–1931), and W. E. B. DuBois (1868–1963), became well known for the ability to articulate how social forces influence our day-to-day interactions, as we will discuss in more detail throughout this book. During the same time period many psychologists were developing some of the prominent research and theories associated with individual behaviors and internal thought processes.

Historical Context of Sociological Social Psychology

The term *sociology* was coined by French social philosopher August Comte (1798–1857). Comte first defined the field of sociology in 1838, later than other sciences such as economics and biology. Comte was a staunch positivist. Positivism is the belief that the scientific method is the best approach to the production of knowledge. Comte attempted to place sociology in the context of more traditional scientific fields. In his view, the complexities of social dynamics would make sociology the most challenging scientific field. We as sociologists think about all the factors that influence what people do on a daily

Psychoanalysis in Psychology

Psychologists generally are interested in internal processes. The German psychologist Sigmund Freud (1856–1939) popularized the idea of the unconscious mind and the development of personality over time. Freud's psychoanalytic method was designed as a means of gaining access to an individual's subconscious thoughts. Psychoanalysis emphasizes the role of conscious and unconscious processes that manifest themselves in everyday life. The role of the psychoanalyst is to access all these inner thoughts and feelings in an effort to liberate individuals from their problems by resolving the internal conflicts that have evolved over time. Hence, the analyst must often reconstruct life events and childhood experiences—a process that may take years of analysis to accomplish (Cockerham 2003). The impact of larger social conditions does enter into the psychoanalytic perspectives, but the analysts tend to focus primarily on internal dynamics. Sociologists, by contrast, are less likely to draw a dividing line between internal and external worlds; rather, we view thoughts and feelings as a continual exchange of information between internal and external sources.

basis—the situational, structural, and historical conditions that lead people to do the things that they do. Although some people believe that social behavior is too complex to understand using the scientific method, we believe that the same features that make sociology a most challenging discipline also make it a most interesting one.

The generation of sociologists who followed August Comte began to make keen observations about the connection of society to the individual. Sociologists such as George Herbert Mead (1863–1931) and William Thomas (1863–1947) helped found a uniquely American school of social psychology at the University of Chicago. Mead studied how social conditions affect our senses of self. Thomas (Thomas and Znaniecki 1958) focused on the role of life histories as a way of assessing the effects of social and historical changes on individuals' lives over time. This research led to the classic book, *The Polish Peasant in Europe and America* (originally published in intervals between 1918 and 1920). The ideas of these early sociologists helped in the creation of symbolic interactionism, a perspective in sociological social psychology that will be reviewed in detail in this and subsequent chapters.

Other major contributors to the development of sociological social psychology include Charles Horton Cooley (1864–1929) and Georg Simmel (1858–1918). Cooley (1909) contributed to the development of sociological social psychology with his theoretical formulation of primary and secondary groups. Primary groups refer to small groups of people with whom we have face-to-face contact, such as our friends and family, whereas secondary groups are larger and less intimate. Cooley argued that primary and secondary groups produce fundamentally different types of interactions. Simmel, a German sociologist at the University of Berlin, viewed society as a complex network of interactions between dyads (two-person groups) and triads (three-person groups) (Simmel 1950). Finally, W. E. B. Dubois, an American sociologist writing in the mid-1800s into the twentieth century, helped in part to elaborate the social psychological dimensions of racial discrimination in the United States.

These sociological social psychologists helped to lay the foundation for the perspectives and theories that modern social psychologists use to study human behavior in a social context. The next section will elaborate on the perspectives that they helped to create.

Charles Horton Cooley and George Herbert Mead are two of the founding sociological social psychologists. Their work inspired generations of sociologists to study social psychology. Their influence led to the development of the Cooley-Mead Award from the Social Psychology Section of the American Sociological Association to recognize outstanding contributions to the field of social psychology. All of the persons profiled in biographies in subsequent chapters were recipients of this prestigious award.

Charles Horton Cooley*

Charles Horton Cooley was born on August 17, 1864, in Ann Arbor, Michigan. He was the son of Mary Elizabeth Horton and the renowned law school professor and State Supreme Court Justice Thomas McIntyre Cooley. After attending the University of Michigan for several years, Cooley graduated with a degree in mechanical engineering. After some work and traveling, he returned to the University of Michigan for graduate work in political economy and sociology in 1890. Cooley received his Ph.D. in philosophy in 1894.

Cooley became an assistant professor of sociology and taught the University of Michigan's first sociology course in 1899. Cooley spent a great deal of time speculating and contemplating the subject of self and its relationship to society. He observed the development of his own children, which he used to help construct his own theories.

Cooley participated in the founding of the American Sociological Society (now American Sociological Association [ASA]) in 1905 and served as its eighth president in 1918. In his work *Personal Competition* (1899), he found that as the United States was expanding and becoming more industrialized, people seemed to become more individualistic and competitive, appearing to exhibit less concern for family and neighborhood. Some of Cooley's other works were inspired by this trend and include *Human Nature and the Social Order* (1902) on symbolism of the self and *Social Organization* (1909) in which he discusses the importance of primary groups. In 1928, Cooley's health began to fail, and in March of 1929, he was diagnosed with cancer. He died shortly after on May 7, 1929.

George Herbert Mead

George Herbert Mead was born on February 27, 1863, in South Hadley, Massachusetts. Mead's family moved to Oberlin, Ohio, in 1870 where his father, Hiram Mead, became a professor at the Oberlin Theological Seminary. Mead earned his master's degree in philosophy at Harvard University; then traveled to Leipzig, Germany, with his close friend Henry Castle and Henry's sister, Helen Castle (who he later married), to pursue graduate work in philosophy and physiological psychology at the University of Leipzig. He later transferred to the University of Berlin to study physiological psychology and economic theory.

Mead's graduate work was interrupted in 1891 by the offer of an instructorship in philosophy and psychology at the University of Michigan. He never completed his Ph.D. In 1894, Mead took a teaching position at the University of Chicago, where he stayed until he died in 1931. Mead went on to make substantial contributions in both social psychology and philosophy. His major contribution to the field of social psychology was his attempt to show how the human self arises in the process of social interaction, especially by the way of linguistic communication (later called symbolic interaction). A compilation of some his best writings can be found in the book *Mind, Self, & Society* (1934).

*Information about Charles Horton Cooley was obtained from the American Sociological Association website (www.asanet.org); details about George Herbert Mead's biography come from Baldwin (1986).

Section Summary

In this section of the chapter, we answered the questions: What is sociology? How does macrosociology differ from microsociology? What are the differences in the ways sociologists and psychologists study social psychology? We defined sociology as the systematic study of society. Some sociologists focus on macro-level processes in society, the study of societies as a whole. Other sociologists focus on micro-level processes, the systematic study of people's thoughts, feelings, and behavior in social context. Although both sociologists and psychologists study social psychology, sociological social psychologists emphasize the impact of large social forces in our lives. Important historical figures in sociological social psychology include George Herbert Mead, Charles Horton Cooley, Georg Simmel, and W. E. B. Dubois, among others.

Your Social Psychological Tool Kit

I remember my first social psychology course. There is so much to know—so many different topics and chapters. I am not really sure how to bring it all together. Human life is so complex....

—Jamal, sophomore Psychology major

Jamal's story is probably a familiar one for many students who are just starting to study the social sciences. Understanding the social contexts of human behavior means that you must be able to incorporate almost all the elements of both the macro and the micro levels of society—how the influence of society plays out in social structures as well as in interactions among individuals. On your journey through social psychology, there are a few essential tools that you can take with you: the concepts and terms that sociologists employ in developing and describing their theories and research. We will be using these concepts throughout this text to help you understand how sociologists develop, carry out, and interpret social psychological research.

The Sociological Imagination

The impact of society in our lives is complex. How do we develop the ability to "see" society in our daily lives? Peter Berger (1973) says that we can see social forces in everyday life through individuals' expressions and behavior. We make choices every day without much conscious thought—such as purchasing food and clothing or spending time with friends and family. How do these choices reflect larger cultural values and norms? Berger stresses the importance of developing the ability to see how what we do in our day-to-day lives reflects larger social forces.

An important tool for seeing such forces in your life is the **sociological imagination**—the ability to see our personal lives in the context of the history, culture, and social structure of the larger society within which we live. C. Wright Mills (1959) argued that sociologists must understand the larger cultural, structural, and historical conditions influencing individuals before arriving at any conclusions about the causes of their decisions or experiences. Specifically, Mills said, "The sociological imagination enables its possessor to understand the larger historical scene in terms of its meaning for the inner life and the external career of a variety of individuals" (p. 5).

The sociological imagination gives social psychologists the vision necessary to assess all the possible social conditions that may influence individuals' thoughts, feelings, and behavior. If we limit our perspective on the social world to explanations that do not take social factors into consideration, we will miss some of the possible causal explanations for behavior. In a classic example, Durkheim (1951, originally 1897) questioned the traditional approach to understanding suicide, which focused on the mental health of the individual. He proposed that suicide rates are influenced by societal conditions, above and beyond personal problems. Durkheim first examined his ideas by comparing suicide rates over time and in different countries. He found that both time and place affected suicide rates—something that would not be true if suicide simply reflected factors internal to an individual. Durkheim concluded that suicide had to be, in part, a manifestation of social issues as well as personal problems. His research showed that groups that are better integrated into society have lower suicide rates than groups with fewer social connections. For instance, married people, who are presumably better integrated into society as part of a social unit, were less susceptible to suicide than singles.

Other Tools in Your Kit

The sociological imagination is a tool that social psychologists can use to understand the influence of society on individuals. What exactly are we looking for? From a social psychological perspective, society exists both within and between individuals. It also takes the form of our positions in society and the expectations associated with those positions, which give us different levels of power and access to resources. When we try to see the larger influences of society, we must consider our relative positions in groups as well as how our culture views those relationships and positions. Society, from this perspective, is only as stable as the people, positions, and relationships that make-up society. In a sense, society exists amid both stability and change, as people either accept existing rules or try to change them to meet the needs of contemporary life. The following concepts will help you know what to look for as you are trying to identify "society" as an influence in your day-to-day life.

Social Norms and Values

Social norms are behavioral guidelines—the rules that regulate our behavior in relationships. If society exists through our relationships with one another, then it is guided by the rules of conduct that apply to those relationships. One of the first things we learn about a society is its rules of conduct. **Values** differ from social norms in that they refer to especially deeply held ideals and beliefs. The laws of a given society codify many of its shared values and norms. For example, murder is considered such a destructive behavior that we impose large penalties for committing such an act. Other lesser violations of norms, such as doing something inappropriate in front of a crowd, may be met only with public embarrassment. You will not go to jail for putting a lampshade on your head, but you may be the target of ostracism from others. Society, then, can influence people's behaviors by establishing both formal and informal rules of conduct.

We can discover a society's formal rules by examining its laws. But the process of identifying informal rules is more complex. People may not even be aware that they are following norms on a day-to-day basis. In *Tally's Corner*, Elliot Liebow (1967) observed a group of poor men living in Washington, D.C.,

Ethnomethodology

Harold Garfinkel (b. 1917) proposed a method of studying society as reflected in our typical, day-to-day interactions that he called **ethnomethodology** (Garfinkel 1967). Ethnomethodology is both a theory and a method of inquiry. That is, it is a theoretical understanding of the linkages between the individual and society, and it is also a methodological approach to studying the relationship between the individual and society. One way that ethnomethodologists study informal social norms is through breaching experiments.

Breaching experiments include any method of violating social order to assess how people construct social reality (Ritzer 1996). Garfinkel was famous for asking students to perform breaching acts and report on reactions to these events. In a classic example, students were instructed to engage in a conversation and insist that their partner explain commonplace remarks. The following excerpt comes from Garfinkel's (1967) book, *Studies in Ethnomethodology*.

SUBJECT: I had a flat tire.

EXPERIMENTER: What do you mean, you had a flat tire?

SUBJECT (appears momentarily stunned and then replies in a hostile manner): What do you mean, "What do you mean?" A flat tire is a flat tire. That is what I meant. Nothing special. What a crazy question.

This interaction demonstrates that there are implicit rules that we expect not to be questioned during a simple exchange. When those rules are broken, there is an emotional reaction (note the hostility of the subject), followed by an attempt to restore order (restating the comment about the flat tire) and explain the interruption; in this case, the subject explains the experimenter's question as simply crazy. Such interactions are essential to the appearance of social order in everyday life. However, we may not be aware of such rules until they are broken in some way. Breaching experiments provide a way of finding and assessing informal norms and values.

---

during the 1960s. The men's lives revolved around a corner carryout restaurant, where some men were waiting for work or just "hanging out." Every man had a different reason for hanging out at the corner—some were waiting for someone to offer a part-time job, others were avoiding their families, and still others were just socializing. Despite their different reasons for being on the corner, all of them converged there on a regular basis, and this served as a norm of street-corner life, although the norm guiding behavior was not driven by the same motivation for each individual. Relationships set up expectations of behavior that can operate above and beyond our thought processes. Alternatively, these norms can serve as a script, offering us a limited set of behavioral options from which we can choose.

Children learn technical and social skills in their interactions with adults and other children.

Roles and Statuses

Another aspect of society consists of the roles and statuses that people occupy. **Status** refers to a person's position in a group or society that is associated with varying levels of prestige and respect. Statuses are often formalized so that the relative standings of group members can be easily identified. In a workplace setting, for instance, a supervisor is paid to manage a group of people and may be given the right to tell people what to do. Other times, status develops more informally.

Our status usually includes a set of expectations about how to behave in a group. These expectations refer to our **roles** in society. Roles and statuses are related but distinct concepts. For instance, medical doctors have relatively high status in Western society. Expectations associated with their roles include looking after the health of their patients. Some business leaders also have high status in society, but expectations for these persons are quite different. In other words, top business leaders and medical doctors may occupy similar status positions, but they hold noticeably different roles in society. Statuses, then, refer to our

Major Institutions in Society

Most of our lives can be studied in the context of social institutions—stable patterns of behavior guided by norms and roles. Institutions provide a context for studying individuals' thoughts, feelings, and behavior. Most societies around the world contain at least the following five institutions:

- Economy and work: Ways of coordinating and facilitating the process of gathering resources and converting them into goods and commodities needed in the society
- Politics, government, and the military: System for preserving order in society
- Family: An institution for regulating sexual relations and child rearing
- Religion: Rituals and beliefs regarding sacred things in society
- Education: The institution devoted to the creation and dissemination of knowledge and information about the larger world

All these institutions help define our roles in society. For instance, our positions in the economy, defined by our jobs and income, have significant impacts on how we live. Our positions also affect the types of people with whom we interact and the ways in which we interact.

---

positions in a group or society, whereas roles refer to the specific expectations about how to behave in those positions.

Organizations and Institutions

Society is also reflected in the regular patterns of behavior and relationships among people. Norms of behavior may include regular work schedules (for example, 9:00 a.m. to 5:00 p.m.) and sleep patterns. Much of this regulation exists within **organizations**—groups that share a common purpose and contain a formal set of rules and authority structure. Our work and school lives revolve around meeting the demands of our superiors within the rules of those organizations. At work, we are paid to produce a product or service, but we must do so within certain guidelines and procedures. At school, we must turn in papers and tests to our teachers to be judged worthy of a passing grade.

When the accumulation of both formal and informal norms produces patterns of behavior for an entire group or even a whole society, these norms, collectively, are often referred to as an institution. A **social institution** consists of patterns of interaction in which the behavior of a large group is guided by the same norms and roles (Jary and Jary 1991). Traditionally, sociologists have divided society into five major institutions: family, economy, religion, education, and government.

Although the norms and rules that govern these institutions may vary by society, almost all human societies have some way of raising children (family), systems of exchange (economy), and an education system. In addition to being found in most or all of the countries in the world today, these institutions have been found to have existed in societies going back thousands of years.

Institutions are different from other sets of relationships in life because they involve complex sets of rules or laws that serve to guide behaviors. For instance, there are many formal and informal rules governing the family in the United States. Laws restrict the number of spouses that are allowed in a family and other behaviors such as spousal or child abuse. There are also informal rules of conduct in the family. For instance, it is not necessarily illegal to have affairs outside of marriage, but opinion polls continually show that most Americans frown on such behavior (Newport 2009). Individuals usually learn the rules associated with a given institution through their interactions with other people in society.

Culture

Each society has its own **culture**—its unique patterns of behavior and beliefs. The norms, roles, and relationships that make up social institutions vary from one society to another, giving each society its own "personality." For example, two societies may have very different sets of expectations associated with being a father. Hence, to study people from different places, we must examine the ways in which these people's lives reflect their cultures. Researchers must also recognize that a given group or society has its own unique set of institutions—different from those that may exist in the researcher's own culture. For example, the media may be a significant institution in American life, but it is probably less important in countries with little access to television or the Internet.

The components of culture include language, symbols, values and beliefs, norms, and material artifacts. Differences in language are often most immediately apparent between societies. We use different words and symbols to represent some of the same objects and ideas. Even subtle differences between cultures can have large implications for how people live their lives. In a classic example, "The Body Ritual of the Nacerima," Horace Miner (1956) described a "foreign" culture in which the primary belief is that the body is ugly and has a natural tendency toward disease. As a result, the "tribe members" visit "magical practitioners" for the mouth and body on a regular basis. Eventually, readers discover that the "Nacirema" are simply "Americans" (Nacirema is American spelled backward)!

Miner's point is that it is hard to understand our own culture unless we step outside it enough to see how what we consider "normal" may look to outsiders. Although we can think independently of the people around us, we often make our choices within cultural limitations. In a simple example, when you are thirsty, you may choose to buy bottled water even when tap water is safe because it is valued as "pure" in your culture; however, this may not be something that

Elements of Culture

Sociological social psychologists must be aware of elements of culture that have effects on our thoughts, feelings, and behavior. These include symbols, values and beliefs, language, norms, and material culture.

- Symbols: Anything that carries a particular meaning recognized by people who share the same culture
- Values and beliefs: Standards by which people assess desirability, goodness, and beauty that serve as both guidelines for living (values) and specific statements that people hold to be true (beliefs)
- Language: A system of symbols that allows people to communicate
- Norms: Rules and expectations for people's behavior within a society
- Material culture: The tangible artifacts of culture—for example, cars, houses, clothing, and computers

The various elements of culture often interact to help us interpret a social situation and decide how to react to other people. People from different cultures may understand the meaning of an action differently and, as a result, may respond with different sets of feelings and actions. To an American, for example, the gesture of raising the middle finger is likely to produce feelings of anger, perhaps leading to an aggressive response. In England, the same gesture may produce no feelings or even be interpreted in a positive manner. Such cultural variations are important to understanding social psychological phenomena.

---

people would do in a society that is more critical of marketers' claims about pureness. Rather, they might see such a purchase as wasteful of money and contributing to environmental degradation from leftover plastic bottles.

In similar fashion, society provides both formal and informal rules for making more important decisions—for example, about marriage and intimate partnership. Some cultures limit marital relationships to a single man and woman. Some Western cultures have recently extended legal marriage to couples of the same sex. Some other cultures allow for multiple partners, but only in the context of marriage. Sociologists try to understand the societal and cultural guidelines that influence the behavior of individuals in a given society.

The social psychological study of culture also emphasizes the ways in which individuals contribute to the development and maintenance of culture in everyday life. How are the formal and informal rules that guide behaviors transmitted from one group to another? How do they change over time? These processes can be studied in the context of socialization among small groups of family members and friends. For instance, Gary Alan Fine (1979) studied a group of youth baseball teams by observing the culture of each group and the changes in those cultures over time. He found that the culture of the group changed as new people entered and left the group but that some consistency was maintained as new members learned the ways of the group from older, more senior team members. These processes, however, were stratified—some children, new or old, had more control over creation and maintenance of culture than others.

Section Summary

The final section of this chapter answered the question: What do I need to know to study the effects of society in my day-to-day life? Here, we introduce an important concept in the field of sociology, the sociological imagination, which is a tool to help you see the larger context of people's decisions and behaviors. In addition, we have given you a tool kit to help you develop the sociological imagination, a kit that includes important concepts that sociologists use in research, including norms, values, statuses, roles, institutions, and culture. All these concepts help to illuminate the effects of society on individuals' thoughts, feelings, and behaviors.

Bringing It All Together

There is so much to study in social psychology. I feel like I can't take it all in sometimes. I look forward to signing up for classes because I know that each one represents another aspect of human life to be studied. I truly wish I had the time to take more classes!

—Jacky, senior Sociology major

Jacky's attitude toward social psychology is reasonable given the size and scope of the field. Social psychologists study many aspects of human life—everything from the social factors influencing feelings of love to studies of behaviors in small groups. You will probably find some of those areas more interesting than others, and you may also find that some areas of social life are not covered in this or any other textbook. As you begin your investigation into sociological social psychology, you should be ready to use your sociological imagination to see how society influences individuals' thoughts, feelings, and behavior.

WHAT IS SOCIAL PSYCHOLOGY?

Arthur Aron and Elaine N. Aron

Arthur Aron and Elaine Aron wanted to get right to the heart of the question: What Is Social Psychology? So they interviewed many social psychologists and asked them various questions: What is the field, exactly? Who were its important founders of the field? What values do social psychologists share?

They concluded that, at the center of it all, social psychology is a field with heart: a passion for the betterment of humankind through theory and research. While individual social psychologists struggle with the apparent dichotomy between theoretical advancements and practical applications, most would agree that the field advances through both. The stories of the founders of social psychology echo this theme of improving the world through a passion for research and theory. Indeed many of the field's founders had the "chutzpah," or courage, to tackle the difficult and volatile social problems of their times in order to make a difference in the world.

First there was Kurt Lewin, who fled Nazi Germany for the democracy of the United States. Lewin could switch from the theoretical to the practical world in a heartbeat. Later there were social psychologists like Muzafer Sherif, who after almost being killed at gunpoint by an occupying army in his native country devoted his life in his adopted country to understanding and eliminating animosity among groups. Currently there are social psychologists like Elliot Aronson, who having solved the problem of school integration over 20 years ago is now studying ways to persuade people to prevent the spread of HIV/AIDS.

You will meet all of these esteemed indivduals—and many others—briefly in this excerpt and later in more depth as you learn about social psychology. Like other social psychologists before you, you may find that the field of social psychology inspirational and its passion contagious.

Imagine you are a skin cell (we know it sounds ridiculous, but do it). Your job is to toss out bundles of chemicals when told to, to shrivel up tight when told to, to stand your ground when bumped, and generally to keep up your borders. Food and water gets delivered when you need it. Now and then a nice thrill runs through you and your neighbors. When you're in the mood, you reproduce yourself. It's a good life.

Given your well-regulated behavior, if you thought about yourself at all you would be unlikely to think of yourself as an independent cell, doing your own thing, free to leave when you felt like it, free to reproduce yourself ad infinitum. You would know that you were part of a body. If you left, you would die. If you quit and the others around you quit, the body would die. If you quit and the others did not quit, you would get shoved aside, you would shrivel up, and . . . But you couldn't quit, anyway. Your place is Left Forearm, Human Being. You know no other life.

Human beings are equally enmeshed in their families, jobs, and society—yet frequently see themselves as independent. In a way, social psychology is something of a crusade: The goal is to make the people of the world realize they are part of a social organism, as much as a cell is part of a body. To social psychologists, it is as though humans are under some spell that keeps them from seeing the social context of their lives. And as psychologists, they want to break that spell.

Why? Some just want you to see the truth. Some hope that when things go wrong, you will know to blame yourself or others a little less sometimes and to blame the wider social situation a little more. Others hope that once you are aware of social influences you will be able to resist them when it would be better to do so. Still others hope you will spontaneously do more for the health of the social organism if you see your dependence on it.

But whatever the reason, most social psychologists strive to make people see that social influences determine their thoughts, attitudes, perceptions, emotions, and even their very selves. Modern social psychology arose in part from the thinking of Charles Horton Cooley, who expressed it vividly

From: Arthur Aron and Elaine N. Aron, reprinted from *The Heart of Social Psychology* (1989).

when he said we possess only a "looking glass self" (1902). Other significant early social psychologists, such as George Herbert Mead and his followers, built their entire theory of social psychology mainly on this theme. The very definition of social psychology is that it studies how people "are influenced by the actual, imagined, or implied presence of others" (Allport, 1968, p. 3).[1]

In every decade, social psychologists have tried to make their point in some new, dramatic, emphatic way. Lewin said it was *outdated* to think of people's behavior as caused only by their inner characteristics. He called that the "Aristotelian approach" because it was concerned with "essences." The new, social psychology approach, he insisted, is to see behavior as an interaction of a person's past social experiences and his or her current social situation. This he called the "Galilean approach," the basis of modern science, which is concerned with "forces."

In the 1960s a personality and social psychologist, Walter Mischel, set psychology on its ear by saying that a knowledge of the inner personalities of people allows even a well-trained psychologist to predict almost nothing about what those people will do in the next moment, whereas knowing concrete facts about their immediate social situation allows anyone to predict a great deal about their behavior. (If you think about it, the fact that you are reading this article right now gives much more information about your behavior—you are sitting still and looking at the page—than any personality test score could possibly tell.)

Virtually all the nearly fifty social psychologists we interviewed in the process of writing this . . . said their main message to students and to the world was, in Russ Fazio's words, "the incredible power of the social." And no doubt we will hear new, more dramatic statements of that point in the future.

It takes a lot of chutzpah to embark on such a campaign. In Western cultures especially, people seem to like to think of themselves as rugged individuals who control their own destiny, succeed or fail according to their own efforts, and base their beliefs and feelings, and certainly their perceptions, on direct, rational, "objective" experience. Is this a good cause for a crusade? Or something more like tilting at windmills? Do you think you really aren't *quite* as tightly enmeshed in society as a cell is embedded in a body?

All right, then cut yourself free and imagine for a few minutes that you are the only person in the world. (Yet you have somehow managed to survive and reach adulthood. Don't ask us how!) Your first thought is probably that you would lack the comforts provided by technology. That is a good point. Science, technology, agricultural techniques—society has developed them all and passed the knowledge on from generation to generation. But that would be the least of your problems. Your very ability to think about the situation would be extremely limited. How would you think without language?

Worse, you would probably be listless and lonely, whether you knew why or not (animals raised in total isolation are not very happy looking beasts either). Any meaning to life beyond survival—love, success, having your efforts appreciated, power, even laughter—almost all the pleasures of life are tightly bound up with other people.

You also would know very little. What is poisonous to eat, when and where it is safe to sleep, the function of your brain, your stomach, your lungs—all these things would have to be learned from scratch, for in fact you only know them because someone else has told you. This authority in turn relied on still others: the few people who actually found out for themselves. If so much of what we accept to be "objectively" true is really social knowledge, think how much more social are your political and moral "realities," such as the importance of democracy or the sacredness of human life.

Now we hope you have gotten the message. But how would you get it across to others? As Ellen Berscheid, an eminent researcher and a recent president of the Society for Personality and Social Psychology, said, "Social influence is one of the great, great influences in nature . . . tremendously powerful . . . yet you can't see it."

Of course, as Berscheid added, you can't see electricity or gravity either. But through ingenious experiments, physicists proved the existence of these basic forces. Similarly, social psychologists are demonstrating the existence of this other basic, powerful, invisible force. . . .

♋ CHUTZPAH: SOCIAL PSYCHOLOGY TAKES ON THE BIG ISSUES

Chutzpah is a Yiddish word meaning the guts to stick your neck out, perhaps even a little *too* far out, and take on something really big. Social psychologists abound in chutzpah, confidently believing that any social question worth debating is worth testing rigorously, if possible with an experiment that sorts out the underlying causes. No area of human concern, from the most pressing practical problems to the most long-standing philosophical issues, is beyond the reach of some determined social psychologist.

A prime example (among hundreds) is Stanley Schachter. So far in his prolific and audacious career, he has studied why people want to be with others, how people know what they feel, what makes people overweight, why people commit crimes, and why people smoke. All these areas have stymied other researchers and the public for years. But whatever the project, in each case Schachter quickly makes breakthroughs. "There's no such thing as a tough area," Schachter has said. "An area's only tough if you don't have an idea" (quoted in Evans, 1976, p. 166). When pressed, Schachter admitted that it's hard to talk about some of these things without sounding pompous. But if I were forced to give advice, I'd say, get problem-oriented, follow your nose and go where problems lead you. Then something opens up that's interesting and that requires techniques and knowledge with which you're unfamiliar, learn them. (p. 168)

It's that simple when you have chutzpah.

The same sentiment was expressed by Robert Zajonc—an eminent social psychologist especially admired for his gutsiness by many of the social psychologists we interviewed. . . . Over the years, Zajonc has been responsible for a series of breakthrough theories and unexpected experimental results, ranging from the arousing effects on the individual of working in the presence of others to long-term changes in the appearance of married partners.

When we asked Zajonc about social psychology, his attitude was like Schachter's. Zajonc said:

All problems are solvable. It is simply a matter of finding the methods. . . . Two weeks before the Wright brothers took off from Kitty Hawk, a man named Simon Newcomb published in *Science* a definitive article showing that it's absolutely impossible to build a machine heavier than air that would fly. So if you did a meta-analysis of all empirical research done before the Wright brothers, the conclusion would be it's pointless. Give up. . . . [But with any problem,] it's just a matter of being clever enough, or lucky enough, to formulate it in a way that makes it solvable.

. . .

In Conclusion: Where Chutzpah Comes From and Where It Goes

. . . To a certain extent it comes from the nature of the field—the study of the interaction between individuals and social forces. In this arena significant conflicts occur; intense influences push and shove, outcomes dramatically affect everyday life. It would almost be hard to plan a social psychology study that would *not* be a potential conversation piece.

Still, other fields of psychology are potentially as relevant and riveting, yet they generally lack this bold approach. That seems to be simply because chutzpah has not been part of their historical development, whereas in social psychology a generous display of chutzpah has been a social norm from the beginning. Idealistic graduate students with unusual ideas to test were sought and encouraged by their departments. Bold studies of real-life situations were more likely to be accepted for publication by the editors of social psychology journals. And within certain limits, the more difficult and controversial a topic, the more admiration its researchers received when they made scientific sense out of it.

Most of the social psychologists we spoke with were proud of this aspect of their field. For example, when we asked Bob Zajonc about chutzpah, he explained:

I think that I would call that aspect taking risks. You don't do interesting research if you don't take risks. Period. If you just prove the obvious, that's not interesting research. The risks may come because the problem is socially delicate, or the risks may come because the problem is intellectually difficult. But usually problems that involve some risks are problems that involve some payoff.

Every discipline has its own history, culture, and social norms. They decide what is worth studying, what methods are appropriate, and what assumptions can be made. These attitudes are passed on from teacher to student and maintained also by journal editors and the hiring practices of academic departments. One can (and probably should, to a certain extent) think of these as limits or blinders placed on the researchers by their field's culture. But as in any culture, these limits also have value: They save the time of those who come after. They don't "reinvent the wheel" or "go down blind alleys." Instead, those who follow are encouraged to build on those who came before. Finally, if it happens that one of a science's norms is not to be conservative but to attack new problems with new methods, then its culture is encouraging its own continual regeneration by more or less protecting its own members from itself. Now that's real chutzpah!

✑ "WE HAVE A DREAM. STILL.": SOCIAL PSYCHOLOGY PERSISTENTLY TACKLES SOCIAL PROBLEMS

Muzafer Sherif told us how he got into social psychology, or "the study of human relations," as he prefers to call it. It was 1919 and the Greeks were arriving to occupy his native province in Turkey. Sherif was only fourteen or fifteen, but "I was always, even at that time, curious about seeing things for myself." So he went down to where the troops were disembarking:

They came . . . and they started killing people right and left. The immediate thing that concerned me was that somebody else beside me was killed . . . . And I thought it was my friend and that I'd be killed too that day. Then the soldier . . . looked at me for a few minutes. He was ready to stab me. Then he walked away.

That enmity that led people to kill each other made a great impression on me. There and then I became interested in understanding why these things were happening among human beings. I didn't know what profession I'd follow—the technical term for it—but I wanted to learn whatever science or specialization was needed to understand this intergroup savagery. I wanted to understand, and I devoted myself to studying human relations.

We have already seen how Hitler caused many social psychologists to direct their efforts toward understanding and preventing all that nazism had been able to do to a nation of normal people. Sherif's story is another verse in the same song. In fact, ask almost any social psychologist why he or she chose the profession, and he or she will tell you something like "I wanted to understand how people could be so cruel." Or so uncaring. Or so stupid. Or the person wanted to fight injustice, understand prejudice, help people get along with one another, prevent war. Or just help others live a happier, more loving, more fulfilling life. It is not true for every last one of them, but it seems to be true for most. It is as though a large number of social psychologists have appointed themselves to be our species' self-improvement committee.

...

Action Research

[. . . Kurt] Lewin started out just interested in psychology, pure and simple. But the events in his native Germany forced him to look around, and he gradually turned more toward social psychology.

He found racial and ethnic prejudice in the United States too, much as he loved the country and wanted not to see faults. Thus, by the early 1940s he had already conducted the famous study of authoritarian and democratic leadership and was saying that it was not enough for psychology to understand behavior: "We must be equally concerned with discovering how people can change their ways so that they learn to behave better" (quoted in Marrow, 1969, p. 158). By the end of the war, Lewin had become committed to his often-cited dictum that there should be "no action without research; no research without action" (quoted in Marrow, 1969, p. 193).

Indeed, by 1946 Lewin had set up not one but two institutes to create and apply knowledge. One of them was the Commission on Community Interrelations (CCI), which he had persuaded the American Jewish Congress to fund as an institute to study and reduce intergroup tensions and prejudice. For its motto, he suggested the two-thousand-year-old saying from the famous rabbi Hillel:

If I am not for myself, who will be for me?
If I am for myself alone, what am I?
And if not now, when?

At the same time, Lewin founded the Center for Group Dynamics at the Massachusetts Institute of Technology. The site was not accidental.[2] MIT focused on science and engineering—pure knowledge, along with its application. Likewise, his new enterprise would integrate theoretical and experimental social psychology with its applications, by creating "experiments in change":

[This goal of integrating the two] can be accomplished . . . if the theorist does not look toward applied problems with highbrow aversion or with a fear of social problems, and if the applied psychologist realizes that there is nothing so practical as a good theory. (Lewin, 1951, p. 169)

...

The first problem CCI took on was an incident between Jewish and Italian-Catholic teenage gangs, especially the latter's disturbance of Yom Kippur services at a synagogue in Coney Island. Lewin created a team to investigate, and it found that the attack was not so much against Jews as it was a venting of frustration due to lack of adequate housing, recreational facilities, and the like. Accordingly, Lewin simultaneously worked with the mayor's office to improve conditions and sent in a staff member, Russell Hogrefe, to work with the gang that had started the trouble. A year later the gang was behaving in much more socially acceptable ways, and CCI's methods of changing the gang's behavior was later adopted by other agencies all over the country.

CCI also took on the problem of quotas for Jews in the admissions policies of universities. Conferring with American Jewish Congress members, Lewin argued that forcing discriminatory policies to be changed would eventually lessen prejudice. This approach would be better in this case, he thought, than relying on decreased prejudice to lead eventually to better policies. As a result of his advice, the American Jewish Congress brought a suit against Columbia University's medical school and won. Lewin's point—that in the case of prejudice you can sometimes "legislate morality"—proved true years later, during and after the civil rights movement, and was no doubt behind the thinking of the Equal Rights Amendment. (It was also a point that later was to become the core of Festinger's cognitive dissonance theory.)

CCI also helped blacks get jobs at New York department stores. The stores argued that white customers would not buy from black sales personnel, but CCI did opinion surveys that demonstrated the argument was not true.

CCI disproved yet another myth, too—that Jews always voted for other Jews. That study was done by Festinger.

Perhaps the most influential study from this period was done by Morton Deutsch and Mary Evans Collins (1951), on integrated housing.

It was a simple study comparing housing projects in New York City with projects in Newark, its neighbor across the Hudson River. The housing projects were nearly identical, except that Newark's were segregated, with blacks in different buildings checkerboarded around the project, whereas

New York's project buildings were thoroughly integrated. The question was, Did living in close proximity increase or decrease prejudice among the races?

Deutsch and Collins found that integration in these projects dramatically decreased prejudice. Those in the integrated buildings seemed to share a growing feeling of their common humanity. Hostility was being replaced by friendliness. Residents wanted to see their buildings even more integrated. In the segregated projects, whites were more prejudiced against blacks, wanted still greater segregation, and expressed more hostility, even toward other whites. It had always been assumed that whites at least had to outnumber blacks for the whites to accept integration. But in fact, the best race relations seemed to be in a project that was 70% black.

The study bore much fruit, most of it sweet. While one prosegregation group used it for evidence that integration should be prevented because otherwise the races would become too friendly (!), most public officials saw the point. Deutsch told us that because of the research, the Newark Housing Authority, where they did the study,

> found themselves under pressure from a lot of citizens groups to desegregate, and with the research results and I think the basic willingness of the Authority, they in fact desegregated the housing project and no longer maintained separate buildings for blacks and whites.

In those postwar years everyone around Lewin felt the heady thrill of maybe being able to do something about social problems. From 1946 to 1950, fifty separate projects were carried out by CCI. Lewin's excitement about the whole thing was extreme even for him. It was a time of great creativity for him. In fact, some of Lewin's associates think his frenetic activity led to his early death in 1947. Not only was he still an active theorist and a social activist, but he was personally raising funds and maintaining public relations for his new institutes.

Gertrud Lewin, Kurt's wife, reminisced about this period:

> Kurt Lewin was so constantly and predominantly preoccupied with the task of advancing the conceptual representation of the social-psychological world, and at the same time he was so filled with the urgent desire to make use of his theoretical insight for building a better world, that it is difficult to decide which of these two sources of motivation flowed with greater energy or vigor. (G. Lewin, 1948, p. xv).

• • •

To Be Objectively Compassionate or Compassionately Objective

A number of social psychologists believe that the most important thing they can do to contribute to the betterment of humankind is to conduct the most purely theoretical, experimental research possible, so that they will discover principles that can be broadly applied. For example, Lee Ross emphasized:

> I think that the classic experiments that have contributed to theory development are more useful to the applied researcher than any particular applied study that has ever been done. . . . Part of it is that most applied research by its very nature has a degree of specificity about it that makes it not terrifically helpful in the way you think about the next situation. A classic theoretical study may be more relevant to the next thing you do than the last applied thing you do.

> If you to understand why social change has been so much harder to accomplish than all the applied psychologists thought it would be, the answers are to be found in theoretical social psychology, not in probing through the notes of applied psychologists.

• • •

What you are hearing is a caution. Traditionally, science is "pure." Physics doesn't worry about whether its discoveries will help space travel or the energy problem. Those problems are left to be solved by engineers and inventors—the people who apply science. Scientists fear that if they limit their thinking to what is needed at the moment, not only will they not make the type of basic discoveries that in the past have proved most fruitful in the long run, but they won't be as objective, being in someone's pay or focused on some one group's problem or out to prove a particular ideological point.

Alice Eagley, a major contributor to the social psychology of gender, spoke to us at length on this point, because her research is so relevant to women's issues. She said, "I find it is very hard to [present a finding to some people] that doesn't fit the liberal feminist ideology—which I share to a great extent." She sees being frequently misquoted and her data misinterpreted as "an interesting case history of science coming into confrontation with social action." But she has a faith that

> if we are good social scientists and tell the truth—use the scientific method—in the long run that is better for women. To suppress a finding and use some other that some kind of audience wants to hear—I think that's selling out as a scientist. It sells a false reality, and what we want for women, and others too, is to understand the reality as it is and to move in terms of that. We cannot build a social movement on shaky ground.

Still, the caution of people like Fazio and Eagley clearly overlies a continuous concern in social psychology for relevance, a concern for people. From many of the social psychologists we talked with, we could hear the constant struggle between the desire to help and the desire to be what they saw as the *most* help, by contributing solid knowledge and not wishful thinking. . . .

Dalmas Taylor, a black social psychologist at the University of Maryland, has his own resolution of this internal conflict what we will call the "two hats solution." He says:

> The problem is that when you are involved in studying something, it requires a certain amount of objectivity and detachment. When you are involved in pursuing a remedy, there is less objectivity and a great deal of attachment. So you essentially end up wearing two hats, playing two different roles. I think that can be done, but it's very *difficult*. . . . What we have is a series of methodological strategies that mitigate our biases, and I think they perform a sufficient check and balance to let us play this dual role with less concern and less error. . . .

Getting the Fruit off the Branch and into the People

The problem, of course, is that if most social psychologists stick to pure science, who is applying all these findings to the problems that they all agree they want solved? Chemical companies apply chemistry, oil companies apply geology, but who applies social psychology? Some ideas are used by advertising and opinion pollsters, but much of the findings would be best used, especially in the opinion of socially concerned social psychologists, in public agencies and institutions like government, schools, services for the disadvantaged, and rehabilitation settings—institutions that often lack the personnel to find out about or apply social science theory and findings to their problems.

For that matter, even the brightest practitioners and social policymakers tend not to know about social psychology findings, probably couldn't understand the jargon if they did read the research journals in which the findings are hidden, and certainly would have a hard time setting any practical implications of "the fundamental attribution error" or "cognitive dissonance" for their own policy or problem area.

This question of how to see that social psychology knowledge is applied has been of particular interest to M. Brewster Smith, a student of Gordon Allport and a social psychologist who has had a long, illustrious career, including presiding over the American Psychological Association and SPSSI. One of Smith's greatest interests is the application of social psychology to the prevention of nuclear war and to political issues generally, and he is able to point to at least a few instances in which social psychology's ideas have reached top decision-makers. For example, Smith cites a speech by Jack Kennedy in 1963 in which JFK proposed a unilateral test ban treaty and invited the Soviets to take other unilateral initiatives; historical evidence suggests that this speech reflected the theories of social psychologist Charles Osgood on conflict reduction, as these theories were apparently well appreciated by those close to the president.

But Smith admits that right now

> there is not any great readiness of the inner circles to pay much attention to our ilk. Therefore our role in these times is more to arm those who are trying to educate the broader public. To present them with perspectives that have not been front and center, like the inherent nature of the conflict process, for example—White's and Bronfenbrenner's stuff on the way each side sees itself as defending, the other side threatening. [Our goal should be] to get those ideas into the social bloodstream.

But it's a frustrating task for a social psychologist. As Ned Jones put it, "I think we have a lot to say—at least as much to contribute as economics and political science." It is therefore not surprising that many social psychologists believe that if they want to see their work applied, they will have to apply it themselves. For example, Don Dutton . . . is now studying the effect of misattribution of arousal on family violence. Elaine Hatfield, perhaps the foremost pioneer in research on love, has an active marital-therapy practice, wherein she directly applies the results of her own and others' research. John Gottman . . . has helped create marital-communication training programs based on his work. And O.J. Harvey, one of the researchers on the Robber's Cave study, has since worked on applying his theories of cognitive flexibility and belief systems to education.

Another approach to getting ideas applied is to make social psychology research so dramatic and obvious that the applications can't be missed. This was Sherif's strategy with the Robber's Cave studies of intergroup conflict and conflict resolution. And it was Phil Zimbardo's strategy with the Stanford prison study . . . he used his very clear, relatively straightforward findings to try to persuade correctional authorities and other public officials to make changes in the prison system.

Last but not least is the approach of teaching. Social psychologists are, after all, usually professors. During their career they may teach many tens of thousands of students, the vast majority of whom will not become social psychologists but will be in a position to use social psychology personally or professionally. Teaching is obviously an important opportunity to point out the practical implications of theories.

The Well-Trained Mind Bears Fruit

We first suggested that there are two branches to this tree of strategies for expressing social concern: a pure science branch and an applied branch. But by now you can see that it might be more accurate to say there are many branches. Or better, a continuum of branches, bearing social psychologists of all types, from those not at all concerned as professionals with any practical implications of social psychology; to those who are concerned but feel pure research and theory serve humankind best in the long run; to those who are also concerned and agree that pure science serves best *but* make an extra, personal effort to get the pure science applied (we just finished describing that branch).

But there is one more limb to the tree, the branch of direct, applied, or "action research." Applied research uses the theories and especially the methods of social psychology to study and solve specific social problems. In fact, maybe the best way to describe this approach is to say it uses the social psychologist's mind as its tool, a mind that has been trained to look at behavior in unique ways. The applied researcher takes as his or her topics not theoretical issues but questions about how to solve specific problems in a real, struggling, social world. The studies done by Lewin's CCI are a perfect example.

Still farther out on the applied continuum are social psychologists who have so devoted themselves to particular applied issues—such as organizational behavior, psychology of law, health psychology, and environmental psychology—that in many cases these specialties have become fields in their own right, spinoffs as it were from the mainstream of social psychology. (Interestingly, because issues of peace and social justice on the whole lack ready-made social institutions to support studies in the manner that medicine, law, and business fund research, these areas of concern have remained closer to the center of social psychology.)

Most social psychologists, however, keep one foot within social psychology proper, even as they explore the "real world." For example, they may offer themselves as consultants or advisers. Some even have private consulting practices in which they help individuals or organizations. Others tackle broad social problems, like child abuse or addictions. But they all tend to make important contributions just because of the perspective they bring to the problem. When Don Dutton began working with battered women's groups, for example, he was impressed by how well social psychology theory and methods had prepared him to be useful "out in the world."

Another example is Craig Haney. After conducting the Stanford prison study, Haney became dissatisfied with what he calls the "trickle down theory of social change"—that you do the research and it goes into journals and somehow gets where it needs to be. The Stanford study drew media attention and opened doors into government and the courts. But it was difficult to get their message across. Haney's solution was to learn more about law and the justice system, and he has made a career out of "making research results directly available to legislative agencies and organizations whose job it is to develop policy, making results have some kind of relevance to the constitutional questions the court is examining."

As a result, Haney has seen social psychology research on, for example, jury selection appear in places like California Supreme Court decisions. One decision, he says, "reads like a social science treatise. It changed the way juries are selected in California. That time the courts were really listening to what was being said."

Yet another example is Daryl Bem, the magician who developed self-perception theory as an alternative to cognitive dissonance theory. Like many social psychologists, Bem entered the field because he thought it was a way to help the world. Remember how he started out in physics at MIT? The social psychologist who changed Bem's mind was Thomas Pettigrew, who at nearby Harvard was teaching a course on race relations and had Freedom Riders up from the South to talk about the civil rights movement (and who has continued to be a central figure in the study of race relations). Pettigrew greatly renewed Bem's interest in social psychology and brought him, as Bem put it, "into the fold."

These days Daryl and his wife, Sandra Bem, are busy applying social psychology methods and ideas to a number of projects, in addition to continuing their more theoretical work. Opportunities come up particularly in her area, sex roles, in which she is one of the leading researchers. Daryl described several cases to us:

> We were asked by the Equal Employment Opportunity Commission to demonstrate that AT&T's advertising practices were perpetuating the segregation of jobs by always showing operators were female and linemen were men. We demonstrated the effect of that in a very simple study. And we won the case. We've done that three times in three different contexts. We consulted for the Highway Patrol in California—there are now women patrol officers. I have the feeling that it's the methods we apply that make the difference. But the results of the studies have the direct effects.

You recall Elliot Aronson, the former student of Leon Festinger who has earned a reputation as one of the outstanding experimentalists in the field. As a young assistant professor at Harvard, Aronson met one of the most senior members of the department, Gordon Allport. Allport had a strong sense of social commitment. For years, Aronson had always thought, as Festinger did, that it was enough to do the research and let someone else apply it. But he remembered Allport telling him that unless you apply the knowledge yourself, no one else will. That thought nagged Aronson, and so about fifteen years ago he substantially broadened the focus of his career.

He had been doing experimental work exclusively, on interpersonal attraction and self-esteem, at the University of Texas, when he became aware of problems in Austin's schools because of desegregation. In some schools, students of different races were staying particularly separate and hostile to each other. This situation tended to lower the self-esteem of the minority-race students, thus hurting their classroom performance and education (and their self-esteem still further)—hardly the intent of desegregation. When violence finally broke out, Aronson got involved and was permanently changed by the experience. He reports:

> My interest in self-esteem made it easy for me to jump into the school system when there was a crisis because of desegregation. But my actual involvement happened by accident. Austin was being desegregated and had riots. One of my former students was the assistant superintendent of schools for Austin, and he had heard me say many times in lectures how applicable this stuff is, so he thought of me to help solve this crisis. Then, once I'd tasted the experience of actually solving a crisis, Gordon Allport's influence became vivid. The laboratory seemed dull after that. Once we got significant results, instead of looking for another hypothesis to test in the laboratory, I was looking for another crisis to solve.

Essentially what Aronson did was apply the lesson from Robber's Cave. Do you remember what finally stopped the war between the Eagles and the Rattlers? A superordinate goal. Aronson decided that the goal for students is to learn. Thus he developed the "jigsaw classroom" (Aronson & Bridgeman, 1979), a method that forces students to cooperate in their learning.

Students meet in a six-person learning groups in which each has one part of the written lesson and teaches it to the others. For the group to get the whole lesson, all its members have to be allowed to present and everyone has to listen to everyone else, regardless of race or ethnic background. Evaluations of the program show that it greatly increases participation by those previously excluded, obviously, and also raises self-esteem, liking for school, positive inter- and intraethnic perceptions, and empathy. Members of minorities also get better grades.

While still an experimentalist, Aronson is now also involved in using social psychology knowledge about attitude change and social cognition to get socioeconomically lower households to make use of energy-efficient technology that is available for free but that up to now has not been adopted by most such households. And most recently he has begun a research project to evaluate the potential application of social psychology principles to making AIDS education more effective.

All in all, he feels the focus of his excitement has shifted from the *process* of research to its *outcome,* to the changes research can make in society:

> The whole idea for me now is to take research beyond the demonstration phase. Since 1971 I've spent a lot of my time in the office of school princi-

pals, trying to get them to understand why the jigsaw classroom would be useful in their schools—and failing more often than succeeding. I don't enjoy that process very much. But the beauty of jigsaw is not that it discovered something new. The beauty of jigsaw is that it packaged some knowledge in a way that works (the evaluations are superb) and that it is easy to use.

Another beauty of the jigsaw classroom for Aronson is the knowledge that it has made a difference in people's lives. He notes, "I still get letters from some of those kids in the classrooms, ones who are now in law school or in medical school, but who say they never would've gotten beyond the eighth grade if it hadn't been for that jigsaw experience."

As a result of his experiences applying social psychology, Aronson's viewpoint on social psychology's role in social change has altered markedly. Says he: "I obviously think it should be a lot stronger than it is now. There should be social psychologists in high-level positions in government."

He seems to be right, if you consider another example—Herbert Kelman—who is merely trying to use social psychology to maintain world peace.

· · ·

Kelman has done most of his workshops with Palestinians and Israelis. Some have been with Egyptians and Israelis and with Greek and Turkish Cypriots. Notes Kelman:

> The whole effort here is designed not just as a learning experience for the participants but as a contribution to the larger political process.

> An example would be a workshop in which Palestinians come to the point where they can see that, for the Israelis, Zionism is a positive concept, that it is an expression of national liberation. They don't become Zionist. They still see it as inimical to their own interest. But they begin to understand that the meaning of Zionism isn't exhausted by the destruction of the Palestinians. And conversely, Israelis begin to understand what the PLO (Palestine Liberation Organization) means to the Palestinians. Again, they don't become supportive of the PLO. But they begin to see that the PLO is not just an agency dedicated to the destruction of Israel, but also a movement of national liberation and self-expression for the Palestinians. That Palestinians who identify with the PLO do so for positive reasons.

> This then leads to the next step. It is possible for an Israeli to be Zionist and for a Palestinian to be a supporter of the PLO and yet be interested in peace. In order to have peace, your enemy doesn't have to abandon his ideology, his commitment.

Mostly Kelman has worked with people who have influence in the decision-making process, sometimes even parliamentarians or party leaders (top leaders being, actually, poor candidates for the process because they "can't just toy with ideas . . . once they say something it becomes a political reality").

Although the conflicts he's worked on are still ongoing, Kelman knows some ideas that have come out of these workshops have reached decision makers and influenced their decisions. The changes have been small, but he sees an impact. And he finds personal satisfaction.

> I'm using everything that I am and that I have. Whatever knowledge and skills and experience and credibility I've built up over the years—I'm utilizing all of it in trying to make a contribution to the resolution of international conflict.

That seems to be a fairly concise description of a fulfilling career. Social psychologists seem to have a lot of such careers, perhaps because so many of them have devoted their lives to trying to help others while simultaneously using their minds to their utmost, with chutzpah and daring, in a cooperative (or playfully competitive) spirit with other bright, sociable people. Whether they choose to pursue pure research with the faith that deep knowledge best serves humankind or take their research out into the schools and social battlefields and find applications or use their minds as tools in applied settings—social psychologists generally show a deep concern for others.

In Conclusion: Science with Compassion

We asked Morton Deutsch to describe what kind of social psychology program he organized at Columbia Teachers College when he went there in 1963. His answer sums up this article very well:

> I wanted to create tough-minded but tender-hearted students . . . people that would be sharp and critical and would know theory and know research methods. . . . But I wanted them also to have a tender heart, to be concerned with social problems. . . . Science is very important. But science without a heart can be destructive. And a heart without a mind is not very valuable. So I think its very important to have both.

Endnotes

[1]Although Allport's definition of the field focuses on social influence, among social psychologists he was unusually partial to the role of personality in social behavior. For example, Tom Pettigrew, who was later winner of both the distinguished Lewin Memorial Award and the Allport Intergroup Relations Research Prize, was a student of Gordon Allport's at Harvard. Pettigrew recalls proudly showing his adviser his first publica-tion—a study showing the relationship between desegregation and various economic and other social statistics. The six-foot-four Allport looked up from his desk and said, "This is all very interesting, but tell me about the wise judge, the brave mayor." The important cause for Allport was the person, not the social situation.

[2]Accident apparently helped a little. Supposedly Lewin would not have minded locating in Berkeley, either, with its warm winters and congenial social and political climate. But the proposed center's letter of acceptance from the University of California came two days too late.

References

Allport, G. W. (1968). The historical background of modern social psychology. In G. Lindzey & E. Aronson (Eds.), *The handbook of social psychology* (Vol. I, 2nd ed., pp. 1-80). Reading, MA: Addison-Wesley.

Aronson, E., & Bridgeman, D. (1979). Jigsaw groups and the desegregated classroom: In pursuit of common goals. *Personality and Social Psychology Bulletin, 5,* 438-66.

Cooley, C. H. (1902). *Human nature and the social order.* New York: Scribner.

Deutsch, M., & Collins, M. E. (1951). *Interracial housing: A psychological evaluation of a social experiment.* Minneapolis: University of Minnesota Press.

Evans, R. I. (1976). *The making of psychology: Discussions with creative contributors.* New York: Knopf.

Lewin, G. (1948). Preface. In D.C. Cartwright (Ed.), *Field theory in social science: Selected theoretical papers by Kurt Lewin* (pp. Vii-xiv). New York: Harper & Brothers.

Lewin, K. (1951). Problems of research in social psychology. In D.C. Cartwright (Ed.), *Field theory in social science: Selected Theoretical papers by Kurt Lewin* (pp. 155-69). New York: Harper & Brothers.

Marrow, A. J. (1969). *The practical theorist.* New York: Basic Books.

☙ Questions

1. Why do Aron and Aron claim that chutzpah is important in the field of social psychology? According to their discussion, why would chutzpah be less important in a field like physics?

2. What do you view as the biggest social problem facing the world today? If you were a social psychologist, how would you study it? Would you first test your theory in a laboratory using a controlled experiment, or would you initially do a field study to understand the problem better? (Note: You may want to check out the index of your social psychology textbook to see what, if anything, has been done on your topic.)

3. Social psychology does have a lot to say: to policy makers, to government officials, to the criminal justice system, to the school system, to city planners, to advertisers, and to everyday people. What is the best way for social psychologists to "get the word out"? Should we hire ourselves out

as consultants? Should we appeal to Congress and the President? Should we seek to educate people? How should we do as you suggest?

4. How did your social psychology professor get into the field? What problem is he or she interested in? Is it a research problem or a social problem? With whom did your professor study in graduate school? With whom did *that* person study? Trace your social psychological heritage as far back as you can—perhaps even back to one of the founders mentioned in this excerpt?

SOCIAL PSYCHOLOGY:
WHO WE ARE AND WHAT WE DO

Abraham Tesser and Jinn Jopp Bau

Institute for Behavioral Research University of Georgia

ॐ

In this study, Abraham Tesser and Jinn Jopp Bau counted how often researchers were mentioned in two important social psychology handbooks, identifying the researchers who had the greatest number of citations. Tesser and Bau called these researchers "the most frequently mentioned contributors," or "FMCs." They determined the FMCs' gender and the years in which they received their PhDs. Then, using a statistical technique called Factor Analysis, they calculated similarity scores based on whether the FMCs' names tended to be discussed within the same social psychological contexts. Tesser and Bau's analysis identified eight major areas of social psychological research, who the important social psychologists are, and what they do.

I have been fascinated with the subject matter and theoretical thinking in social and personality psychology since I began graduate school. Now, on the thresh old of a new millennium, it is the field of social psychology as it currently stands that I attempt to describe—because I am a psychologist, I focus on the people that do social psychology. Who are they? Where are they now and where do they come from? What are the topics that drive their inquiry, exploration, and analysis?

A current description of the field should be comprehensive, and there should be some defensible criterion for including this and excluding that. A reflex for many of us is to take a data-driven approach—that is, to focus on something that can be counted and analyzed. In this instance, a data-driven approach may be no more valid than a qualitative narrative. However, it has the advantage of making many of us, myself included, more comfortable.

Where might we find something to count that would give a good description of the field? One could collect new data, perhaps a survey of the membership of the Society of Personality and Social Psychology. Respondents could be asked to indicate their own research interests, the areas they consider to be most important, and the people who they believe currently have the most influence in the field. The result of such a survey would be instructive. However, such an approach is expensive, subject to distortion by subject loss, and likely to reflect mostly the current top-of-the-head thinking of the respondent rather than a more thoughtful analysis.

Another reasonable solution would be to sample the currently available textbooks. The table of contents for many texts, however, are formulaic and may unduly reflect "tradition" in their coverage: in many instances the coverage is more superficial than might be the case in more sophisticated sources. Perhaps the ideal approach would be to sample the authors and content of our best journals. This would be timely, and the content would have the appropriate depth. Regrettably, however, such an approach would have required more resources than I had for this particular project. I settled on a compromise somewhere between the textbook approach and the journal approach. Much of what follows is based on analysis of the author index of two recently published handbooks of social psychology: *Handbook of Social Psychology* (Gilbert et al., 1998) and *Social Psychology: Handbook of Basic Principles* (Higgins & Kruglanski, 1996).

The fourth edition of the *Handbook of Social Psychology* (GFL Handbook; Gilbert et al., 1998) was published in 1998 by McGraw-Hill. It was edited by Daniel T. Gilbert, Susan T. Fiske, and Gardner Lindzey and consists of 2 volumes and 37 chapters. The GFL Handbook, starting with the first edition in 1935, has been a standard reference work in social psychology. It is intended to cover the breadth of the field. I believe that the McGraw-Hill volumes are highly successful in achieving their goals. The current edition, was, at the time of this writing, the most timely and comprehensive single collection for serious scholarship in social psychology that was

From: Abraham Tesser and Jinn Jopp Bau, reprinted from *Personality and Social Psychology Review* 6, no. 1 (February 2002), by permission of Sage Publications, Inc.

available. Moreover, the authors are recognized experts in each of their fields.

Any one work is likely to reflect, at least in part, idiosyncrasies associated with the editors, specific authors, and publishers. To derive a more general picture it is probably prudent to have at least one other comprehensive description of the field from which to draw. The Higgins and Kruglanski (1996) handbook, *Social Psychology: Handbook of Basic Principles* (HK Handbook) published by Guilford Press, appeared in 1996. This single-volume handbook contains 28 chapters and also attempts a comprehensive view of the field of social psychology but from a different perspective. Instead of an organization around areas of social psychology, this volume is organized around basic principals and processes. According to the authors' preface, other works of this type focused on social psychological phenomena and social issues. The HK Handbook "complements these by searching for specific principles underlying many different social-psychological phenomena rather than focusing on the phenomena themselves" (Higgins & Kruglanski, 1996, p. vii). Like the GFL Handbook, the HK Handbook is a well-respected source work. It is edited and written by some of the field's best-known experts. Because the handbooks differ with respect to organization, editors, authors (to some extent), and publisher, what is common to both volumes should give us a more general view of social psychology in the closing decade of the second millennium than either volume considered by itself.

❧ WHO ARE WE?

The first set of questions that I address concern the people who are currently influential in the construction of our discipline. It turns out that there are a lot more people contributing to the discipline than I would have guessed. In the GFL Handbook there are over 10,000 persons (10,020 to be exact) named in the index as being cited in the text at least once. However, the number of contributors falls quickly as we raise the number of mentions. (Note that I use the word *mentions* as shorthand for the number of pages on which a person is cited at least once.) Thus, although there are almost 6,000 contributors cited on only one page of the text (5,959 to be exact), there are fewer than 1,800 (1,760 exactly) mentioned on two pages and substantially less than half that number cited on three different pages. Indeed, the 90th percentile for mentions is somewhere between only four and five mentions over all 37 chapters of the two-volume set.

This dramatic falloff in citations is nicely illustrated in Figure 1, in which the number of investigators is plotted against the number of text pages on which they were cited in the GFL Handbook. In approximate numbers, 10,000 were mentioned on at least one page, 4,000 were mentioned on two or more pages, 2,000 on three or more pages, and so on. So, there are a lot of us. However, the number of us whose contributions are broad enough or important enough to be mentioned in multiple contexts quickly drops off.

Table 1 *Twenty-Five Most Frequently Mentioned Contributors*

Contributors	M N(z)	GFL Handbook N(z)	GFL Handbook N	HK Handbook N(z)	HK Handbook N
Higgins, E. T.	3.33	1.52	75	5.13	141
Fiske, S. T.	3.30	4.10	130	2.50	85
Bargh, J. A.	2.79	1.85	82	3.72	111
Chaiken, S.	2.34	1.85	82	2.83	92
Kelley, H. H.	2.13	1.85	82	2.40	83
Eagly, A. H.	1.94	2.32	92	1.56	65
Taylor, S. E.	1.89	1.85	82	1.93	73
Petty, R. E.	1.77	1.94	84	1.60	66
Jones, E. E.	1.58	2.79	102	0.38	40
Cacioppo, J. T.	1.56	1.34	71	1.79	70
Fazio, R. H.	1.02	1.19	68	0.85	50
Nisbett, R. E.	0.95	1.66	78	0.24	37
Gilbert, D. T.	0.88	1.38	72	0.38	40
Schwarz, N.	0.84	0.12	45	1.56	65
Brewer, M. B.	0.83	1.76	80	−0.09	30
Markus, H. R.	0.81	1.19	68	0.43	41
Ross, L.	0.74	0.91	62	0.57	44
Festinger, L.	0.74	1.05	65	0.43	41
Zajonc, R. B.	0.69	1.29	70	0.10	34
Zanna, M. P.	0.65	1.10	66	0.19	36
Kruglanski, A. W.	0.63	−0.54	31	1.79	70
Snyder, M.	0.51	0.91	62	0.10	34
Berscheid, E.	0.51	1.05	65	−0.04	31
Smith, E. R.	0.48	0.77	59	0.19	36
Kahneman, D.	0.39	0.35	50	0.43	41

Note: GFL = Gilbert, Fiske, and Lindzey (1998); HK = Higgins and Kruglanski (1996).

Who are the people that are making contributions important enough to be mentioned in multiple contexts? To answer this question, we focused on those contributors whose work is mentioned on 20 or more pages in the two-volume GFL Handbook and 12 or more pages in the single-volume HK Handbook. These cutoffs are arbitrary, but they helped us develop a workable sample (*n* = 154 in the GFL Handbook and *n* = 194 in the HK Handbook). We then compared the names on each list and generated a list of all the people who are mentioned on both lists.

Are the same top people identified in both volumes? The answer is yes, for the most part. Almost 70% (*n* = 106) of the 154 persons identified as being cited most frequently on the GFL Handbook list are also among the most cited in the HK Handbook. The agreement goes beyond simply identifying the same people. Even within this highly restricted sample (e.g., 106 out of more than 10,000 in the GFL Handbook), there is good agreement as to the rank ordering. The correlation between number of mentions in GFL and HK is .63.

Table 1 presents the names of the 25 most frequently mentioned contributors (FMCs) across both handbooks. Because the handbooks differ in number of pages, chapters, and volumes, the mean and standard deviation in mention frequency should also differ. Therefore, Table 1 presents the raw number of mentions in the handbooks (N in the GFL, N in the HK), and the standardized number of mentions ($N(z)$ in the GFL, $N(z)$ in the HK). The standardized number of mentions is the z score derived separately for each handbook. The final rank order was based on the mean z score obtained by averaging over the GFL and the HK z scores. (The reliability of this combined ranking, based on the Spearman–Brown formula, is .77.) The top-20 list holds few surprises. It includes Tory Higgins, Susan Fiske, John Bargh, Shelly Chaiken, Hal Kelley, Alice Eagly, Shelley Taylor, Rich Petty, Ned Jones, John Cacioppo, and other very well-known giants in the field.

Earlier I mentioned the possibility of doing the kind of analyses presented here using textbooks or journals as the source of information. Gordon and Vicari (1992) examined such sources in social psychology for the 1980s. In one of their analyses, they rank ordered the 104 most frequently cited contributors across eight leading textbooks of the period 1987 to 1990. In another, they rank ordered the top 100 contributors (in terms of authorship, weighted for order of authorship in multiple author pieces) across three of our most prestigious journals for the period 1980 to 1989: *Journal of Personality and Social Psychology, Journal of Experimental Social Psychology,* and *Personality and Social Psychology Bulletin.*

A comparison of the present FMCs with the lists published by Gordon and Vicari (1992) may be of interest. An overlap between this list and their lists provides further validity for our data. An overlap implies that there is at least some temporal stability in the leaders of the field. It also goes beyond the overlap between the GFL and HK Handbooks noted earlier. The earlier analysis implies some generality across handbooks. An overlap between our data and the Gordon and Vicari data would imply that this list is not due to something special about handbooks but that they reflect the field more generally.

Analyses reveal both temporal stability in the list and generality across sources of data. The overlap among the present FMCs and the most frequently textbook cited authors for the late 1980s is over 50%: 53 of the 104 contributors identified as most frequently cited in textbooks are also among our FMCs. Further, the FMCs identified by the earlier textbooks are higher on the FMC list ($M = .29$) than the FMCs not so identified ($M = -.29$). There is also some overlap between our FMCs and the list of most frequent contributors to the three major journals in the 1980s. A third of the 100 most frequent contributors in the 1980s is on our list of FMCs. Also, FMCs identified as being a heavy contributor to the journals in the 1980s have higher standard scores ($M = .31$)

than FMCs that are not so identified ($M = -.14$). It is interesting to note that our handbook data are more closely related to the textbooks citations list than it is to publication of journal articles list. Interpreting such a difference is very difficult. There are differences in time of publication, intended audience, emphasis on history, and so forth, as well as source. However, it is tempting to speculate that gatekeepers of organized representations of the field— that is, handbook and textbook writers—may be paying more attention to and agreeing on the "importance" or interest value of primary publications rather than the simple presence (frequency) of publications.

As a tribute to what all of these FMCs have done for the field, the complete list of all 106 names is presented in Table 2. They are in alphabetical order so you can easily see if the person who inspired you most is on the list—or, perhaps more likely, so you can see if your own name, your major professor's name, or your graduate school rival's name is on the list.

. . .

CHARACTERISTICS OF THE FMCs

Now that we have an idea of who are among the most influential social psychologists of the 1990s, do we know anything else about them? Yes, we do. I looked up each of the FMCs in the American Psychological Association (APA) directory (*2000 APA Membership Register,* 2000) and the American Psychological Society directory (*Membership Directory of the American Psychological Society,* 1998), checked the Internet, wrote directly to a few colleagues, and used my own knowledge to fill in some of the information about each of these people.

Gender

The FMCs are mostly male, about 83%. Only 18 of the 106 FMCs are female. Clearly the number of women in the sample is not representative of our discipline. According to the 1997 APA Directory Survey (APA Research Office, n.d.), with new member updates for 1998, Division 8 (Society for Personality and Social Psychology) of the APA is 65% male. Overall, there is proportionally twice the number of women in the division as a whole as there are among the FMCs. More interesting, however, is the gender breakdown by status in the division. As can be seen in Figure 1, almost 50% of the members at the Associate level are women. This drops to 21% at the Fellow level, a figure that is only 4% higher than the proportion in our elite sample.

The gender difference has no easy explanation. Indeed, many of us in social psychology are engaged in showing how such differences can emerge even if there are no differences in ability or productivity. Part of it, at least, may be a simple cohort effect. Indeed, the average degree date (see the following) for male FMCs is more than a decade later than it is

Table 2 *All Frequently Mentioned Contributors*

Contributors	M N(z)	GFL Handbook N(z)	N	HK Handbook N(z)	N	Contributors	M N(z)	GFL Handbook N(z)	N	HK Handbook N(z)	N
Abelson, R. P.	−0.13	0.16	46	−0.42	23	Kruglanski, A. W.	0.63	−0.54	31	1.79	70
Ajzen, I.	−0.39	−0.59	30	−0.19	28	Kunda, Z.	−0.64	−1.06	20	−0.23	27
Allport, G. W.	−0.22	0.07	44	−0.51	21	Levine, J. M.	−0.32	−0.21	38	−0.42	23
Asch, S. E.	−0.36	0.12	45	−0.84	14	Lewin, K.	−0.10	0.02	43	−0.23	27
Banaji, M. R.	−0.72	−0.49	32	−0.94	12	Mackie, D. M.	−0.15	−0.21	38	−0.09	30
Bandura, A.	−0.53	−0.73	27	−0.33	25	Markus, H. R.	0.81	1.19	68	0.43	41
Bargh, J. A.	2.79	1.85	82	3.72	111	Martin, L. L.	−0.10	−1.01	21	0.80	49
Baumeister, R. F.	0.36	0.91	62	−0.19	28	McGuire, W. J.	−0.46	−0.31	36	−0.61	19
Bem, D. J.	−0.72	−0.54	31	−0.89	13	Messick, D. M.	−0.79	−1.06	20	−0.51	21
Berscheid, E.	0.51	1.05	65	−0.04	31	Miller, D. T.	−0.06	−0.45	33	0.33	39
Bond, M. H.	−0.97	−1.06	20	−0.89	13	Mills, J.	−0.97	−1.06	20	−0.89	13
Brehm, J. W.	−1.00	−1.06	20	−0.94	12	Mischel, W.	−0.22	−0.77	26	0.33	39
Brewer, M. B.	0.83	1.76	80	−0.09	30	Moreland, R. L.	−0.67	−0.54	31	−0.80	15
Brown, J. D.	−0.81	−0.96	22	−0.66	18	Nisbett, R. E.	0.95	1.66	78	0.24	37
Brown, R. J.	−0.11	0.54	54	−0.75	16	Petty, R. E.	1.77	1.94	84	1.60	66
Bruner, J. S.	0.04	−0.45	33	0.52	43	Pittman, T. S.	−0.65	−0.40	34	−0.89	13
Buss, D. M.	−0.15	0.12	45	−0.42	23	Pratto, F.	−0.95	−1.06	20	−0.84	14
Cacioppo, J. T.	1.56	1.34	71	1.79	70	Pruitt, D. G.	−0.41	−0.45	33	−0.37	24
Cantor, N. E.	−0.64	−0.96	22	−0.33	25	Pyszczynski, T. A.	−0.76	−1.06	20	−0.47	22
Carlston, D. E.	−0.53	−0.77	26	−0.28	26	Reis, H. T.	−0.39	−0.26	37	−0.51	21
Carver, C. S.	−0.34	−0.82	25	0.14	35	Rholes, W. S.	−0.55	−1.06	20	−0.04	31
Chaiken, S.	2.34	1.85	82	2.83	92	Ross, L.	0.74	0.91	62	0.57	44
Cialdini, R. B.	−0.22	0.35	50	−0.80	15	Ross, M.	−0.43	−0.73	27	−0.14	29
Clark, M. S.	−0.81	−1.01	21	−0.61	19	Ruble, D. N.	−0.17	−0.21	38	−0.14	29
Cooper, J.	−0.60	−0.87	24	−0.33	25	Schachter, S.	−0.15	0.26	48	−0.56	20
Crocker, J.	−0.22	0.12	45	−0.56	20	Scheier, M. F.	−0.55	−0.96	22	−0.14	29
Darley, J. M.	−0.29	−0.26	37	−0.33	25	Schwarz, N.	0.84	0.12	45	1.56	65
Davis, K. E.	−0.88	−0.96	22	−0.80	15	Sherman, S. J.	−0.57	−0.96	22	−0.19	28
Deaux, K.	−0.62	−0.31	36	−0.94	12	Singer, J. E.	−0.79	−0.96	22	−0.61	19
Deutsch, M.	−0.29	−0.45	33	−0.14	29	Smith, E. R.	0.48	0.77	59	0.19	36
Devine, P. G.	0.13	0.30	49	−0.04	31	Snyder, M.	0.51	0.91	62	0.10	34
Eagly, A. H.	1.94	2.32	92	1.56	65	Srull, T. K.	−0.06	−0.68	28	0.57	44
Ekman, P.	−0.62	−0.40	34	−0.84	14	Stangor, C.	−0.62	−0.82	25	−0.42	23
Fazio, R. H.	1.02	1.19	68	0.85	50	Steele, C. M.	−0.43	0.07	44	−0.94	12
Festinger, L.	0.74	1.05	65	0.43	41	Strack, F.	−0.24	−0.92	23	0.43	41
Fishbein, M.	−0.57	−0.73	27	−0.42	23	Swann, W. B., Jr.	−0.27	−0.31	36	−0.23	27
Fiske, S. T.	3.30	4.10	130	2.50	85	Tajfel, H.	−0.18	−0.02	42	−0.33	25
Gilbert, D. T.	0.88	1.38	72	0.38	40	Taylor, S. E.	1.89	1.85	82	1.93	73
Greenberg, J.	−0.53	−0.68	28	−0.37	24	Tesser, A.	0.13	0.12	45	0.14	35
Greenwald, A. G.	−0.50	−0.21	38	−0.80	15	Tetlock, P. E.	−0.06	0.26	48	−0.37	24
Hamiliton, D. L.	−0.50	−0.68	28	−0.33	25	Thibaut, J. W.	0.08	−0.16	39	0.33	39
Hastie, R.	−0.22	−0.31	36	−0.14	29	Triandis, H. C.	−0.67	−0.40	34	−0.94	12
Heider, F.	−0.27	−0.21	38	−0.33	25	Turner, J. C.	−0.01	−0.16	39	0.14	35
Higgins, E. T.	3.33	1.52	75	5.13	141	Tversky, A.	0.32	0.40	51	0.24	37
Hilton, J. L.	−0.76	−1.06	20	−0.47	22	Wegener, D. T.	−0.27	−0.16	39	−0.37	24
Hixon, J. G.	−0.90	−0.87	24	−0.94	12	Wegner, D. M.	0.15	0.30	49	0.00	32
Hogg, M. A.	−0.41	−0.68	28	−0.14	29	Wicklund, R. A.	−0.95	−0.96	22	−0.94	12
James, W.	−0.67	−1.06	20	−0.28	26	Wilson, T. D.	−0.62	−0.31	36	−0.94	12
Janis, I.	−0.86	−0.96	22	−0.75	16	Wood, W.	−0.69	−0.73	27	−0.66	18
Jones, E. E.	1.58	2.79	102	0.38	40	Wyer, R. S., Jr.	−0.10	−0.12	40	−0.09	30
Kahneman, D.	0.39	0.35	50	0.43	41	Zajonc, R. B.	0.69	1.29	70	0.10	34
Kelley, H. H.	2.13	1.85	82	2.40	83	Zanna, M. P.	0.65	1.10	66	0.19	36
Kenny, D. A.	−0.15	0.40	51	−0.70	17						
Kitayama, S.	0.04	0.49	53	−0.42	23						

Note: GFL = Gilbert, Fiske, and Lindzey (1998): HK = Higgins and Kruglanski (1996).

for women, 1965 versus 1978, respectively. To look at it another way, the are no women among the quartile of FMCs with the oldest degrees, four in the next quartile, seven in the next, and seven in the quartile containing FMCs with the most recent degrees. We see in the next section that the most productive among us have been around for a while. Thus, although the gender difference may reflect bias, it also may simply reflect the demographics of the field for the period in which the work was done.

It is noteworthy that the female FMCs, as few as there are, are on average more influential than the men. The mean number of standard mentions (averaged over HK and GFL Handbooks) is .34 for women versus –.07 for men. Because of the huge skew in the mentions data, however, the median of the standard mentions (averaged over HK and GFL Handbooks) may be a more appropriate index of central tendency. Here, too, the women do a bit better than the men with respective medians of –.16 versus –.27.

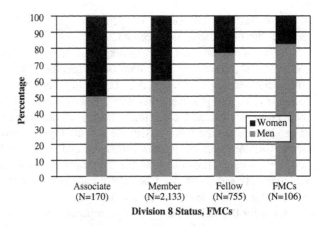

Figure 1 Gender distribution in APA's Division 8 by membership status and in the current set of FMCs. (Source of Division 8 data is an APA Research Office document titled "1997 APA Directory Survey, with new member updates for 1998," n.d.)

Age of Degree

How long have our FMCs been at it? One piece of information posted for each contributor is the year in which his or her PhD was awarded. This distribution of these years is shown in Figure 2 (*N* = 106).

There are several observations to make about this distribution. First, there is some, but not very much, focus on our history. There is very little acknowledgement of our classical roots in philosophy; rather, we tend to cite modern contributors to social psychology. The person with the oldest degree to appear on this list is William James, who received his MD degree in 1869. He is followed in time by Kurt Lewin (1916). Fritz Heider (1920). Gordon Allport (1922), and Solomon Asch (1932); with those five names, we are already into the 1940s.

Figure 2 shows a steady decrease in the number of persons frequently mentioned as their degree gets more than 20 years from the handbook publication dates. Indeed, 88% of this group of contributors were alive when the handbooks were published. This emphasis on the work of contemporary scientists probably reflects a number of things. The discipline has been growing, and there were simply fewer social psychologists around in the olden days (i.e., pre-1977); or, it could reflect the emphasis on newer, often more sophisticated research findings (Reis & Stiller, 1992); or it could reflect the lack of a "standard paradigm" with well-developed historical roots. Therefore, we are not particularly driven by historical tradition as reflected in the work of a pantheon of early giants. Perhaps this is a good thing for a scientific discipline with an empirical base.

On the other hand, it does take some time to build a career. Figure 2 clearly shows a drop in the number of FMCs with degrees more than 20 years old, but it also shows a drop in the number of contributors with degrees less than 20 years old. Ninety percent of the sample received their

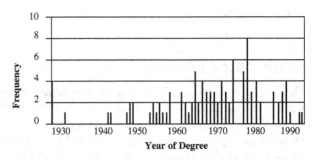

Figure 2 Frequency distribution of year of highest degree for group of FMC's. Note that the year 1930 represents the year 1930 and all of the previous years.

degree in 1950 or more recently. Only 15% of the sample received their doctoral degree more recently than 1985, and 15% received their degree in 1954 or earlier. So 70% of our frequent contributors received their degree in a 35-year window. Half of our frequent contributors received their degree in an 18-year window between 1961 and 1978. The handbooks were published in 1996 and 1998. The contributions of FMCs are acknowledged 20 to 37 years after the degree. In round numbers, it takes an average of 20 to 35 years of productivity to be recognized as particularly influential in our field, and that recognition appears to continue for about 20 to 30 years.

A comparison between Division 8 Fellows (APA Research Office, n.d.) and our HK and GFL Handbook FMCs may be of interest. The FMCs are a bit younger than the Fellows: Using 1997, the average publication date of the handbooks, as the standard, about 46% of the FMCs had their degree less than 25 years compared to about 25% of the Fellows; that is, almost 75% of the Fellows have had their degrees for more than 25 years and only about 54% of the Fellows have had their degrees for more than 25 years—and that includes the FMCs who are deceased.

There is one obvious potential explanation for why our elite FMC sample is younger than our respected Fellows. Once Fellow status is achieved, it is held for life. Persons may continue to be Fellows even after they are actively producing scholarship. By contrast, a particular work does not continue to be cited unless the work is seminal and the topic remains lively. Citations depend on their timeliness and relevance to question at hand, regardless of the investigator's previous achievements. Fellow status depends critically on a corpus of work that may take many years to accumulate.

Even for the FMCs, however, it is unusual to have one's work recognized by frequent citations very early in one's career—that is, within the first 15 years. Therefore, I would like to recognize the eight most recent graduates in this category by mentioning their names in the order of their degree date: Duane Wegener, 1994; J. G. Hixon, 1991; Felicia Pratto, 1988; Shinobu Kitayama, 1987; and the wonderful class of 1986—Mahzarin Banaji, Trish Devine, Jonathon Brown, and Chuck Stangor.

. . .

Contributor Factors

The first rotated factor, at 56%, easily accounts for the lion's share of the explained variance in FMC similarity. Indeed, it accounts for more than four and a half times the variance of its nearest competitor. I am sure that you did not need convincing, but the 1990s is clearly a decade of social psychology that belongs to Social Cognition. There are many FMCs with substantial loadings on this factor. Table 3 lists the 20 FMCs with the highest loading on this factor. The presence of names like Don Carlston, Tom Srull, Eliot Smith, William Rholes, Bob Wyer, Dave Hamilton, John Bargh, Tory Higgins, Lenny Martin, and Jerry Bruner make the identity of this factor as Social Cognition fairly easy.

It is worth pointing out that this appears to be a unidirectional factor. The loadings range from very high positive numbers to numbers around zero. Table 3 includes the two individuals with the lowest (most negative) loading on this factor to illustrate the point. I make note of it because unidirectionality in these factors appears to be the usual case and it makes sense. For example, one may do social cognition research and that would be reflected in a positive loading; or, one may do work that is largely independent of social cognition and that would result in a low loading on the factor. It is difficult, however, to even conceptualize what it means to make contributions that are so antithetical to the social cognition area so as to result in a substantial negative loading on the factor.

The second factor accounted for approximately 12% of the explained variance. Table 4 shows the 20 top loading and the 3 lowest loading FMCs. This factor, like Factor 1, appears

Table 3 *FMC Factor 1: Social Cognition*

Contributor	Factor Loading
Carlston, D. E.	.92
Srull, T. K.	.92
Smith, E. R.	.92
Rholes, W. S.	.89
Wyer, R. S., Jr.	.85
Hamilton, D. L.	.81
Bargh, J. A.	.81
Higgins, E. T.	.81
Martin, L. L.	.80
Bruner, J. S.	.78
Strack, F.	.76
Schwarz, N.	.76
Hastie, R.	.76
Sherman, S. J.	.76
Stangor, C.	.76
Devine, P. G.	.73
Fiske, S. T.	.71
Banaji, M. R.	.71
Pratto, F.	.69
Gilbert, D. T.	.69
Pruitt, D. G.	−.12
Deutsch, M.	−.15

Note: FMC = frequently mentioned contributor.

easy to identify. The FMCs who lead the list have all made substantial and highly visible contributions to the attitudes area. They include Wendy Wood, Irv Janis, Bill McGuire, Rich Petty, Alice Eagly, Duane Wegener, Shelley Chaiken, John Cacioppo, Marty Fishbein, and Icek Ajzen.

Factor 3 accounted for 9% of the explained variance. I have named it *Motivated Attribution,* but the commonality among the highest loading contributors is not as clear to me as it was for Factors 1 and 2. Names like Jones, Miller, Darley, and Hilton have clear connections to attribution theory; people like Ross, Kunda, Pyszczynski, and Greenberg have clearly addressed motivational issues in attribution—as has nearly everyone else on the list. There are at least a couple of other themes as well: Several of the FMCs have reported research on self-confirmation and interpersonal aspects of attribution theory—for example, Snyder, Swann, Darley, and Hilton. There is even a Princeton connection: Darley, Kunda, Hilton, Swann, Miller, and Jones. Table 5 lists the 20 highest loading FMCs and a couple of low-loading FMCs.

Factor 4 accounted for 8% of the explained variance (see Table 6). The people who lead this factor are Mike Scheier, Chuck Carver, Walter Mischel, Bob Wicklund, Albert Bandura, Dan Wegner, Roy Baumeister, Nancy Cantor, Jack

Table 4 *FMC Factor 2: Attitudes*

Contributor	Factor Loading
Wood, W.	.93
Janis, I.	.93
McGuire, W. J.	.92
Petty, R. E.	.90
Eagly, A. H.	.90
Wegener, D. T.	.89
Chaiken, S.	.88
Cacioppo, J. T.	.86
Fishbein, M.	.77
Ajzen, I.	.74
Mackie, D. M.	.71
Zanna, M. P.	.68
Bem, D. J.	.67
Greenwald, A. G.	.67
Cialdini, R. B.	.66
Fazio, R. H.	.56
Tesser, A.	.65
Cooper, J.	.65
Festinger, L.	.64
Kruglanski, A. W.	.57
Reis, H. T.	−.07
Bond, M. H.	−.10

Note: FMC = frequently mentioned contributor.

Table 5 *FMC Factor 3: Motivated Attribution*

Contributor	Factor Loading
Darley, J. M.	.77
Greenberg, J.	.75
Pyszczynski, T. A.	.74
Kunda, Z.	.73
Hilton, J. L.	.72
Swann, W. B., Jr.	.70
Miller, D. T.	.65
Snyder, M.	.63
Jones, E. E.	.59
Ross, M.	.58
Crocker, J.	.57
Pittman, T. S.	.57
Heider, F.	.56
Kruglanski, A. W.	.56
Nisbett, R. E.	.55
Taylor, S. E.	.50
Ross, L.	.48
Davis, K. E.	.47
Tetlock, P. E.	.46
Tversky, A.	.45
Moreland, R. L.	−.14
Ekman, P.	−.16

Note: FMC = frequently mentioned contributor.

Brehm, and William James. It is not difficult to recognize this as a factor having to do with research on the self.

The fifth factor accounted for 5% of the explained variance and is host to people like Dean Pruitt, John Thibaut, Morton Deutsch, David Messick, John Levine, Dick Moreland, Hal Kelley, Jud Mills, Solomon Asch, and Bob Cialdini. It looks like we have gone from the intrapersonal focus associated with social cognition, attitudes, attribution, and self to a concern with the interpersonal. I have named this factor *Interpersonal Influence*, but the presence of people like Berscheid, Clark, and Mills also gives the factor a hint of relationship research. Table 7 lists the 20 highest loading FMCs on this factor.

The sixth factor also accounted for 5% of the explained variance (see Table 8). This factor appears to go a step up on the scale from intrapersonal and interpersonal to intergroup relations. I think that the label *Intergroup Relations and Stereotypes* captures much of what is common to the work of the highest loading people on this dimension. Some of these people are Henri Tajfel, John Turner, Michael Hogg, Kay Deaux, Rupert Brown, Marilynn Brewer, Jenny Crocker,

Mahzarin Banaji, Claude Steele, and Dick Mooreland. Table 8 presents the names of all the FMC with loadings above .30. In the case of this factor only, there are FMCs with negative loadings greater than .2. Their names and loadings are in the table, but no interpretation is offered.

It seems unlikely to me that the Factor 7 would have emerged only 10 years ago. It accounts for only 3% of the explained variance, and it appears to reflect the field's great interest in questions of psychological universality. The cultural approach focuses on plasticity of cognition and belief; the evolutionary approach focuses on our common biological origins. I am basing my interpretation of the factor on the first six names on the list. Thus, Kitayama, Bond, Triandis, and Markus are strongly associated with cultural psychology and Ekman and Buss with universals in behavior. However, other themes can be gleaned from this list of contributors. For example, there is a strong emotion thread with names like Ekman, James, Schacter, Singer, and Zajonc. All FMCs with loading of .3 or higher are listed in Table 9.

The final factor accounted for 3% of the common variance. Like Factor 5, this appears to be concerned with

Table 6 *FMC Factor 4: Self*

Contributor	Factor Loading
Scheier, M. F.	.92
Carver, C. S.	.90
Mischel, W.	.82
Wicklund, R. A.	.80
Bandura, A.	.78
Wegner, D. M.	.72
Baumeister, R. F.	.69
Cantor, N. E.	.69
Brehm, J. W.	.68
James, W.	.54
Brown, J. D.	.53
Tesser, A.	.40
Steele, C. M.	.39
Bem, D. J.	.37
Swann, W. B., Jr.	.36
Taylor, S. E.	.34
Pyszczynski, T. A.	.34
Ruble, D. N.	.32
Greenberg, J.	.31
Pittman, T. S.	.30
Moreland, R. L.	−.08
Levine, J. M.	−.09

Note: FMC = frequently mentioned contributor.

Table 7 *FMC Factor 5: Interpersonal Influence*

Contributor	Factor Loading
Pruitt, D. G.	.88
Thibaut, J. W.	.88
Deutsch, M.	.87
Messick, D. M.	.84
Levine, J. M.	.78
Moreland, R. L.	.78
Kelley, H. H.	.76
Mills, J.	.54
Asch, S. E.	.52
Cialdini, R. B.	.49
Festinger, L.	.49
Lewin, K.	.48
Ross, L.	.47
Clark, M. S.	.47
Kenny, D. A.	.45
Hogg, M. A.	.44
Berscheid, E.	.40
Nisbett, R. E.	.39
Miller, D. T.	.38
Turner, J. C.	.36
Pratto, F.	−.11
Banaji, M. R.	−.16

Note: FMC = frequently mentioned contributor.

Table 8 *FMC Factor 6: Intergroup Relations and Stereotypes*

Contributor	Factor Loading
Tajfel, H.	.84
Turner, J. C.	.83
Hogg, M. A.	.79
Deaux, K.	.79
Brown, R. J.	.78
Brewer, M. B.	.61
Crocker, J.	.53
Banaji, M. R.	.46
Steele, C. M.	.41
Moreland, R. L.	.36
Levine, J. M.	.36
Stangor, C.	.35
Allport, G. W.	.34
Bond, M. H.	.33
Mackie, D. M.	.31
Messick, D. M.	.30
Kahneman, D.	−.20
Brehm, J. W.	−.22
Tversky, A.	−.24
Schachter, S.	−.32
Singer, J. E.	−.34

Note: **FMC** = frequently mentioned contributor.

Table 9 *FMC Factor 7: Culture and Evolution*

Contributor	Factor Loading
Kitayama, S.	.86
Bond, M. H.	.84
Triandis, H. C.	.81
Markus, H. R.	.78
Ekman, P.	.54
Buss, D. M.	.44
Lewin, K.	.43
Davis, K. E.	.39
James, W.	.37
Nisbett, R. E.	.36
Asch, S. E.	.36
Schachter, S.	.33
Ross, L.	.31
Singer, J. E.	.31
Bruner, J. S.	.30
Zajonc, R. B.	.30
Mills, J.	−.09
Hilton, J. L.	−.11

Note: FMC = frequently mentioned contributor.

Table 10 *FMC Factor 8: Interpersonal Relationships*

Contributor	Factor Loading
Reis, H. T.	.82
Clark, M. S.	.75
Berscheid, E.	.71
Mills, J.	.63
Kenny, D. A.	.47
Ekman, P.	.47
Buss, D. M.	.43
Singer, J. E.	.41
Schachter, S.	.37
Swann, W. B., Jr.	.31
Kelley, H. H.	.31
Pittman, T. S.	.31
Snyder, M.	.30
Ajzen, I.	−.18
Fishbein, M.	−.19

Note: FMC = frequently mentioned contributor.

interpersonal relationships. The emphasis here, however, seems to be on relationships rather than influence. Thus, the highest loading FMCs are Harry Reis, Peggy Clark, Ellen Berscheid, and Jud Mills. David Buss contributes to the relationship literature from an evolutionary perspective and also has a substantial loading on this factor. Also, like Factor 7, there is a dose of emotion research in this factor with Ekman, Schacter, and Singer having noteworthy loadings. Table 10 lists the FMCs with loadings greater than .30.

· · ·

Summary of Similarity

The affinities of the heavy contributors to the discipline appear to make sense. The factors are relatively easy to interpret, and they seem, to me at least, to do a good job of capturing much of what is common to what social psychologists do. They span the intrapersonal and the interpersonal. They show our classic concern with attitudes and our love affair with social cognition and social influence. We see our recent and very popular interest in stereotypes and ingroup-outgroup phenomena. There is also a relatively clear factor reflecting our needed, broadening focus on the issues of biology (evolution) and culture.

Clearly these factors are not totally comprehensive. There is no "aggression" or "altruism" factor. There are other specific domains that might have emerged. Nevertheless, the factors that emerged do paint a broad-brush picture of what social psychology was like in the last decade of the 20th century and who was doing what.

CONCLUSION

To know a scientific discipline is, at least in part, to know something about the people who are constructing that discipline. I have attempted to provide you with a snapshot, a picture of the people constructing social psychology on the cusp of the 21st century. The persons who have been identified will come as no surprise to active scholars in the area. Not present are many people whose work I admire and who I would vote to have on such a list. I will not mention specific names because I am sure to make some egregious omission. However, there are at least two general categories that appear underrepresented. As I see the field of scholars at the moment, I am convinced that this data underrepresents the scholarship of women and of persons outside the United States, particularly Western Europe and Australia.

The factors that describe how we organize ourselves also will not be a total surprise to active scholars in the discipline. Whether this is an accurate description of the field at this moment is an open question. The factor structure has more familiarity than we would expect if the discipline was changing and the factor structure reflected the cutting edges of those changes. The discipline is changing, but there is a lag in what is reflected in the handbooks. However, I am not sure how, precisely, to characterize those changes other than to mention the obvious trend in psychology as a whole toward a greater emphasis on neuroscience approaches.

This description is static and has a built-in lag. A scientific discipline, like a living organism, changes continuously. Social psychology is no exception. Indeed, there is already a new handbook. Nevertheless, I found it interesting to learn more about who was constructing the discipline in the 1990s and how they were organized. I hope you did as well.

REFERENCES

2000 APA membership register. (2000). Washington, DC: American Psychological Association.

Gilbert, D. T., Fiske, S. T., & Lindzey, G. (Eds.). (1998). *The handbook of social psychology* (4th ed.). Boston: McGraw-Hill.

Gordon. R., & Vicari, P. J. (1992). Eminence in social psychology: A comparison of textbook citation. Social Sciences Citation Index and research productivity ranking. *Personality and Social Psychology Bulletin, 18,* 26–38.

Higgins. E. T., & Kruglanski, A. W. (Eds.). (1996). *Social psychology: Handbook of basic principles.* New York: Guilford.

Membership Directory of the American Psychological Society. (1998). Washington, DC: American Psychological Society.

Questions

1. How might Tesser and Bau's results have been biased by their methods? That is, they used two handbooks of social psychology to determine the FMCs. How might their results have been different if they counted citations in journals

instead? How might their results have been different if they counted citations in textbooks?

2. Why do Tesser and Bau find a gender bias in FMCs? Can you think of another explanation? If their reasoning is correct, what might the field look like in about ten years?

3. According to Tesser and Bau's analysis, what were the major areas of social psychological research in the 1990s? Look up the areas of research in your social psychology text book or on a psychology database such as Psych Articles. What are the important findings in these areas? Which do you think you might like to study?

4. Do you recognize any of Tesser and Bau's FMC names? Can you imagine your name being on a similar list in the future? Look up these people in your social psychology textbook or on a psychology data base such as Psych Articles. What kinds of research are the FMCs currently doing?

How Sociologists
Do Research

From: *Sociology: A Down-to-Earth Approach, 2010 Census Update,* Tenth Edition
by James M. Henslin.

South Korea

Chung Sung-Jun/Getty Images

C indy Hudo, a 21-year-old mother of two in Charleston, South Carolina, who was charged with the murder of her husband, Buba, said:

I start in the car, and I get down the road, and I see Buba walking, and he's real mad. . . . I pull over, you know, and [I said] "I didn't know to pick you up. You know, I'm sorry." And he didn't even say nothing to me. He just started hitting on me. And that's all I wanted to do, was just get home, because I was just self-conscious. I don't want nobody to see him hitting me, because I didn't want him to look bad.

"I don't want nobody to see him hitting me, because I didn't want him to look bad."

I had to go to work in a half-hour, because I was working a double-shift. And he told me I had forty minutes to get all my furniture out of the house and get my clothes and be out or he was going to throw them out. And I was sitting there, because I could talk him down. You know, because I didn't want to leave him. I just talked to him. I said, "Buba, I don't want to leave." I said, "This is my house." And then he told me . . . (unclear) . . . "my kids." And I said, "No, you're not taking my kids from me. That's too much." And so I said, "Just let me leave. Just let me take the kids. And, you know I'll go, and you know, I won't keep the kids from you or nothing like that." And he said, "I'm going to take them, and you're getting out."

[After they went inside their trailer, Buba threatened to shoot Cindy. He loaded a shotgun, pointed it at her, and said]: "The only way you're going to get out of this is if you kill me, and I'll—I'll kill you." [Buba gave me the shotgun and] turned around and walked right down the hall, because he knew I wouldn't do nothing. And I just sat there a minute. And I don't know what happened. I just, you know, I went to the bedroom, and I seen him laying there, and I just shot him. He moved. I shot him again because I thought he was going to get up again. . . .

I loved him too much. And I just wanted to help him.

Source: Transcript, ABC Television, *20/20,* October 18, 1979.

What Is a Valid Sociological Topic?

Sociologists do research on just about every area of human behavior. On the macro level, they study such broad matters as race relations (Schaefer 2008), the military (Caforio 2006), and multinational corporations (Kristensen and Morgan 2006). On the micro level, they study such individualistic matters as pelvic examinations (Henslin and Biggs 1971/2007), how people interact on street corners (Whyte 1989, 2001), and even shyness (Scott 2006). Sociologists study priests and prostitutes, cops and criminals, as well as all kinds of people in between. In fact, no human behavior is ineligible for sociological scrutiny—whether that behavior is routine or unusual, respectable or reprehensible.

What happened to Cindy and Buba, then, is also a valid topic of sociological research. But exactly *how* would you research spouse abuse? As we look at how sociologists do research, we shall try to answer this question.

Common Sense and the Need for Sociological Research

First, why do we need sociological research? Why can't we simply depend on common sense, on "what everyone knows"? Commonsense ideas may or may not be true. Common sense, for example, tells us that spouse abuse has a significant impact on the lives of the people who are abused.

Although this particular idea is accurate, we need research to test commonsense ideas, because not all such ideas are true. After all, common sense also tells us that if a woman is abused, she will pack up and leave her husband. Research, however, shows that the reality of abuse is much more complicated than this. Some women do leave right away, some even after the first incident of abuse. For a variety of reasons, however, some women suffer abuse for years. The main reason is that they feel trapped and don't perceive any viable alternatives.

This brings us to the need for sociological research, for we may want to know why some women put up with abuse, while others don't. Or we may want to know something entirely different, such as why men are more likely to be the abusers. Or why some people abuse the people they say they love.

In order to answer a question, we need to move beyond guesswork and common sense. We want to *know* what is really going on. To find out, sociologists do research on about every aspect of social life. Let's look at how they do their research.

A Research Model

As shown in Figure 1 on the next page, scientific research follows eight basic steps. This is an ideal model, however, and in the real world of research some of these steps may run together. Some may even be omitted.

1. Selecting a Topic

The first step is to select a topic. What do you want to know more about? Many sociologists simply follow their curiosity, their drive to learn more about social life. They become interested in a particular topic and they pursue it, as I did in studying the homeless. Some sociologists choose a topic because funding is available for that topic, others because a social problem such as domestic violence is in the news and they want to help people better understand it—and perhaps to help solve it. Let's use spouse abuse as our example.

Barry Batchelor/PA Photos/Landov

Because sociologists find all human behavior to be valid research topics, their research runs from the unusual to the routines of everyday life. Their studies range from broad scale social change, such as the globalization of capitalism, to smaller scale social interaction, such as people having fun.

2. Defining the Problem

The second step is to define the problem, to specify what you want to learn about the topic. My interest in the homeless increased until I wanted to learn about homelessness across the nation. Ordinarily, sociologists' interests are much more focused than this; they examine some specific aspect of the topic, such as how homeless people survive on the streets. In the case of spouse abuse, sociologists may want to know whether violent and nonviolent husbands have different work experiences. Or they may want to learn what can be done to reduce spouse abuse.

The topics that sociologists study are far-ranging. In fact, sociologists do research on any aspect of social life that interests them. The "problem" can be as earth shattering as trying to figure out why nations would ever contemplate nuclear war, as perplexing as understanding how "good" people can torture and kill, or as simple as wanting to find out why Native Americans like Westerns.

3. Reviewing the Literature

You must read what has been published on your topic. This helps you to narrow the problem, identify areas that are already known, and learn what areas need to be researched. Reviewing the literature may also help you to pinpoint the questions that you will ask. You might even find out that the problem has been answered already. You don't want to waste your time rediscovering what is already known.

4. Formulating a Hypothesis

The fourth step is to formulate a **hypothesis,** a statement of what you expect to find according to predictions from a theory. A hypothesis predicts a relationship between or among **variables,** factors that change, or vary, from one person or situation to another. For example, the statement "Men who are more socially isolated are more likely to abuse their wives than are men who are more socially integrated" is a hypothesis.

Your hypothesis will need **operational definitions**—that is, precise ways to measure the variables. In this example, you would need operational definitions for three variables: social isolation, social integration, and spouse abuse.

5. Choosing a Research Method

You then need to decide how you are going to collect your data. Sociologists use seven basic **research methods** (or *research designs*), which are outlined in the next section. You will want to choose the research method that will best answer your particular questions.

6. Collecting the Data

When you gather your data, you have to take care to assure their **validity;** that is, your operational definitions must measure what they are intended to measure. In this case, you must be certain that you really are measuring social isolation, social integration, and spouse abuse—and not something else. Spouse abuse, for example, seems to be obvious. Yet what some people consider to be abuse is not regarded as abuse by others. Which definition will you choose? In other words, you must state your operational definitions so precisely that no one has any question about what you are measuring.

You must also be sure that your data are reliable. **Reliability** means that if other researchers use your operational definitions, their findings will be consistent with yours. If

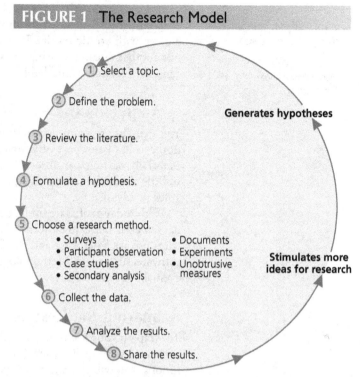

FIGURE 1 The Research Model

① Select a topic.
② Define the problem.
③ Review the literature.
④ Formulate a hypothesis.
⑤ Choose a research method.
  • Surveys
  • Participant observation
  • Case studies
  • Secondary analysis
  • Documents
  • Experiments
  • Unobtrusive measures
⑥ Collect the data.
⑦ Analyze the results.
⑧ Share the results.

Generates hypotheses

Stimulates more ideas for research

Source: Modification of Figure 2.2 of Schaeffer 1989.

hypothesis a statement of how variables are expected to be related to one another, often according to predictions from a theory

variable a factor thought to be significant for human behavior, which can vary (or change) from one case to another

operational definition the way in which a researcher measures a variable

research method (or research design) one of seven procedures that sociologists use to collect data: surveys, participant observation, case studies, secondary analysis, documents, experiments, and unobtrusive measures

validity the extent to which an operational definition measures what it is intended to measure

reliability the extent to which research produces consistent or dependable results

your operational definitions are sloppy, husbands who have committed the same act of violence might be included in some research but excluded from other studies. You would end up with erratic results. If you show a 10 percent rate of spouse abuse, for example, but another researcher using the same operational definitions determines it to be 30 percent, the research is unreliable.

7. Analyzing the Results

You can choose from a variety of techniques to analyze the data you gather. If a hypothesis has been part of your research, now is when you will test it. (Some research, especially participant observation and case studies, has no hypothesis. You may know so little about the setting you are going to research that you cannot even specify the variables in advance.)

With today's software, in just seconds you can run tests on your data that used to take days or even weeks to perform. Two basic programs that sociologists and many undergraduates use are Microcase and the Statistical Package for the Social Sciences (SPSS). Some software, such as the Methodologist's Toolchest, provides advice about collecting data and even about ethical issues.

8. Sharing the Results

To wrap up your research, you will write a report to share your findings with the scientific community. You will review how you did your research, including your operational definitions. You will also show how your findings fit in with what has already been published on the topic and how they support or disagree with the theories that apply to your topic.

When research is published, usually in a scientific journal or a book, it "belongs" to the scientific community. Your findings will be available for **replication;** that is, others can repeat your study to see if they come up with similar results. As Table 1 on the next page illustrates, sociologists often summarize their findings in tables. As finding is added to finding, scientific knowledge builds.

Let's look in greater detail at the fifth step to see what research methods sociologists use.

THE FAR SIDE® BY GARY LARSON

© 1984 FarWorks, Inc. All Rights Reserved/Dist. by Creators Syndicate

"Anthropologists! Anthropologists!"

A major concern of sociologists and other social scientists is that their research methods do not influence their findings. Respondents often change their behavior when they know they are being studied.

Research Methods

As we review the seven research methods (or *research designs*) that sociologists use, we will continue our example of spouse abuse. As you will see, the method you choose will depend on the questions you want to answer. So that you can have a yardstick for comparison, you will want to know what "average" is in your study. Table 2 discusses ways to measure average.

Surveys

Let's suppose that you want to know how many wives are abused each year. Some husbands also are abused, of course, but let's assume that you are going to focus on wives. An appropriate method for this purpose would be the **survey,** in which you would ask individuals a series of questions. Before you begin your research, however, you must deal with practical matters that face all researchers. Let's look at these issues.

TABLE 1   How to Read a Table

Tables summarize information. Because sociological findings are often presented in tables, it is important to understand how to read them. Tables contain six elements: title, headnote, headings, columns, rows, and source. When you understand how these elements fit together, you know how to read a table.

1. The **title** states the topic. It is located at the top of the table. What is the title of this table? Please determine your answer before looking at the correct answer at the bottom of this page.

2. The **headnote** is not always included in a table. When it is, it is located just below the title. Its purpose is to give more detailed information about how the data were collected or how data are presented in the table. What are the first eight words of the headnote of this table?

3. The **headings** tell what kind of information is contained in the table. There are three headings in this table. What are they? In the second heading, what does *n* = 25 mean?

4. The **columns** present information arranged vertically. What is the fourth number in the second column and the second number in the third column?

5. The **rows** present information arranged horizontally. In the fourth row, which husbands are more likely to have less education than their wives?

6. The **source** of a table, usually listed at the bottom, provides information on where the data in the table originated. Often, as in this instance, the information is specific enough for you to consult the original source. What is the source for this table?

Comparing Violent and Nonviolent Husbands

Based on interviews with 150 husbands and wives in a Midwestern city who were getting a divorce.

Husband's Achievement and Job Satisfaction	Violent Husbands *n* = 25	Nonviolent Husbands *n* = 125
He started but failed to complete high school or college.	44%	27%
He is very dissatisfied with his job.	44%	18%
His income is a source of constant conflict.	84%	24%
He has less education than his wife.	56%	14%
His job has less prestige than his father-in-law's.	37%	28%

Source: Modification of Table 1 in O'Brien 1975.

Some tables are much more complicated than this one, but all follow the same basic pattern.

ANSWERS

1. Comparing Violent and Nonviolent Husbands
2. Based on interviews with 150 husbands and wives
3. Husband's Achievement and Job Satisfaction, Violent Husbands, Nonviolent Husbands. The *n* is an abbreviation for number, and *n* = 25 means that 25 violent husbands were in the sample.
4. 56%, 18%
5. Violent Husbands
6. A 1975 article by O'Brien

Selecting a Sample.   Ideally, you might want to learn about all wives in the world. Obviously, your resources will not permit such research, and you will have to narrow your **population,** the target group that you are going to study.

Let's assume that your resources (money, assistants, time) allow you to investigate spouse abuse only on your campus. Let's also assume that your college enrollment is large, so you won't be able to survey all the married women who are enrolled. Now you must

population a target group to be studied

TABLE 2 Three Ways to Measure "Average"

The Mean	The Median	The Mode
The term *average* seems clear enough. As you learned in grade school, to find the average you add a group of numbers and then divide the total by the number of cases that you added. Assume that the following numbers represent men convicted of battering their wives:	To compute the second average, the *median*, first arrange the cases in order—either from the highest to the lowest or the lowest to the highest. That arrangement will produce the following distribution.	The third measure of average, the *mode*, is simply the cases that occur the most often. In this instance the mode is 57, which is way off the mark.

EXAMPLE (Mean):
```
  321
  229
   57
  289
  136
   57
1,795
```

EXAMPLE (Median):
```
   57      1,795
   57        321
  136        289
  229   or   229
  289        136
  321         57
1,795         57
```

EXAMPLE (Mode):
```
  [57]
  [57]
  136
  229
  289
  321
1,795
```

The Mean	The Median	The Mode
The total is 2,884. Divided by 7 (the number of cases), the average is 412. Sociologists call this form of average the *mean*. The mean can be deceptive because it is strongly influenced by extreme scores, either low or high. Note that six of the seven cases are less than the mean. Two other ways to compute averages are the median and the mode.	Then look for the middle case, the one that falls halfway between the top and the bottom. That number is 229, for three numbers are lower and three numbers are higher. When there is an even number of cases, the median is the halfway mark between the two middle cases.	Because the mode is often deceptive, and only by chance comes close to either of the other two averages, sociologists seldom use it. In addition, not every distribution of cases has a mode. And if two or more numbers appear with the same frequency, you can have more than one mode.

sample the individuals intended to represent the population to be studied

random sample a sample in which everyone in the target population has the same chance of being included in the study

stratified random sample a sample from selected subgroups of the target population in which everyone in those subgroups has an equal chance of being included in the research

respondents people who respond to a survey, either in interviews or by self-administered questionnaires

questionnaires a list of questions to be asked of respondents

self-administered questionnaires questionnaires that respondents fill out

select a **sample,** individuals from among your target population. How you choose a sample is crucial, for your choice will affect the results of your research. For example, married women enrolled in introductory sociology and engineering courses might have quite different experiences. If so, surveying just one or the other would produce skewed results.

Because you want to generalize your findings to your entire campus, you need a sample that accurately represents the campus. How can you get a representative sample?

The best way is to use a **random sample.** This does *not* mean that you stand on some campus corner and ask questions of any woman who happens to walk by. *In a random sample, everyone in your population (the target group) has the same chance of being included in the study.* In this case, because your population is every married woman enrolled in your college, all married women—whether first-year or graduate students, full- or part-time—must have the same chance of being included in your sample.

How can you get a random sample? First, you need a list of all the married women enrolled in your college. Then you assign a number to each name on the list. Using a table of random numbers, you then determine which of these women will become part of your sample. (Tables of random numbers are available in statistics books and online, or they can be generated by a computer.)

A random sample will represent your study's population fairly—in this case, married women enrolled at your college. This means that you can generalize your findings to *all* the married women students on your campus, even if they were not included in your sample.

What if you want to know only about certain subgroups, such as freshmen and seniors? You could use a **stratified random sample.** You would need a list of the married women in the freshman and senior classes. Then, using random numbers, you would select a sample from each group. This would allow you to generalize to all the freshman and senior married women at your college, but you would not be able to draw any conclusions about the sophomores or juniors.

Asking Neutral Questions.   After you have decided on your population and sample, your next task is to make certain that your questions are neutral. Your questions must allow **respondents,** the people who answer your questions, to express their own opinions. Otherwise, you will end up with biased answers—which are worthless. For example, if you were to ask, "Don't you think that men who beat their wives should go to prison?" you would be tilting the answer toward agreement with a prison sentence. The *Doonesbury* cartoon below illustrates another blatant example of biased questions. For examples of flawed research, see the Down-to-Earth Sociology box on the next page.

Questionnaires and Interviews.   Even if you have a representative sample and ask neutral questions, you can still end up with biased findings. **Questionnaires,** the list of questions to be asked, can be administered in ways that are flawed. There are two basic techniques for administering questionnaires. The first is to ask the respondents to fill them out. These **self-administered questionnaires** allow a larger number of people to be sampled at a lower cost, but the researchers lose control of the data collection. They don't know the conditions under which people answered the questions. For example, others could have influenced their answers.

The second technique is the **interview.** Researchers ask people questions, often face to face, sometimes by telephone or e-mail. The advantage of this method is that the researchers can ask each question in the same way. The main disadvantage is that interviews are time-consuming, so researchers end up with fewer respondents. Interviews can also create **interviewer bias;** that is, the presence of interviewers can affect what people say. For example, instead of saying what they really feel, respondents might give "socially acceptable" answers. Although they may be willing to write their true opinions on an anonymous questionnaire, they won't tell them to another person. Some respondents even shape their answers to match what they think an interviewer wants to hear.

In some cases, **structured interviews** work best. This type of interview uses **closed-ended questions**—each question is followed by a list of possible answers. Structured interviews are faster to administer, and they make it easier to *code* (categorize) answers so

Sociologists usually cannot interview or observe every member of a group or participant in an event that they want to study. As explained in the text, to be able to generalize their findings, they select samples. Sociologists would have several ways to study this protest in San Francisco against U.S. foreign policy.

interview direct questioning of respondents

interviewer bias effects that interviewers have on respondents that lead to biased answers

structured interviews interviews that use closed-ended questions

closed-ended questions questions that are followed by a list of possible answers to be selected by the respondent

Improperly worded questions can steer respondents toward answers that are not their own, which produces invalid results.

Down-to-Earth Sociology

Loading the Dice: How *Not* to Do Research

The methods of science lend themselves to distortion, misrepresentation, and downright fraud. Consider these findings from surveys:

Americans overwhelmingly prefer Toyotas to Chryslers.
Americans overwhelmingly prefer Chryslers to Toyotas.

Obviously, these opposite conclusions cannot both be true. In fact, both sets of findings are misrepresentations, even though the responses came from surveys conducted by so-called independent researchers. These researchers, however, are biased, not independent and objective.

It turns out that some consumer researchers load the dice. Hired by firms that have a vested interest in the outcome of the research, they deliver the results their clients are looking for (Armstrong 2007). Here are six ways to load the dice.

1. **Choose a biased sample.** If you want to "prove" that Americans prefer Chryslers over Toyotas, interview unemployed union workers who trace their job loss to Japanese imports. The answer is predictable. You'll get what you're looking for.

2. **Ask biased questions.** Even if you choose an unbiased sample, you can phrase questions in such a way that you direct people to the answer you're looking for. Suppose that you ask this question:

We are losing millions of jobs to workers overseas who work for just a few dollars a day. After losing their jobs, some Americans are even homeless and hungry. Do you prefer a car that gives jobs to Americans, or one that forces our workers to lose their homes?

This question is obviously designed to channel people's thinking toward a predetermined answer—quite contrary to the standards of scientific research. Look again at the Doonesbury cartoon on the previous page.

3. **List biased choices.** Another way to load the dice is to use closed-ended questions that push people into the answers you want. Consider this finding:

U.S. college students overwhelmingly prefer Levis 501 to the jeans of any competitor.

fotoshoot/Alamy Royalty Free

Sound good? Before you rush out to buy Levis, note what these researchers did: In asking students which jeans would be the most popular in the coming year, their list of choices included no other jeans but Levis 501!

4. **Discard undesirable results.** Researchers can keep silent about results they find embarrassing, or they can continue to survey samples until they find one that matches what they are looking for. As has been stressed in this chapter, research must be objective if it is to be scientific. Obviously, none of the preceding results qualifies. The underlying problem with the research cited here—and with so many surveys bandied about in the media as fact—is that survey research has become big business. Simply put, the money offered by corporations has corrupted some researchers.

The beginning of the corruption is subtle. Paul Light, dean at the University of Minnesota, put it this way: "A funder will never come to an academic and say, 'I want you to produce finding X, and here's a million dollars to do it.' Rather, the subtext is that if the researchers produce the right finding, more work—and funding—will come their way."

The first four sources of bias are inexcusable, intentional fraud. The next two sources of bias reflect sloppiness, which is also inexcusable in science.

5. **Misunderstand the subjects' world.** This route can lead to errors every bit as great as those just cited. Even researchers who use an adequate sample and word their questions properly can end up with skewed results. They may, for example, fail to anticipate that people may be embarrassed to express an opinion that isn't "politically correct." For example, surveys show that 80 percent of Americans are environmentalists. Most Americans, however, are probably embarrassed to tell a stranger otherwise. Today, that would be like going against the flag, motherhood, and apple pie.

6. **Analyze the data incorrectly.** Even when researchers strive for objectivity, the sample is good, the wording is neutral, and the respondents answer the questions honestly, the results can still be skewed. The researchers may make a mistake in their calculations, such as entering incorrect data into computers. This, too, of course, is inexcusable in science.

Sources: Based on Crossen 1991; Goleman 1993; Barnes 1995; Resnik 2000; Hotz 2007.

they can be fed into a computer for analysis. As you can see from Table 3, the answers listed on a questionnaire might fail to include the respondent's opinions. Consequently, some researchers prefer **unstructured interviews.** Here the interviewer asks **open-ended questions,** which allow people to answer in their own words. Open-ended questions allow you to tap the full range of people's opinions, but they make it difficult to compare answers. For example, how would you compare the following answers to the question "Why do you think men abuse their wives?"

"They're sick."

"I think they must have had problems with their mother."

"We oughta string 'em up!"

TABLE 3	Closed and Open–Ended Questions	
A. Closed–Ended Question	**B. Open–Ended Question**
Which of the following best fits your idea of what should be done to someone who has been convicted of spouse abuse? 1. probation 2. jail time 3. community service 4. counseling 5. divorce 6. nothing—it's a family matter	What do you think should be done to someone who has been convicted of spouse abuse?

Establishing Rapport.   Research on spouse abuse brings up another significant issue. You may have been wondering if your survey would be worth anything even if you rigorously followed scientific procedures. Will women who have been abused really give honest answers to strangers?

If your method of interviewing consisted of walking up to women on the street and asking if their husbands had ever beaten them, there would be little basis for taking your findings seriously. Researchers have to establish **rapport** ("ruh-POUR"), a feeling of trust, with their respondents, especially when it comes to sensitive topics—those that elicit feelings of embarrassment, shame, or other deep emotions.

We know that once rapport is gained (often by first asking nonsensitive questions), victims will talk about personal, sensitive issues. A good example is rape. To go beyond police statistics, each year researchers interview a random sample of 100,000 Americans. They ask them whether they have been victims of burglary, robbery, or other crimes. After establishing rapport, the researchers ask about rape. They find that rape victims will talk about their experiences. The National Crime Victimization Survey shows that the actual incidence of rape is about 40 percent higher than the number reported to the police—and that attempted rapes are *nine* times higher than the official statistics (*Statistical Abstract* 2009: Tables 303, 304).

A new technique to gather data on sensitive areas, Computer-Assisted Self-Interviewing, overcomes lingering problems of distrust. In this technique, the interviewer gives a laptop computer to the respondent, then moves aside, while the individual enters his or her own answers into the computer. In some versions of this method, the respondent listens to the questions on a headphone and answers them on the computer screen. When the respondent clicks the "Submit" button, the interviewer has no idea how the respondent answered any question (Mosher et al. 2005).

Participant Observation (Fieldwork)

In the second method, **participant observation** (or **fieldwork**), the researcher *participates* in a research setting while *observing* what is happening in that setting. But how is it possible to study spouse abuse by participant observation? Obviously, this method does not mean that you would sit around and watch someone being abused. Spouse abuse, however, is a broad topic, and many questions about abuse cannot be answered adequately by any method other than participant observation.

Let's suppose that you are interested in learning how spouse abuse affects wives. You might want to know how the abuse has changed the wives' relationship with their husbands. How has it changed their hopes and dreams? Or their ideas about men? Certainly it has affected their self-concept as well. But how? Participant observation could provide insight into such questions.

For example, if your campus has a crisis intervention center, you might be able to observe victims of spouse abuse from the time they report the attack through their participation in counseling. With good rapport, you might even be able to spend time with them in other

unstructured interviews interviews that use open-ended questions

open-ended questions questions that respondents answer in their own words

rapport (ruh-POUR) a feeling of trust between researchers and the people they are studying

participant observation (or fieldwork) research in which the researcher participates in a research setting while observing what is happening in that setting

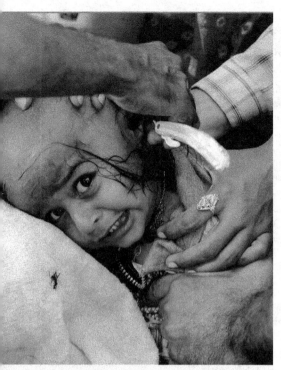

Dinodia/The Image Works

Participant observation, participating and observing in a research setting, is usually supplemented by interviewing, asking questions to better understand why people do what they do. In this instance, the sociologist would want to know what this hair removal ceremony in Gujarat, India, means to the child's family and to the community.

settings, observing further aspects of their lives. What they say and how they interact with others might help you to understand how the abuse has affected them. This, in turn, could give you insight into how to improve college counseling services.

Participant observers face two major dilemmas. The first is **generalizability,** the extent to which their findings apply to larger populations. Most participant observation studies are exploratory, documenting in detail the experiences of people in a particular setting. Although such research suggests that other people who face similar situations react in similar ways, we don't know how far the findings apply beyond their original setting. Participant observation, however, can stimulate hypotheses and theories that can be tested in other settings, using other research techniques. A second dilemma is the extent to which the participant observers should get involved in the lives of the people they are observing. Consider this as you read the Down-to-Earth Sociology box on the next page.

Case Studies

To do a **case study,** the researcher focuses on a single event, situation, or even individual. The purpose is to understand the dynamics of relationships, power, or even the thought processes that led to some particular event. Sociologist Ken Levi (2009), for example, wanted to study hit men. He would have loved to have had a large number of hit men to interview, but he had access to only one. He interviewed this man over and over again, giving us an understanding of how someone can kill others for money. Sociologist Kai Erikson (1978), who became intrigued with the bursting of a dam in West Virginia that killed several hundred people, focused on the events that led up to and followed this disaster. For spouse abuse, a case study would focus on a single wife and husband, exploring the couple's history and relationship.

As you can see, the case study reveals a lot of detail about some particular situation, but the question always remains: How much of this detail applies to other situations? This problem of generalizability, which plagues case studies, is the primary reason that few sociologists use this method.

Secondary Analysis

In **secondary analysis,** a fourth research method, researchers analyze data that others have collected. For example, if you were to analyze the original interviews from a study of women who had been abused by their husbands, you would be doing secondary analysis. Ordinarily, researchers prefer to gather their own data, but lack of resources, especially money, may make this impossible. In addition, existing data could contain a wealth of information that wasn't pertinent to the goals of the original researchers, which you can analyze for your own purposes.

Like the other methods, secondary analysis also poses its own problems. How can a researcher who did not carry out the initial study be sure that the data were gathered systematically and recorded accurately and that biases were avoided? This problem plagues researchers who do secondary analysis, especially if the original data were gathered by a team of researchers, not all of whom were equally qualified.

Documents

The fifth method that sociologists use is the study of **documents,** recorded sources. To investigate social life, sociologists examine such diverse documents as books, newspapers, diaries, bank records, police reports, immigration files, and records kept by organizations. The term *documents* is broad, and it also includes video and audio recordings.

To study spouse abuse, you might examine police reports and court records. These could reveal what percentage of complaints result in arrest and what proportion of the men arrested are charged, convicted, or put on probation. If these were your questions, police statistics would be valuable (Kingsnorth and MacIntosh 2007).

generalizability the extent to which the findings from one group (or sample) can be generalized or applied to other groups (or populations)

case study an analysis of a single event, situation, or individual

secondary analysis the analysis of data that have been collected by other researchers

documents in its narrow sense, written sources that provide data; in its extended sense, archival material of any sort, including photographs, movies, CDs, DVDs, and so on

Down-to-Earth Sociology

Gang Leader for a Day: Adventures of a Rogue Sociologist

Next to the University of Chicago is an area of poverty so dangerous that the professors warn students to avoid it. One of the graduate students in sociology, Sudhir Venkatesh, the son of immigrants from India, who was working on a research project with William Julius Wilson, decided to ignore the warning.

With clipboard in hand, Sudhir entered "the projects." Ignoring the glares of the young men standing around, he went into the lobby of a high-rise. Seeing a gaping hole where the elevator was supposed to be, he decided to climb the stairs, where he was almost overpowered by the smell of urine. After climbing five flights, Sudhir came upon some young men shooting craps in a dark hallway. One of them jumped up, grabbed Sudhir's clipboard, and demanded to know what he was doing there.

Sudhir blurted, "I'm a student at the university, doing a survey, and I'm looking for some families to interview."

One man took out a knife and began to twirl it. Another pulled out a gun, pointed it at Sudhir's head, and said, "I'll take him."

Then came a series of rapid-fire questions that Sudhir couldn't answer. He had no idea what they meant: "You flip right or left? Five or six? You run with the Kings, right?"

Grabbing Sudhir's bag, two of the men searched it. They could find only questionnaires, pen and paper, and a few sociology books. The man with the gun then told Sudhir to go ahead and ask him a question.

Sweating despite the cold, Sudhir read the first question on his survey, "How does it feel to be black and poor?" Then he read the multiple-choice answers: "Very bad, somewhat bad, neither bad nor good, somewhat good, very good."

As you might surmise, the man's answer was too obscenity laden to be printed here.

As the men deliberated Sudhir's fate ("If he's here and he don't get back, you know they're going to come looking for him"), a powerfully built man with a few glittery gold teeth and a sizable diamond earring appeared. The man, known as J.T., who, it turned out, directed the drug trade in the building, asked what was going on. When the younger men mentioned the questionnaire, J.T. said to ask *him* a question.

Amidst an eerie silence, Sudhir asked, "How does it feel to be black and poor?"

"I'm not black," came the reply.

"Well, then, how does it feel to be African American and poor?"

"I'm not African American either. I'm a nigger."

Sudhir was left speechless. Despite his naïveté, he knew better than to ask, "How does it feel to be a nigger and poor?"

As Sudhir stood with his mouth agape, J.T.

Paresh Gandhi Courtesy of Sudhir Venkatesh, Columbia University

Sudhir Venkatesh, who now teaches at Columbia University, New York City.

added, "Niggers are the ones who live in this building. African Americans live in the suburbs. African Americans wear ties to work. Niggers can't find no work."

Not exactly the best start to a research project.

But this weird and frightening beginning turned into several years of fascinating research. Over time, J.T. guided Sudhir into a world that few outsiders ever see. Not only did Sudhir get to know drug dealers, crackheads, squat- beatings by drug crews, drive-by shootings done by rival gangs, and armed robberies by the police.

How Sudhir got out of his predicament in the stairwell, his immersion into a threatening underworld—the daily life for many people in "the projects"—and his moral dilemma at witnessing so many crimes are part of his fascinating experience in doing participant observation of the Black Kings.

Sudhir, who was reared in a middle-class suburb in California, even took over this Chicago gang for a day. This is one reason that he calls himself a rogue sociologist—the decisions he made that day were serious violations of law, felonies that could bring years in prison. There are other reasons, too: During the research, he kicked a man in the stomach, and he was present as the gang planned drive-by shootings.

Sudhir eventually completed his Ph.D., and he now teaches at Columbia University.

Based on Venkatesh 2008.

But for other questions, those records would be useless. If you want to learn about the victims' social and emotional adjustment, for example, those records would tell you little. Other documents, however, might provide answers. For example, diaries kept by victims could yield insight into their reactions to abuse, showing how their attitudes and

The *research methods* that sociologists choose depend partially on the questions they want to answer. They might want to learn, for example, which forms of publicity are more effective in increasing awareness of spouse abuse as a social problem.

Jim West/Alamy

experiment the use of *control* and *experimental groups* and *dependent* and *independent variables* to test causation

experimental group the group of subjects in an experiment who are exposed to the independent variable

control group the subjects in an experiment who are not exposed to the independent variable

relationships change. If no diaries were available, you might ask victims to keep diaries. Perhaps the director of a crisis intervention center might ask clients to keep diaries for you—or get the victims' permission for you to examine records of their counseling sessions. To my knowledge, no sociologist has yet studied spouse abuse in this way.

Of course, I am presenting an ideal situation, a crisis intervention center that opens its arms to you. In actuality, the center might not cooperate at all. It might refuse to ask victims to keep diaries—or it might not even let you near its records. *Access,* then, is another problem that researchers face. Simply put, you can't study a topic unless you can gain access to it.

Experiments

Do you think there is a way to change a man who abuses his wife into a loving husband? No one has made this claim, but a lot of people say that abusers need therapy. Yet no one knows whether therapy really works. Because **experiments** are useful for determining cause and effect (discussed in Table 4 on the next page), let's suppose that you propose an experiment to a judge and she gives you access to men who have been arrested for spouse abuse. As in Figure 2 below, you would randomly divide the men into two groups. This helps to ensure that their individual characteristics (attitudes, number of arrests, severity of crimes, education, race–ethnicity, age, and so on) are distributed evenly between the groups. You then would arrange for the men in the **experimental group** to receive some form of therapy. The men in the **control group** would not get therapy.

FIGURE 2   The Experiment

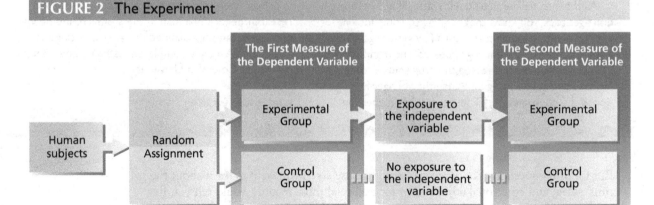

Source: By the author.

TABLE 4   Cause, Effect, and Spurious Correlations

Causation means that a change in one variable is caused by another variable. Three conditions are necessary for causation: correlation, temporal priority, and no spurious correlation. Let's apply each of these conditions to spouse abuse and alcohol abuse.

(1) The first necessary condition is *correlation*.

If two variables exist together, they are said to be correlated. If batterers get drunk, battering and alcohol abuse are correlated.

Spouse Abuse + Alcohol Abuse

People sometimes assume that correlation is causation. In this instance, they conclude that alcohol abuse causes spouse abuse.

Alcohol Abuse ⟶ Spouse Abuse

But *correlation never proves causation. Either* variable could be the cause of the other. Perhaps battering upsets men and they then get drunk.

Spouse Abuse ⟶ Alcohol Abuse

(2) *temporal priority*.

Temporal priority means that one thing happens before something else does. For a variable to be a cause (*the independent variable*), it must *precede* that which is changed (*the dependent variable*).

precedes
Alcohol Abuse ⟶ Spouse Abuse

If the men had not drunk alcohol until after they beat their wives, obviously alcohol abuse could not be the cause of the spouse abuse. Although the necessity of temporal priority is obvious, in many studies this is not easy to determine.

(3) The third necessary condition is *no spurious correlation*.

This is the necessary condition that really makes things difficult. Even if we identify the correlation of getting drunk and spouse abuse and can determine temporal priority, we still don't know that alcohol abuse is the cause. We could have a *spurious correlation*; that is, the cause may be some underlying third variable. These are usually not easy to identify. Some sociologists think that male culture is that underlying third variable.

Male Culture ⟶ Spouse Abuse

Socialized into dominance, some men learn to view women as objects on which to take out their frustration. In fact, this underlying third variable could be a cause of both spouse abuse and alcohol abuse.

Male Culture ⟶ **Spouse Abuse** / **Alcohol Abuse**

But since only some men beat their wives, while all males are exposed to male culture, other variables must also be involved. Perhaps specific subcultures that promote violence and denigrate women lead to both spouse abuse and alcohol abuse.

Male Subculture ⟶ **Spouse Abuse** / **Alcohol Abuse**

If so, this does *not* mean that it is the only causal variable, for spouse abuse probably has many causes. Unlike the movement of amoebas or the action of heat on some object, human behavior is infinitely complicated. Especially important are people's *definitions of the situation*, including their views of right and wrong. To explain spouse abuse, then, we need to add such variables as the ways that men view violence and their ideas about the relative rights of women and men. It is precisely to help unravel such complicating factors in human behavior that we need the experimental method.

MORE ON CORRELATIONS

Correlation simply means that two or more variables are present together. The more often that these variables are found together, the stronger their relationship. To indicate their strength, sociologists use a number called a *correlation coefficient*. If two variables are always related, that is, they are always present together, they have what is called a *perfect positive correlation*. The number 1.0 represents this correlation coefficient. Nature has some 1.0's, such as the lack of water and the death of trees. 1.0's also apply to the human physical state, such as the absence of nutrients and the absence of life. But social life is much more complicated than physical conditions, and there are no 1.0's in human behavior.

Two variables can also have a *perfect negative correlation*. This means that when one variable is present, the other is always absent. The number –1.0 represents this correlation coefficient.

Positive correlations of 0.1, 0.2, and 0.3 mean that one variable is associated with another only 1 time out of 10, 2 times out of 10, and 3 times out of 10. In other words, in most instances the first variable is *not* associated with the second, indicating a weak relationship. A strong relationship may indicate causation, but not necessarily. Testing the relationship between variables is the goal of some sociological research.

independent variable a factor that causes a change in another variable, called the dependent variable

dependent variable a factor in an experiment that is changed by an independent variable

unobtrusive measures ways of observing people so they do not know they are being studied

Your **independent variable,** something that causes a change in another variable, would be therapy. Your **dependent variable,** the variable that might change, would be the men's behavior: whether they abuse women after they get out of jail. Unfortunately, your operational definition of the men's behavior will be sloppy: either reports from the wives or records indicating which men were rearrested for abuse. This is sloppy because some of the women will not report the abuse, and some of the men who abuse their wives will not be arrested. Yet it may be the best you can do.

Let's assume that you choose rearrest as your operational definition. If you find that the men who received therapy are *less* likely to be rearrested for abuse, you can attribute the difference to the therapy. If you find *no difference* in rearrest rates, you can conclude that the therapy was ineffective. If you find that the men who received the therapy have a *higher* rearrest rate, you can conclude that the therapy backfired.

Ideally, you would test different types of therapy. Perhaps only some types work. You might even want to test self-therapy by assigning articles, books, and videos.

Unobtrusive Measures

Researchers sometimes use **unobtrusive measures,** observing the behavior of people who are not aware that they are being studied. For example, social researchers studied the level of whisky consumption in a town that was legally "dry" by counting empty bottles in trashcans (Lee 2000). Researchers have also gone high-tech in their unobtrusive measures. To trace customers' paths through stores, they attach infrared surveillance devices to shopping carts. Grocery chains use these findings to place higher-profit items in more strategic locations (McCarthy 1993). Casino operators use chips that transmit radio frequencies, allowing them to track how much their high rollers are betting at every hand of poker or blackjack (Sanders 2005; Grossman 2007). Billboards read information embedded on a chip in your car key. As you drive by, the billboard displays *your* name with a personal message (Feder 2007). The same device can *collect* information as you drive by. Cameras in sidewalk billboards scan the facial features of people who pause to look at its advertising, reporting their sex, race, and how long they looked (Clifford 2008). The billboards, which raise ethical issues of invasion of privacy, are part of marketing, not sociological research.

It would be considered unethical to use most unobtrusive measures to research spouse abuse. You could, however, analyze 911 calls. Also, if there were a public forum held by abused or abusing spouses on the Internet, you could record and analyze the online conversations. Ethics in unobtrusive research are still a matter of dispute: To secretly record the behavior of people in public settings, such as a crowd, is generally considered acceptable, but to do so in private settings is not.

Deciding Which Method to Use

How do sociologists choose among these methods? Four primary factors affect their decision. The first is *access to resources*. They may want to conduct a survey, for example, but if their finances won't permit this, they might analyze documents instead. The second is *access to subjects*. Even though they prefer face-to-face interviews, if the people who make up the sample live far away, researchers might mail them questionnaires or conduct a survey by telephone or e-mail. The third factor concerns the *purpose of the research*. Each method is better for answering certain types of questions. Participant observation, for example, is good at uncovering people's attitudes, while experiments are better at resolving questions of cause and effect. Fourth, *the researcher's background or training* comes into play. In graduate school, sociologists study many methods, but they are able to practice only some of them. After graduate school, sociologists who were trained in quantitative research methods, which emphasize measurement and statistics, are likely to use surveys. Sociologists who were trained in qualitative research methods, which emphasize observing and interpreting people's behavior, lean toward participant observation.

How Hwee Young/epa/Corbis

To prevent cheating by customers and personnel, casinos use *unobtrusive measures*. In the ceiling above this blackjack table are video cameras that record every action. Observors are also posted there.

Controversy in Sociological Research

Sociologists sometimes find themselves in the hot seat because of their research. Some poke into private areas of life, which upsets people. Others investigate political matters, and their findings threaten those who have a stake in the situation. When researchers in Palestine asked refugees if they would be willing to accept compensation and not return to Israel if there were a peace settlement, most said they would take the buyout. When the head researcher released these findings, an enraged mob beat him and trashed his office (Bennet 2003). In the following Thinking Critically section, you can see how even such a straightforward task as counting the homeless can land sociologists in the midst of controversy.

ThinkingCRITICALLY

Doing Controversial Research—Counting the Homeless

What could be less offensive than counting the homeless? As sometimes occurs, however, even basic research lands sociologists in the midst of controversy. This is what happened to sociologist Peter Rossi and his associates.

There was a dispute between advocates for the homeless and federal officials. The advocates claimed that 3 to 7 million Americans were homeless; the officials claimed that the total was about 250,000. Each side accused the other of gross distortion—the one to place pressure on Congress, the other to keep the public from knowing how bad the situation really was. But each side was only guessing.

Only an accurate count could clear up the picture. Peter Rossi and the National Opinion Research Center took on that job. They had no vested interest in supporting either side, only in answering this question honestly.

The challenge was immense. The *population* was evident—the U.S. homeless. A *survey* would be appropriate, but how do you survey a *sample* of the homeless? No one has a list of the homeless, and only some of the homeless stay at shelters. As for *validity*, to make certain that they were counting only people who were really homeless, the researchers needed a good *operational definition* of homelessness. To include people who weren't really homeless would destroy the study's *reliability*. The researchers wanted results that would be consistent if others were to *replicate*, or repeat, the study.

As an operational definition, the researchers used "literally homeless," people "who do not have access to a conventional dwelling and who would be homeless by any conceivable definition of the term." With funds limited, the researchers couldn't do a national count, but they could count the homeless in Chicago.

By using a *stratified random sample*, the researchers were able to generalize to the entire city. How could they do this since there is no list of the homeless? They did have a list of the city's shelters and a map of the city. A stratified random sample of the city's shelters gave them access to the homeless who sleep in the shelters. For the homeless who sleep in the streets, parks, and vacant buildings, they used a stratified random sample of the city's blocks.

Their findings? On an average night, 2,722 people are homeless in Chicago. Because people move in and out of homelessness, between 5,000 and 7,000 are homeless at

Research sometimes lands sociologists in the midst of controversy. As described here, the results of a study to determine how many homeless people there are in the United States displeased homeless advocates. Homelessness is currently growing at such a pace that many U.S. cities have set up "tent cities." Shown here is a tile worker in St. Petersburg, Florida, who lost his home and lives in a tent.

Diez, Cherie/St. Petersburg Times/Rapport Press via Newscom

some point during the year. On warm nights, only two out of five sleep in the shelters, and even during Chicago's cold winters only three out of four do so. Seventy-five percent are men, 60 percent African Americans. One in four is a former mental patient, one in five a former prisoner. Projecting these findings to the United States yields a national total of about 350,000 homeless people.

This total elated government officials and stunned the homeless advocates. The advocates said that the number couldn't possibly be right, and they began to snipe at the researchers. This is one of the risks of doing research, for sociologists never know whose toes they will step on. The sniping made the researchers uncomfortable, and to let everyone know they weren't trying to minimize the problem, they stressed that these 350,000 Americans live desperate lives. They sleep in city streets, live in shelters, eat out of garbage cans, and suffer from severe health problems.

The controversy continues. With funding at stake for shelters and for treating mental problems and substance abuse, homeless advocates continue to insist that at least 2 million Americans are homeless. While the total is not in the millions, it has doubled recently to 672,000. As a sign of changing times, veterans, many of them emotionally disturbed, make up 15 percent of this total.

Sources: Based on Anderson 1986; Rossi et al. 1986; Rossi et al. 1987; Rossi 1989, 1991, 1999; Bialik 2006; Chan 2007; National Coalition for the Homeless 2008; Preston 2008.

Gender in Sociological Research

You know how significant gender is in your own life, how it affects your orientations and your attitudes. You also may be aware that gender opens and closes doors to you. Because gender is also a factor in social research, researchers must take steps to prevent it from biasing their findings. For example, sociologists Diana Scully and Joseph Marolla (1984, 2007) interviewed convicted rapists in prison. They were concerned that their gender might lead to *interviewer bias*—that the prisoners might shift their answers, sharing certain experiences or opinions with Marolla, but saying something else to Scully. To prevent gender bias, each researcher interviewed half the sample. Later in this chapter, we'll look at what they found out.

Gender certainly can be an impediment in research. In our imagined research on spouse abuse, for example, could a man even do participant observation of women who have been beaten by their husbands? Technically, the answer is yes. But because the women have been victimized by men, they might be less likely to share their experiences and feelings with men. If so, women would be better suited to conduct this research, more likely to achieve valid results. The supposition that these victims will be more open with women than with men, however, is just that—a supposition. Research alone will verify or refute this assumption.

Gender is significant in other ways, too. It is certainly a mistake to assume that what applies to one sex also applies to the other (Bird and Rieker 1999; Neuman 2006). Women's and men's lives differ significantly, and if we do research on just half of humanity, our research will be vastly incomplete. Today's huge numbers of women sociologists guarantee that women will not be ignored in social research. In the past, however, when almost all sociologists were men, women's experiences were neglected.

Gender issues can pop up in unexpected ways in sociological research. I vividly recall this incident in San Francisco.

The streets were getting dark, and I was still looking for homeless people. When I saw someone lying down, curled up in a doorway, I approached the individual. As I got close, I began my opening research line, "Hi, I'm Dr. Henslin from. . . ." The individual began to scream and started to thrash wildly. Startled by this sudden, high-pitched scream and by the rapid movements, I quickly backed away. When I later analyzed what had happened, I concluded that I had intruded into a woman's bedroom.

This incident also holds another lesson. Researchers do their best, but they make mistakes. Sometimes these mistakes are minor, and even humorous. The woman sleeping in the doorway wasn't frightened. It was only just getting dark, and there were many people on the street. She was just assertively marking her territory and letting me know in no uncertain terms that I was an intruder. If we make a mistake in research, we pick up and go on. As we do so, we take ethical considerations into account, which is the topic of our next section.

Ethics in Sociological Research

In addition to choosing an appropriate research method, we must also follow the ethics of sociology (American Sociological Association 1999). Research ethics require honesty, truth, and openness (sharing findings with the scientific community). Ethics clearly forbid the falsification of results. They also condemn plagiarism—that is, stealing someone else's work. Another ethical guideline states that research subjects should generally be informed that they are being studied and should never be harmed by the research. Ethics also require that sociologists protect the anonymity of those who provide information. Sometimes people reveal things that are intimate, potentially embarrassing, or otherwise harmful to themselves. Finally, although not all sociologists agree, it generally is considered unethical for researchers to misrepresent themselves.

Sociologists take their ethical standards seriously. To illustrate the extent to which they will go to protect their respondents, consider the research conducted by Mario Brajuha.

Protecting the Subjects: The Brajuha Research

Mario Brajuha, a graduate student at the State University of New York at Stony Brook, was doing participant observation of restaurant workers. He lost his job as a waiter when the restaurant where he was working burned down—a fire of "suspicious origin," as the police said. When detectives learned that Brajuha had taken field notes (Brajuha and Hallowell 1986), they asked to see them. Because he had promised to keep the information confidential, Brajuha refused to hand them over. When the district attorney subpoenaed the notes, Brajuha still refused. The district attorney then threatened to put Brajuha in jail. By this time, Brajuha's notes had become rather famous, and unsavory characters—perhaps those who had set the fire—also wanted to know what was in them. They, too, demanded to see them, accompanying their demands with threats of a different nature. Brajuha found himself between a rock and a hard place.

For two years, Brajuha refused to hand over his notes, even though he grew anxious and had to appear at several court hearings. Finally, the district attorney dropped the subpoena. When the two men under investigation for setting the fire died, the threats to Brajuha, his wife, and their children ended.

Misleading the Subjects: The Humphreys Research

Sociologists agree on the necessity to protect respondents, and they applaud the professional manner in which Brajuha handled himself. Although it is considered acceptable for sociologists to do covert participant observation (studying some situation without announcing that they are doing research), to deliberately misrepresent oneself is considered unethical. Let's look at the case of Laud Humphreys, whose research forced sociologists to rethink and refine their ethical stance.

Laud Humphreys, a classmate of mine at Washington University in St. Louis, was an Episcopal priest who decided to become a sociologist. For his Ph.D. dissertation, Humphreys (1971, 1975) studied social interaction in "tearooms," public restrooms where some men go for quick, anonymous oral sex with other men.

Humphreys found that some restrooms in Forest Park, just across from our campus, were tearooms. He began a participant observation study by hanging around these restrooms. He found that in addition to the two men having sex, a third man—called a "watch queen"—served as a lookout for police and other unwelcome strangers.

Drew Crawford/The Image Works

Ethics in social research are of vital concern to sociologists. As discussed in the text, sociologists may disagree on some of the issue's finer points, but none would approve of slipping LSD to unsuspecting subjects like these Marine recruits in basic training at Parris Island, South Carolina. This was done to U.S. soldiers in the 1960s under the guise of legitimate testing—just "to see what would happen."

Humphreys took on the role of watch queen, not only watching for strangers but also observing what the men did. He wrote field notes after the encounters.

Humphreys decided that he wanted to learn about the regular lives of these men. For example, what was the significance of the wedding rings that many of the men wore? He came up with an ingenious technique: Many of the men parked their cars near the tearooms, and Humphreys recorded their license plate numbers. A friend in the St. Louis police department gave Humphreys each man's address. About a year later, Humphreys arranged for these men to be included in a medical survey conducted by some of the sociologists on our faculty.

Disguising himself with a different hairstyle and clothing, Humphreys visited the men's homes. He interviewed the men, supposedly for the medical study. He found that they led conventional lives. They voted, mowed their lawns, and took their kids to Little League games. Many reported that their wives were not aroused sexually or were afraid of getting pregnant because their religion did not allow them to use birth control. Humphreys concluded that heterosexual men were also using the tearooms for a form of quick sex.

This study stirred controversy among sociologists and nonsociologists alike. Many sociologists criticized Humphreys, and a national columnist even wrote a scathing denunciation of "sociological snoopers" (Von Hoffman 1970). One of our professors even tried to get Humphreys' Ph.D. revoked. As the controversy heated up and a court case loomed, Humphreys feared that his list of respondents might be subpoenaed. He gave me the list to take from Missouri to Illinois, where I had begun teaching. When he called and asked me to destroy it, I burned the list in my backyard.

Was this research ethical? This question is not decided easily. Although many sociologists sided with Humphreys—and his book reporting the research won a highly acclaimed award—the criticisms continued. At first, Humphreys defended his position vigorously, but five years later, in a second edition of his book (1975), he stated that he should have identified himself as a researcher.

How Research and Theory Work Together

Research cannot stand alone. Nor can theory. As sociologist C. Wright Mills (1959) argued so forcefully, research without theory is simply a collection of unrelated "facts." But theory without research, Mills added, is abstract and empty—it can't represent the way life really is.

Research and theory, then, are both essential for sociology. Every theory must be tested, which requires research. And as sociologists do research, they often come up with surprising findings. Those findings must be explained, and for that we need theory. As sociologists study social life, then, they combine research and theory.

The Real World: When the Ideal Meets the Real

Although we can list the ideals of research, real-life situations often force sociologists to settle for something that falls short of the ideal. In the following Thinking Critically section, let's look at how two sociologists confronted the ideal and the real.

ThinkingCRITICALLY

Are Rapists Sick? A Close-Up View of Research

Two sociologists, Diana Scully and Joseph Marolla, whose research was mentioned earlier, were not satisfied with the typical explanation that rapists are "sick," psychologically disturbed, or different from other men. They developed the hypothesis that rape is like most human behavior—learned through interaction with others. That is, some men learn to think of rape as appropriate behavior.

To test this hypothesis, it would be best to interview a random sample of rapists. But this is impossible. There is no list of all rapists, so there is no way to give them all the same chance of being included in a sample. You can't even use prison populations to select a random sample, for many rapists have never been caught, some who were caught were found not guilty, and some who were found guilty were given probation. And as we know from DNA testing, some who were convicted of rape are innocent. Consequently, Scully and Marolla confronted the classic dilemma of sociologists—either to not do the research or to do it under less than ideal conditions.

They chose to do the research. When they had the opportunity to interview convicted rapists in prison, they jumped at it. They knew that whatever they learned would be more than we already knew. They sent out 3,500 letters to men serving time in seven prisons in Virginia, the state where they were teaching. About 25 percent of the prisoners agreed to be interviewed. They matched these men on the basis of age, education, race–ethnicity, severity of offense, and previous criminal record. This resulted in a sample of 98 prisoners who were convicted of rape and a control sample of 75 men convicted of other offenses.

As noted earlier, because the sex of the interviewer can bias research results, Scully and Marolla each interviewed half the sample. It took them 600 hours to gather information on the prisoners, including their psychological, criminal, and sexual history. To guard against lies, they checked what the individuals told them against their institutional records. They used twelve scales to measure the men's attitudes about women, rape, and themselves. In order to find out what circumstances the men defined as rape or when they viewed the victim as responsible, they also gave the men nine vignettes of forced sexual encounters and asked them to determine responsibility in each one.

Scully and Marolla discovered something that goes against common sense—that most rapists are not sick and that they are not overwhelmed by uncontrollable urges. The psychological histories of the rapists and the nonrapists were similar. These men rape for a variety of reasons: to "blow off steam" over problems they are having with others, to get sex, to feel powerful, and to hurt women (Monahan et al. 2005). Some rape spontaneously, while others plan their rapes. Some rape as a form of revenge, to get even with someone, not necessarily their victim. For some, rape is even a form of recreation, and they rape with friends on weekends.

Scully and Marolla also found support for what feminists had been pointing out for years, that power is a major element in rape. Here is what one man said:

> Rape gave me the power to do what I wanted to do without feeling I had to please a partner or respond to a partner. I felt in control, dominant. Rape was the ability to have sex without caring about the woman's response. I was totally dominant.

To discover that most rape is calculated behavior—that rapists are not "sick"; that a motivating force can be power, not passion; that the behavior stems from the criminal pursuit of pleasure, not from mental illness—is significant. It makes the sociological quest worthwhile.

In comparing their sample of rapists with their control group of nonrapists, Scully and Marolla also made another significant finding: The rapists are more likely to believe "rape myths." They are more likely to believe that women cause their own rape by the way they act and the clothes they wear, that a woman who charges rape has simply changed her mind after participating in consensual sex, and that most men accused of rape are innocent.

Connecting Research and Theory

Such findings go far beyond simply adding to our storehouse of "facts." As indicated in Figure 1, research stimulates both the development of theory and the need for more research. Scully and Marolla suggest that rape myths act as neutralizers, that they allow "potential rapists to turn off social prohibitions against injuring others."

This hypothesis needs to be confirmed by other research. It also pinpoints the need to determine how such myths are transmitted. Which male subcultures perpetuate them? Do the mass media contribute to these myths? Do family, religion, and education create respect for females and help keep males from learning such myths? Or do they somehow contribute to these myths? If so, how?

Sociologists have begun to build on this path-breaking research, which was done, as usual, under less than ideal conditions. The resulting theorizing and research may provide the basis for making changes that reduce the incidence of rape in our society.

Sources: Marolla and Scully 1986; Scully 1990; Scully and Marolla 1984, 2007.

Sociology needs more of this type of research—imaginative and sometimes daring investigations conducted in an imperfect world under less than ideal conditions. This is really what sociology is all about. Sociologists study what people do—whether their behaviors are conforming or deviant, whether they please others or disgust them. No matter what behavior is studied, systematic research methods and the application of social theory take us beyond common sense. They allow us to penetrate surface realities so we can better understand human behavior—and, in the ideal case, make changes to help improve social life.

SUMMARY *and* REVIEW

What Is a Valid Sociological Topic?

Any human behavior is a valid sociological topic, even disreputable behavior. Spouse abuse is an example. Sociological research is based on the sociologist's interests, access to subjects, appropriate methods, and ethical considerations.

Common Sense and the Need for Sociological Research

Why isn't common sense adequate?

Common sense doesn't provide reliable information. When subjected to scientific research, commonsense ideas often are found to be limited or false.

A Research Model

What are the eight basic steps of sociological research?

(1) Selecting a topic, (2) Defining the problem, (3) Reviewing the literature, (4) Formulating a **hypothesis,** (5) Choosing a research method, (6) Collecting the data, (7) Analyzing the results, and (8) Sharing the results.

Research Methods

How do sociologists gather data?

To collect data, sociologists use seven **research methods** (or research designs): **surveys, participant observation** (fieldwork), **case studies, secondary analysis, documents, experiments,** and **unobtrusive measures.**

How do sociologists choose a research method?

Sociologists choose their research method based on questions to be answered, their access to potential subjects, the resources available, their training, and ethical considerations.

Controversy in Sociological Research

Why is sociological research often controversial?

Some people get upset because sociologists do research on disreputable or illegal activities or on personal or intimate areas of life. Other people get upset when research findings go against their interests or biases.

Gender in Sociological Research

What is the relationship between gender and research?

There are two aspects. First, findings based on samples of men do not necessarily apply to women and findings based on samples of women do not necessarily apply to men. Second, in some kinds of research, such as studying abused spouses, rape victims, and rapists, the gender of the researcher could affect findings.

Ethics in Sociological Research

How important are ethics in sociological research?

Ethics are of fundamental concern to sociologists, who are committed to openness, honesty, truth, and protecting their subjects from harm. The Brajuha research on restau-

rant workers and the Humphreys research on "tearooms" were cited to illustrate ethical issues that concern sociologists.

How Research and Theory Work Together

What is the relationship between theory and research?

Theory and research depend on one another. Theory generates questions that need to be answered by research, and sociologists use theory to interpret the data they gather. Research, in turn, helps to generate theory: Findings that don't match what is expected can indicate a need to modify theory.

THINKING CRITICALLY

1. Should sociologists be allowed to do research on disreputable or disapproved behavior? On illegal behavior? Why or why not?

2. What factors make for *bad* sociological research? How can these be avoided?

3. What ethics govern sociological research?

4. Is it right (or ethical) for sociologists to not identify themselves when they do research? To misrepresent themselves? What if identifying themselves as researchers will destroy their access to a research setting or to informants?

ADDITIONAL RESOURCES

What can you find in MySocLab? mysoclab www.mysoclab.com

- Complete Ebook
- Practice Tests and Video and Audio activities
- Mapping and Data Analysis exercises

- Sociology in the News
- Classic Readings in Sociology
- Research and Writing advice

Where Can I Read More on This Topic?

Bryman, Alan. *Social Research Methods,* 3rd ed. Oxford: Oxford University Press, 2008. An overview of the research methods used by sociologists, with an emphasis on the logic that underlies these methods.

Creswell, John W. *Research Design: Qualitative, Quantitative, and Mixed Methods Approaches,* 3rd ed. Beverly Hills, Calif.: Sage, 2008. This introduction to research methods walks you through the research experience and helps you to understand when to use a particular method.

Drew, Paul, Geoffrey Raymond, and Darin Weinberg. *Talk and Interaction in Social Research Methods.* Thousand Oaks, Calif.: Sage, 2006. The authors stress the importance of talk in a variety of social research methods.

Lee, Raymond M. *Unobtrusive Methods in Social Research.* Philadelphia: Open University Press, 2000. This overview of unobtrusive ways of doing social research summarizes many interesting studies.

Lomand, Turner C. *Social Science Research: A Cross Section of Journal Articles for Discussion and Evaluation,* 5th ed. Los Angeles: Pyrczak, 2007. This overview of the methods of research used by sociologists includes articles on current topics.

Neuman, W. Lawrence. *Social Research Methods: Qualitative and Quantitative Approaches,* 6th ed. Boston: Allyn and Bacon, 2006. This "how-to" book of sociological research describes how sociologists gather data and the logic that underlies each method.

Schuman, Howard. *Method and Meaning in Polls and Surveys.* Cambridge, Mass.: Harvard University Press, 2008. Examines how the wording of questions can change findings and how to understand the results of surveys.

Whyte, William Foote. *Creative Problem Solving in the Field: Reflections on a Career.* Lanham, Md.: AltaMira Press, 1997. Focusing on his extensive field experiences, the author provides insight into the researcher's role in participant observation.

Wysocki, Diane Kholos, ed. *Readings in Social Research Methods,* 3rd ed. Belmont, Calif.: Wadsworth, 2008. The authors of these articles provide an overview of research methods.

Writing Papers for Sociology

Booth, Wayne C., Gregory G. Colomb, and Joseph M. Williams. *The Craft of Research,* 3rd ed. Chicago: University of Chicago Press, 2008. How to plan a paper, build an argument, anticipate and respond to the reservations of readers, and create introductions and conclusions that answer the demanding question, "So what?"

Richlin-Klonsky, Judith, William G. Roy, Ellen Strenski, and Roseann Giarusso, eds. The Sociology Writing Group. *A Guide to Writing Sociology Papers,* 6th ed. New York: Worth, 2007. The guide walks students through the steps in writing a sociology paper, from choosing the initial assignment to doing the research and turning in a finished paper. Also explains how to manage time and correctly cite sources.

SOCIAL PSYCHOLOGY'S THREE LITTLE PIGS*

Donelson R. Forsyth

Virginia Commonwealth University

In this article, Donelson Forsyth uses the fable of the three little pigs to illustrate three perspectives on the nature of scientific research. The debate over the relative merits of these three perspectives has been raging since the field of social psychology emerged. The first little pig represents basic science, or the study of theoretically meaningful questions through rigorous scientific methods of research. The second little pig represents applied science or the tackling of practical problems. The third little pig represents the best combination of both: action research. Action research is applied research that seeks to solve practical problems by the application of theory. The "big bad wolf" in this story can represent many things: reality, funding opportunities, denial of tenure or promotion, peer review for publication, null results, etc.

There are many subtleties in this paper that will amuse you depending on how much you know about research and social psychology. For example, the so-called Journal for Purely Scientific Pigs (JPSP) is meant as a mock acronym of the Journal of Personality and Social Psychology, *also abbreviated JPSP. Similarly, the yearly reunions are references to the annual meetings of the American Psychological Association or similar associations.*

As with all such allegories, the simple appearance of this fable masks its deeper truth.

Not-so-long-ago in a not-so-far-away land lived three little pigs. These three little pigs grew up in the same neighborhood, attended the same schools, and shared the same passion: houses. The three were fascinated by the various types of structures inhabited by pigs the world over, and they whiled away many a happy hour puzzling over the nature and design of such dwellings. They could think of nothing more meaningful than dedicating their lives to the scientific study of houses and the ways they can be improved and repaired.

As they grew older, however, the pigs gradually grew apart in values, beliefs, and goals. The first pig became intrigued with understanding how houses worked, and embarked on a systematic study of foundations, arches, doors, and windows. So he bought a big armchair in which to sit in his straw house and develop theory. He converted his pig pen into an elaborate laboratory where he could test out hypotheses, and erected a large sign for all to see. The sign read: Scientific Pig. Using his armchair and laboratory, he developed a particularly interesting theory about round houses that had no windows or doors. Although no one had found any of these houses, other scientifically minded pigs thought the work was interesting.

The second pig was also interested in the theory behind houses, arches and doorways. The second pig, however, wanted to use this knowledge to improve houses; to repair misshapen houses and possibly make houses of tomorrow better than houses of today. So this pig put a sign in front of his pen that read "Practical Pig," and began helping other pigs build and repair their houses. Soon, Practical Pig had made so much money that he could afford to build a breathtakingly beautiful house of sticks on a large tract of land in the country.

What, in the meantime, was the third pig doing? Well, it seems that he too was trying diligently to understand the nature of houses. Although Scientific Pig and Practical Pig only spoke to one another once a year at their annual reunion, the third pig often visited each one to talk about houses and ideas for improving them. When Scientific Pig would describe his studies of round houses, the third pig would ask what the studies say about the structural dynamics of houses in general. And when Practical Pig would talk about building houses out of sticks, the third pig would ask why sticks rather than stone? After many conversations and much research on houses, the third pig managed to build a house that, though it lacked the beauty of Practical Pig's house, was more useful than the round houses that the Scientific Pig studied.

"Social Psychology's Three Little Pigs," by Donelson R. Forsyth, reprinted from *The State of Social Psychology*, edited by Mark R. Leary, 1989, Sage. Copyright © by Select Press. pp. 63–65.

From: Donelson R. Forsyth, reprinted from *The State of Social Psychology*, edited by Mark R. Leary (1989), by permission of Sage Publications, Inc.

One day a pig-hungry wolf came to town. When he came to the first pig's pen the wolf said, "I am hungry, and must have a pig for breakfast."

Scientific Pig, rising up from his arm chair said, "Why eat me? Can't you see the long-term importance of my work on round houses?

"No," answered the wolf as he bit off the poor Scientific Pig's head.

You see, although the first pig had fashioned a marvelous round house of straw and mortar with strong arches and walls, it had no window or doors. It was a fine model to be used for testing predictions about houses, but it didn't protect him from the wolf. The third pig had warned him that building houses with doors would yield both better data as well as safety from predators, but he hadn't heeded his friend's warnings.

Sadly, the second pig was also eaten, for although he had built what seemed to be a safe house, Practical Pig decided to use sticks for the walls. Although the first pig had found that "weightbearing, rigid barriers fashioned from the woody fibers of trees and shrubs can be rendered discohesive through exposure to focused atmospheric air pressure of excessive magnitude," the Practical Pig felt that the first pig's studies were so artificial that they didn't have any relevance for "real" houses. In fact, he had let his subscription to the *Journal for Purely Scientific Pigs* (or, *JPSP*) lapse, so he didn't even know about the problems with sticks. So when the wolf huffed and puffed and blew, the house tumbled down and the second pig fell victim.

The third pig survived (of course). When he saw the wolf approach, he ran into his house and locked the door. The wolf pushed on the house, but the foundation and structure were too strong. He tried blowing on the house, but the stone walls held secure. He tried climbing on the roof, but the carefully crafted masonry gave him no purchase. The hungry wolf, relenting, then left the third pig in peace.

The moral of the story is taken from the monument that the third pig erected to the memory of his departed childhood friends. It read:

Knowledge cannot prosper
When science is one-sided,
The basic and applied must be
United, not divided.

(Postscript: It should also be noted that although the third pig mourned the passing of his two friends, he was glad to finally get control of the editorial boards of the leading journals in the field.)

ENDNOTE

Author's Note: This paper is based on an allegory presented at the 10th Annual Meeting of the Society of Southeastern Social Psychology, November 1987, in Athens, Georgia. Thanks are extended to Leo Simonetta, Steve Danish, and Mark Leary for their help in writing the allegory.

✌ Questions

1. In your opinion, what does the "big bad wolf" represent?

2. Can this story apply to fields other than social psychology, such as chemistry, architecture, or economics? Why or why not?

3. What other stories could describe the field of social psychology or social psychological research? Can the story of Little Red Riding Hood apply to the process of research, for example?

What Does It Mean to Be Human?: Human Nature, Society, and Culture

JOEL M. CHARON

The popular television series "The Twilight Zone" of the 1960s was exciting and sometimes eerie. As an audience we seemed to know that a surprise—scary, wondrous, or both—awaited us at the end if we patiently followed the story. One episode that has stayed with me concerned a journey by American astronauts who landed on a distant planet. They befriended the inhabitants (who looked very human) and were pleased to find themselves in a luxurious home, much like one they might have had on earth. However, they eventually became aware that they could not leave the home, that they had become prisoners. Then a wall opened up and revealed a large pane of glass with spectators peering in. The astronauts were on display under the label "*Homo Sapiens* from the Planet Earth."

Since then, I have been bothered by a question that probably few people asked after seeing that episode: What would those creatures from earth that we call human beings have to do in the cage for those outside to understand what human beings are really like? Phrasing the question differently: What is the human being? What makes us "human" and not something else? In what ways are we like all other living creatures? What do we have in common with other animals?

65

How are we different? Of course, these questions have probably teased the thinking person from the very beginning of human existence. Look around. We see worms, dogs, cats, bees, ants, and maybe fish. Are we unique? All species of animals are unique. But how are we unique? What is our essence as a species? What would the astronauts in the cage have to do to reveal the essence of the species they represent?

We might begin by recognizing that we share many qualities with other animals. Human beings are mammals, which means we are warm-blooded, we give birth to live young, the female nurses the young, and we have hair covering parts of our body. We are also primates; therefore, we are mammals who are part of an order within nature that is characterized by increasing manual dexterity, intelligence, and the probability of some social organization.

Philosophers have made various claims about what our outstanding characteristic, our key quality, is. They have pointed to our ability to make and use tools, to love, to know right from wrong, to feel, to think, or to use language. Religious leaders emphasize that we have a soul and a conscience. They may also stress that we are created in God's image (thus, we are closest to God) or that we are selfish and sinful (thus, we are similar to other animals). The more cynical critic maintains that we are the only animal that makes war on its own kind (even though other animals are clearly aggressive toward members of their own species).

Psychologists may focus on the fact that humans are instinctive, that they are driven by their nonconscious personality, that they are conditioned like many other animals, or that, unlike other animals, they act in the world according to the ideas and perceptions they learn. Most will maintain that human beings develop traits early in life out of an interplay of heredity and environment.

Sociologists, too, have much to say about the nature of the human being. They maintain that our unique qualities are that we are

1. *social,* in that our lives are linked to others and to society in many complex ways;

2. *cultural,* in that what we become is not a result of instinct but of the ideas, values, and rules developed in our society.

Without these two core qualities, we would not be *what we are.* Put us in a zoo, take away either quality, and visitors to the zoo would see something very different. To understand human beings as a species, therefore, it is important to understand how these two core qualities enter into our lives. It is also important to recognize the complex interrelationship between the social and the cultural: Our culture *arises from* our social life, and the continuation of our social life *depends on* our culture.

☺ Human Beings Are Social Beings

. . .

What does it mean to be "social"? On the simplest level it means that *humans need others for their very survival.* Infants need adults for their physical survival: for food, shelter, and protection. A great deal of evidence suggests that infants also need adults for emotional support, affection, and love. Normal growth—even life itself—seems to depend on this support. Studies of infants brought up in nurseries with very little interaction with adults show us that these babies suffer physical, intellectual, and emotional harm and that this harm is lasting (Spitz, 1945). Of course, the horrible discovery in 1990 of infants brought up in Romanian government nurseries attests to the same problems: Neglecting the basic emotional needs of children brings severe retardation of growth and often death.

Adults also need other people. We depend on others for our physical survival (to grow and transport our food, to provide shelter and clothing, to provide protection from enemies, and almost all the things we take for granted). As adults we also depend on others for love, support, meaning, and happiness. Human survival, therefore, is a social affair: Almost all of our needs—physical and emotional—are met through interaction with others.

Learning How to Survive

To be social also means that much of what we become depends on socialization. *Socialization* is the process by which the various representatives of society—parents, teachers, political leaders, religious leaders, the news media—teach people the ways of society and, in so doing, form their basic qualities. Through socialization people learn the ways of society and internalize those ways—that is, make them their own.

Back to survival, for a moment: Others are important not only for fulfilling our needs, but also for *teaching us how to survive.* We know how to do very little instinctively (suck, defecate, breathe, sweat, cry, see, hear, and other simple reflexes). But we are not born knowing how to deal with our environment. As newcomers we do not know how to get along in our world. We do not know how to deal with other people, weather, food sources, shelter, and so on. We do not know how to survive through instinct, necessitating our social nature. We do not have to learn that we need to eat, but we do learn how to get food (to grow it, hunt it, fish it, or buy it). In most societies (though not all) we must also learn how to build a shelter, use weapons, make clothing, and handle other people, to name only a few of the things that matter. In fact, we must learn thousands of things if we are to survive in the society we live in, from learning the ABCs to learning how to discourage others from robbing us to learning how best to dress and talk so we can be popular. In short, human beings live in a world where *socialization is necessary for survival.*

Individual Qualities

Besides showing us how to survive, *socialization is also necessary for creating our individual qualities.* Our talents, tastes, interests, values, personality traits, ideas, and morals are not qualities we have at birth but qualities we develop through socialization in the context of the family, the school, our peers, the community, and even the media.

We become what we do because of a complex mixture of heredity and socialization. We may have certain biological predispositions, but how others act toward us, what they teach us, and the opportunities they provide for us are all important for what we become. As we interact with others, we choose the directions we will take in life: crime or legitimate business, school or on-the-job training, the single life or the married life, life on the farm or life in the city. Some of us may have all kinds of talent, but whether we direct it toward making money through selling illegal drugs or helping people solve their problems through psychoanalysis depends on our interactions and resulting socialization.

The treatment of women in our society highlights this point. Actually, if we are going to be more accurate, this description is most applicable to white women born in America. In colonial days women were socialized to become the property of men. It was socialization not only by parents, neighbors, religion, and friends that accomplished this, but also by limited opportunities for women in the larger society, and this prohibition told women what they must become to be useful in society. Eventually, the relationship between white women and men was altered as women were increasingly socialized to take care of the household in return for male economic support. In the twentieth century, and especially after World War II, this relationship moved toward a more equal one. As economic opportunities opened up, white women joined the paid labor force in real numbers. Their success in the political, educational, and economic worlds altered the expectations in society for women, and it increasingly altered the female role. After the war, our view of the differences between women and men continued to blur. By the 1990s, an acceptance of the idea that women can do almost anything traditionally reserved for men had clearly evolved, even though opportunities remained limited. Such an idea influences the socialization of children; that socialization affects choices made in life. I never dreamed 25 years ago that women would ever compete in horse racing, bodybuilding, or fast-pitch softball. I never imagined that women would be successfully competing with men in the armed services, on police forces, and in business. My imagination was limited by my own socialization, which carefully distinguished what men could do from what women could do. Opportunity and socialization have influenced each other, and the result is a society less differentiated and stratified on the basis of gender. Although barriers will continue to exist in society for a long time, we are clearly living within a real-life experiment that offers clear support for the idea that socialization is very powerful for what people become!

It is important to see that socialization is very complex. It involves not only learning things but also modeling one's behavior on that of individuals whom one respects, being socialized by perceived opportunities "for people like us," and being influenced by one's successes and failures. When we see socialization this way, we can better understand the harmful effects of discrimination, segregation, and persecution. To be put down by others directly has an impact; to see others like oneself in a deprived existence has an effect on the value one places on oneself as well as the expectations that one develops for oneself. Of course, some individuals overcome such conditions, but these exceptions do not disprove the power of socialization. Indeed, they help clarify the importance of socialization as we try to identify the conditions that encourage individuals to be different from those around them. Socialization helps explain why poverty is so powerful a force on what children choose to do with their adult lives.

We can also turn this explanation around. The opportunities that wealthy and privileged people have in society socialize their children to seek directions closed to most other people in society: prestigious high schools and colleges, providing professional training that helps ensure high placement in society and a life of affluence. Robert Coles (1977) describes the final result of socialization in the wealthy class to be "entitlement": The children of the affluent learn that they are entitled to certain things in their lives that other children cannot take for granted and often do not even know exist. "The child has much, but wants and expects more, all assumed to be his or hers by right— at once a psychological and material inheritance that the world will provide" (p. 55). In what their parents give and teach, affluent children learn what they have a right to expect from life, what is their *due* because of who they are.

Socialization may not determine all that we are, but its influence cannot be easily denied. Much of what each of us has become can be traced to our interaction with others, and thus, our individual qualities are in this sense really *social ones.* The sociologist emphasizes how socialization influences our choices, abilities, interests, values, ideas, and perspective—in short, the directions we take in our lives. And, socialization is not something that happens to us in childhood alone; instead, it continues throughout our lives. At every stage we are being taught or shown by others how we should act, what we should think, and who we are. Early socialization may be the most important, but later socialization may reinforce these early directions or lead us in new ones. Socialization forms the individual actor and is the third way we are social beings: by our very nature.

Basic Human Qualities

We have looked at three ways in which we are social: Our survival depends on others, we learn how to survive through what is taught to us by others, and we develop our individual qualities largely through socialization by others. A fourth quality of the human being attests to the importance of our social life: our very humanity.

At what point does the human being *become* human? Religious leaders differ: Some argue that it is at the point of conception, while others say that it occurs when the fetus can survive on its own or at birth or after one year of survival. Indeed, in some religious perspectives children are not really fully human; and for some, women are less than fully human. Religious leaders in every society have joined in defining certain immoral or different people as less than human and thus nondeserving of human rights. Political leaders also define what constitutes a human with full human rights (this is sometimes based on citizenship, ethnic-group membership, religion, gender, and even correct political beliefs). Philosophers, psychologists, biologists, and artists also have their views. Although this is a highly emotional topic, it is a very important one. It revolves around the question of human essence. If we believe in soul, we will use that as the defining quality. If we believe in God-given human rights at the point of conception, we will use that as the defining quality. Philosophers might focus on mind as the defining quality, psychologists human intelligence, and biologists the fertilization of the egg or the birth or development of the mature fetus.

It is in fact a religious, political, and scientific question, and there is little agreement. Scientists typically attempt to identify certain attributes that make human beings human: intelligence, problem-solving ability, language use, or culture, for example. Sociologists typically focus on three interrelated qualities: the use of symbols, the development of self, and thinking. It is only when these three qualities are in evidence that human beings are able to act like the animal we call human. Perhaps the sociologist exaggerates, but there is something very important here: these three qualities, central to the human being, *are socially created.* In this sense, our very humanity is developed only through social interaction. We are unfinished beings at birth, potentially able to act as other humans do, but that potential is realized only through our social life. Let us examine briefly each of these qualities.

The Use of Symbols The more we understand about human beings, the more centrally important becomes their use of *symbols*. A symbol is something that stands for something else and that we use in place of that something else for purposes of communication. Although we communicate through the use of nonintentional body language, unconscious facial expressions, and so on, symbols have the additional quality of being understood by the user. Symbolic communication is meaningful: It represents something to the one who communicates as well as to the one receiving the communication.

Words are the best example of symbols. They stand for whatever we decide they do. We use words intentionally to communicate something to others, and we use words to think with. Besides words, however, we also decide that certain acts are symbolic (shaking hands, kissing, raising a hand). And humans also designate certain objects to be symbolic: flags, rings, crosses, and hairstyles, for example. Such objects are not meaningful in themselves, but they are designated to be.

Where do such representations come from? It is true that many other animals communicate with one another: wagging tails, making gestures, giving off smells, and growling, for example. The vast majority of these behaviors, however, are instinctive. They are not learned, and they are universal to the species. They are performed by the organism automatically and usually do not appear to have any meaning to the user. . . . The closer we get to the human being in the animal kingdom, however, the more the forms of communication take on a different quality: The acts represent something else only because it is agreed on in social interaction. In other words, *the tools of communication are socially based.* Because the meanings of symbols are socially based, what something represents is pointed out—intentionally taught—to the organism. . . .

This ability *to create and use symbols that are understood by the user is part of our social essence.* And this ability is so important to us that it undoubtedly qualifies as a central human quality alongside our social essence. Consider what we do with symbols: We use them *to communicate* ideas, feelings, intentions, identities; *to teach others* what we know; *to communicate* to others and *to cooperate* with others in organization; and *to learn* roles, ideas, values, rules, and morals. We can hand down to future generations what we have learned, and they are able to build on what others have taught; symbols make *the accumulation of knowledge possible.* We use symbols *to think* with: to contemplate the future, apply the past, figure out solutions to problems, consider how our acts might be moral or immoral, generalize (about anything, such as all living things, all animals, or all human beings), and make subtle distinctions between smart and not-so-smart candidates for office. Our whole lives are saturated with the use of symbols. And, far from being created by nature for us, symbols are created by human beings in social interaction. It is through social interaction that our representations are developed, communicated, and understood by us.

Selfhood   In a similar way, humans develop self-awareness only through interaction with others, and self-awareness, too, qualifies as a central human quality. Humans develop a realization that they exist as objects in the environment. . . . This self-realization should not be taken for granted. It arises through the acts of others. We see ourselves through the eyes, words, and actions of others; it is clearly through socialization that we come to see ourselves as objects in the environment. Selfhood develops in stages, and each stage depends on a social context. Through interaction with significant others, we first come to be aware of the self, and we see it through the eyes of one other person at a time. (Children may see themselves through the eyes of their mother, then their father, then their nursery school teacher, then Mister Rogers—all in the same day.) Over time, our significant others merge into a whole, into "them," "society," "other people," or what George Herbert Mead calls a "generalized other," and we begin to use the generalized other to see and direct ourselves. We then see ourselves in relation to a group or society, in relation to many people simultaneously. We thus guide our own acts in line with an organized whole: our family, our elementary school, the United States, all people in our church, or all humanity. We see and understand a relationship between our acts and these other organized wholes.

Selfhood makes possible many human qualities—from the ability to assess our place in a situation or in the universe to the ability to judge our own behavior or general worth in life to the ability to control our own actions through directing ourselves in situations.

Specifically, we are able to do three things because we have a self. First, *we can see and understand the effects of our own actions, and we are able to see and understand the effects of the acts of others on us.* We are thus able to plan strategy, alter our directions, and interpret situations as we act. For example, in choosing a major, students can examine themselves: their abilities, interests, values, and past achievements

They can evaluate their experiences, future chances, and possible occupational opportunities. They will probably try to imagine what they would look like in a certain occupation and whether the work would be enjoyable.

Second, *selfhood also brings us the ability to judge ourselves:* to like or dislike who we are or what we do, to feel proud or mortified. We develop a self-concept, an identity and self-love or self-hate.

Third, *self also means self-control,* our ability to direct our own actions. We can hold back; we can let go at will; we can go one direction, and upon evaluation, decide to tell ourselves to go quite another. We are not simply subject to our environment—we are able to alter our own acts as we make decisions, and we are able to do something other than what we have been taught to do.

The more we investigate the meaning and importance of having a self, the more obvious it can be recognized as one of our central qualities. And it is *a socially developed quality:* Without *our* dependence on social interaction, selfhood would certainly not exist.

Mind George Herbert Mead made sociologists aware that the ability to think is intimately related to selfhood and symbol use. Mead called this ability *mind.* Humans, like all other animals, are born with a brain, but the mind—the ability to think about our environment—is a socially created quality. Symbols are agreed-on representations that we use for communication. When we use them to communicate to our *self,* we call this thinking; and all this *communication* that we call thinking, Mead called mind. Humans do not simply respond to their environment; they point things out to themselves, manipulate the environment in their heads, imagine things that do not even exist in the physical world, consider options, rehearse their actions, and consider how others will act. . . . This ability, so central to what humans are, is made possible through symbols and self, which (as we saw above) are possible only through social interaction.

To be social, therefore, means that humans need others to survive and socialization to learn to survive. Socialization also creates our individual qualities. And social interaction is important for developing our essence: It creates our central qualities of symbol use, self-hood, and mind.

A Life of Interaction Within Society

Humans are social in a fifth sense, however. For whatever reason, *we live our entire lives interacting and embedded in society.* Observe our species: We are not simply around others all the time, we are doing things *with* others. Anyone watching human beings objectively should be amazed at how much their lives are affected by one another. We are constantly *social actors:* We impress others, communicate to others, escape others, con others, try to influence others, watch others entertain, display affection to others, play music or create art for others, and so on. Almost everything we do has an element of the social—it takes other people into account. As a result, we also end up *interacting* with others, and therefore, what we do affects what the others do. Action is built up back and forth as we do things together: cooperate, discuss, argue, teach, engage in conflict, play, make love, play tennis, or rear children. We are constantly involved in social action and social interaction, and this again is evidence of how important our social life is to what we are.

But we are also *embedded in social organization.* Our whole lives exist within groups, formal organizations, communities, and society. We live an organized existence, not an existence apart from others. Almost everyone spends his or her life in a world of *social rules* (morals, laws, customs) and *social patterns* (established systems of inequality, types of families, schools, and religious worship, for example), a world that directs much of what he or she does. As we try to understand what human beings are objectively, we inevitably see animals who are born into a society they did not create, who are very likely to live their entire existence there, and who will find life filled with belonging to a host of groups, formal organizations, and one or a few communities. To observe humans in an environment that does not include a larger social organization is not to observe them as they actually live their lives. We are not solitary beings, but social ones: We exist within a social organization.

To emphasize the idea that human beings are social by their very nature is to see something very profound about what we are. Take away our social life and there is nothing left that we might call human. Our very survival depends on society; much of what we are both as individuals and as a species depends on socialization, and almost everything we do is based on and includes a strong element of social action, social interaction, and social organization.

☺ Human Beings Are Cultural Beings

To say that human beings are cultural is to maintain that we are characterized by several other qualities not described above. Many animals are social, but what makes some animals cultural? The answer to this question entails determining what the foundation of a society is. Most social animals live together out of *instinct*. Nature commands that they cooperate, and it directs exactly how that cooperation should take place. Worker bees, queen bees, and other bees do not understand what they are doing, nor do they figure out how to play their various roles. Instead, they are born with instincts that control their behavior, making cooperation possible.

Some animals learn how to act in society, but much of that learning is *imitative*. They watch and do what others do. In this way they learn their place in the organization. In still other animal societies, adults actually teach the young what to do. This teaching is instinctive; that is, nature commands the organism how the young are to be trained. Now, it is difficult to determine how close to culture some animals come, but it is clear that human beings are cultural, and their social organization is founded on culture, not on *instinct, simple imitation, or species-based teaching.*

As cultural beings, humans act in society as they do because they share a view of their environment. This shared view is sometimes called culture. *Culture* is a set of ideas, values, and norms (procedures, customs, laws, morals) that people use as a guide to understanding and self-control. It is how we are able to know how to act around one another in a cooperative manner. Humans discuss their world, learn about their world, and teach what they learn. Knowledge is not lost with the individual organism but is passed down to others. There is a heritage that each individual within society learns and uses. People are not simply trained; with culture they are able to *understand* what they and others are doing and are supposed to do. Because of this cultural quality, societies differ considerably from one another. Each has a somewhat unique approach to living. Culture distinguishes organizations of people.

On the one hand, culture means that we see the world according to our social life; on the other hand, it means that we give meaning to our world. We do not merely respond to a world that acts as a stimulus on us. Instead, we understand it through the meanings that we learn in interaction. As our culture changes, so does our understanding of the world and our action in it.

Even our internal world is cultural, not simply physical. Our physical internal state may change as something happens to us (as someone points a gun at us or surprises us or tells us he or she loves us). But a change in our internal state does not automatically produce a response. Responses are defined, controlled, and directed by us, and they are guided by what our culture teaches. Between the internal physical response and what we do lies culture. Although many animals cry out toward their environment in what we might call "anger," human beings have the ability to understand that quality in themselves. They are taught by other people to distinguish anger from love, jealousy, pride, hatred, and fear. The culture that we learn tells us when it is appropriate to get angry and when it is appropriate to show it. We learn how to control anger, how to express anger, and how to feel sorry, guilty, or happy about our anger. It also teaches us many ideas about anger . . . , and we apply these ideas to understanding our internal responses. Even the word *anger*—the label we give our internal state—is cultural. Experts are able to show us different types of anger and different levels of it. We can even learn when anger is "healthy" and "unhealthy," and we can learn how and when it can be "useful" or "harmful" to our goals.

We also label and act toward other people culturally, not "naturally." We see middle-class people and working-class people, conformists and nonconformists, nice people and nasty people. These labels are cultural. They help us divide up reality, and behavior that we perceive as deviant at one time or in one society may not be perceived that way in another (for example, polygamy, homosexuality, cocaine use, and divorce).

Through all of his work, Max Weber emphasizes the important point that we all live in a world of meaning. To understand human action, he argues, we must understand how people define their world, how they think about it. That thinking is anchored in a socially created culture. Weber focuses his attention on the influence of religious culture. He shows, for example, that in the seventeenth century, Protestantism was an important influence on the way people acted in the work world. In his view, Protestantism fostered a strong work ethic in society, encouraging individuals to strive for economic success. We are not isolated beings; through our social life we develop our thinking about the world, which, in turn, influences how we act in that world.

☺ The Importance of It All

What difference does it really make that we are social and cultural beings? To be social and cultural means, first of all, that *we are not set at birth but can become many different things and can go in many different directions.* Because we are social and cultural, we are capable of becoming a saint or sinner, a warrior or business executive, a farmer or nurse. One can become only what one knows, and that depends on what one learns. Although biology may have something to do with differentiating us from one another, making it possible for some of us to excel in various spheres rather than others, our flexibility is still great, and thus society, culture, and socialization play an important role in what we all become.

Societies based on culture rather than instinct, imitation, or universal-species teaching, will *vary greatly in what they emphasize, and thus, what they socialize their populations to become.* We can become a peaceful people or a people who worship militarism. As a people we can come to believe that the most important goal in life is to make money, or we can believe that the good life is one of unselfish giving. We can emphasize past, present, or future; people or things; competition or cooperation; this life or an afterlife; rock music or opera. Nature does not command what a society becomes, just as it does not command what an individual becomes. Social interaction and culture do, and thus we have evolved a wide diversity of societies. This also means that as new circumstances and problems arise, people can reach new understandings and change their ways. It means that, in contrast to other primates, humans are able to evaluate their ways and improve their cooperative endeavors. How a society comes to define reality changes and this, in turn, changes the direction of society. Agricultural societies become industrial societies, peaceful societies turn their attention to war or architecture; tastes in food and music, technology, and employment possibilities change over time.

To be social and cultural also means that to a great extent each of us is controlled by other people. We are located within a set of social forces that shape and control what we do, what we are, and what we think. The culture that we learn becomes a part of our very being and comes to influence every aspect of our lives. Unlike other animals, it is not nature that commands us. Nor, unlike what most of us may think, is it free choice that characterizes many of our decisions. We are social and cultural beings, and it is impossible to escape the many complex influences that fact has on us.

Our relationship with our environment also changes because we are social and cultural. It is not a fixed response to a stimulus that characterizes what we do. Instead, socialization into a society with culture means that we begin to *understand our environment;* we now have the tools of ideas, values, morals, goals from which to approach life. We can do more with our surroundings than simply respond to them. We can shape it to fit our goals, we can better determine what we should do in relation to it, we can guide our actions by a set of rules or values that we understand. By not simply responding to the environment, we are able to shape it to some extent. Through the use of symbols, self, and mind—all arising from a society that socializes us into its culture—we are able to figure out our world and develop ideas uniquely our own. In short, it is because we are both social and cultural that we are able to think about our world and control what we do in it. Humans are not passive fixed responders, but active thinking actors.

☻ *Summary and Conclusion*

Look around you. Look in your classroom, on the campus mall, in your dorm, home, or apartment. Look at television, on the street, in the department store. Watch football games, symphony concerts, and serious drama. What is it that you see? What is the real essence of that being you see that we call human? The sociological answer is that you see:

1. A being who is *social* in nature, who survives through a dependence on others, who learns how to survive from others, who develops both human qualities and individual qualities through socialization, and who lives life embedded in society.

2. A being who is *cultural* in nature, who interprets the world according to what he or she learns in society, and, therefore, a being whose nature is not fixed by biology but who is tremendously diverse.

It may eventually be found that alcoholism, homosexuality, intelligence, athletic skill, and so on have biological bases. It would be a mistake, however, to isolate and claim that it is only biology that matters. All of our qualities as individuals are encouraged or discouraged by society and its culture. Our rules, our ways of viewing others and ourselves, our rewards and punishments, and the expectations we have for ourselves and others are all social. In fact, it is critical to recognize that although biology may matter in explaining individual differences, it matters far less in explaining differences between groups of people. Groups of people differ primarily because of social and cultural differences.

References

Coles, R. (1977). Entitlement. *The Atlantic.*

MacIver, R. M. (1931). *Society: Its structure and changes.* New York: Ray Long and Richard R. Smith.

McCall, G. J., & Simmons, J. L. (1978). *Identities and interactions.* New York: Free Press.

Mead, G. H. (1925). The genesis of the self and social control. *International Journal of Ethics, 35,* 251–277.

Spitz, R. A. (1945). Hospitalism: An inquiry into the genesis of psychiatric conditions in early childhood. In A. Freud et al (Eds.), *The psychoanalytic study of the child.* New York: International University Press.

☁ ☁ ☁

The girl in the window

Lane DeGregory, Tampa Bay Times Staff Writer Published Thursday, July 31, 2008

Dani, 9, has a new family now, and a new chance at life thanks to her brother William, 10, and parents Diane and Bernie Lierow.
[MELISSA LYTTLE | Times]

Part One: The Feral Child

PLANT CITY—The family had lived in the rundown rental house for almost three years when someone first saw a child's face in the window.

A little girl, pale, with dark eyes, lifted a dirty blanket above the broken glass and peered out, one neighbor remembered.

Everyone knew a woman lived in the house with her boyfriend and two adult sons. But they had never seen a child there, had never noticed anyone playing in the overgrown yard.

The girl looked young, 5 or 6, and thin. Too thin. Her cheeks seemed sunken; her eyes were lost.

The child stared into the square of sunlight, then slipped away.

Months went by. The face never reappeared.

Just before noon on July 13, 2005, a Plant City police car pulled up outside that shattered window. Two officers went into the house—and one stumbled back out.

From: Lane DeGregory, reprinted from the *Tampa Bay Times*, July 31, 2008.

83

Clutching his stomach, the rookie retched in the weeds.

Plant City Detective Mark Holste had been on the force for 18 years when he and his young partner were sent to the house on Old Sydney Road to stand by during a child abuse investigation. Someone had finally called the police.

They found a car parked outside. The driver's door was open and a woman was slumped over in her seat, sobbing. She was an investigator for the Florida Department of Children and Families.

"Unbelievable," she told Holste. "The worst I've ever seen."

The police officers walked through the front door, into a cramped living room.

"I've been in rooms with bodies rotting there for a week and it never stunk that bad," Holste said later. "There's just no way to describe it. Urine and feces—dog, cat and human excrement—smeared on the walls, mashed into the carpet. Everything dank and rotting."

Tattered curtains, yellow with cigarette smoke, dangling from bent metal rods. Cardboard and old comforters stuffed into broken, grimy windows. Trash blanketing the stained couch, the sticky counters.

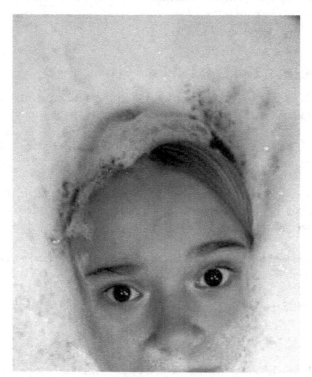

No one has any way of telling what lies behind Dani's big brown eyes and vacant stare.
[MELISSA LYTTLE | Times]

The floor, walls, even the ceiling seemed to sway beneath legions of scuttling roaches.

"It sounded like you were walking on eggshells. You couldn't take a step without crunching German cockroaches," the detective said. "They were in the lights, in the furniture. Even inside the freezer. The freezer!"

While Holste looked around, a stout woman in a faded housecoat demanded to know what was going on. Yes, she lived there. Yes, those were her two sons in the living room. Her daughter? Well, yes, she had a daughter…

The detective strode past her, down a narrow hall. He turned the handle on a door, which opened into a space the size of a walk-in closet. He squinted in the dark.

At his feet, something stirred.

• • •

First he saw the girl's eyes: dark and wide, unfocused, unblinking. She wasn't looking at him so much as through him.

She lay on a torn, moldy mattress on the floor. She was curled on her side, long legs tucked into her emaciated chest. Her ribs and collarbone jutted out; one skinny arm was slung over her face; her black hair was matted, crawling with lice. Insect bites, rashes and sores pocked her skin. Though she looked old enough to be in school, she was naked—except for a swollen diaper.

"The pile of dirty diapers in that room must have been 4 feet high," the detective said. "The glass in the window had been broken, and that child was just lying there, surrounded by her own excrement and bugs."

When he bent to lift her, she yelped like a lamb. "It felt like I was picking up a baby," Holste said. "I put her over my shoulder, and that diaper started leaking down my leg."

The girl didn't struggle. Holste asked, What's your name, honey? The girl didn't seem to hear.

He searched for clothes to dress her, but found only balled-up laundry, flecked with feces. He looked for a toy, a doll, a stuffed animal. "But the only ones I found were covered in maggots and roaches."

Choking back rage, he approached the mother. How could you let this happen?

"The mother's statement was: 'I'm doing the best I can,' "the detective said. "I told her, 'The best you can sucks!' "

He wanted to arrest the woman right then, but when he called his boss he was told to let DCF do its own investigation.

So the detective carried the girl down the dim hall, past her brothers, past her mother in the doorway, who was shrieking, "Don't take my baby!" He buckled the child into the state investigator's car. The investigator agreed: They had to get the girl out of there.

"Radio ahead to Tampa General," the detective remembers telling his partner. "If this child doesn't get to a hospital, she's not going to make it."

• • •

Her name, her mother had said, was Danielle. She was almost 7 years old.

She weighed 46 pounds. She was malnourished and anemic. In the pediatric intensive care unit they tried to feed the girl, but she couldn't chew or swallow solid food. So they put her on an IV and let her drink from a bottle.

Aides bathed her, scrubbed the sores on her face, trimmed her torn fingernails. They had to cut her tangled hair before they could comb out the lice.

Her caseworker determined that she had never been to school, never seen a doctor. She didn't know how to hold a doll, didn't understand peek-a-boo. "Due to the severe neglect," a doctor would write, "the child will be disabled for the rest of her life."

Hunched in an oversized crib, Danielle curled in on herself like a potato bug, then writhed angrily, kicking and thrashing. To calm herself, she batted at her toes and sucked her fists. "Like an infant," one doctor wrote.

She wouldn't make eye contact. She didn't react to heat or cold—or pain. The insertion of an IV needle elicited no reaction. She never cried. With a nurse holding her hands, she could stand and walk sideways on her toes, like a crab. She couldn't talk, didn't know how to nod yes or no. Once in a while she grunted.

She couldn't tell anyone what had happened, what was wrong, what hurt.

Dr. Kathleen Armstrong, director of pediatric psychology at the University of South Florida medical school, was the first psychologist to examine Danielle. She said medical tests, brain scans, and vision, hearing and genetics checks found nothing wrong with the child. She wasn't deaf, wasn't autistic, had no physical ailments such as cerebral palsy or muscular dystrophy.

The doctors and social workers had no way of knowing all that had happened to Danielle. But the scene at the house, along with Danielle's almost comatose condition, led them to believe she had never been cared for beyond basic sustenance. Hard as it was to imagine, they doubted she had ever been taken out in the sun, sung to sleep, even hugged or held. She was fragile and beautiful, but whatever makes a person human seemed somehow missing.

Armstrong called the girl's condition "environmental autism." Danielle had been deprived of interaction for so long, the doctor believed, that she had withdrawn into herself.

The most extraordinary thing about Danielle, Armstrong said, was her lack of engagement with people, with anything. "There was no light in her eye, no response or recognition. . . . We saw a little girl who didn't even respond to hugs or affection. Even a child with the most severe autism responds to those."

Danielle's was "the most outrageous case of neglect I've ever seen."

• • •

The authorities had discovered the rarest and most pitiable of creatures: a feral child.

The term is not a diagnosis. It comes from historic accounts—some fictional, some true—of children raised by animals and therefore not exposed to human nurturing. Wolf boys and bird girls, Tarzan, Mowgli from *The Jungle Book*.

It's said that during the Holy Roman Empire, Frederick II gave a group of infants to some nuns. He told them to take care of the children but never to speak to them. He believed the babies would eventually reveal the true language of God. Instead, they died from the lack of interaction.

Then there was the Wild Boy of Aveyron, who wandered out of the woods near Paris in 1800, naked and grunting. He was about 12. A teacher took him in and named him Victor. He tried to socialize the child, teach him to talk. But after several years, he gave up on the teen and asked the housekeeper to care for him.

"In the first five years of life, 85 percent of the brain is developed," said Armstrong, the psychologist who examined Danielle. "Those early relationships, more than anything else, help wire the brain and provide children with the experience to trust, to develop language, to communicate. They need that system to relate to the world."

The importance of nurturing has been shown again and again. In the 1960s, psychologist Harry Harlow put groups of infant rhesus monkeys in a room with two artificial mothers. One, made of wire, dispensed food. The other, of terrycloth, extended cradled arms. Though they were starving, the baby monkeys all climbed into the warm cloth arms.

"Primates need comfort even more than they need food," Armstrong said.

The most recent case of a feral child was in 1970, in California. A girl whom therapists came to call Genie had been strapped to a potty chair until she was 13. Like the Wild Boy, Genie was studied in hospitals and laboratories. She was in her 20s when doctors realized she'd never talk, never be able to take care of herself. She ended up in foster care, closed off from the world, utterly dependent.

Danielle's case—which unfolded out of the public spotlight, without a word in the media—raised disturbing questions for everyone trying to help her. How could this have happened? What kind of mother would sit by year after year while her daughter languished in her own filth, starving and crawling with bugs?

And why hadn't someone intervened? The neighbors, the authorities—where had they been?

"It's mind-boggling that in the 21st century we can still have a child who's just left in a room like a gerbil," said Tracy Sheehan, Danielle's guardian in the legal system and now a circuit court judge. "No food. No one talking to her or reading her a story. She can't even use her hands. How could this child be so invisible?"

But the most pressing questions were about her future.

When Danielle was discovered, she was younger by six years than the Wild Boy or Genie, giving hope that she might yet be teachable. Many of her caregivers had high hopes they could make her whole.

Danielle had probably missed the chance to learn speech, but maybe she could come to understand language, to communicate in other ways.

Still, doctors had only the most modest ambitions for her.

"My hope was that she would be able to sleep through the night, to be out of diapers and to feed herself," Armstrong said. If things went really well, she said, Danielle would end up "in a nice nursing home."

• • •

Danielle spent six weeks at Tampa General before she was well enough to leave. But where could she go? Not home; Judge Martha Cook, who oversaw her dependency hearing, ordered that Danielle be placed in foster care and that her mother not be allowed to call or visit her. The mother was being investigated on criminal child abuse charges.

"That child, she broke my heart," Cook said later. "We were so distraught over her condition, we agonized over what to do."

Eventually, Danielle was placed in a group home in Land O'Lakes. She had a bed with sheets and a pillow, clothes and food, and someone at least to change her diapers.

In October 2005, a couple of weeks after she turned 7, Danielle started school for the first time. She was placed in a special ed class at Sanders Elementary.

"Her behavior was different than any child I'd ever seen," said Kevin O'Keefe, Danielle's first teacher. "If you put food anywhere near her, she'd grab it" and mouth it like a baby, he said. "She had a lot of episodes of great agitation, yelling, flailing her arms, rolling into a fetal position. She'd curl up in a closet, just to be away from everyone. She didn't know how to climb a slide or swing on a swing. She didn't want to be touched."

It took her a year just to become consolable, he said.

By Thanksgiving 2006—a year and a half after Danielle had gone into foster care—her caseworker was thinking about finding her a permanent home.

A nursing home, group home or medical foster care facility could take care of Danielle. But she needed more.

"In my entire career with the child welfare system, I don't ever remember a child like Danielle," said Luanne Panacek, executive director of the Children's Board of Hillsborough County. "It makes you think about what does quality of life mean? What's the best we can hope for her? After all she's been through, is it just being safe?"

That fall, Panacek decided to include Danielle in the Heart Gallery—a set of portraits depicting children available for adoption. The Children's Board displays the pictures in malls and on the Internet in hopes that people will fall in love with the children and take them home.

In Hillsborough alone, 600 kids are available for adoption. Who, Panacek wondered, would choose an 8-year-old who was still in diapers, who didn't know her own name and might not ever speak or let you hug her?

● ● ●

The day Danielle was supposed to have her picture taken for the Heart Gallery, she showed up with red Kool-Aid dribbled down her new blouse. She hadn't yet mastered a sippy cup.

Garet White, Danielle's care manager, scrubbed the girl's shirt and washed her face. She brushed Danielle's bangs from her forehead and begged the photographer to please be patient.

White stepped behind the photographer and waved at Danielle. She put her thumbs in her ears and wiggled her hands, stuck out her tongue and rolled her eyes. Danielle didn't even blink.

White was about to give up when she heard a sound she'd never heard from Danielle. The child's eyes were still dull, apparently unseeing. But her mouth was open. She looked like she was trying to laugh.

Click.

Part Two: Becoming Dani

Teenagers tore through the arcade, firing fake rifles. Sweaty boys hunched over air hockey tables. Girls squealed as they stomped on blinking squares.

Bernie and Diane Lierow remember standing silently inside GameWorks in Tampa, overwhelmed. They had driven three hours from their home in Fort Myers Beach, hoping to meet a child at this foster care event.

But all these kids seemed too wild, too big and, well, too worldly.

Bernie, 48, remodels houses. Diane, 45, cleans homes. They have four grown sons from previous marriages and one together. Diane couldn't have any more children, and Bernie had always wanted a daughter. So last year, when William was 9, they decided to adopt.

Their new daughter would have to be younger than William, they told foster workers. But she would have to be potty-trained and able to feed herself. They didn't want a child who might hurt their son, or who was profoundly disabled and unable to take care of herself.

On the Internet they had found a girl in Texas, another in Georgia. Each time they were told, "That one is dangerous. She can't be with other children."

That's why they were at this Heart Gallery gathering, scanning the crowd.

Bernie's head ached from all the jangling games; Diane's stomach hurt, seeing all the abandoned kids; and William was tired of shooting aliens.

Diane stepped out of the chaos, into an alcove beneath the stairs. That was when she saw it. A little girl's face on a flier, pale with sunken cheeks and dark hair chopped too short. Her brown eyes seemed to be searching for something.

Diane called Bernie over. He saw the same thing she did. "She just looked like she needed us."

• • •

Bernie and Diane are humble, unpretentious people who would rather picnic on their deck than eat out. They go to work, go to church, visit with their neighbors, walk their dogs. They don't travel or pursue exotic interests; a vacation for them is hanging out at home with the family. Shy and soft-spoken, they're both slow to anger and, they say, seldom argue.

They had everything they ever wanted, they said. Except for a daughter.

But the more they asked about Danielle, the more they didn't want to know.

She was 8, but functioned as a 2-year-old. She had been left alone in a dank room, ignored for most of her life.

No, she wasn't there at the video arcade; she was in a group home. She wore diapers, couldn't feed herself, couldn't talk. After more than a year in school, she still wouldn't make eye contact or play with other kids.

No one knew, really, what was wrong with her, or what she might be capable of.

"She was everything we didn't want," Bernie said.

But they couldn't forget those aching eyes.

• • •

When they met Danielle at her school, she was drooling. Her tongue hung from her mouth. Her head, which seemed too big for her thin neck, lolled side to side.

She looked at them for an instant, then loped away across the special ed classroom. She rolled onto her back, rocked for a while, then batted at her toes.

Diane walked over and spoke to her softly. Danielle didn't seem to notice. But when Bernie bent down, Danielle turned toward him and her eyes seemed to focus.

He held out his hand. She let him pull her to her feet. Danielle's teacher, Kevin O'Keefe, was amazed; he hadn't seen her warm up to anyone so quickly.

Bernie led Danielle to the playground, she pulling sideways and prancing on her tiptoes. She squinted in the sunlight but let him push her gently on the swing. When it was time for them to part, Bernie swore he saw Danielle wave.

That night, he had a dream. Two giant hands slid through his bedroom ceiling, the fingers laced together. Danielle was swinging on those hands, her dark eyes wide, thin arms reaching for him.

• • •

Everyone told them not to do it, neighbors, co-workers, friends. Everyone said they didn't know what they were getting into.

So what if Danielle is not everything we hoped for? Bernie and Diane answered. You can't pre-order your own kids. You take what God gives you.

They brought her home on Easter weekend 2007. It was supposed to be a rebirth, of sorts—a baptism into their family.

"It was a disaster," Bernie said.

They gave her a doll; she bit off its hands. They took her to the beach; she screamed and wouldn't put her feet in the sand. Back at her new home, she tore from room to room, her swim diaper spewing streams across the carpet.

She couldn't peel the wrapper from a chocolate egg, so she ate the shiny paper too. She couldn't sit still to watch TV or look at a book. She couldn't hold a crayon. When they tried to brush her teeth or comb her hair, she kicked and thrashed. She wouldn't lie in a bed, wouldn't go to sleep, just rolled on her back, side to side, for hours.

All night she kept popping up, creeping sideways on her toes into the kitchen. She would pull out the frozen food drawer and stand on the bags of vegetables so she could see into the refrigerator.

"She wouldn't take anything," Bernie said. "I guess she wanted to make sure the food was still there."

When Bernie tried to guide her back to bed, Danielle railed against him and bit her own hands.

In time, Danielle's new family learned what worked and what didn't. Her foster family had been giving her anti-psychotic drugs to mitigate her temper tantrums and help her sleep. When Bernie and Diane weaned her off the medication, she stopped drooling and started holding up her head. She let Bernie brush her teeth.

• • •

Bernie and Diane already thought of Danielle as their daughter, but legally she wasn't. Danielle's birth mother did not want to give her up even though she had been charged with child abuse and faced 20 years in prison. So prosecutors offered a deal: If she waived her parental rights, they wouldn't send her to jail.

She took the plea. She was given two years of house arrest, plus probation. And 100 hours of community service.

In October 2007, Bernie and Diane officially adopted Danielle. They call her Dani.

• • •

"Okay, let's put your shoes on. Do you need to go potty again?" Diane asks.

It's an overcast Monday morning in spring 2008 and Dani is late for school. Again. She keeps flitting around the living room, ducking behind chairs and sofas, pulling at her shorts.

After a year with her new family, Dani scarcely resembles the girl in the Heart Gallery photo. She has grown a foot and her weight has doubled.

All those years she was kept inside, her hair was as dark as the dirty room she lived in. But since she started going to the beach and swimming in their backyard pool, Dani's shoulder-length hair has turned a golden blond. She still shrieks when anyone tries to brush it.

The changes in her behavior are subtle, but Bernie and Diane see progress. They give an example: When Dani feels overwhelmed she retreats to her room, rolls onto her back, pulls one sock toward the end of her toes and bats it. For hours. Bernie and Diane tell her to stop.

Now, when Dani hears them coming, she peels off her sock and throws it into the closet to hide it.

She's learning right from wrong, they say. And she seems upset when she knows she has disappointed them. As if she cares how they feel.

Bernie and Diane were told to put Dani in school with profoundly disabled children, but they insisted on different classes because they believe she can do more. They take her to occupational and physical therapy, to church and the mall and the grocery store. They have her in speech classes and horseback riding lessons.

Once, when Dani was trying to climb onto her horse, the mother of a boy in the therapeutic class turned to Diane.

"You're so lucky," Diane remembers the woman saying.

"Lucky?" Diane asked.

The woman nodded. "I know my son will never stand on his own, will never be able to climb onto a horse. You have no idea what your daughter might be able to do."

Diane finds hope in that idea. She counts small steps to convince herself things are slowly improving. So what if Dani steals food off other people's trays at McDonald's? At least she can feed herself chicken nuggets now. So what if she already has been to the bathroom four times this morning? She's finally out of diapers.

It took months, but they taught her to hold a stuffed teddy on the toilet so she wouldn't be scared to be alone in the bathroom. They bribed her with M&M's. "Dani, sit down and try to use the potty," Diane coaxes. "Pull down your shorts. That's a good girl."

• • •

Every weekday, for half an hour, speech therapist Leslie Goldenberg tries to teach Dani to talk. She sits her in front of a mirror at a Bonita Springs elementary school and shows her how to purse her lips to make puffing sounds.

"Puh-puh-puh," says the teacher. "Here, feel my mouth." She brings Dani's fingers to her lips, so she can feel the air.

Dani nods. She knows how to nod now. Goldenberg puffs again.

Leaning close to the mirror, Dani purses her lips, opens and closes them. No sound comes out. She can imitate the movement, but does't know she has to blow out air to make the noise.

She bends closer, scowls at her reflection. Her lips open and close again, then she leaps up and runs across the room. She grabs a Koosh ball and bounces it rapidly.

She's lost inside herself. Again.

But in many ways, Dani already has surpassed the teacher's expectations, and not just in terms of speech. She seems to be learning to listen, and she understands simple commands. She pulls at her pants to show she needs to go to the bathroom, taps a juice box when she wants more. She can sit at a table for five-minute stretches, and she's starting to scoop applesauce with a spoon. She's down to just a few temper tantrums a month. She is learning to push buttons on a speaking board, to use symbols to show when she wants a book or when she's angry. She's learning it's okay to be angry: You can deal with those feelings without biting your own hands.

"I'd like her to at least be able to master a sound board, so she can communicate her choices even if she never finds her voice," Goldenberg says. "I think she understands most of what we say. It's just that she doesn't always know how to—or want to—react."

Dani's teacher and family have heard her say only a few words, and all of them seemed accidental. Once she blurted "baaa," startling Goldenberg to tears. It was the first letter sound she had ever made.

She seems to talk most often when William is tickling her, as if something from her subconscious seeps out when she's too distracted to shut it off. Her brother has heard her say, "Stop!" and "No!" He thought he even heard her say his name.

Having a brother just one year older is invaluable for Dani's development, her teacher says. She has someone to practice language with, someone who will listen. "Even deaf infants will coo," Goldenberg said. "But if no one responds, they stop."

• • •

William says Dani frightened him at first. "She did weird things." But he always wanted someone to play with. He doesn't care that she can't ride bikes with him or play Monopoly. "I drive her around in my Jeep and she honks the horn," he says. "She's learning to match up cards and stuff."

He couldn't believe she had never walked a dog or licked an ice cream cone. He taught her how to play peek-a-boo, helped her squish Play-Doh through her fingers. He showed her it was safe to walk on sand and fun to blow bubbles and okay to cry; when you hurt, someone comes. He taught her how to open a present. How to pick up tater tots and dunk them into a mountain of ketchup.

William was used to living like an only child, but since Dani has moved in, she gets most of their parents' attention. "She needs them more than me," he says simply.

He gave her his old toys, his "kid movies," his board books. He even moved out of his bedroom so she could sleep upstairs. His parents painted his old walls pink and filled the closet with cotton-candy dresses.

They moved a daybed into the laundry room for William, squeezed it between the washing machine and Dani's rocking horse. Each night, the 10-year-old boy cuddles up with a walkie-talkie because "it's scary down here, all alone."

After a few minutes, while his parents are trying to get Dani to bed, William always sneaks into the living room and folds himself into the love seat.

He trades his walkie-talkie for a small stuffed Dalmatian and calls down the hall, "Good night, Mom and Dad. Good night, Dani."

Some day, he's sure, she will answer.

• • •

Even now, Dani won't sleep in a bed.

Bernie bought her a new trundle so she can slide out the bottom bunk and be at floor level. Diane found pink Hello Kitty sheets and a stuffed glow worm so Dani will never again be alone in the dark.

"You got your wormie? You ready to go to sleep?" Bernie asks, bending to pick up his daughter. She's turning slow circles beneath the window, holding her worm by his tail. Bernie lifts her to the glass and shows her the sun, slipping behind the neighbor's house.

He hopes, one day, she might be able to call him "Daddy," to get married or at least live on her own. But if that doesn't happen, he says, "That's okay too. For me, it's all about getting the kisses and the hugs."

For now, Bernie and Diane are content to give Dani what she never had before: comfort and stability, attention and affection. A trundle, a glow worm.

Now Bernie tips Dani into bed, smooths her golden hair across the pillow. "Night-night," he says, kissing her forehead.

"Good night, honey," Diane calls from the doorway.

Bernie lowers the shade. As he walks past Dani, she reaches out and grabs his ankles.

Part Three: The Mother

She's out there somewhere, looming over Danielle's story like a ghost. To Bernie and Diane, Danielle's birth mother is a cipher, almost never spoken of. The less said, the better. As far as they are concerned Danielle was born the day they found her. And yet this unimaginable woman is out there somewhere, most likely still on probation, permanently unburdened of her daughter, and thinking— what? What can she possibly say? Nothing. Not a thing. But none of this makes any sense without her.

Michelle Crockett lives in a mobile home in Plant City with her two 20-something sons, three cats and a closet full of kittens. The trailer is just down the road from the little house where she lived with Danielle.

On a steamy afternoon a few weeks ago, Michelle opens the door wearing a long T-shirt. When she sees two strangers, she ducks inside and pulls on a housecoat.

She's tall and stout, with broad shoulders and the sallow skin of a smoker. She looks tired, older than her 51 years.

"My daughter?" she asks. "You want to talk about my daughter?" Her voice catches. Tears pool in her glasses.

The inside of the trailer is modest but clean: dishes drying on the counter, silk flowers on the table. Sitting in her kitchen, chain-smoking 305s, she starts at the end: the day the detective took Danielle.

"Part of me died that day," she says.

• • •

Michelle says she was a student at the University of Tampa when she met a man named Bernie at a bar. It was 1976. He was a Vietnam vet, 10 years her senior. They got married and moved to Las Vegas, where he drove a taxi.

Right away they had two sons, Bernard and Grant. The younger boy wasn't potty-trained until he was 4, didn't talk until he was 5. "He was sort of slow," Michelle says. In school, they put him in special ed.

Her sons were teenagers when her husband got sick. Agent Orange, the doctors said. When he died in August 1997, Michelle filed for bankruptcy.

Six months later, she met a man in a casino. He was in Vegas on business. She went back to his hotel room with him.

"His name was Ron," she says. She shakes her head. "No, it was Bob. I think it was Bob."

• • •

For hours Michelle Crockett spins out her story, tapping ashes into a plastic ashtray. Everything she says sounds like a plea, but for what? Understanding? Sympathy? She doesn't apologize. Far from it. She feels wronged.

Danielle, she says, was born in a hospital in Las Vegas, a healthy baby who weighed 7 pounds, 6 ounces. Her Apgar score measuring her health was a 9, nearly perfect.

"She screamed a lot," Michelle says. "I just thought she was spoiled."

When Danielle was 18 months old, Michelle's mobile home burned down, so she loaded her two sons and baby daughter onto a Greyhound bus and headed to Florida, to bunk with a cousin.

They lost their suitcases along the way, she says. The cousin couldn't take the kids. After a week, Michelle moved into a Brandon apartment with no furniture, no clothes, no dishes. She got hired as a cashier at Publix. But it was okay: "The boys were with her," she says. She says she has the paperwork to prove it.

• • •

She goes to the boys' bathroom, returns with a box full of documents and hands it over.

The earliest documents are from Feb. 11, 2002. That was when someone called the child abuse hotline on her. The caller reported that a child, about 3, was "left unattended for days with a retarded older brother, never seen wearing anything but a diaper."

This is Michelle's proof that her sons were watching Danielle.

The caller continued:

"The home is filthy. There are clothes everywhere. There are feces on the child's seat and the counter is covered with trash."

It's not clear what investigators found at the house, but they left Danielle with her mother that day.

Nine months later, another call to authorities. A person who knew Michelle from the Moose Lodge said she was always there playing bingo with her new boyfriend, leaving her children alone overnight.

"Not fit to be a mother," the caller said.

The hotline operator took these notes: The 4-year-old girl "is still wearing a diaper and drinking from a baby bottle. On-going situation, worse since last August. Mom leaves Grant and Danielle at home for several days in a row while she goes to work and spends the night with a new paramour. Danielle . . . is never seen outside the home."

Again the child abuse investigators went out. They offered Michelle free day care for Danielle. She refused. And they left Danielle there.

Why? Didn't they worry about two separate calls to the hotline, months apart, citing the same concerns?

"It's not automatic that because the home is dirty we'd remove the child," said Nick Cox, regional director of the Florida Department of Children and Families. "And what they found in 2002 was not like the scene they walked into in 2005."

The aim, he said, is to keep the child with the parent, and try to help the parent get whatever services he or she might need. But Michelle refused help. And investigators might have felt they didn't have enough evidence to take Danielle, Cox said.

"I'm concerned, though, that no effort was made to interview the child," he said.

"If you have a 4-year-old who is unable to speak, that would raise a red flag to me. "I'm not going to tell you this was okay. I don't know how it could have happened."

· · ·

Michelle insists Danielle was fine.

"I tried to potty-train her, she wouldn't train. I tried to get her into schools, no one would take her," she says in the kitchen of her trailer. The only thing she ever noticed was wrong, she says, "was that she didn't speak much. She talked in a soft tone. She'd say, 'Let's go eat.' But no one could hear her except me."

She says she took Danielle to the library and the park. "I took her out for pizza. Once." But she can't remember which library, which park or where they went for pizza.

"She liked this song I'd sing her," Michelle says. "Miss Polly had a dolly, she was sick, sick, sick . . ."

Michelle's older son, Bernard, told a judge that he once asked his mom why she never took Danielle to the doctor. Something's wrong with her, he remembered telling her. He said she answered, "If they see her, they might take her away."

· · ·

A few months after the second abuse call, Michelle and her kids moved in with her boyfriend in the rundown rental house in Plant City. The day the cops came, Michelle says, she didn't know what was wrong.

The detective found Danielle in the back, sleeping. The only window in the small space was broken. Michelle had tacked a blanket across the shattered glass, but flies and beetles and roaches had crept in anyway.

"My house was a mess," she says. "I'd been sick and it got away from me. But I never knew a dirty house was against the law."

The cop walked past her, carrying Danielle.

"He said she was starving. I told him me and my sisters were all skinny till we were 13.

"I begged him, 'Please, don't take my baby! Please!' "

She says she put socks on her daughter before he took her to the car, but couldn't find any shoes.

• • •

A judge ordered Michelle to have a psychological evaluation. That's among the documents, too.

Danielle's IQ, the report says, is below 50, indicating "severe mental retardation." Michelle's is 77, "borderline range of intellectual ability."

"She tended to blame her difficulties on circumstances while rationalizing her own actions," wrote psychologist Richard Enrico Spana. She "is more concerned with herself than most other adults, and this could lead her to neglect paying adequate attention to people around her."

She wanted to fight for her daughter, she says, but didn't want to go to jail and didn't have enough money for a lawyer.

"I tried to get people to help me," Michelle says. "They say I made her autistic. But how do you make a kid autistic? They say I didn't put clothes on her—but she just tore them off."

After Danielle was taken away, Michelle says, she tripped over a box at Wal-Mart and got in a car accident and couldn't work anymore. In February, she went back to court and a judge waived her community service hours.

She's on probation until 2012.

She spends her days with her sons, doing crossword puzzles and watching movies. Sometimes they talk about Danielle.

• • •

When Danielle was in the hospital, Michelle says, she and her sons sneaked in to see her. Michelle took a picture from the file: Danielle, drowning in a hospital gown, slumped in a bed that folded into a wheelchair.

"That's the last picture I have of her," Michelle says. In her kitchen, she snubs out her cigarette. She crosses to the living room, where Danielle's image looks down from the wall.

She reaches up and, with her finger, traces her daughter's face. "When I moved here," she says, "that was the first thing I hung."

She says she misses Danielle.

"Have you seen her?" Michelle asks. "Is she okay?"

•••

Is she okay?

Danielle is better than anyone dared hope. She has learned to look at people and let herself be held. She can chew ham. She can swim. She's tall and blond and has a little belly. She knows her name is Dani.

In her new room, she has a window she can look out of. When she wants to see outside, all she has to do is raise her arms and her dad is right behind her, waiting to pick her up.

Chapter 3
Socialization

I was just 14, and my friend and I became volunteers at a local hospital. Because we had these uniforms on, patients, their families, nurses, and other staff were treating us like we knew what we were doing. But it was just a summer volunteer job, and I was sure I would mess it up! It was strange, but after about a month, I really felt competent at getting the patients where they had to be. I was proud when people asked me questions and I had learned the answers. The hospital setting was routine, but there was some real drama in the hallways and being a part of that place was something I really liked. Now I'm planning to go to medical school.

—Maya, senior Biology major

How individuals attempt to align their own thoughts, feelings, and behavior to fit into society or groups is called **socialization** (Corsaro and Fingerson 2003; Stryker 2002). As with Maya's story, socialization can occur informally through observation and interaction. Socialization can also be more formal as children enter educational institutions to learn the appropriate skills necessary to successfully enter the economy of a given society. Although most people associate socialization with children's development, adults continue to be socialized over the course of their lives, learning norms and values in new social contexts as well as age-appropriate ways to think, feel, and behave (Crosnoe and Elder 2004; Elder 1994; Mortimer and Simmons 1978). In the preceding example, Maya is socialized as a hospital worker—she learns what it means to be that kind of person, interacts with others on the basis of that role, and finally comes to feel that the role is central to who she is.

Agents of Socialization

Earlier we defined agents of socialization as groups most influential in the process of teaching children the norms and values of a particular culture. It is important to understand that sociologists generally view agents of socialization as mediators of the larger society, rather than direct causes of socialization (Corsaro and Eder 1995). That is, families may affect child development directly

From: *Social Psychology: Sociological Perspectives*, Second Edition by David E. Rohall, Melissa A. Milkie, and Jeffrey W. Lucas.

through their parenting techniques, but those techniques reflect larger cultural patterns. The famous pediatrician Dr. Spock wrote *The Common Sense Book of Baby and Child Care* in 1946 with several follow-up versions printed over the last several decades. His ideas helped to change the way parents thought about parenting, emphasizing more flexible parenting techniques. Spock encouraged parents to be more emotionally attached to children and less strict in their discipline. Children were to be thought of as individuals rather than subjects of training and development. Through the middle of the twentieth century, Spock and other child specialists moved families away from traditional parenting styles. In a sense, parents implemented larger societal changes in attitudes toward children (as individuals) and parenting styles more generally (loving and affectionate and independent) as displayed in Spock's books.

There are many agents of socialization. Here, we emphasize only some of the most important ones: families, school, and peers. We also discuss the media as a source of socialization in Western societies.

Families

Families are considered the first or primary agent of socialization because virtually all children are raised from infancy with one to two parents and often siblings. However, the family has changed dramatically over the last century. For example, people in Western countries are having fewer children—almost half the world's population in 2000 lived in countries that were at or below replacement level (the point at which populations stabilize), primarily in richer, Western nations such as Italy and Germany (Morgan 2003). Since 1970, the number of individuals living alone in the United States has increased from 16% of households to 25%. The traditional family, married couples with children, has declined from 40% of households to just 24%, with a corresponding increase in the number of nontraditional households (e.g., single parents).

Family Structure and Children. Structural changes in the family are important to track because they can have ramifications for child socialization. Only about one in three children live in a family with a stay-at-home parent; the rest are in dual-earner, single-parent, or other types of families (Waite and Gallaher 2000). Children from single-parent families often struggle for at least two reasons (Gecas 1992; Waite and Gallaher 2000). First, single-parent families earn less money than their married counterparts, partly because there is one less person to contribute to the household income and also because women are more likely to be single parents than men (Demo 1992). (In 2002, the gender-wage gap in the United States was 23 cents; women earned about 77 cents for every dollar earned by men.) Hence, single parents typically lack the fiscal resources found in two-parent families.

Second, single-parent families may lack the same social resources available to two-parent families. Children in single-parent households often rely on one person to provide the love and discipline found in families with two caregivers (Gecas 1992; Waite and Gallaher 2000), although extended families may be

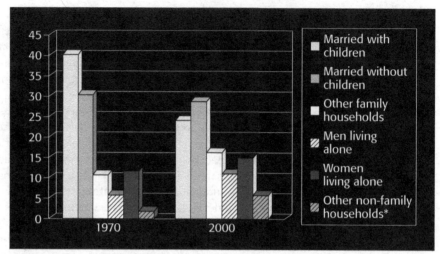

Changes in U.S. Household Composition, 1970 and 2000

*Mostly single men and women.

Source: U.S. Census Bureau, Current Population Survey, March Supplements: 1970 to 2000.

involved in raising the child. Single parents have less time and energy to devote to their children as well. However, the bond between a single parent and child may be strengthened because of the amount of intimacy available in a dyad compared to a triad.

These dynamics may disproportionately affect some minority groups because some family demographics vary by race. According to the 2000 U.S. census, African Americans, for example, have larger families on average than the overall population, and these families are also more likely to be single-parent households (McKinnon and Bennett 2005). Hence, we would expect family socialization to be different in African American families than among whites and other racial groups. African American families are less likely to have the resources found among white families but may have other strengths. For instance, in one study, researchers found that African American women rated the families they grew up in as more cohesive, expressive, and lower in conflict than white women (Clay et al. 2007).

The effects of family structure on children's health and well-being has been well documented in the area of divorce. Children of divorced parents tend to divorce or cohabit at higher rates than children from intact families (Thornton, Axinn, and Xie 2007; Wolfinger 2005). They also report higher levels of distress and more behavioral problems than their counterparts in stable families (Amato and Cheadle 2008; McCabe 1997). The effects of living with the same- or opposite-sex parent for children living in single-parent households has also been questioned, although evidence suggests that parent–child gender differences may not be important for child outcomes (Powell and Downey 1997). Sibling order and configuration is another family structure element that may importantly influence how children are socialized, although findings are mixed as to its effects

(Steelman et al. 2002; Freese, Powell and Steelman 1999). These findings, however, can vary significantly by the outcome being examined (e.g., cognitive verses behavioral), parenting style, status, and resources available to families before, during, and after a divorce (Campana et al. 2008; Fomby and Cherlin 2007). In a larger historical framework, the meaning of "family" is broadening to include cohabiters, those single (as parents or not) by choice, gay/lesbian families, and hybrids of these and other forms of family. We are just now starting to understand what these family forms look like and how they impact people's lives. Rosanna Hertz (2006) interviewed 65 Boston-area middle-class women who chose to be single mothers. She found that many of them stumbled into single motherhood but decided to go it alone rather than marry someone who did not meet their expectations. The state of being single was found to be a bit unstable as these women entered and left romantic relationships with lovers and co-parents over time. What type of person today opts out of the "traditional family" (a two-parent, married household)? According to Michael Rosenfeld (2007), those not choosing the pathway of the traditional family tended to be people "who live on their own, who support themselves, who postpone marriage, and who have access to higher education" (p. 121).

Class, Race, and Gender Socialization in Families. A family's social class position is another important structural dimension affecting socialization processes. Income differences not only influence the resources available to raise children, but they can also actually affect socialization processes themselves (Gecas 1992; Kohn 1969). Compared to working-class families, middle-class families differ in the values and behaviors taught to children as well as how they teach them those things. Middle-class families tend to stress autonomy and individual development over conformity. In addition, middle-class families are less likely to use punitive child-rearing practices than their counterparts in the working class. Middle-class children, as a result, are more likely to value independence later in life than working-class children. The result of these socialization processes is that working-class youth often grow up less confident in institutional settings such as schools and workplaces (Lareau 2003). Middle-class children usually grow up with more cultural capital that helps them to find and maintain higher status jobs.

The family can also be a source of **racial socialization**, learning about one's ethnic and racial identity in a given culture. Families may pass on their cultural heritage to their children in the form of racial or ethnic pride, history, and heritage. Minority parents can also help prepare their children for racial bias in the future (Hughes 2003; Hughes and Johnson 2001). Racial socialization is important because a strong ethnic identity is associated with greater psychological well-being (Yip 2005).

Families are a key component of **gender socialization**, the learning of expectations about how to behave related to one's gender (Gecas 1992). How children come to appropriate thoughts, feelings, and behaviors associated with age, gender, or other roles is not completely understood. On one level, children simply model the behavior of their parents. We know that mothers continue to do more housework than men, and men work more outside of the home

(Bianchi, Robinson, and Milkie 2006; Robinson and Godbey 1997). These differences can have long-lasting consequences for gendered behavior. Mick Cunningham (2001), for instance, found that fathers' participation in routine housework when their children were very young had positive effects on their sons' later participation in housework, whereas mothers' employment during their daughters' formative years decreased the relative contributions of daughters to housework later in life. Therefore, teaching gender-role attitudes may influence future behavior, but so do parental characteristics and behaviors.

Some research examines how children conceive of gender roles at different developmental stages. Melissa Milkie and her colleagues (1997) analyzed over 3,000 essays in which children were asked to explain why they had the "best" mother or father. Their results generally support findings that show the significance traditional gender roles play in family relationships. However, they also found that children generally downplayed the significance of father's labor force participation, rarely mentioning the breadwinner role central to most men's parenting. Comparing essays written in 1979 and 1980 with those written in the early 1990s, they found that the latter cohort of children deemphasized the parent as a caretaker role, moving toward viewing them in a more recreational role, especially fathers. Hence, children's perceptions of family roles change over time.

Families are a place to learn fundamental beliefs about the world. The transmission of values from generation to generation seems obvious: Our parents tell us right from wrong, and we generally accept those things to be true. However, children often modify their parents' values or adopt altogether new ones. Jennifer Glass and her colleagues (1986) studied the transmission of gender, political, and religious ideology among members of three-generation families (youth, parents, and grandparents). They found very little convergence of parent–child attitudes. Rather, they found that status inheritance—the maintenance of class position—was the primary means of maintaining attitude similarities. Hence, families not only teach and model values to their children, they also impart their social positions, which ultimately tends to produce similar values and beliefs.

Socialization of values and beliefs can occur on multiple levels at the same time. For instance, family influences can be observed in the context of larger social forces, including peers, the media, or other social institutions. Jonathan Kelley and Nan Kirk De Graaf (1997) studied religious beliefs in the context of family upbringing and nations' religious environments. They found that people in more religious nations adopt more orthodox values than those living in more secular nations. However, they also found that family religiosity had a stronger effect than national religiosity on children's religiosity in secular nations; the converse is true in orthodox nations. Thus, the socialization processes found among friends and family can be influenced by larger social and cultural contexts.

Adults in Families. The life-course perspective makes it clear that children are not the only ones who are socialized. As young adults move from their childhood family into forming families of their own, they must learn to adapt to adult family roles such as spouse or parent. It is not just a passive adaptation to roles; rather, people make choices about when and how to enter into different roles. One of the great challenges for adults trying to craft meaningful lives is to attempt to weave together important roles such as being a husband or wife, a mother or father, and a paid work role. Life-course sociologists study what happens when people enter into or exit from various roles, and how that affects future sequencing of their life trajectories or pathways. We are aware, for example, that becoming a parent as a teenager greatly affects the kind of education and work roles that women enter. Life-course sociologists also are concerned with the mental health consequences of family–work trajectories. Kei Nomaguchi and Melissa Milkie (2003) found that entering parenthood affects well-being, but its effects vary by gender and marital status. For married women, those becoming parents were better off than those who remained childless; for unmarried men, those who became fathers over the five-year time frame were more depressed than nonfathers.

School Contexts

Schools are a second major agent of socialization. Although technically designed to impart knowledge about many subjects, the classroom is also a place to learn norms of behavior and to (re)produce workers of various types. Children are placed in large, homogeneous classrooms in which peer influences dominate the social context, above and beyond the effects of families. Sociologists have studied the socialization processes that occur in schools including the learning of official curriculum, the learning goals imposed by the state, and the unofficial curriculum, that which is imparted through teachers and peers in school settings that include the teaching of values and beliefs from the larger culture (Brint, Contreras, and Matthews 2001; Weisz and Kanpol 1990).

Classroom Structure and Socialization Processes.

Much like the family group structures, the classroom represents a group, albeit a much larger one, from which children learn about the world. Because one or two adults typically attend to classes of 20 or 30 children, classroom settings are less intimate and provide children less exposure to adult behavior than home settings. Classrooms are also unique in that they contain children of the same age group and are divided relatively equally by sex, at least in Western nations (Gecas 1992). Hence, classrooms have less direct adult–child interaction than home environments and more competition for attention and resources among children.

Classrooms are also bureaucratically structured in a way that limits child–adult bonds (children leave a teacher after the successful completion of one school year) and emphasizing rationalization and competition among similar age groups (Gecas 1992). The large status gap among students and teachers may influence the development of a student subculture in which the students form a homogeneous subgroup relative to their higher-status teachers. Much like the division of labor in families, school bureaucracies and hierarchies may contribute to the socialization of rationality and order associated with Western culture.

We can apply the same socialization processes found in the family to school contexts. However, schools have different structural features that affect those processes. For instance, obedience to rules becomes paramount in bureaucratic settings such as schools. In addition, teachers and administrators have formal rewards and punishments available, such as grades and detentions, to encourage the maintenance of social order in the classroom.

The increased emphasis on peers, as well as the notion of adults as "outsiders" who merely impose rules and restrictions, may help to explain the development of popular media portrayals of a rebellious student culture. The film *Fast Times at Ridgemont High* (1982) portrayed a California high school almost devoid of any supervision. Students had a subculture in which parents and other adults were outsiders while students developed a social hierarchy within the school structure. Actor Sean Penn played a character, Jeff Spicoli, a drug-using surfer on the fringe of society. This position in the high-school subculture made him one of the cool people in the film, someone who did not live by society's norms and values. Similar portrayals of student life are seen in movies such as *Mean Girls* (2004), which humorously details the sometimes viscous competition among teenage girls, and *American Pie* (1999), a film about four young men who vow to lose their virginity before prom night.

Some research shows that larger schools lead students to be less attached to their schools than students in smaller schools. These students are also less likely to bond with their teachers and less likely to participate in extracurricular activities (Crosnoe, Johnson, and Elder 2004). However, there is no single model of school organization and culture that applies to all educational settings, especially in the U.S. school system, which is decentralized (Hedges and Schneider 2005). The culture of any given school can be considered a negotiated thing—an ongoing interaction among educational leaders (Hallett 2007). Students clearly play a role in this relationship, making staff rethink policies and procedures that they wish to implement. Hence, creation of school culture includes many layers of social dynamics ranging from the development of educational goals and standards on the national level to the negotiated order found within each classroom.

Pygmalion Effect and Children's Social Statuses. Teachers' interactions with children affect the values and beliefs of children much the same as parents' interactions. However, teachers do not share the same relationships with their students as do the students' parents. For instance, if you are reading this book as part of a class, your parents probably care more about your grade in the class than does your professor. The social distance among teachers and students can open the door to subtle forms of bias, some negative and some positive.

In a classic study, *Pygmalion in the Classroom*, researchers Robert Rosenthal and Lenore Jacobson (1968) gave a group of elementary students an intelligence test at the beginning of the school year. They then randomly selected a small percentage of the students and told teachers that these were the students who should be expected to "bloom" intellectually over the coming year. The researchers' statements were not true, but the teachers believed that the randomly selected students possessed great potential. Rosenthal and Jacobson

then retested the students at the end of the year. They found that those students who were randomly deemed to be "bloomers" at the beginning of the year showed a 12-point average improvement in their intelligence test scores compared to an 8-point average improvement among students who had not been labeled. Hence, teacher expectations can influence students' intellectual development. This dynamic is often called the **Pygmalion effect**.

The ramifications of the Pygmalion study can be applied to processes that occur in relation to other types of labels and categorizations of students. Students deemed "slow learners" at a young age may be influenced by expectations in the classroom that limit their academic responsibilities or generally expect less from them. Similarly, children from racial minorities and other disadvantaged groups may find additional hurdles to their intellectual development because of potentially biased interactions with teachers and other important cultural gatekeepers (Alexander, Entwisle, and Thompson 1987; Cooper and Allen 1998).

Being a member of a minority group may influence classroom processes in other ways. According to the U.S. Census Bureau, in 2005 African Americans represented about 13% of the American population. Hence, a fully integrated classroom of 20 students may have only 2 or 3 African Americans. Although classrooms may be homogeneous in terms of age, the minority members of the classroom may feel strain in the face of their differences from majority members. In other words, these students stand out from the rest of the class. Morris Rosenberg (see Elliott 2001; Rosenberg 1986) called this feeling **contextual dissonance**. Minority students feel many of the same peer pressures found in more homogeneous classrooms but also must cope with the feeling that they stand apart from other students. Rosenberg's research shows that contextual dissonance, whether based on class, race, or ability, may reduce students' sense of self-esteem.

Peer Culture

Most of our discussion of socialization agents has emphasized the passive nature of child development: children learn social expectations by modeling and "taking in" family and teacher behavior. School adds the influence of peers to socialization processes, but most research continues to emphasize children as recipients of some formal developmental goals. More recent research and theory has started to examine how children actively participate in the socialization process (Corsaro 2005; Jencks 1996). Much of this work has emphasized children's peer cultures.

Peer-Group Structures. The most important difference between school and peer-group culture is the voluntary nature of peer-group affiliation. Children have more flexibility in a peer-group context than they do inside the classroom. They may also choose to structure their relationships to include like-minded others. In addition, children can choose to leave the group, unlike their family and school groups (Corsaro 2005; Gecas 1992; Jencks 1996). In some sense, peer groups serve to teach children how to think more independently from institutional and adult constraints. Much of our adult life is spent navigating formal and informal contexts, including work, school, family, and friends. The increasing influence of peer groups into the teen years prepares children to manage complex role relationships with guidance not often found in their immediate families.

In one sense, children's peer culture is largely egalitarian because it is free of institutional restraints. However, research shows that children learn to stratify at very young ages. Patricia Adler and Peter Adler (Adler 1996; Adler and Adler 1998) conducted an extensive study of elementary schoolchildren to understand children's hierarchies, using both interview data and personal observations. Their research showed that children form friendship cliques that represent their relative status in children's culture, largely derived from the larger adult culture. These cliques can be divided into four major groups:

1. The popular clique
2. The wannabes
3. Middle friendship circles
4. Social isolates

The **popular clique** includes children with active social lives and with the largest number of friends. They also have the most control over their peers' culture. That is, the kids among the popular crowd had more say in the activities and the definition of *cool* than children in other cliques. It is estimated that the popular clique represents about a third of children (Adler and Adler 1998).

The **wannabes** represent children that want to be popular but do not quite get accepted into this group. Although they are occasionally accepted into the popular clique's activities, they never sustain that status in the group. This group represents about 10% of children. The **middle friendship circles**, in contrast, represent about half of children. This group forms smaller circles of friends and is less hierarchical than the two previous groups. They do not seek popularity but obtain social comfort from their small circles of friends and family.

The final group, the **social isolates**, represents less than 10% of children. This group has trouble establishing any relationships with kids in the other cliques. These children may have behavioral problems or simply have trouble relating to other children. Adler and Adler (1998) observed that many of these children turned to each other as a source of comfort, although this method was not always successful because many isolates want to avoid the stigma associated with being an isolate (Kless 1992). Many of them simply spent time alone, drifting around the playgrounds, watching the other children play.

Peer-Group Socialization Processes. Viktor Gecas (1992) argued that peer-group socialization includes three areas of child development:

1. Development and validation of the self
2. Development of competence in the presentation of self
3. Acquisition of knowledge not provided by parents or schools

Peers provide additional information from which to evaluate our senses of worth. This process can occur through informal interactions, through the remarks and reactions our friends make about our behaviors. Because peer associations are more voluntary than family and school contexts, rewards and punishments offered by peers can have a particularly powerful effect on individual self-evaluations.

Children must also learn subtle aspects of social life. They must learn how to interact in different social contexts. A small part of this "act" is related to manners of behavior, such as the appropriate fork to use at the dinner table. It also includes appropriate greetings and salutations and things to do to avoid causing a fight. Although some of these things are learned at home, many of them fall in the purview of peer relationships. Peer groups provide knowledge unique to a given age group or generation. In other words, parental norms may not be appropriate for same-aged peer groups. Examples of conflict between family and peer-group norms are numerous. Think about a time when you wanted to wear a particular piece of clothing or jewelry when you were living with your parents. Your choices may have been driven by the latest fashion or fad. One example is a teenager who is given a pair of jeans with the word "Squeeze" at the backside of the waistline. The teenager sees nothing wrong with this word as she accepts the jeans from her friend, only to find out that the choice of jeans is seen as inappropriate by her parents. She argues that "all of the kids are doing it," leading her parents to investigate. The parents talk to other parents and find that their daughter is correct—many of the kids are wearing this style at school. The girl's parents' standard of dress diverged from that of her peers. The girl is left to battle over these two different standards, much like you probably did.

Finally, peers also help us develop knowledge about the world that we tend not to get from traditional sources. One example is the transmission of knowledge about sexual behavior. Parents and teachers may share some rudimentary information about the process of having sex and its consequences. However, these sources of information do not always review the more subtle aspects of sexual behavior, what "turns on" the other person, what activities are deemed "normal," and so on. Individuals may feel more comfortable discussing such topics with their peers or finding information from the media than with their parents or teachers. Peer discussions and interactions also give people an opportunity to think and decide about such things in a less-stressful environment.

Kathleen Bogle (2008) investigated the culture of what she calls "hooking up" on college campuses. Hooking up refers to sexual activities that occur outside of committed relationships. Interviewing 76 men and women on college campuses, she provides a detailed review of the practice, discussing how it develops among college students but then ends after college. The role of peers in college becomes most pronounced in this practice because it develops and is taught among peers, not from any other agent of socialization. The structure of college life makes peer influence especially prominent with dense living arrangements mixed with little authoritative oversight.

Other Socializing Agents: The Role of Media

media

There are almost certainly other agents of socialization in your life that we have not discussed. You may have been influenced by a small town community, a religious group, or some other group unique to your life. The media is a particularly prominent agent in the Western world and is a growing influence on the rest of the world. Americans spend at least 15 hours a week on average watching television (Robinson and Godbey 1997). Children's viewing of television and the use of electronic media has increased in recent years too (Brown and Marin 2009). A major way that agents of socialization affect us is merely through observation and adaptation: We watch other people do things and adopt those behaviors over time. Hence, watching people on television may provide role models for our own behavior. It also provides scripts with which we can use during interactions with other people. Over two hundred studies have been conducted to assess the relationship between watching television and the incidence of violence (Comstock 2008). Most of this research shows that there is at least a correlation between watching violent programming and violent behavior. Some scholars question whether correlational research, research in which viewing behavior is connected to aggressive behavior at one time period, adequately accounts for the long-range effects of television violence and violent behavior (Grimes and Bergen 2008), but the best research using longitudinal data does suggest that exposure to violent programming at an early age leads to later aggressive behavior (Brown and Marin 2009; Wilson 2008).

Similar types of research have been conducted to determine if the content of television programming affects our thoughts, feelings, or behavior. Sociologists are especially interested in knowing if the effects of gender and racial stereotypes exist on television and other media and whether these stereotypes lead to sexist or racist outcomes. If we see racism and sexism on television, we may feel that these behaviors are acceptable and even adapt them into our own repertoire of attitudes and behaviors. Studies show that negative stereotypes do exist in television and video games, among other sources of media (Dill and Thill 2007; Mastro, Behm-Morawitz, and Kopacz 2008; Saeed 2007). Other research shows that watching sexual content on television is associated with increased pregnancy among teens (12–17 years of age) (Martino et al. 2008). The content of television programming does seem to impact people's lives.

Watching people live out different lifestyles on television may engender more tolerance toward these behaviors. Indeed one of the most important influences of the media is as a pervasive presence throughout society in helping to define what is "normal" (Milkie 1999). In a Brazilian study of television viewing, for instance, heavy television watchers reported holding more liberal attitudes toward blacks and were more supportive of interracial marriage than those who watched less television (Leslie 1995). Socialization is a process but the content and methods of transmitting culture can vary from place to place.

Adult Socialization

Although most of our discussion of socialization processes has focused on children, many of these socialization dynamics continue into adulthood. We learn new skills (social and otherwise) and social roles over time. We must be able to take the role of the other as we become parents, workers, and change careers, among other life events. As such, we adapt new and drop old aspects of our identity. For instance, if you become an accountant, you will have to work with different sets of people than when you are in school—people will likely interact with more formality and expect more consistent work patterns than among college students. You would probably anticipate this change entering a new profession. But what if you decide to go to graduate school and get a Ph.D. in sociology? How would you act as a professor on campus? You may contemplate what you remember from your former professors and adopt some of their behaviors.

Like childhood socialization, adult socialization can be a reciprocal process: just as we are socialized into a new role, other people are also being socialized by us. For instance, Allison Hicks (2008) studied the socialization of new prison chaplains. Prison chaplains expected to serve as agents of socialization for inmates, trying to help them rehabilitate (resocialize) their spiritual and social lives. However, Hicks found that they had to modify these expectations to meet the demands of the institution and the apparent lack of desire among prisoners to change. They began to redefine the concept of rehabilitation to include institutional goals, which included a stronger focus on safety and security needs in the prison environment. Hicks's work shows the multiple levels of socialization going on in this setting: prison chaplains trying to socialize inmates, inmates' effects on chaplains, and the influence of institutional conditions on interactions between these two groups.

SOCIALIZATION

The Process of Fitting *into* Society

From: *Think Sociplogy 2010*, by John D. Carl.

SOCIALIZATION

"People

don't come to Temple City to be discovered, they come to be left alone . . . Before the disruption of that quiet [street] in November of 1970, the residents of one small house behind the row of royal palms were known to their neighbors as the quietest family of all.

"The disruption was spectacular—enough so to earn a week's worth of stories in the Los Angeles Times . . . *"GIRL, 13, PRISONER SINCE INFANCY, DEPUTIES CHARGE; PARENTS JAILED," . . . "MYSTERY SHROUDS HOME OF ALLEGED CHILD PRISONER."*

"The ensuing inquiries found the girl to be a teenager, though she weighed only fifty-nine pounds and was only fifty-four inches tall. She was in much worse physical shape than at first suspected: she was incontinent, could not chew solid food and could hardly swallow, could not focus her eyes beyond twelve feet, and, according to some accounts, could not cry . . . She could not hop, skip, climb, or do anything requiring the extension of her limbs . . . [and] she could not talk . . .

"The girl is referred to not by her real name but by her scientific alias, Genie—the name used in the symposium papers, the psychology magazines, and the textbooks contrived in order to protect the child's identity.

"The story of Genie, has come to seem to me . . . twin histories; that of a young woman trying desperately, heroically, and ultimately unsuccessfully, to transcend the confining horrors of her childhood, and that of researchers . . . In a mutual quest, the successes and failures of scientist and subject became linked.

"Genie had appeared to them out of a little room and they had thought . . . that here was someone of whom they might ask questions and whom might be able to respond . . . It turned out the scientists had not freed Genie from the little room; instead she had ushered them in."[1]

The Process of Fitting *into* Society

In *Genie: A Scientific Tragedy*, Russ Rymer chronicles how **Genie's father locked her in a small room, fearing his daughter was mentally retarded.**

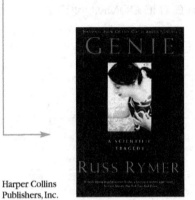

Harper Collins
Publishers, Inc.

In a dark, gloomy room, a 13-year-old girl sits tied to a toddler's potty chair. Left for days on end, she rarely sees the light of day or interacts with others. Guttural utterances and a few recognizable words are all that she can muster. Unfortunately, this girl isn't some fictional character from a movie; she's an actual girl whom scientists dubbed "Genie." Equipped with absolutely no social skills, Genie materialized from her room into a human society with which she had no experience.

When Genie was finally rescued in November of 1970, experts found that a lack of nurturing and care had left her ill prepared to interact with others.

Thinking about Genie, I'm reminded of my own children and how important it is to speak to them, read to them, and interact with them. Such interaction is vital for a child to know who he or she is. Rymer's work explores the questions: What happens to someone who lives in absolute isolation during his or her formative years? What can science do for such a person? And, does a lack of early socialization pose long-term problems for a person?

get the topic: WHAT IS SOCIALIZATION?

SOCIALIZATION is the process that teaches the norms, values, and other aspects of a culture to new group members.

How do you know what language to speak? What does a red light mean? From the minute you are born, you are being socialized into the world around you. At a football game I recently attended, a young man did not remove his hat during the national anthem. Offended, an older man reached over and snatched the hat off the young man's head. Each man's values, in terms of respect for his country, were miles apart. How did they learn these differing values? Through socialization, of course.

Socialization is the process that teaches the norms, values, and other aspects of a culture to new group members. As such, it is a lifelong process of creating and maintaining group membership. Countless sociologists and psychologists have studied how people become socialized, which has led to the development of several socialization theories.

Socialization theory claims that the person we become is the result of our environment. According to sociologist Talcott Parsons, socialization requires people to learn and internalize society's values.[2] In other words, we accept and integrate the values of the group as our own. These social values constantly surround us, but they often go unexamined.

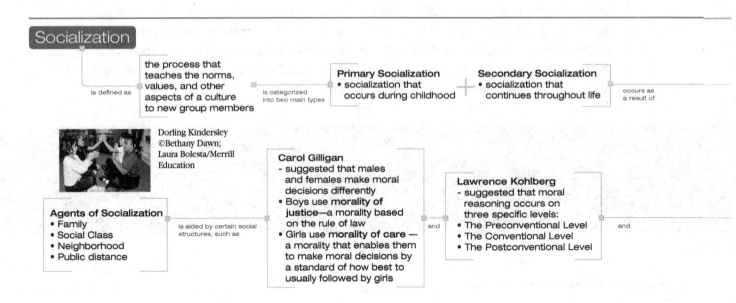

Socialization

is defined as → the process that teaches the norms, values, and other aspects of a culture to new group members

is categorized into two main types →

Primary Socialization
• socialization that occurs during childhood

Secondary Socialization
• socialization that continues throughout life

occurs as a result of

Dorling Kindersley ©Bethany Dawn; Laura Bolesta/Merrill Education

Agents of Socialization
• Family
• Social Class
• Neighborhood
• Public distance

is aided by certain social structures, such as →

Carol Gilligan
- suggested that males and females make moral decisions differently
• Boys use **morality of justice**—a morality based on the rule of law
• Girls use **morality of care** — a morality that enables them to make moral decisions by a standard of how best to usually followed by girls

and →

Lawrence Kohlberg
- suggested that moral reasoning occurs on three specific levels:
• The Preconventional Level
• The Conventional Level
• The Postconventional Level

and

At what point in our lives does socialization take place? Parsons and Bales argue that most socialization occurs during childhood.[3] Orville Brim refers to this early socialization as **primary socialization**.[4] Parents are their children's first teachers; they pass on values, rules, language, religious beliefs, and an unending list of social norms. However, socialization is also reciprocal because children also influence their parents. Before I had children, I thought I knew about parenting, but each child teaches me something new as I try to socialize them. Because socialization is an unending cycle, we are at times the "socializer" and at other times the "socialized."[5] This dynamic, whereby socialization continues throughout our lives is considered **secondary socialization**.[6] As you experience life-changing events—like going to college, beginning a career, or getting married—new socialization occurs. At each stage of life, we encounter new norms, values, and expectations. We learn to accept and integrate them as we adapt to our environment. In a sense, the socialization process makes us who we are. Why might Genie's lack of primary socialization have lasting effects on her life?

The Nature vs. Nurture Debate — What Makes Us Who We Are?

As one theorist said, "We, and all other animals, are machines created by our genes."[7] Pure **"nature"** theorists believe that the genes we get from our parents at conception are the primary causes of human behaviors—in short, our genetic makeup determines who we are. For example, a biologist studying Genie might argue that her genetics determined how she coped with and survived her predicament. Had her genetic makeup been different, she might have emerged from the room with little or no side effects.

In the 20th century, social scientists began to fight biologists' belief that nature is the sole determinant of who we are. Those who believe in **"nurture,"** like philosopher John Locke, propose that our environment influences the way we think, feel, and behave.[8] Supporters of this idea assert that socialization molds us like pieces of clay, particularly during early childhood. Many nurture theorists believe that a social process teaches people who they are and how they fit into their world. For some-

PRIMARY SOCIALIZATION is socialization that occurs during childhood.

SECONDARY SOCIALIZATION is the dynamic whereby socialization continues throughout our lives.

NATURE THEORY states that the genes we get from our parents at conception are the primary causes of human behaviors.

NURTURE THEORY states that our environment influences the way we think, feel, and behave.

one like Genie, who lacked such nurturing, her ability to cope within society could be greatly affected.

Extreme proponents on both sides of the nature/nurture debate have difficulty sorting out this issue. Although it is true that our genes do not necessarily dictate our destiny, it's also true that our biological makeup is what interacts with the environment in the first place. Noted biologist and author Paul Ehrlich supports a blended point of view. In Ehrlich's book he notes, "We can't partition the responsibility for aggression, altruism, or charisma between DNA and upbringing. In many such cases, trying to separate the contributions of nature and nurture to an attribute is rather like trying to separate the contributions of length and width to the area of a rectangle, which at first glance also seems easy. When you think about it carefully, though, it proves impossible."[9]

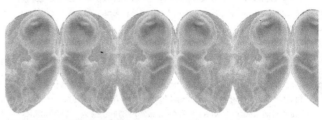

Does our genetic makeup really determine who we will become? Or do other factors come into play, such as the way our parents care for us? Where do you stand on the nature vs. nurture debate?

Nature
• the belief that genetic and biological heredity are the primary causes of human behaviors

or

Nurture
• the belief that the way in which we think, feel, and behave are the results of our environment

has inspired many theorists to explain how people become socialized, such as

Charles H. Cooley
• proposed the theory of "looking-glass self," which states that the self develops through a process of reflection

and

George Herbert Mead
- proposed that the self consists of two parts the "I" and the "Me"
- suggested that the self develops in three stages:
• The Imitation Stage
• The Play Stage
• The Game Stage

and

Jean Piaget
- proposed that people go through a four-stage process of cognitive development:
• The Sensorimotor Stage
• The Preoperational Stage
• The Concrete Operational Stage
• The Formal Operational Stage

and

Erik Erikson
- proposed that people develop a personality in eight psychosocial stages
- at each stage we experience a crisis that upon resolving will have an effect on our ability to deal with the next one
The Eight Stages:
• Infancy
• Toddlerhood
• Preschooler
• Elementary School

• Adolescence
• Young Adulthood
• Middle Adulthood
• Late Adulthood

Trish Gant ©Dorling Kindersley

THINK SOCIOLOGICALLY

Rhesus Monkey Study

Which is more important to our survival—nature or nurture? To find out, researchers Harry and Margaret Harlow conducted numerous experiments with rhesus monkeys.[10] One of the most famous was designed to test which need is greater: the need for physical contact or the need for biological sustenance. The Harlows raised monkeys in isolation and eventually presented them with two artificial "mothers." The first "mother"—which was simply a hard wire frame with a wooden head—provided food. The other "mother" provided no food at all but was made of soft, cuddly material. The Harlows noticed that frightened baby monkeys sought comfort with the soft "mother" and not with the "mother" that fed them. They drew the conclusion that the key component of infant-mother bonding is not the providing of food, but the presence of comfort. The Harlows' findings, while not directly applicable to human development, support the idea that socialization, i.e., nurture, is a key building block in normal development.

The Harlows' conclusion supports Genie's story. The Genie team concluded that she was not retarded from birth, but due to her deprivation early in life, she would never be "normal." Her arrested development proves how sustenance is actually secondary to comfort as a necessary component for human development. Genie's growth as a person was stunted due to her lack of socialization.

FERAL AND ISOLATED CHILDREN

Tales of **feral**, or wild, children raised by animals are not limited to works of fiction like *Tarzan* or *The Jungle Book*. Newspapers and tabloids often feature sensational headlines about the discoveries of such children. Unfortunately, there are too many stories about children held captive at the hands of abusive and/or mentally unstable parents. Although these stories are staples on the nightly news, we rarely explore or even think about what happens to these children as a result of their isolation. How does human contact, or the lack thereof, affect the people we become?

In April 2008, the story of Josef Fritzl — an Austrian father who had imprisoned his daughter in a basement dungeon for 24 years—attracted worldwide coverage on all the cable news networks. During this time, Fritzl repeatedly abused and raped his imprisoned daughter Elisabeth, even impregnating her seven times. One child died, Fritzl and his wife were raising three children, and the remaining three were left in the dungeon with little human contact. Until the rescue, the three isolated children had never seen the light of day, and they communicated using only simple grunts and gestures.[11] The future of the Fritzl children and their mother remains to be seen. They've surely got intense therapy and a long struggle ahead of them. Will the children ever become socialized?

Some clues might be found when looking back at the story of Genie, who was discovered in California in 1970. When authorities removed the child from her home, they immediately began to care for her.[12] A group of experts, known as "the Genie team," observed that Genie could not walk normally and understood only a few words. Additionally, she had problems eating solid food and still needed diapers. However, after her rescue, Genie made rapid progress. She quickly learned to dress and go to the toilet herself. She also learned to walk more normally. Her language skills began to develop, and within a few months, her vocabulary of only five to ten words had expanded to more than 100 words.[13]

Unfortunately, despite the massive efforts to help Genie, she never caught up with her peers. "The Genie team" concluded that her delayed progress was the result of missing key points in her social development. Because this lack of socialization kept her brain from fully developing, Genie must now live in a home for mentally retarded adults.[14]

Not all feral children have such difficulty becoming socialized. Isabelle, a feral child whose

Average Vocabularies of Children by Age

2000 words	
1500 words	
1000 words	
500 words	
0 words	

12-18 months   2 years   3 years   4 years   5 years

Source: Based on *Stages of Language Development* by Louis De Maio.   Shutterstock

<<< **Shortly after Genie's rescue, she developed a vocabulary of more than 100 words.**
How does Genie's vocabulary compare to children raised in a more "typical" way?

grandfather locked her in a darkened room with her deaf-mute mother, was discovered at age six. She communicated only through gestures, which her mother taught her. Experts put Isabelle through a rigorous socialization process. Surprisingly, Isabelle learned quickly. After two months, she was able to speak in sentences, and after about 18 months she had a vocabulary of 1500–2000 words. Ultimately, Isabelle was able to go to school and function normally with children her own age.[15]

Humans need other humans in order to live and to develop normally. Our human nature is not necessarily instinctual. If it were, Genie would have been able to catch up developmentally to her peers.

Deprivation of human interaction is perhaps more detrimental to humans than being underfed or physically abused. If we are to achieve our full potential, we need others to socialize us. The nurturing we experience in our early lives ultimately affects who we are and who we will become.

Theorists on Socialization

Socialization is a process that theorists have been studying for decades. Many of these theorists, from sociologists to psychologists, have made significant contributions to our understanding of the development of self and the development of morality. Like a never-ending college course, we're enrolled in "socialization" until the day we die. In that sense, we're constantly learning about ourselves.

COOLEY'S LOOKING–GLASS SELF

Charles H. Cooley is one of the central theorists of the development of the self. His notion of the **"looking-glass self"** proposes that, like a mirror, the self develops through a process of reflection. That said, one's self is also established through interactions with others. According to Cooley, this process contains three steps:

1. We imagine how our behaviors will look to others.
2. We interpret others' reactions to our behaviors.
3. We develop a self-concept.[16]

Although Cooley's ideas were developed more than a century ago, modern scholars remain interested in them. King-To Yeung and John Levi Martin, contemporary sociologists who study the processes of the "looking-glass self," used Cooley's theory to test the internalization of self-understanding.[17] Their research found general support for the theory that our self-concept involves interpreting and internalizing others' perceptions about us. Yeung and Martin showed that the importance of our relationships is the key factor in determining how we internalize others' perceptions of us. This is why our parents influence us more than our local bank tellers do.[18]

GEORGE HERBERT MEAD — THE THREE STAGES OF THE "I-ME" SELF

Another theory about how humans develop the self was explored in symbolic interactionist George Herbert Mead's *Mind, Self, and Society*. For Mead, the self is that part of personal identity that has both self-aware-

FERAL means wild.

LOOKING-GLASS SELF is the theory that the self develops through a process of reflection, like a mirror.

"I" SELF is the subjective part of the self.

"ME" SELF is the objective part of the self.

IMITATION STAGE is Mead's first stage of development, which is the period from birth to about age 2, and is the stage at which children merely copy the behaviors of those around them.

PLAY STAGE is Mead's second stage of development, which occurs around the ages of 2-4 years, during which children play roles and begin to take on the characteristics of important people in their world.

GAME STAGE is Mead's third stage of development that never truly ends, and is the stage in which we begin to understand that others have expectations and demands placed upon them.

THE GENERALIZED OTHER is our sense of others.

ness and self-image.[19] Like Cooley, Mead agreed that the development of self involves interaction with others.

For Mead, though, the self consists of two parts: the "I" and the "Me." These two parts essentially create the self through their interaction. The **"I" Self** is the part of us that is an active subject, our subjective sense of who we are. It seeks self-fulfillment, asking, "What do *I* want?" In contrast, the **"Me" Self** is the objective part of the self; the part of our self-concept that questions how others might interpret our actions. The "Me" understands the symbols that others give us, and seeks to find favorable reactions to our behaviors from others.[20]

According to Mead, the self develops in three stages. The first is the **imitation stage**, which is the period from birth to about age 2. At this stage, children merely copy the behaviors of those around them. They don't attribute meaning to their actions, nor do they understand the implications of their behavior. For instance, when you see your baby sister clapping her hands, she's probably just imitating something she's seen and not actually giving you a round of applause.

Children enter the **play stage** around the ages of 2–4 years. Here, children play roles and begin to take on the characteristics of important people in their world. By playing roles, children see others as separate from themselves. They understand that their actions can affect other people, and vice versa. Mead claimed that, through play, children learn to find a sense of who they are and how to best interact with others in their society. At this stage, you're likely to see little boys tie blankets around their necks and pretend to be superheroes.

During our early school years, we enter what Mead called the **game stage**, a stage that never truly ends. It is in the game stage that we begin to understand that others have expectations and demands placed upon them. Mead termed this sense of others **"the generalized other."**

Through understanding others we are able to adjust or evaluate our own behavior based on factors such as culture and society. Developing a concept of the generalized other helps us understand other people's roles, norms, and expectations. This concept is important if we are to fit into society and live intimately with others.[21] The idea of little league sports best represents this stage.

When children are involved in a team sport like baseball or basketball, they must understand each position's roles and responsibilities in order to play the game. Not everyone can hit or shoot; everyone has a job to do or we can't play the game.

Socialization

PSYCHOSOCIAL CRISIS is a crisis occurring during each of Erikson's stages that will be resolved either positively or negatively, and each outcome will have an effect on our ability to deal with the next one.

COGNITIVE DEVELOPMENT is a person's ability to think and reason.

SENSORIMOTOR STAGE is the stage (birth to 2 years) at which infants learn to experience and think about the world through their senses and motor skills.

PREOPERATIONAL STAGE is the stage (ages 2 through 7 years) at which the ability to speak grows rapidly.

CONCRETE OPERATIONAL STAGE is the stage (ages 7 through 12 years) at which children can think about objects in the world in more than one way and start to understand causal connections in their surroundings.

FORMAL OPERATIONAL STAGE is the stage (ages 12 years and above) at which people become able to comprehend abstract thought.

Erik Erikson's Eight Stages of Development

Erik Erikson proposed that humans develop a personality in eight psychosocial, or psychological and social, stages. During each stage, we experience a particular **psychosocial crisis** that will be resolved either positively or negatively, and each outcome will have an effect on our ability to deal with the next one.[22]

According to Erikson, the crisis at each stage of development must be resolved positively before you can successfully master subsequent stages. Think back to Genie. She was imprisoned from the infancy stage through the elementary school stage, so did she ever truly become socialized? The answer is no. Although Genie did make some initial progress, she regressed after her first foster parents severely punished her for vomiting. Genie refused to open her mouth for fear it might happen again and responded in the only way she knew how: silence.[23] Genie's case helps illustrate Erikson's theory that failing to master one stage can mean that a person will fail the subsequent stages.

Jean Piaget's Theory of Cognitive Development

While Erikson's research focused on personality development, the work of Jean Piaget focused on **cognitive development**, which relates to a person's ability to think and reason. Since the way we think helps shape our self-concept, cognition (thinking) plays a significant role in socialization. Simply put, Piaget found that children don't think like adults. His four-stage theory of cognitive development has become an important basis for much educational theory, particularly as it applies to teaching young children.

When my daughter was an infant, nearly everything she touched went directly into her mouth. It didn't matter if it was a stuffed panda, board book, or a long red millipede. If she could reach it, it was going in her mouth. According to Piaget, this is the way babies learn. At the **sensorimotor stage** (birth to age 2 years), infants learn to experience and think about the world through their senses and motor skills. During this period, children develop a sense of "object permanence," the understanding that objects outside themselves still exist even when they are not in view.[24] For example, play "peek-a-boo" with an infant and you'll notice that the baby expresses surprise when you cover your face, followed by great joy when you reveal it. Near the end of the sensorimotor stage, peek-a-boo loses its allure and object permanence exists.

At the **preoperational stage** (ages 2 through 7 years), the ability to speak grows rapidly. Although children have already learned some words and phrases, their ability to use and interpret symbols is limited. Children will generally identify objects by a single characteristic. If you show a child the letters *C-A-T*, for example, the child is likely to read each individual letter aloud. It is unlikely that she will link them together into the word *cat*. Linking multiple symbols together is difficult for a preoperational thinker. By the end of this stage, however, a child can say the word *ball*, draw a picture of a ball, point to a ball on the floor, and understand that all of these mean the same thing.[25]

Each of the theorists—Cooley, Mead, Erikson, and Piaget—provides a different view of the development of self. **All these theorists agree that a person's development continues throughout life. These theories present human development as a type of staircase process.** Children who miss one or more stages of socialization generally fail to reach successful completion of their development, as was the case for Genie.

During the **concrete operational stage** (ages 7 through 12 years), children can think about objects in the world in more than one way and start to understand causal connections in their surroundings. They can think logically about some objects and events. For example, they learn that even though a plain sheet of white paper is folded into a paper airplane, it is still that same piece of white paper. Children at this stage can also imagine what other people might be thinking or feeling. Piaget believed we can't understand the "position" of others until we have passed through some developmental state. Children gain this ability during the concrete operational stage.[26]

Only at the **formal operational stage** (ages 12 years and above) do people become able to comprehend abstract thought. Because they're testing their ability to reason and comprehend the complexities of their world, children at this stage often argue with those in authority. Unsure of themselves, they're testing their thinking. Understanding abstract mathematical principles, such as algebra, becomes possible at this stage, and we become able to understand more deeply the interactions of concrete reality with abstract ideals.[27]

Piaget argued that it could be frustrating and traumatizing to force children to learn ahead of their cognitive capacities. In other words, it serves no purpose to try to teach geometry to a first-grader. Expecting a child to act like an adult is both impossible and unfair.[28]

Erikson's Eight Stages of Development

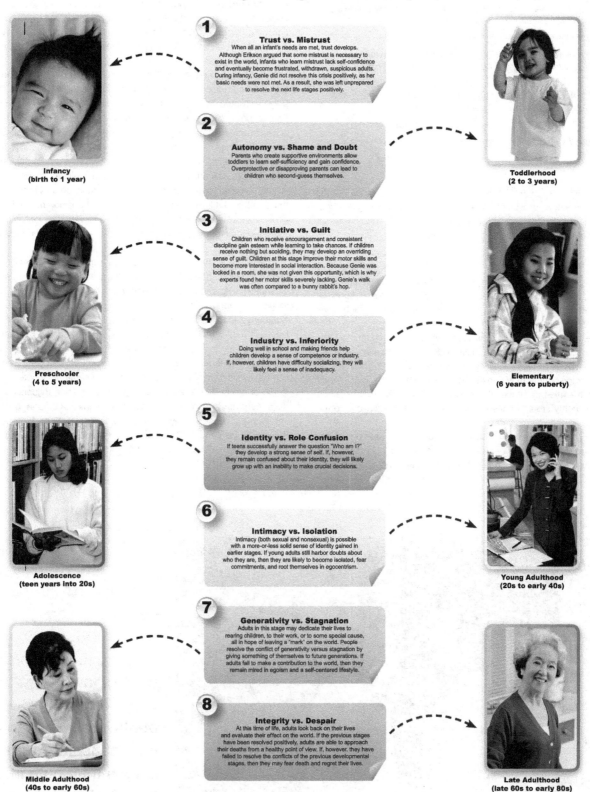

Infancy
(birth to 1 year)

1 **Trust vs. Mistrust**
When all an infant's needs are met, trust develops. Although Erikson argued that some mistrust is necessary to exist in the world, infants who learn mistrust lack self-confidence and eventually become frustrated, withdrawn, suspicious adults. During infancy, Genie did not resolve this crisis positively, as her basic needs were not met. As a result, she was left unprepared to resolve the next life stages positively.

2 **Autonomy vs. Shame and Doubt**
Parents who create supportive environments allow toddlers to learn self-sufficiency and gain confidence. Overprotective or disapproving parents can lead to children who second-guess themselves.

Toddlerhood
(2 to 3 years)

Preschooler
(4 to 5 years)

3 **Initiative vs. Guilt**
Children who receive encouragement and consistent discipline gain esteem while learning to take chances. If children receive nothing but scolding, they may develop an overriding sense of guilt. Children at this stage improve their motor skills and become more interested in social interaction. Because Genie was locked in a room, she was not given this opportunity, which is why experts found her motor skills severely lacking. Genie's walk was often compared to a bunny rabbit's hop.

4 **Industry vs. Inferiority**
Doing well in school and making friends help children develop a sense of competence or industry. If, however, children have difficulty socializing, they will likely feel a sense of inadequacy.

Elementary
(6 years to puberty)

Adolescence
(teen years into 20s)

5 **Identity vs. Role Confusion**
If teens successfully answer the question "Who am I?" they develop a strong sense of self. If, however, they remain confused about their identity, they will likely grow up with an inability to make crucial decisions.

6 **Intimacy vs. Isolation**
Intimacy (both sexual and nonsexual) is possible with a more-or-less solid sense of identity gained in earlier stages. If young adults still harbor doubts about who they are, then they are likely to become isolated, fear commitments, and root themselves in egocentrism.

Young Adulthood
(20s to early 40s)

7 **Generativity vs. Stagnation**
Adults in this stage may dedicate their lives to rearing children, to their work, or to some special cause, all in hope of leaving a "mark" on the world. People resolve the conflict of generativity versus stagnation by giving something of themselves to future generations. If adults fail to make a contribution to the world, then they remain mired in egoism and a self-centered lifestyle.

8 **Integrity vs. Despair**
At this time of life, adults look back on their lives and evaluate their effect on the world. If the previous stages have been resolved positively, adults are able to approach their deaths from a healthy point of view. If, however, they have failed to resolve the conflicts of the previous developmental stages, then they may fear death and regret their lives.

Middle Adulthood
(40s to early 60s)

Late Adulthood
(late 60s to early 80s)

Socialization

Source: Based on *Childhood and Society* by Erik Erikson.

PRECONVENTIONAL LEVEL is the first stage of moral development that lasts through the elementary school years; at this level, children make their moral judgements within a framework of hedonistic principles.

HEDONISM is seeking pleasure over pain.

CONVENTIONAL LEVEL is the second stage of moral development that arises before puberty and uses the lens of norms and rules to determine what is right and wrong.

POSTCONVENTIONAL LEVEL is the third stage of moral development that refers to a morality based on abstract principles.

MORALITY OF JUSTICE is morality based on the rule of law.

MORALITY OF CARE is morality decided by a standard of how best to help those who are in need.

Theories of Moral Development

How do we know what's right and what's wrong? Do girls learn about morals differently from boys? These are just two of the questions that theories of moral development seek to answer.

Kohlberg's Theory of Moral Development

Building upon the work of Piaget, the prominent theorist Lawrence Kohlberg suggested that moral reasoning occurs on three specific levels: preconventional, conventional, and postconventional. Each level describes different ways in which we make moral decisions.[29]

During the **preconventional level,** which lasts through the elementary school years, children make their moral judgments within a framework of **hedonism**—seeking pleasure over pain.[30] In other words, children judge right from wrong on the basis of what feels good or right to them. If a little boy notices that drawing on the walls results in a visit to the "naughty stool," chances are he won't take the crayons to the walls again.

The **conventional level** arises before puberty and uses the lens of norms and rules to determine what is right and wrong.[31] Basically, what is "right" is obedience to the rules. Rather than question the logic behind why those rules were established, a child simply does what he or she is told. The child may not understand *why* kicking his sister is wrong; he just understands that he shouldn't do it because "Mommy says so." Following the expectations of the family or group is valuable in and of itself. Doing your duty and respecting authority are the hallmarks of this level of development.

Kohlberg's third stage of moral development, the **postconventional level**, refers to a morality based on abstract principles. These may be rooted in political beliefs, religious beliefs, or a combination of both. Kohlberg suggests that the "good" includes adherence to agreed-upon principles rather than rules.[32] Such principles guide all decisions and provide a seamless web of morality for us all. For example, during the civil rights movement of the 1950s and 1960s, countless African American college students held sit-ins at segregated lunch counters, museums, libraries, and many other public places. Although their behavior broke the Jim Crow laws of the time, these students believed their behavior was "right" because they were drawing attention to laws that were morally wrong.

Although Kohlberg's own research supported his theory, more recent scholars question some of his assumptions. For example, Charles Helwig and Urszula Jasiobedzka found that children's moral judgments about law and lawbreaking occur earlier in life than Kohlberg's theory proposed.[33] Preschoolers may abide by the rules because they believe rule-breaking is wrong. In addition, moral reasoning doesn't always correlate with moral behavior. Using Kohlberg's schema, Colby and Damon showed that people at the highest levels of moral development act the same as people at lower levels of moral development. Instead, the situation influences people's behavior.[34] Take speeding, for example. Although everyone knows it's against the law, many people speed when they believe they won't be caught. These and other questions about Kohlberg's theory of moral development led Carol Gilligan to propose another point of view in 1982.

<<< It's hard to imagine that the simple act of sitting at a lunch counter could be illegal. **The unfairness of laws** such as these **led many students of all races to hold peaceful sit-ins across the South in hopes of abolishing Jim Crow laws.**

Corbis/Bettmann

Carol Gilligan and the "Morality of Care"

Carol Gilligan suggested that Kohlberg's theories were valid, though only when discussing the development of male morality. To Gilligan, his conclusions were biased against women because Kohlberg only studied men initially.[35] This, in turn, led him to erroneously assume men and women developed moral decisions similarly without actually studying women. Do men and women approach moral decisions differently?

I recently faced a moral decision while shopping at my local discount store. The cashier gave me $10 too much change. Being a bit of a miser, I immediately noticed her mistake. I'm human, so I considered keeping the money, but then I began to wonder what might happen if I took the money. Was it my fault that the cashier made a mistake? Would she get in trouble when she came up short at the end of her shift? All of these thoughts ran through my mind. Of course, I gave her the money back. Gilligan would argue that my gender influenced the way I approached my decision; women would follow a slightly different process.

After investigating women's experiences with morality, Gilligan concluded that moral decisions arise from two different principles: the morality of justice and the morality of care. She agreed that boys primarily follow what she called a **morality of justice**, a morality based on the rule of law. However, girls learn a **morality of care**, which enables them to make moral decisions by a standard of how best to help those who are in need.[36]

To study the differences between moral development in boys and girls, Gilligan proposed a real-life moral dilemma to young male and female subjects. Gilligan used the story of "Mr. Heinz and the Druggist," a tale that Kohlberg also used in his research. The general idea of the story is this: Mr. Heinz's wife is sick with a potentially fatal disease. Luckily, their small-town pharmacy is the only place around that carries the life-saving medication that his wife needs. The problem is the drug costs an astronomical $10,000, and the druggist refuses to sell it for any less. Should Mr. Heinz steal the drug?

Gilligan found that most male subjects used logic when answering the question. Many boys believed that Mr. Heinz should steal the medication, even though it's legally wrong. Boys reasoned that the judge would likely be lenient on Mr. Heinz because of the circumstances. In short, the boys answered the question like a math problem: $x + y = z$. The girl subjects, however, considered the personal relationships involved. Girls worried that Mr. Heinz might go to jail, which could make his wife sicker and leave no one around to care for her or provide her with medicine. They also tried to think of other ways for Mr. Heinz to get the drug so that he would not have to leave his wife. Girls were more concerned about how Mr. Heinz's actions would affect the dynamic between him and his wife.

Modern research provides mixed support for Gilligan's assertion of gender differences in moral reasoning. In short, it appears that girls and boys learn *both* morality of care and morality of justice. The two types of morality are not exclusive to one gender over the other.[37] Some findings show that since girls advance through the stages of moral development faster than boys, they actually develop postconventional morality at earlier ages.[38] The most important aspect, perhaps, is the link between ego development and the moralities of care and justice. Because girls develop faster than boys, they present a morality of care more quickly than boys.[39]

Either way, Gilligan and Kohlberg both agree that moral reasoning follows a developmental process and that the surroundings affect that process. Although the precise gender differences may not be as clearly distinguished as Gilligan initially believed, and Kohlberg's age groups may be more flexible than he proposed, both theories show that we learn to make moral decisions in different ways.

Kohlberg and Gilligan's Theories of Moral Development

"Both boys and girls go through the same three stages—preconventional, conventional, and postconventional—to develop their morality."
— Lawrence Kohlberg

From top: Shutterstock; Getty Images; Photo by Jerry Bauer. Courtesy of Harvard Graduate School of Education

"Boys and girls develop their morality differently. Boys generally develop a morality of justice, while girls develop a morality of care."
— Carol Gilligan

Socialization

Agents of Socialization

We learn socialization with outside help from different **agents of socialization**, which are the people and groups that shape our self-concept, beliefs, and behavior. So what social structures, or agents, help us become socialized?

THE FAMILY: PARENTING STYLES AND RECIPROCAL SOCIALIZATION

Few things in life shape us more than our parents. Because both my parents worked full time, I learned at an early age that one must work to live. I started working at 13 and am still working today, as evidenced by my writing this book on nights, weekends, and summer vacations. My parents also valued education. Although they never completed college, they encouraged us kids to go. Sometimes, I wonder what my life would have been like if I had had different parents. What if my parents were drug addicts? Or illiterate? Or members of the wealthiest elite in the country (my personal favorite)? My point is merely that children don't select their parents, and yet family is one of the most important agents of socialization.

When parents socialize their children, they do so in two different ways. First, they create safe environments by providing emotional support through love, affection, and nurturing. Second, parents provide social control by teaching their children appropriate behaviors. Parents do this by using force, coercion, threats, or rewards.[40] If parents are not successful at providing these things for their children, the results can be disastrous. Genie's father, for example, locked her in a dark room on a potty for days on end. She didn't receive the love and nurturing she needed as a child, which led to socialization problems after she was rescued.

Sociologist Diana Baumrind explored how parental discipline affects children. Although disciplining children is a cultural universal, the manner in which it occurs varies by culture and family style. Baumrind observed that parenting styles have a substantial effect on individual socialization outcomes.[41] Parents who practice an **authoritative style** listen to their children's input while consistently enforcing the preset rules. Children reared in such an environment integrate into the world with the most ease because they exhibit high levels of self-esteem and possess the capacities for independence and cooperation with others.

Whereas authoritative parents practice a balanced style of child-rearing, permissive and authoritarian parents represent opposite extremes, and neither produces positive outcomes. **Permissive style** parents provide high levels of support but an inconsistent enforcement of rules. This results in a child who does not understand boundaries and expectations. The teenagers on MTV's *My Super Sweet 16* who are showered with lavish gifts and extravagant parties by their affluent parents may be ill-equipped to deal with the disappointments and responsibilities that are sure to come later in life. Conversely, children reared by **authoritarian style** parents experience high levels of social control but low levels of emotional support. Such children understand the rules but have no relational reasons to obey them when their parents are not looking. Often, the most rebellious youths are by-products of very strict households. Baumrind suggests that these two styles of parenting produce children with lower self-esteem and less self-assurance.[42]

Three Parenting Styles

Permissive Style

Authoritative Style

Authoritarian Style

Source: Based on *Current Patterns of Parental Authority* by Diana Baumind.
From top: Shutterstock; Shutterstock; Shutterstock

▶▶▶ GO GL🌐BAL

Parenting in Asian Cultures

Do the parenting styles that Baumrind describes apply in all cultures? Ruth Chao studied how the parenting styles of Chinese families affected children.[43] In order to explore the perception of Chinese schoolchildren as successful and well behaved, Chao observed how parents interacted with their children.[44] The mothers she observed provided high levels of control, but also high levels of sacrifice and personal closeness to their children. Parents in China expect their children to meet high standards of both individual achievement and social conformity. In general, Chinese children meet these standards. The parents in this culture are authoritative; children receive adequate emotional support and know that their hard work will gain the family's approval.

In another study, sociologist Min Zhou proposed that Confucian philosophy, with its emphasis on family loyalty, acts as a social control mechanism that supports Asian children's success.[45] Studies of Vietnamese immigrant children living in enclaves in the United States show similar findings to those of Chao. They show that second-generation immigrant children who remain linked to their families and culture have better outcomes with regard to educational attainment and the likelihood that they will stay in school.[46] Culture plays an important role in psychologists' and sociologists' interpretations about family socialization.

SOCIAL CLASS: OPPORTUNITIES FOR SOCIALIZATION

Family isn't the only agent of socialization; our social class also affects us. Numerous studies show connections between social class and socialization. Melvin Kohn's research found that working-class parents focus on their children's obedience to authority, whereas middle-class parents showed greater concern about the motivations for their children's behavior.[47] Because working-class parents are closely supervised at their jobs, they are more likely to demand this same conformity from their children. Therefore, the mother who is used to punching a clock at the assembly line is more likely to expect a home environment in which her children do their chores at set times.

Our social class affects us in many ways that we do not anticipate and may not even recognize. The availability of piano lessons, art classes, and little-league sports teams all socialize children; however, these experiences are typically available only to middle- and upper-income families. Children of less affluent families tend to miss these socialization opportunities. Social class affects not only the type of experiences we have, but also their quality and quantity.

NEIGHBORHOOD

Anyone who's ever visited a dormitory building before making a decision to live there believes that the "right" dorm matters. The same is true of choosing a neighborhood in which to live because your social class is often tied to the kind of neighborhood you live in. Noted sociologist William J. Wilson looked at how inner-city poverty brought with it the disadvantages of poor schools, weak social structures, high crime rates, and rampant drug use.[48] Wilson argued that poor people are truly disadvantaged because their community offers few role models for anything else. Children who grow up in these communities are likely to make poor decisions. Studies have shown that neighborhood has significant negative effects on IQ, teen pregnancy, and high school dropout rates.[49]

Neighborhoods also influence economically privileged children. Children who grow up in more affluent neighborhoods often do better in

AGENTS OF SOCIALIZATION are the people and groups who shape our self-concept, beliefs, and behavior.

AUTHORITATIVE STYLE is a parenting style in which parents listen to their children's input while consistently enforcing the preset rules.

PERMISSIVE STYLE is a parenting style in which parents provide high levels of support but an inconsistent enforcement of rules.

AUTHORITARIAN STYLE is a parenting style with which children experience high levels of social control but low levels of emotional support.

RESOCIALIZATION is the process of learning new norms, values, attitudes, and behaviors, and abandoning old ones.

TOTAL INSTITUTIONS are places in which the most effective forms of resocialization can occur because they isolate people from outside influences so they can be reformed and controlled.

school, have lower rates of teen pregnancy, and higher IQ scores.[50] Neighborhoods can also predict how far you may go in school, showing that the higher the socioeconomic status of the neighborhood, the higher the educational attainment.[51] Neighborhood effects also apply to voluntary associations for children. A predicting factor in the sport children will play is correlated to their neighborhoods.[52] For example, a sport like skiing that requires expensive equipment is more likely to played by children of well-to-do families because they can afford the upkeep and travel to the slopes.

Of course, just because parents are affluent does not mean that they will be great parents or that their children will be successfully socialized. The reverse is also true; a parent who has very limited financial means may be a very good parent.

Can We Be "Resocialized"? Experiencing the Total Institution

Resocialization is the process of learning new norms, values, attitudes, and behaviors and abandoning old ones. This process involves more than the kinds of secondary socialization that occur when we marry or take a new job. Yoda, the noted Jedi philosopher, says it best in the film *The Empire Strikes Back;* sometimes, "You must unlearn what you have learned."

The most effective forms of resocialization occur in **total institutions** that isolate people from outside influences so they can be reformed and controlled.[53] People may enter total institutions voluntarily, as in the case of non-draftees that enlist in military boot camps, or involuntarily, as in the case of inmates in mental institutions and prisons. Regardless, total institutions have certain characteristics:

1. There is one authority, and activities take place in specific locations.

2. Carefully structured activities control the participants.

3. Authorities carefully screen all information from outside the institution.

4. Rules and roles are clearly defined.

5. A strict hierarchy exists within the institution.

6. Total institutions restrict individual choice.

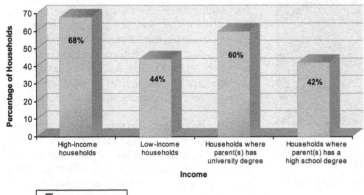

The Effect of Income and Education on Children's Participation in Organized Sports in Canada

Percentage of Households

- High-income households: 68%
- Low-income households: 44%
- Households where parent(s) has university degree: 60%
- Households where parent(s) has a high school degree: 42%

Income

■ Participation in Organized Sports

Source: Based on "Organized Sports Participation Among Children," 2005.

Socialization

think sociologically: HOW DO THE THREE THEORETICAL PARADIGMS VIEW SOCIALIZATION?

Symbolic Interactionism and Resocialization

We've seen how symbolic interactionists interpret society's symbols as a means for people to create a sense of self. We've also learned how the self develops under ordinary conditions. But how might development inside a total institution affect a person's sense of self?

Sociologist Harold Garfinkel explored the similarities in the ways prison inmates and military enlistees are resocialized upon entering those total institutions.[54] Garfinkel points out that these institutions "welcome" new members through some form of degrading ceremony designed to humiliate the person. This humiliation is required to "break them down" so that resocialization is possible. Inmates and enlistees may both have their heads shaved and their "street clothes" taken away. After putting on uniforms, their individual style of dress is erased in order to look like everyone else. In boot camp and under the control of the institution, the new recruit has no choice in when he or she will eat, sleep, or bathe. Similarly, inmates receive numbers to replace their names, are given uniforms to wear, and are told where they will sleep, when they will eat, and how they will spend their allocated "free" time. In both cases, the goal is to strip away former identity and resocialize the person into someone who will be obedient to commands.

Through resocialization, the institution controls all aspects of a person's life.[55] The techniques that total institutions use change the inmate or soldier's internal thinking, which in turn changes his or her sense of self.

Getty Images

∧
∧   **Prison inmates are stripped of their individual**
∧   **identities so that they can be transformed into**
people who willingly follow the orders of those
in authority.

Functionalism

While symbolic interactionists study the effect of institutions on individuals, functionalists examine how certain institutions, specifically religion and education, function in society. An institution's function, and the individual's relationship to that institution, helps determine what role it plays in the development of self.

RELIGION

In every U.S. election, Christian fundamentalists are a key voting bloc that politicians court by campaigning on "family values." Though the idea of such values is malleable depending on the issues, it's clear that the members of this group share a common set of beliefs that finds its foundation in religion.

From Muslim practitioners to Orthodox Jews and Buddhist monks, all world religions provide frames of reference for believers. These frameworks include beliefs, values, and behaviors in keeping with the teachings of that religion. Religions teach about life, death, and all of life's transitions in between. The religious socialization that results from this teaching process has measurable effects.

Sociologists Charles Tittle and Michael Welch studied the links between religiosity and juvenile delinquency and found that they were inversely related. The more religious the juvenile, the less likely he or she is to be delinquent.[56] Harold Grasmick and colleagues found weaker, but similar, results with respect to adults and behaviors such as tax cheating and littering.[57] This research shows that religion can play a role in forming our behavior.

EDUCATION

Out of a typical seven-hour school day, students in secondary schools in the United States spend only about three hours doing academic activities.[58] Instead, students are learning the **"hidden curriculum"**–lessons taught in school that are unrelated to academic learning. School teaches you to deal with peers who are sometimes cruel.[59] If students successfully negotiate the dangers of their neighborhoods and the various power struggles that go on in their schools, they feel a sense of satisfaction. Mock elections and saluting the flag help foster citizenship among students. Schools also socialize children by setting regulations that structure the school day. Students must show up on time, get along with others, follow teachers' expectations, wait in lines, and follow the rules.[60]

When families and schools cooperate to teach children to follow the rules, they help create a society that has fewer lawbreakers. When neighborhoods support these ideals, children grow up feeling part of something important. In the event that the family is dysfunctional, or the school does not work, or the neighborhood is infecting them with negative ideas about the society, this too socializes children. Negative outcomes usually result. Society functions best when social institutions cooperate.

Socialization

Conflict Theory—What Forces Socialize Us?

Recall that conflict theory suggests that power relationships influence our perceptions. To guide our actions, societies use **gender socialization** to teach their members how to express their masculinity or femininity. **Gender** refers to the expectations of behavior and attitude that a society considers proper for males and females. If and when these expectations limit one gender in favor of the other, it usually occurs as a result of differences in power.

> **HIDDEN CURRICULUM** refers to the lessons taught in school that are unrelated to academic learning.
>
> **GENDER SOCIALIZATION** teaches members of society how to express their masculinity or femininity.
>
> **GENDER** is the expectations of behavior and attitude that a society considers proper for males and females.
>
> **MASS MEDIA** include any print or electronic resource that is used to communicate to a wide audience.

Conflict theorists often argue that **men use their power to dominate and limit women.**

MAKE CONNECTIONS

Fictional Tales and Gender

From *Aesop's Fables* to the Brothers Grimm, folktales symbolize the innocence of childhood. But a closer analysis shows how these folktales shape how children perceive gender. Most folktales follow a typical pattern in which a dependent woman relies exclusively on a strong man to save her from harm. Think about the story of Rapunzel—the girl with the long, golden hair who is trapped in a tower by a witch. In the story, Rapunzel is merely a piece of property, given away by her father in exchange for his life. While trapped in the tower, Rapunzel is dependent on the witch and unable to escape. Rapunzel, afraid of the witch's wrath, remains in the tower alone and refuses the prince's help to escape. The prince goes blind because he is unable to save the beauty. Young children, especially young girls, who read these tales internalize the idea that being submissive and reliant on men is a desired trait.

These stereotypes are not just a part of archaic folktales; they also appear in modern works of fiction. Television programs like *Grey's Anatomy* and *Desperate Housewives* feature female characters who reinforce generalizations about gender roles. That said, there are a number of stereotype-breaking charac-ters like those featured on *Buffy the Vampire Slayer* and *Lost*. Even in the *Harry Potter* series, Hermione Granger, Harry's sidekick, is a secondary character and yet she is always saving the day. Real life does not work as it does in fiction. Not all men can be heroes, and passivity and dependency rarely bring women success in the modern world.

>>> **ACTIVITY** Think about a movie or TV show you've seen or a book you've read recently. What gender stereotypes, if any, are depicted on the screen or the page? Does the work defy any traditional gender stereotypes? Write a paragraph analyzing the work you chose.

GENDER BIAS IN THE MEDIA

When Senator Hillary Clinton ran for the Democratic nomination in the 2008 presidential race, one of the major issues involved how the pundits and politicos treated the first viable woman to run for the highest office in the land. Clinton's supporters pointed to the disproportionate amount of attention given to their candidate's appearance and noted a perceived gender bias in the coverage of her campaign.

Any print or electronic resource that is used to communicate to a wide audience is referred to as **mass media**.

Products of mass media—books, magazines, television, radio, movies, music, and newspapers—are everywhere, and their influence on culture is inescapable. **The media play a role in our socialization because they transmit stories, values, and attitudes.**

Consider the effect the media have in determining gendered stereotypes through sexual imagery. Kirstie Farrar and her colleagues reviewed the sexual images that aired during "prime-time" television hours. They found that images on shows like *The Bachelor* and *One Tree Hill* tended to reinforce the notion that women are primarily sexual objects.[61] These and other images supported the dominant male/submissive female paradigm. They also found that 64 percent of the television shows during the 2000–2001 season contained sexual messages, and that sexual intercourse occurred in 14 percent of the shows. For conflict theorists, these findings suggest that such imagery is an effort by those in power to maintain it. Men are the primary decision makers for large media corporations, so are they responsible for perpetuating these ideas about gender roles?

Because of the way gender roles are defined in society, it can take several years to see through the generalizations. I can remember realizing during my freshman year in college that my father and I had never hugged, primarily because of gender ideals about men touching each other. The next time I returned home, I gave him a big hug as soon as he answered the door. From that day forth, hugging was no longer taboo at our house. In this simple way, my father and I changed our gender socialization.

Socialization

WRAP YOUR MIND AROUND THE THEORY

In order for a society to function, **functionalists argue that people adapt their behavior to the norms and values of the institutions in that society.**

FUNCTIONALISM

According to functionalists, socialization occurs when people internalize society and enact its norms, values, and roles. In high schools across the country, students struggle with the choice to conform and practice "normal" behavior or to think outside the box. Those who step outside the box are often stigmatized and labeled as "different." These individuals are not "functioning" because they don't conform to the rules set by the society's institutions. Institutions, such as religion and education, serve their function. To keep a society running smoothly, people adapt to the norms and values of their particular institutions. In short, people become socialized when they learn and accept what a society expects of them.

CONFLICT THEORY

Conflict theorists believe that the "haves" and the "have-nots" are socialized differently. Children who come from middle- and upper-class backgrounds are more likely to participate in organized sports, take music or art lessons, and have Internet access in their homes. Taking part in activities such as these teaches children how to interact with others and learn what society expects of them. Impoverished children sometimes find themselves at a disadvantage because they are less likely to have these experiences. Of course, material wealth is not the only determinant of whether one becomes socialized. However, parents' material wealth does put some children at an advantage.

HOW DO PEOPLE BECOME SOCIALIZED?

SYMBOLIC INTERACTIONISM

Symbolic interactionists believe that socialization is the major determinant of human nature. People develop their sense of self by incorporating how others interpret their behavior. The symbols we encounter, such as other people's interpretations of our behavior, help shape who and what we become. Genie, the feral child discovered in 1970, was not given the opportunity to interact with others during her formative years. As a result, she was unable to fully develop her own identity when she was thrust into the social world. As we saw in Mead's theory of the "I" and the "Me," people develop their sense of self though their interaction with others.

Children who participate in organized sports learn how to interact with others in the social world. **Having little or no opportunities to play sports can limit a child's socialization.**

If the students in class snicker and whisper while the child gives his report, how might the child interpret these symbols? How might he feel about himself?

discover sociology in action:
HOW DOES UNDERSTANDING SOCIALIZATION HELP US IMPROVE THE COMMUNITY?

Applying Sociological Thinking in the World, Social Policy, and Title IX

Auguste Comte, the founder of sociology, urged us to use our knowledge about society to improve society. Lawmakers have used that philosophy to enact various **social policies**, deliberate strategies designed to correct recognized social problems. The 1972 educational amendment, commonly known as **Title IX**, is one such attempt to implement sociological knowledge. Named the Patsy T. Mink Equal Opportunity in Education Act in honor of its principle author—a Hawaiian congresswoman who felt that gender discrimination in public schools must be stopped—the act prohibits the exclusion of any person from participation in an educational program on the basis of gender.[62]

Title IX became important when it was used to allocate funding for extracurricular activities like sports. Before 1972, very few girls were involved in sports partly because few sports existed for girls. In the three decades since Title IX, however, those numbers have skyrocketed:

- Female participation in high school sports has increased 800 percent.
- Female participation in intercollegiate athletics has increased 400 percent.
- Girls now make up 42 percent of high school athletes.

> **SOCIAL POLICIES** are deliberate strategies designed to correct recognized social problems.
>
> **TITLE IX** is a 1972 educational amendment that prohibits the exclusion of any person from participation in an education program on the basis of gender.

- Women now make up 42 percent of Division I varsity college athletes.
- Women receive 43 percent of Division I athletic scholarship dollars.
- Women's college sports receive about one dollar for every two spent on men's programs.[63]

You can see that a social policy designed to give equal opportunities to both genders has increased women's athletic participation. However, these numbers also indicate that the goal of actual equality has not yet been met. Today, girls may have many more athletic role models than they did 30 years ago, but they do not yet receive equal funding for sports programs in their schools. Although women outnumber men on college campuses, funding remains largely in the hands of male sports. A quick look at the difference in television budgets between the men's and women's NCAA Final Four basketball tournaments demonstrates the disparity. Sports play a big role in a child's socialization, and both genders should have the opportunity to participate equally.

ACTIVITIES

1. How does your college deal with Title IX? Are male and female scholarships equal? Are they in compliance?
2. What agents of socialization influenced you the most when you were growing up? What influences you the most now?
3. Read stories of feral children, such as Genie. What is the importance of early socialization on development? Have researchers made any strides in socializing feral children?
4. Visit a developmental disability hospital in your area and talk to the staff and parents. Can the best efforts at socialization overcome nature? Write about your findings.

From Classroom to Community Children's Hospital

When David, one of my sociology students, decided to do his service learning project at a local children's hospital for the developmentally disabled, he was not prepared for the experiences he was about to have.

"Before I started my volunteerism," he said,

> "I had a clear understanding of the socialization process. I'd studied Genie and knew how difficult it was to socialize children who had developmental delays."

David realized that many of the children, unlike Genie, came from loving families and had received all kinds of therapy from a very early age. But David found that despite all the assistance they received, something about their development was delayed.

"Some children had physical delays, while others had cognitive ones," he recalled. David was particularly interested in a 12-year-old boy who was born deaf, blind, and mentally retarded.

"He was a really difficult case because I couldn't figure out how to communicate with him. He interacted mostly through touch. Yet when you reached out to help him, he often hit you and wildly swung his arms around in the air."

Children with development delays that influence communication often experience problems with socialization.

> "It seemed that about all my patient could do was hit people and eat.

I could not help but wonder how this boy would come to know who he was and where he fit in the world. Without communication, it seems almost impossible."

WHAT IS SOCIALIZATION?

the process that teaches the norms, values, and other aspects of a culture to new group members

HOW DO THE THREE THEORETICAL PARADIGMS VIEW SOCIALIZATION?

functionalism: institutions, like religion and education, are useful in socializing individuals

conflict theory: societies use gender socialization to teach members how to express their femininity and masculinity

symbolic interactionism: total institutions are successful in resocializing people by altering their sense of self

HOW DOES UNDERSTANDING SOCIALIZATION HELP US IMPROVE THE COMMUNITY?

through social policies that are designed to give equal opportunities to both genders

get the topic: WHAT IS SOCIALIZATION?

The Nature vs. Nurture Debate—
　What Makes Us Who We Are?
Theorists on Socialization
Agents of Socialization

Can We Be "Resocialized"? Experiencing the
　Total Institution
Symbolic Interactionism and Resocialization
Functionalism

Conflict Theory—What Forces Socialize Us?
Applying Sociological Thinking in the World,
　Social Policy, and Title IX

Theory

FUNCTIONALISM

- socialization occurs when people internalize society and enact its norms, values, and roles
- people who don't internalize norms are stigmatized and labeled as "different"
- people become socialized when they learn and accept what society expects of them

CONFLICT THEORY

- the "haves" and the "have-nots" are socialized differently

- taking part in activities teaches children how to interact with others and learn what society expects of them
- children who come from middle- and upper-class backgrounds are more likely to participate in organized activities than some impoverished children who are unable to participate

SYMBOLIC INTERACTIONISM

- socialization is the major determinant of human nature
- people develop their sense of self by incorporating how others interpret their behavior

Key Terms

socialization is the process that teaches the norms, values, and other aspects of a culture to new group members.

primary socialization is socialization that occurs during childhood.

secondary socialization is the dynamic whereby socialization continues throughout our lives.

nature theory states that the genes we get from our parents at conception are the primary causes of human behaviors.

nurture theory states that our environment influences the way we think, feel, and behave.

feral means wild.

looking-glass self is the theory that the self develops through a process of reflection, like a mirror.

"I" self is the subjective part of the self.

"me" self is the objective part of the self.

imitation stage is Mead's first stage of development, which is the period from birth to about age 2, and is the stage at which children merely copy the behaviors of those around them.

play stage is Mead's second stage of development, which occurs around the ages of 2–4 years, during which children play roles and begin to take on the characteristics of important people in their world.

game stage is Mead's third stage of development that never truly ends, and is the stage in which we begin to understand that others have expectations and demands placed upon them.

the generalized other is our sense of others.

psychosocial crisis is a crisis occurring during each of Erikson's stages that will be resolved

either positively or negatively, and each outcome will have an effect on our ability to deal with the next one.

cognitive development is a person's ability to think and reason.

sensorimotor stage is the stage (birth to age 2 years) at which infants learn to experience and think about the world through their senses and motor skills.

preoperational stage is the stage (ages 2 through 7 years) at which the ability to speak grows rapidly.

concrete operational stage is the stage (ages 7 through 12 years) at which children can think about objects in the world in more than one way and start to understand causal connections in their surroundings.

(continued)

formal operational stage is the stage (ages 12 years and above) at which people become able to comprehend abstract thought.

preconventional level is the first stage of moral development that lasts through elementary school years; at this level, children make their moral judgments within a framework of hedonistic principles.

hedonism is seeking pleasure over pain.

conventional level is the second stage of moral development that arises before puberty and uses the lens of norms and rules to determine what is right and wrong.

postconventional level is the third stage of moral development that refers to a morality based on abstract principles.

morality of justice is morality based on the rule of law.

morality of care is morality decided by a

standard of how best to help those who are in need.

agents of socialization are the people and groups who shape our self-concept, beliefs, and behavior.

authoritative style is a parenting style in which parents listen to their children's input while consistently enforcing the preset rules.

permissive style is a parenting style in which parents provide high levels of support but an inconsistent enforcement of rules.

authoritarian style is a parenting style with which children experience high levels of social control but low levels of emotional support.

resocialization is the process of learning new norms, values, attitudes, and behaviors and abandoning old ones.

total institutions are places in which the most effective forms of resocialization can

occur because they isolate people from outside influences so they can be reformed and controlled.

hidden curriculum refers to the lessons taught in school that are unrelated to academic learning.

gender socialization teaches members of society how to express their masculinity or femininity.

gender is the expectations of behavior and attitude that a society considers proper for males and females.

mass media include any print or electronic resource that is used to communicate to a wide audience.

social policies are deliberate strategies designed to correct recognized social problems.

Title IX is a 1972 educational amendment that prohibits the exclusion of any person from participation in an educational program on the basis of gender.

Sample Test Questions

These multiple-choice questions are similar to those found in the test bank that accompanies this textbook.

1. During which of Erikson's eight stages would a person develop a strong sense of self?
   a. Trust vs. mistrust
   b. Initiative vs. guilt
   c. Industry vs. inferiority
   d. Identity vs. role confusion

2. According to Piaget, at what stage of cognitive development does a child's ability to speak grow rapidly?
   a. Sensorimotor stage
   b. Preoperational stage
   c. Concrete operational stage
   d. Formal operational stage

3. The preconventional level, conventional level, and postconventional level are stages of
   a. moral development.
   b. social development.
   c. creative development.
   d. language development.

4. Which of the following is *not* an example of a total institution?
   a. A prison
   b. The military
   c. A university
   d. A rehabilitation clinic

5. Which researcher developed the morality of care and the morality of justice?
   a. Erik Erikson
   b. Carol Gilligan
   c. Lawrence Kohlberg
   d. George Herbert Mead

ESSAY

1. How did Piaget describe the stage at which a child learns to speak?
2. What is the difference between authoritative style and authoritarian style parenting?
3. Why is resocialization important in total institutions?
4. Conflict theorists often argue that men use their power to dominate and limit women. Provide an example of gender bias in the media and explain how it supports this theory.
5. In the terms of Erikson's theory, how was Genie's development stunted?

WHERE TO START YOUR RESEARCH PAPER

For more information on "Child of our Time: Socialization Information from British Broadcasting Service" (a BBC interactive discussion on socialization of children with links to online quizzes and expert opinions), go to http://www.open2.net/childofourtime/tv_pages/art_socialization_1.htm

For in-depth articles on the field of evolutionary psychology, relating the development of the brain and how social settings influence a person's development, go to http://www.psych.ucsb.edu/research/cep/

To find data on child socialization and marital adjustment, go to http://www.parentsurf.com

For more information on education and health care for parents and children, go to http://www.kidsource.com/

To learn more about how media influences society (particularly the sociological perspective on media and society), go to http://www.public.asu.edu/~zeyno217/365/notes1.html

To find more information on Mama Feeta and her work in caring for the children of war-torn Liberia, go to http://www.shinefoundation.org/

For more information on centers that work with people who have developmental delays, go to http://www.miusa.org/ncde/

ANSWERS: 1. d; 2. b; 3. a; 4. c; 5. b

Remember to check www.thethinkspot.com **for additional information, downloadable flashcards, and other helpful resources.**

Endnotes

1. Brief excerpts as submitted (six paragraphs in total) from *Genie* by Russ Rymer. Copyright © 1993 by Russ Rymer. A portion of this book appeared in somewhat different form in The New Yorker magazine. Reprinted by permission of HarperCollins Publishers.

2. Talcott Parsons, *The Social System* (New York: Free Press, 1951).

3. Talcott Parsons and Robert Bales, *Socialization and the Interaction Process* (New York: Free Press, 1955).

4. Orville G. Brim, Jr., "Socialization Through the Life Cycle," In: Orville Brim and Stanton Wheeler (eds.), *Socialization after Childhood: Two Essays* (New York: Wiley, 1966).

5. Theodore E. Long and Jeffrey K. Hadden, "Reconception of Socialization," *Sociological Theory.* 1985. 3(1): 39–49.

6. Orville G. Brim, Jr., "Socialization Through the Life Cycle," In: Orville Brim and Stanton Wheeler (eds), *Socialization after Childhood: Two Essays.* (New York: Wiley, 1966).

7. Richard Dawkins, *The Selfish Gene* (Oxford: Oxford University Press, 1989).

8. W. L. Reese, *Dictionary of Philosophy and Religion: Eastern and Western Thought* (Atlantic Highlands, NJ: Humanities Press Inc., 1987).

9. Paul R. Ehrlich, *Human Natures: Genes, Cultures, and the Human Prospect* (Island Press. Washington, D.C., 2000), p. 6, at http://books.google.com/books?id5mHFsScY8ewMC&dq5Human/Natures/Paul/Ehrlich&pg5PP1&ots5XW4w7TDMLU&sig5MjKy9QADe0TPCKe0fZZ8h_ahKLM&hl5en&sa5X&oi5book_result&resnum51&ct5result.

10. Harry F. Harlow and Margaret Harlow, "Social Deprivation in Monkeys," *Scientific America,* 1962. November: 137–146.

11. Susan Donaldson James, "Wild Child Speechless After Tortured Life," *ABC News,* May 7, 2008, at http://abcnews.go.com/Health/story?id54804490; "What Drove Father Who Built House of Horror?" *CNN News,* April 29, 2008, at http://www. cnn.com/2008/WORLD/europe/04/29/austria.cellar.profile/. Accessed November 12, 2008.

12. Russ Rymer, *Genie: An Abused Child's Flight from Silence* (New York, NY: Harper-Collins Publishers, 1993).

13. Ibid.

14. Ibid.

15. Louis De Maio, "Stages of Language Development," at www.mnstate.edu/pccp/stages%20of%20%20language%20development.pdf, Accessed June 5, 2008; "Isabelle," http://www.feralchildren.com/en/showchild.php?ch5isabelle, Accessed June 26, 2008.

16. Charles H. Cooley, *Human Nature and the Social Order* (New York: Schocken Books, 1902, 1964).

17. King-To Yeung and John L. Martin, "The Looking Glass Self: An Empirical Test and Elaboration," *Social Forces,* 2003. 81(3): 843–879.

18. Ibid.

19. George Herbert Mead, *Mind, Self, and Society,* Charles W. Morris, ed. (Chicago: University of Chicago Press, 1934, 1962).

20. Ibid.

21. Ibid.

22. Erik Erikson, *Childhood and Society* (New York: Norton Press, 1963).

23. "Secret of the Wild Child," *Nova,* March 4, 1997, http://www.pbs.org/wgbh/nova/transcripts/2112gchild.html, Accessed November 12, 2008.

24. Jean Piaget and Barbel Inhelder, *The Psychology of the Child* (New York: Basic Books, 1969, 2000).

25. Ibid.

26. Ibid.

27. Ibid.

28. Ibid.

29. Lawrence Kohlberg, *The Psychology of Moral Development: The Nature and Validity of Moral Stages* (New York: Harper & Row, 1981).

30. Ibid.

31. Ibid.

32. Ibid.

33. Charles Helwig and Urszula Jasiobedzka, "The Relation Between Law and Morality: Children's Reasoning about Socially Beneficial and Unjust Laws," *Child Development,* 2001. 72: 1382–1394.

34. Anne Colby and William Damon, *Some Do Care: Contemporary Lives of Moral Commitment* (New York: Free Press, 1992).

35. Carol Gilligan, *In a Different Voice: Psychological Theory and Women's Development* (Cambridge, MA: Harvard University Press, 1982).

36. Ibid.

37. Elliott Turiel, "The Development of Morality," In: W. Damon (ed.), *Handbook of Child Psychology,* 5th ed., Vol. 3, 863–932 (New York: Wiley, 1998).

38. Eva A. Skoe and Alethia Gooden, "Ethics of Care and Real-Life Moral Dilemma Content in Male and Female Early Adolescents," *Journal of Early Adolescence,* 1993. 13(2): 154–167.

39. Eva A. Skoe and Rhett Diessner, "Ethics of Care, Justice, Identity and Gender: An Extension and Replication," *Merrill–Palmer Quarterly,* 1994. 40: 102–119. Eva A. Skoe and Anna L. von der Lippe, "Ego Development and the Ethics of Care and Justice: The Relations Among Them Revisited," *Journal of Personality,* 2002. 70(4): 485–508.

40. Andrew J. Cherlin, *Public and Private Families: An Introduction,* 2nd ed. (Boston: McGraw–Hill College, 1999).

41. Diana Baumrind, "Current Patterns of Parental Authority," *Developmental Psychology Monographs,* 1971. 4(1, pt. 2):103; Diana Baumrind, "Parental Disciplinary Patterns and Social Competence in Children," *Youth and Society,* 1978. 9: 239–276. Diana Baumrind, "The Discipline Controversy Revisited," *Family Relations,* 1996. 5(4): 405–415.

42. Ibid.

43. Ruth K. Chao, "Beyond Parental Control and Authoritarian Parenting Style: Understanding Chinese Parenting Through the Cultural Notion of Training," *Child Development,* 1994. 65(4): 1111–1119.

44. Ibid.

45. Min Zhou, *Chinatown: The Socioeconomic Potential of an Urban Enclave* (Philadelphia, PA: Temple University Press, 1992).

46. Min Zhou and Carl L. Bankston, III, "Social Capital and the Adaptation of the Second Generation: The Case of Vietnamese Youth in New Orleans," *The New Second Generation,* Alejandro Portes (ed.), (New York: Russell Sage Foundation, 1996), 197–220.

47. Melvin L Kohn, "Social Class and Parent-Child Relationships: An Interpretation," *American Journal of Sociology,* 1963. 571–580.

48. William J. Wilson, *The Truly Disadvantaged: The Inner City, The Underclass, and Public Policy* (Chicago: University of Chicago Press, 1987).

49. Jeanne Brooks–Gunn, Greg Duncan, Pamela Klebanove, and Naomi Sealand, "Do Neighborhoods Influence Child and Adolescent Development?" *American Journal of Sociology,* 1993. 99(2): 353–395.

50. Ibid.

51. Gary Solon, Marianne Page, and Greg J. Duncan, "Correlations Between Neighboring Children and Their Subsequent Educational Attainment," *Review of Economics and Statistics,* 2000. 82(3): 383–393.

52. John D. Carl, "Social Capital and Sport Participation," Ph.D. dissertation, Department of Sociology, University of Oklahoma, Norman, OK, 2002.

53. Erving Goffman, *Asylums: Essays on the Social Situation of Mental Patients and Other Inmates* (Chicago: Aldine, 1961).

54. Harold Garfinkel, "Conditions of Successful Degradation Ceremonies," *American Journal of Sociology,* 1956. 61(2): 420–424.

55. Howard S. Becker, "The Politics of Presentation: Goffman and Total Institutions," *Symbolic Interaction,* 2003. 26(4): 659–669.

56. Charles Tittle and Michael Welch, "Religiosity and Deviance: Toward a Contingency Theory of Constraining Effects," *Social Forces,* 1983. 61(3): 653–682.

57. Harold Grasmick, Karyl Kinsey, and Kent Smith, "Framing Justice: Taxpayer Evaluations of Personal Tax Burdens, *Law and Society Review.* 1991. 25: 845–873.

58. "Prisoners of Time," Education Commission of the States, April 1994, www.eric.ed.gov/ERICDocs/data/ericdocs2sql/content_storage_01/0000019b/80/1b/b9/60.pdf, Accessed November 12, 2008..

59. Annette Hemmings, "The 'Hidden' Corridor Curriculum," *High School Journal,* 2000. 83(2): 1–10.

60. Philip Jackson, *Life in Classrooms* (New York, NY: Holt, Rinehart, and Winston, 1968).

61. Kirstie Farrar, Dale Kunkel, Erica Biely, Keren Eyal, Rena Fandrich, and Edward Donnerstein, "Sexual Messages During Primetime Programming," *Sexuality & Culture,* 2003. 7(3): 7–38.

62. "Patsy T. Mink Equal Opportunity in Education Act," *K12 Academics,* http://www.k12academics.com/patsy_t_mink_equal_opportunity_education_act.htm, Accessed June 27, 2008.

63. NWLC: National Women's Law Center, "Quick facts on women and girls in athletics," June 2002, http://www.nwlc.org/pdf/quickfacts_June2002.pdf; NWLC: National Women's Law Center, "The Battle for Gender Equity in Athletics: Title IX at Thirty," 2002, http://www.nwlc.org/pdf/Battle%20for%20Gender%20Equity%20in%20Athletics%20Report.pdf.

Chapter 4
Identity and the Self

I am a mother, first and foremost. So if my baby gets sick, I just can't study as much as I want to. Sometimes my grades suffer. And sometimes I am frustrated by all the things I can't do. The other day, some of the people in my class were talking about a big party that they went to. That kind of "fun" stuff is almost always out of the question now. But, you know, people tell me I am a really good mom to my baby, and I feel like I am working for something—I am making a good life for her.

—Marsha, junior Sociology major

Marsha has a lot of roles to juggle. But for her, being a mother is her most salient, important identity. As a result, when she has to choose how to use her time, she will often spend it with her child. And, she explains her behavior to herself and others based on her identities. Her story also reveals that she feels good about who she is and what she is capable of doing as a mom.

Most of us have some familiarity with the concepts of self, identity, and personality. We may explain our behaviors by saying we did something because "that's the way I am." Sociologists believe that a significant part of what people might call *personality* is socially constructed. If objects, social relationships, and society are constructed via social interactions, then our selves and identities must also reflect social conditions.

Sociologists do not study personality per se but rather the **self**, a process in which we construct a sense of who we are through interaction with others. Because the self is a process, it changes over time. We can take snapshots of our senses of self at given times, but they regularly get updated as we interact with people and adapt to new events and transitions in our lives. That snapshot, or the outcome of the self process at a given point in time, is the **self-concept**. Morris Rosenberg (1986) defined the self-concept as the sum total of thoughts and feelings we have about ourselves as objects. Essentially, the "self process" creates the "self-concept," or understandings we have about ourselves. The self-concept is an "object" or thing, and just like other things, such as a baseball, a hat, or any other physical object, we can talk about and reflect on our self-concept. Scholars examining the self-concept focus on **self-identities** (the kind of person we see ourselves as) and on **self-evaluations** (judgments we make of ourselves). The

From: *Social Psychology: Sociological Perspectives*, Second Edition by David E. Rohall, Melissa A. Milkie, and Jeffrey W. Lucas.

three self-evaluations we will discuss in this chapter are self-esteem, mastery, and mattering.

Social psychologists approach the study of the self in diverse ways, often dependent on the broad theoretical traditions in which they work. Some symbolic interactionists focus on the self as a process, examining how we present ourselves to others in interaction, and how we make meaning of who we are, in concert with significant others. Other, more structural symbolic interactionists focus on how, through interaction, our self comes to reflect the structure of society in a stable understanding of who we are. Because society is highly differentiated, the self is composed of multiple, complex parts. Social structure and personality scholars explicitly consider how social-structural conditions, notably our positions and statuses in society, affect the self-concept. ("Social structure and the self-concept" may in fact be a better title for this field of study than "social structure and personality.") Finally, group processes scholars emphasize the role of group processes in affecting identities. We will address the following questions in this chapter:

- What are the components of the self?
- What are interactionist theories of the self and identity?
- What are three dimensions of the self-concept? What do we know from research on the self-concept?
- How do group processes affect identity?

The Self as a Process

When I first came to college, I was such a party animal. I would miss most of my classes and just get drunk or high. There was always a party to go to. I am not sure why I became that way. I did well in high school and was always a "good girl" growing up. I guess going to college just changed me. Maybe I took advantage of the freedom of being away from home. It was so funny to be called a "party girl" in college! Well, when my parents heard about my grades, the funding stopped, and I had to drop out. I started taking classes at a local college. I didn't go back to being a "good girl" but I was certainly not the party girl anymore. I guess place and time can change you.

—Quinn, junior Journalism major

According to the symbolic interactionist perspective, the self is a process, just like the construction of any social reality. We give meaning to our self in many different ways. Are we good or bad people? How well do we do the tasks we set out to do? We continually take information from the world around us to answer these types of questions. The subtle feedback that we get over many experiences with significant others shapes us. It's not that we fail an exam and simply think that we are bad students. An exam is only one experience in our role as students, and we will assess many other aspects of the environment, such as how many students failed, how difficult the class is, and so on. We do sometimes make conscious choices to become certain kinds of people; we may try to lose weight, to become an accountant, or to appear more intelligent. The process involves grafting on thoughts and behaviors necessary to achieve the best outcomes for ourselves in interactions. For instance, if a graduate student concerned about her status in an intellectual community enters a room full of older professors, she may start acting more mature, using formal language, and trying to make clear, cogent statements to the people around her. This process may only last the duration of the meeting, with her goal being to look intelligent in front of the professors. However, the "act" of being more mature and intelligent may become a more permanent part of her sense of self as she interacts more with professors and students similar to her. How could her behavior become a permanent part of her sense of self? Over time she may begin to think of herself as "smart," and her "student" identity may become more salient in future interactions with people.

In Quinn's example, going away to college changed the ways she thought, felt, and behaved. Instead of being the "good girl" that she was at home, she started missing classes and going to more parties. Her networks and her priorities changed in her new social environment. The changes had some long-term consequences for her sense of self. Even when she was forced to go home, she never totally relinquished her party identity. Quinn is able to dialogue about herself as an object. She can see how she is now and compare it to the past. Furthermore, she is able to negotiate her sense of self using the alternatives available to her. When she was faced with returning home, she recognized that it limited her ability to "party," but she did not completely submit to her previous sense of self.

In this section of the chapter, we examine the way that the self is constructed and how we incorporate societal roles and expectations into our senses of self.

The I, the Me, and Self Narratives

We use symbols and language to communicate with other people, but we also use language to think internally, a process that Herbert Blumer (1969) calls **self-indication**. We can have conversations with our selves just as we can with other people. Further, we can internally negotiate the meanings of objects, including our sense of self. In fact, there are several situations in which internal dialogues are the only appropriate ways to assess meaning.

According to George Herbert Mead (1934), a large part of our internal dialogues occur as interplay between two characters within ourselves: the I and the Me. The **Me** is the organized set of attitudes toward the self, based on the views of significant others, such as friends and family, as well as society as a whole. The **I** refers to our active self; the I is the one on stage, in the moment, talking to other people. The "I" and the "Me" form a constant dialectic regarding our thoughts, feelings, and behaviors. This internal dialogue reflects the importance we give to social conditions when deciding how to think, feel, or behave. In some sense, society resides in the Me. Because we have human agency, the ability to make choices about our actions, the "I" is able to act based on the "Me" in a number of different ways. Ellen Granberg (2006) studied the ways that individuals use agency and internal thought

Freud's Approach to Personality

The psychoanalytic approach to personality assumes that people are largely irrational, trying to manage passions and inner conflicts from the past. The approach is largely associated with Sigmund Freud (1859–1939), an Austrian psychologist. Freud was one of the first to popularize the idea that we have an "unconscious" mind—that there are things going on in the brain that affect our thoughts, feelings, and behavior of which we are unaware. According to Freud, only through psychotherapy can we tap this inner room. Freud argued that personalities are made of three components: the Id that houses our basic instincts, seeking only pleasure or carnal fulfillment; the Ego, which helps to restrain the Id until it can achieve its wants in a reasonable way given different physical and social conditions; and the Superego, which houses an individual's ideals, larger social and cultural norms, and standards. In some sense, the Ego and Superego contain elements of society, where we learn specific ways to constrain the Id. These internal processes share some things in common with the relationship between the "I" and the "Me" outlined by Mead, with one dimension of our selves interacting with other aspects of the self on a day-to-day basis.

processes during a specific form of self change: weight loss. Using in-depth interviews with 10 men and 36 women who had lost weight and sustained the weight loss for at least three months, she found that weight (or being overweight) was a major part of their identities and that images of their possible identities, what their identities could be in the future, was a source of motivation to lose weight. They had images that losing weight would change the way they would live (e.g., buying smaller-sized clothing) and their interactions with other people. These images helped them sustain their dieting. Did the reality of weight loss meet these images? Not always. Granberg found that the weight loss was accompanied by different sets of feedback from other people, and the reality of the weight loss did not always live up to their ideals. As a result, respondents had to negotiate new senses of self that blended some of their own reflections on the self-change process with the social feedback from others.

The use of narratives and storytelling is an important part of the symbolic interaction process. They can also be used to understand how individuals conceive of their senses of self. Think about how you talk about yourself to other people. You probably do not share your internal conversations reflecting the I and the Me. Rather, you probably share stories about your life relevant to the discussion. In the process you reveal important events and how you interpreted those events. Perhaps you share about a wild trip to a foreign country where you experiment with different foods and cultures. What does that say about you? First, that you are the type of person willing to make such a journey. Second, that you are the type of person willing to share intimate details of such a journey. Third, it tells the people around you that you enjoy trying new things. The telling of the story helps to solidify this identity too—the storytelling process helps to make the self-image more concrete to self and others because it becomes the memory by which you will reference in future interactions or internal discussions when confronting new information about the self (e.g., when someone presents you with a really crazy idea, are you going to be open to it or not?). The nature of an autobiography exemplifies this perspective: We write the stories of our lives to give people a better sense of who we are. Just as narrative can be used to understand how people construct the meaning of social life, we can study **self narratives**, how individuals construct the meaning of their identities using personal stories (Brockmeier and Carbaugh 2001; Gergen and Gergen 1997). In a sense, if social life is a story, we are a character in that larger story with our own story to tell. In a study of survivors of childhood sexual abuse, Thomas DeGloma (2007) found two groups of survivors: those survivors who accept that they had been abused and have recovered, and those that do not accept that they have been abused and cope with their situation by retracting their story, claiming it as a false memory. The researcher found that both groups used autobiographical revisions of their abuse stories to help maintain their current identities. Self narratives are not simply a list of stories that occur in our lives but the reformatting of multiple stories to make a single, coherent sense of self over time.

Identity Theory

Identity theory (which derives from the symbol interaction perspective) emphasizes the enduring nature of our thoughts about who we are. **Identity** refers to our internalized, stable sense of who we are, including role identities, social categories, and personal characteristics (Burke 2003). Hence, identity includes our understanding of our unique nature (personality) as well as our social roles. **Role identities** are the internalized expectations associated with different positions. Some examples of role identities are college student, politician, or brother. For adults, the most important role identities typically stem from work and family positions. **Social categories** include identities related to social groups to which we belong, such as Canadian, woman, or Latino. Last, **personal characteristics** include anything we use to describe our individual nature, such as being kind or generous or athletic.

Identity theory examines the ways society shapes how we view ourselves and how those views, or identities, affect our behavior.

Sheldon Stryker (2002) offered five principles that are at the root of identity theory:

1. Behavior is based on an already defined and classified world.
2. Positions in society are among the things classified in the world.
3. People develop their identities based on their positions in society.
4. We incorporate our social positions into our senses of identity; our positions become part of our senses of self.
5. Social behavior is derived from the shaping and modifying of the expectations of our positions.

The theory is rather simple and eloquent and tries to predict behavior when people have choices. The premise is that society affects self, which affects behavior. Styker's definition of society refers to patterns of commitments to other people. Commitment includes the number of significant others tied to a given identity or to being a certain kind of person and the intensity of those bonds. Commitment shapes the salience of an identity, which in turn shapes how we will behave. For instance, living with many close friends in a sorority house makes a "Greek" identity very salient and, according to identity theory, would make us act in ways to express the meaning of being Greek or, more specifically, say, a Gamma Phi Beta (wearing symbols, talking like others, doing the philanthropy of that organization) when we have the opportunity to do so.

Identity theory extends symbolic interactionist principles by focusing on the social construction of the self (principles #3 and #4) and the belief that there is an existing social reality that we use as the basis for self-identification processes (principles #1 and #2). Thereafter, identities generate behavior (#5), but we are able to "make" or play out roles in somewhat unique ways. That is, how we act in a given situation is contingent on the meanings we give our identities. According to identity theory, then, we use identities to guide our own behavior, but that behavior depends on the meaning of the identity.

Consider two fathers. How they act out their father roles (or behave as fathers) can be quite different. Their behavior will depend on both the salience and the meaning of the father identity. In one study, Thomas Rane and Brent McBride (2000) found that fathers who considered the nurturing aspect of the father role more meaningful to their sense of identity interacted with their children more often than those who did not. If being a good father means being more attentive to children's needs, then how should the father act? He should probably spend more time with them.

There is often some latitude in acting out identities; for example, it is generally viewed as important for fathers to provide for children, but emphasis on the nurturing aspect is fine, too. We also assess our identities when we are with other people, making sure that they correspond with our senses of self. We make small adjustments to our behavior to maintain our identities (Cast 2003a). We may do the same for other people, too, helping them maintain their senses of identity through our interactions with them (Cast 2003b). Ultimately, these identity processes are designed to make the world controllable; self-confirmation can provide us a guide in awkward social situations and an emotional anchor in an otherwise changing world (Stets and Burke 2005).

The tendency to seek confirmation of self-meanings is the basis of **identity control theory**. This theory proposes that self-consistency is as important or more important to people than maintaining a positive self-image. If that is true, how do individuals maintain their senses of self amid so many different social situations? Why do people change? Sheldon Stryker's and Richard Serpe's (1982, Serpe 1987; Serpe and Stryker 1987, 1993) studies of youth entering college found that transitioning students employed both affective and interactional commitment to identities to help maintain their original senses of self when entering college. Affective commitment refers to our personal desire to maintain an identity, while interactional commitment refers to maintaining relationships with people in different social spheres related to our identities. Being an environmentalist may be important to you, but you may not have close ties to other environmentalists. They also found that students tended to find groups that helped them to maintain their senses of identity. When such groups were not available to them, the students' initial identities began to change. Thus, while we seek to maintain identities that are important to us, we make changes when social resources are not available to stabilize our senses of self. In this way, our social relationships provide a mooring, a place of refuge and stability, for our identities (Cassidy and Trew 2001).

Some recent studies employing identity control theory have focused on self-change and stability among newly married couples (see Burke 2006; Cast and Cantwell 2007; Stets and Cast 2007). As people enter these relationships, they must negotiate new role relationships, working with their partner to determine how they should act as spouses. Partners bring images of themselves and the other into marriages (e.g., intelligence, attractiveness, likeability). This line of research shows a general decline in the difference between self-views and spouses' views over time. What is more, spouses will change their senses of self to match the other's view whether it is positive or negative! If we think we are unintelligent but our spouse thinks we are smart, we are likely to develop a more positive sense of self. However, we are equally likely to do the reverse: we will develop a more negative sense of self if our spouse has a negative view of us. How do we negotiate our sense of self in these relationships? Peter Burke (2006) argues that we make small changes in our self over time as we engage in routine activities. During those activities, we provide verbal and nonverbal feedback about our thoughts, feelings, and behavior that we use in our internal dialogue between the I and the Me. As more information about the self is gained over time, we begin to rethink our sense of who we are. We are not likely to see large-scale changes in our identities at any moment but small changes in the self over time.

Dramaturgical Sociology and the Presentation of Self

Symbolic interaction emphasizes the fact that humans have agency, the power to act independently of constraints. Thus, individuals can act apart from their senses of self. You may consider yourself to be a below average student but decide to "act" like a good one in front of a professor. The study of how we present ourselves, playing roles and managing impressions during interactions with other people, is called **dramaturgical sociology**. Dramaturgical sociology is most closely associated with Erving Goffman (1922–1982). It includes the study of impression formation and the management of impressions. It is also associated with short-term changes in the self through the impression processes.

In a sense, identity and affect control theories incorporate elements of dramaturgical sociology. These theories posit that when our identity does not match the environment, we change in some way to ensure that the two are commensurate. The theories assume that we have some control over what others think about us in a given interaction, a basic premise of dramaturgical sociology. Dramaturgical sociology also incorporates that idea that we can choose to act different than our identities during social exchanges and that we have to practice identities before fully incorporating them into our senses of self. Our personal sense of identity and our perceptions of the conceptions people have of us form a constant dialectic under the heading of impression management.

Impression Management

Erving Goffman (1959) believed that we seek information from people when we come in contact with them. We use such information to help establish expectations of our behavior and that of the people around us. Information comes from the physical attributes of the other people—their race or gender, for instance—as well as our histories with those people. We also have some control over the information we give to other people. For instance, we can dress formally to give people the impression that we are mature and serious. Similarly, we can wear jeans and a T-shirt if we want to look relaxed. The former dress may help get a job, whereas the latter is more appropriate among friends and family.

Impression management refers to the ways individuals seek to control the impressions they convey to other people. Impression management is a social process, involving more than just our own behavior. For instance, you can try to impress a potential employer by wearing nice clothing but cannot ensure that the employer finds the dress appropriate. Hence, there are **impressions given** and **impressions given off**—the impression you believe that you are giving and the impression the other person has of you.

Goffman argued that we are driven to maintain positive impressions, probably because outcomes of interactions are to avoid embarrassment or to enhance our personal position in an interaction (Gawley 2008; Scheff 2006). You would feel embarrassed if you tried to present yourself as a serious job candidate but lost your keys and spilled coffee. To avoid this impending embarrassment, we may plan ahead by not bringing coffee to the affair or having a spare set of keys available in case of such an emergency. Alternatively, we may contemplate the way we react to embarrassing interactions to make them appear better than they are (e.g., making a joke about the incident to show that you are not concerned about it). Goffman also observed that other people are driven to help support our impressions. For instance, the employer may make a joke about your clumsiness or give you an opportunity to explain why you are especially clumsy that day. You might respond in agreement, finding an excuse like the wobbly new shoes you are wearing. Thus, both of you have found a way to make the impression as favorable as possible under those conditions.

The motivation to support others' impressions is somewhat self-serving. First, helping other people maintain their impressions helps maintain the interaction, helping us predict future behavior and making it easier for us to know what to do. Second, we may need support in our own impression management efforts later in the interaction. Helping the other person makes it more likely that the other person will reciprocate support for us.

Front Stage, Back Stage

Goffman described two regions of impression formation and management. Goffman's **front stage** is the place where we present ourselves to others. The **backstage** is the region where we relax our impression management efforts, and we may practice our performances (Goffman 1959). We think of the job interview as the front stage, trying to look and act in a way that will make a certain impression and allow us to reach a goal—employment. When you see your friends (your backstage), you may express a very different attitude toward the job and the employer. Similarly, you may want to sound serious and polite when you approach a professor about a test grade, then report your anger and disgust about the grade and the professor with your friends in the campus dining hall after the meeting. This usually works fine, unless your "backstage" is revealed; that is, if your friends point out to you that your professor is eating her lunch right behind you.

Spencer Cahill and his colleagues (1985) studied behavior in public bathrooms, assessing the role social structure plays in the most "private" or "backstage" areas of our lives. He and his colleagues observed and took notes of behavior for hundreds of hours in the bathrooms of malls, student unions, restaurants, and other places over a nine-month period. Among other things, they found that bathrooms serve as a place to "retire" from front-stage performances. The researchers showed that bathrooms serve as "self-service" repair shops, where individuals can take off their "fronts." Mirrors allow us to check our front (e.g., makeup, clothing) before facing the public again. Bathrooms also serve as a retreat from embarrassment, a place to prepare for publicly awkward situations—giving people a "staging area" for their public performances.

The relationship between the front and back stages makes it difficult to assess the honesty of other people. If you find out that your friend is having an affair with your boyfriend, you start to question whether anything this person says to you is true. Is she just "putting on an act" of kindness and loyalty when she is around you but then portraying her true self when she is with your boyfriend? How do you know when someone is being honest with you? It is hard to say. In a participant-observation study of working-class white men, Monica McDermott (2006) found that her subjects were friendly and civil toward African Americans during everyday interactions but tended to express hostility about them when only around other whites. They were also reluctant to discuss race around strangers of any race (ostensibly because they feared reprisals for revealing their true beliefs).

The Importance of Self-Presentations: Some Tips

Our presentations of self do make a difference in the world. People evaluate other people based on their front-stage performances. That may be why the men in the previously cited study refused to talk about race when in the presence of strangers. People also judge us on our looks and mannerisms. Our use of language, for instance, affects people's assessment of our competency (Lewandowski and Harrington 2006; Nath 2007). People who employ more formal language (verbal and through e-mail exchanges) are generally given higher evaluations than people who use more informal language.

How do you build a good first impression? There are impression-consulting companies that can help if you have the money. They may not call themselves impression-management companies—maybe image consultants—but they do provide tips for how to dress and act for success. However, acting out a social identity simply requires a good sociological imagination. If you know how people behave in different societal roles, you can adopt similar mannerisms to reproduce those impressions. In a participant observation of high-school students, for instance, learning how to "perform"—to present one's self in public—takes some work. Consider two musicians, both of whom are equally talented, but one of them smiles and dances with the music while she performs while the other regularly looks down at her instrument and makes very few gestures while playing. Which one do you think will be more popular with the crowd? How do people learn to be good performers? The short answer is practice. In a qualitative study of amateur musicians, Marcus Aldredge (2006) found that musicians use less formal settings such as open-mic nights to develop their musical skills while learning how to perform in front of live audiences. At first, Aldredge observes, many musicians are nervous about being in front of a crowd, and it can make it hard for them to play well. Over time they become more relaxed while performing. They also use audience reactions to assess their performances. This process does not occur overnight, it takes many nights of stress and anxiety before musicians learn how to perform well in front of a crowd. In short, like any other skill, developing good impression management skills takes three things: practice, practice, practice!

Self-Esteem

Self-esteem is the positive or negative evaluation of our self as an object (Rosenberg 1986). It answers the question, How good am I? In addition to thoughts about how worthy we are, social psychologists also understand self-esteem to be the emotional reactions to the self (Hewitt 2003a). Thus, self-esteem has at least two dimensions; we can both cognitively and affectively react to the self. For instance, we may think very highly of ourselves and concurrently feel good about ourselves. Alternatively, we can think poorly of ourselves and feel bad too. Self-esteem is global or specific; that is, an overall sense of worth or a sense of worth based on specific roles or spheres of life. Academic self-esteem is our worth as a student (Rosenberg, Schooler, and Schoenbach 1989).

If you enter the term *self-esteem* into an Internet search engine, you will find dozens of Web sites designed to sell products guaranteed to boost your self-esteem. Self-esteem has become a common expression in the Western world; parents try to build their children's self-esteem, and many people participate in self-esteem-boosting programs. Much of the early research in self-esteem suggested that it is at the core of psychological development (see Elliott 1986; Owens and Stryker 2001; Rosenberg 1986); that is, all other aspects of our life will fail without positive self-esteem. For instance, a person with low self-esteem may find it more difficult to finish a college program, believing that she does not "have what it takes." Therefore, the logic goes, we must first build strong self-esteem and then worry about the other details of life. But this is not quite true. Instead, successful social experiences and a lifetime of supportive interactions with significant others are primary

Children learn positive self-esteem and mastery at the earliest ages through their accomplishments and positive interactions with friends and family.

in creating self-esteem; it cannot be quickly "built" and then used as a tool for success (Rosenberg, Schooler, and Schoenbach 1989).

Self-concept theorists often study the effects of social structure and culture on self-esteem. For instance, people who work in jobs that require little supervision from others and who engage in intellectually complex tasks have higher self-esteem years later than others who perform more mundane work (Schooler and Oates 2001). Another study examined how girls were affected by unrealistic images of female beauty prominent in the media (Milkie 1999). For white girls, even when they were critical of the "perfect" images, the images depressed self-esteem, because girls still made social comparisons with models and assumed that boys bought into the images and viewed the real girls more negatively. But black girls' self-esteem was not affected by these comparisons—they understood that significant others did not believe the images were a standard for African American beauty. Hence, our status and social relationships help us interpret information from the media and other sources in assessing our self-worth.

The importance of self-esteem, according to some scholars, is profound. Many social psychologists believe that self-esteem serves as a basis for motivation of the self process. Viktor Gecas (2001) argued that self-esteem may be a more important motivational force for us than other self processes. Gecas says that individuals are motivated by the **self-consistency motive** to maintain a consistent sense of self and the **self-esteem motive**, the desire to maintain positive self-images. For example, the threat of bad grades (which could produce lower academic self-esteem) may motivate us to study harder for class. It may motivate us to leave school and find an alternative source of esteem. However, someone who receives lower grades may come to see herself as a bad student and work less hard as a student to maintain her negative sense of self.

The set of research discussed earlier shows that self-esteem is, in part, derived from social interaction. In fact, there are four sources of the self-concept: social comparisons, reflected appraisals, psychological centrality, and self-perceptions (Gecas 1982; Rosenberg 1986). **Social comparisons** refer to using other people and groups as a point of reference for our thoughts, feelings, and behaviors. **Reflected appraisals** are the ways that we believe others view us. **Psychological centrality** is our ability to shift aspects of the self to become more or less important to our overall self-concept. Finally, **self-perceptions** are observations of our behavior and its consequences.

An internal dialogue forms the self. Positive or negative evaluations of your self (self-esteem) are the result of your internal dialogue, compiling self-perceptions, social comparisons, and reflected appraisals. Marsha, in the vignette at the start of the chapter, indicated that she felt good about herself as a mother. Her mothering self-esteem was built through all the processes described. She probably made social comparisons with other student mothers and believed that, compared to them, she was doing quite well taking care of her baby. Through interacting with others, her parents, her partner, her friends, and her baby, she is able to form a view of how they viewed her mothering (or reflected appraisals). In terms of psychological centrality, her mothering identity is very important and thus provides a positive global sense of worth as well. And finally, by observing her own behaviors—sacrificing time at parties and studying when necessary—she sees evidence that she is a good mother.

Research generally supports the self-esteem dynamics reviewed. Levels and sources of self-esteem are found to be different for people in various social categories. For instance, of the four sources of the self-concept, reflected appraisals, or our sense of how others view us, have the strongest effect on self-esteem for both men and women, although the effects on women are somewhat stronger than men (Schwalbe and Staples 1991). Research also shows that self-esteem is relatively high for most people, and there is a tendency to focus on positive outcomes of interactions for ourselves—we tend to assess our actions more positively than other people's actions (Allison et al. 2006; Rosenberg 1986). These findings support the idea that self-esteem serves as primary element of the self-concept.

Self-Concept, Self-Esteem, and Identity

Roy F. Baumeister

ℰ

Who are you? What kind of person are you? How good are you? According to Roy Baumeister your answers to these questions form, in turn, your identity, self-concept, and self-esteem. Your identity is who you are as a unique person. Your self-concept is your beliefs about who you are, such as your personality attributes. Your self-esteem is how you feel about yourself in general (i.e., whether you think you are pretty good, so-so, or not so good, overall).

In this excerpt focusing on self-esteem, Baumeister reviews research on elements that build, maintain, and affect self-esteem; differences between people with high and low self-esteem; ways that self-esteem helps us cope with negative events; and defense mechanisms that help us preserve our self-esteem.

...

ℰ Self-Esteem

Of all the aspects of the self-concept, one of the most important is self-esteem. When researchers set out to study the self-concept, they usually end up studying self-esteem. This is partly because self-esteem is so important: self-esteem affects many different actions and reactions. It is also easy and convenient to measure.

No single measure of self-esteem is used by everyone. Rather, there are many such measures, partly because the topic is quite important and partly because researchers criticize each other's ways of measuring it. As already noted, one approach has been to look for discrepancies between the real self and the ideal self. Another way is to ask a series of simple questions about global self-regard (Rosenberg, 1965). The most common approach is to ask a series of questions about different attributes and add them up. The problem is that such a measure might not lend the right importance to the various attributes or dimensions. Most of the common self-esteem measures tend to emphasize social self-esteem, for example. To get an understanding of this approach, read the Activity Box on Measuring Self-Esteem.

The results of these self-esteem measures yield a continuum of scores. Although everyone speaks of high and low self-esteem as if these were distinct types, they are not types in the sense of distinct clusters of scores. Rather, there is a continuum, and people may range anywhere along it. Dividing the scores into high and low self-esteem groups is done for the sake of conceptual convenience (that is, it makes results easier to talk about). Sometimes researchers divide their scores into two groups for analyzing their data; they compare the typical behaviors of high versus low self-esteem groups. There are some minor statistical problems with that approach (for example, it ignores the fact that the highest score in the low-esteem group is probably closer to the lowest score in the high-esteem group than to the lowest score in the low-esteem group), but these can safely be overlooked in making rough comparisons.

Self-Esteem and Self-Concept

Self-esteem is essentially the evaluative dimension of the self-concept. Any piece of information about the self may be incorporated into the self-concept. The information only affects self-esteem once it takes on a value judgment: Is it good or bad? High self-esteem denotes thinking well of oneself. This may include a healthy self-confidence and proper appreciation of one's genuine accomplishments and abilities. It may also exaggerate or distort the truth wildly. High self-esteem can mean being conceited, egotistical, arrogant, and narcissistic. The common thread is thinking well of oneself—regardless of whether this is justified or not.

In theory, low self-esteem is the opposite of high self-esteem, and so it should mean having a negative, unflattering view of self. In practice, however, relatively few people are firmly convinced that they are bad. Most researchers define "low self-esteem" as scoring in the bottom half or bottom third of a sample of scores on a self-esteem scale. An examination of these scores shows that usually they are in the middle range of possible scores, because almost no one scores at the low end (Baumeister, Tice, and Hutton, 1989). In other words, in response to self-esteem scale questions such as "Do

"Self-Concept, Self-Esteem, and Identity" by R. Baumeister from *Personality: Contemporary Theory and Research*, 2ed., Nelson-Hall Publishers. Copyright © 1999 by R. Baumeister.

From: Roy F. Baumeister, reprinted from *Personality: Contemporary Theory and Research*, Second Edition (1999), by permission of the author.

Measuring Your Self-Esteem

Most measures of self-esteem rely on asking a person to rate him- or herself on various dimensions. Here are some sample items that are similar to those used on actual scales. Try to rate yourself on each one- Give yourself a numerical rating from 0 to 6 on each scale, such that 0 = Very often, or Very much, and 6 = Almost never, or Not at all.

1. How often do you feel superior to most other people?

2. How often do you think that one day you will accomplish great things?

3. Do you worry about making a good impression on other people?

4. Do you frequently fear that other people will dislike you or think badly of you?

5. When you complete an assignment or test, do you usually have the feeling that you did a poor or inadequate job?

6. Do you consider yourself more physically attractive than the average person you know?

7. How often do you do things that seem clumsy or uncoordinated?

Self-esteem is scored by computing a total based on the number of points per item. For questions 3, 4, 5, and 7, your rating (0 to 6) is your score. The other three items (1, 2, and 6) are reverse scored, that is, you compute your score by subtracting your rating from 6. For example, it you responded to question 2 by rating yourself 4, your score would be 6 – 4 = 2.

These questions refer to various areas or facets of self-esteem. Questions 1 and 2 refer to "global self-esteem," that is, the person's overall appraisal of self. Questions 3 and 4 measure social self-esteem, that is, feeling of confidence and inhibition about getting along with other people. Question 5 refers to school (intellectual) abilities (confidence in your ability to do good work). Questions 6 and 7 refer to body image; 6 is concerned with attractiveness, and 7 is concerned with physical skills and ability.

Most self-esteem scales use more items than these (see Fleming and Courtney, 1984, for a good example of a complete scale), so you should not place much trust in the reliability of your total score from these few items. Still, you can get a rough idea of how self-esteem is measured by considering these items and similar ones.

you often feel inferior to other people?" a high self-esteem person will answer "Never," but a typical low self-esteem person will say "Sometimes" rather than "Frequently." Hardly anyone says "Frequently."

Thus, low self-esteem is the absence of positives more than the presence of negative beliefs about the self (Baumeister, 1993). People with high self-esteem hold firm, highly favorable beliefs about themselves. People with low self-esteem lack those beliefs, but they generally do not hold firm *unfavorable* beliefs about themselves.

A powerful and influential line of research on the self-conceptions that accompany different levels of self-esteem was conducted by Campbell (1990; Campbell and Lavallee, 1993). The broad conclusion is that low self-esteem is marked by self-concept confusion. That is, people with high self-esteem have clear, consistent, and definite ideas about themselves, whereas people with low self-esteem do not. When people with low self-esteem answered questions about themselves, they differed from people with high self-esteem in several key ways. They tended to give uncertain answers or say they did not know. They gave contradictory or inconsistent answers to similar questions. They gave different answers to the same questions on different occasions. All of these suggest that low self-esteem is marked by a lack of firm self-knowledge. Once again, then, low self-esteem is not a

matter of being convinced that you are bad. More commonly, it is simply the lack of firm conviction that you are good.

Roots of Self-Esteem

The roots of self-esteem were the target of many years of research by Coopersmith (1967). He concluded that three factors contributed to high self-esteem among children. The first was unconditional positive regard, which means that parents (or others) should convey to the child the message that the child is loved no matter what. Many parents give the impression that they love their child only when the child behaves well. However, if a child is to build a strong, healthy self-concept, the foundation is apparently the sense that one is loved and valued regardless of how one behaves.

The second factor identified by Coopersmith was the existence of clear and strong standards. That is, parents can build self-esteem by setting firm, definite criteria as to how the child should behave and expecting the child to live up to them. These include rules and limits on what the child is allowed to do. The modern self-esteem movement's message has been misinterpreted by many modern parents. They believe that in order to build self-esteem they should approve of the child's behavior no matter whether it is good or not. In fact, however, Coopersmith found that children ended up with higher self-esteem if they knew definitely what was expected of them and if these expectations were clear and consistent.

The third ingredient was that parents should give the child freedom, latitude, and respect for behavior that lies within the limits. In particular, it is important that parents show some positive approval when the child does live up to expectations. Some parents tend to make rules and set expectations but only show any feelings when the child falls short. It is better for self-esteem, apparently, if parents also express pride and other positive feelings when the child succeeds.

One might think that the first and second features contradict each other: The first says to love the child no matter what, whereas the second says to set firm rules and punish the child when the child performs badly. The resolution of this seeming contradiction is that it is fine, even desirable, to disapprove of specific behaviors, but parents should continue to feel and show love for the child. When the child disobeys, or fails to complete chores, or does badly in school, the ideal parental message is, "I love you, but I hate what you are doing." The parents who can effectively combine steady love with firm rules (and consistent punishments), as well as giving the child freedom and approval for behavior that satisfies these rules, will likely raise the child with the strongest, healthiest self-esteem.

Why Care about Self-Esteem?

People everywhere care about self-esteem. Anything that gives a boost in self-esteem is almost universally welcome, and by the same token hardly anyone enjoys events that constitute a blow or loss to their self-esteem. Yet, as we shall see, self-esteem does not lead in any palpable, direct way to significant material benefits. Self-esteem does not make people richer, smarter, better liked, or more successful. In a few small ways, people with high self-esteem do better than others, and in a few other ways they do worse, and the overall effect is quite small. Why are people so concerned with something that seems to mean so little?

The emotional implications of self-esteem contain an answer, but only a partial one. People do feel better when their self-esteem is high or rising, and they feel bad when self-esteem is low or dropping. So it is only natural that they should become concerned about self-esteem. Yet this answer is hardly satisfactory, because it raises the question of why emotions should be so strongly tied to something that has little practical value. We have emotions for good reasons. They help us adapt to the world and pass on our genes to the next generation. Fear makes us avoid danger. Love makes us stay with desirable partners, especially when we may reproduce. Anger helps us assert our rights and tackle obstacles. But why should self-esteem be linked to emotions?

At present, several possible answers have been suggested, but none is fully satisfactory. One answer is that people are driven by fear of death, and self-esteem helps comfort them in the face of human mortality (Becker, 1973;

Greenberg, Pyszczynski, and Solomon; 1986; Pyszczynski, Greenberg, and Soloman, in press). Critics of this view point out that self-esteem does not seem to correlate with death anxiety and that high self-esteem would seemingly make death seem worse, not better (because the value of one's own life is higher). In support of this view, however, researchers have shown that high self-esteem seems to hold back anxiety in response to cues designed to evoke thoughts of death and pain (Greenberg, Solomon, Pyszczynski, Rosenblatt, Burling, Lyon, Simon, and Pinel, 1992).

Another view is that self-esteem is sought because it is a valuable aid in coping with stress, trauma, and misfortunes (Steele, 1988). Self-esteem may be of little value under normal circumstances, but in response to adversity people need self-esteem to keep their spirits up and to keep striving for positive outcomes. Self-esteem is thus a valuable resource. This theory does correspond well with the actual, limited benefits of self-esteem, especially the emotional benefits and the improved capacity to persist in the face of failure, but it is not clear that people want self-esteem merely in order to have a resource in case they encounter misfortune. Even when times are good, people seem to want self-esteem. Moreover, this theory still does not explain why it is that people should find that self-esteem helps them cope with failure or misfortune.

A third view is that self-esteem is a sociometer, that is, an internal measure of how well one is connected to other human beings (Leary, Tambor, Terdal, and Downs, 1995). There is a large amount of evidence that forming good social relations and getting along with others is conducive to health, happiness, and well-being, as well as the evolutionary criteria of survival and reproduction. It is fair to say that human beings are partly driven by a fundamental and powerful need to belong (Baumeister and Leary, 1995). Self-esteem may be fairly unimportant in terms of its direct consequences, but it could be important as an inner meter that keeps track of this all-important project of forming and maintaining social bonds. (By analogy, the gas gauge in the car has no direct importance for helping the car run, but it is important as a measure of something crucial, namely, how much fuel the car has.) To support this theory, Leary, Tambor, Terdal, and Downs (1995) showed that self-esteem rises based on events that are linked to social inclusion, such as being accepted by others, proving one's competence, being found attractive, and so forth. Meanwhile, events that can lead to social rejection also tend to lower self-esteem. Moreover, we have already seen that self-esteem is strongly (inversely) correlated with social anxiety, which means that low self-esteem is often linked to a fear of social rejection.

The sociometer theory is a novel solution to the question of why self-esteem matters. It leaves several issues unresolved, however. Can people have high self-esteem even if they do not have strong social connections and relationships? And how can some people have low self-esteem even when they seem to be well connected to family and friends? Still, it is probably no mere coincidence that the main criteria on which self-esteem is based—being likable, attractive, and competent—are the same criteria that groups use to include or exclude individuals.

Is High Self-Esteem a Good Thing?

Interest in self-esteem has extended beyond the research community to society at large. California created a state task force to develop ideas for raising the self-esteem of all residents in the belief that self-esteem would serve as a "social vaccine" to combat a broad array of personal and social problems, including drug abuse, teen pregnancy, crime, school failure, debt, and mental illness (California Task Force, 1990). Many school systems now devote considerable time and effort to boosting self-esteem, even devoting class time to this end rather than to academic topics.

Although belief remains strong in the positive value of self-esteem, the research evidence does not justify it. Even while the California Task Force was touting the benefits of self-esteem, a group of researchers they commissioned to study those benefits published a contrary conclusion: "The news most consistently reported, however, is that the associations between self-esteem and its expected consequences are mixed, insignificant, or absent" (Mecca, Smelser, and Vasconcellos, 1989, p. 15). Raising self-esteem does not appear to be an effective way to prevent teen pregnancy, drug abuse, school failure, or the like.

The link to violence may even be the opposite of what the self-esteem movement assumed. A large-scale review of the research literature by Baumeister, Smart, and Boden (1996) found that the evidence massively contradicted the theory that low self-esteem causes violence. In general, violence seems to occur primarily among people who hold favorable, even inflated views of themselves—and who then encounter someone who questions or challenges their high self-esteem. From gang members who shoot someone who "disses" (shows disrespect to) them, to adults who beat their spouses and lovers to prove that they should be the boss in the family, to playground bullies who victimize other children to prove their own superiority, to tyrannical governments headed by megalomanical dictators, to nations who make war to avenge threats to their honor, to ethnic groups who oppress or attack others based on flimsy notions of racial pride, the same pattern was found over and over: Threatened egotism is the decisive cause of violence and aggression. Not all high self-esteem causes aggression, but when self-esteem consists of inflated, exaggerated, or narcissistic notions of personal superiority, the results can be dangerous.

This is not to say that self-esteem is all bad or irrelevant. Low self-esteem is strongly correlated with depression (Tennen and Affleck, 1993) and social anxiety (Leary and Kowalski, 1995), although it is not clear which causes which. People with low self-esteem have a more difficult time than others recovering from traumas and setbacks, which may represent a greater general vulnerability to life's misfortunes (Steele,

1988; Taylor, 1983, 1989). They also tend to give up more readily in the face of failure, in contrast to the persistence and determination to succeed shown by people with high self-esteem (Shrauger and Sorman, 1977).

Thus, researchers are slowly moving toward a more balanced view of self-esteem that acknowledges both its advantages and its disadvantages, as well as recognizing that its causal impact on important social and personal problems may be far weaker than previously hoped. Low self-esteem is linked to social anxiety and shyness, which can impair people's chances of making friends and getting along with others (Leary and Kowalski, 1995; Schlenker and Leary, 1982)—but people with inflated (high) self-esteem tend to irritate others and turn them off. In the long run these self-centered, conceited individuals show poor social skills and psychological maladjustment (Colvin, Block, and Funder, 1995). Low self-esteem is associated with some patterns of self-defeating behavior, such as giving up too easily—but high self-esteem is associated with other patterns such as overconfidence (Heatherton and Ambady, 1993). When things are going well, people with high self-esteem manage themselves better than those with low self-esteem; they make appropriate commitments and select optimal performance goals. But in response to an ego threat, people with high self-esteem often become irrational and set unrealistic, macho goals for themselves, which may lead to costly failures (Baumeister, Heatherton, and Tice, 1993; McFarlin and Blascovich, 1981).

Much of the down side of high self-esteem seems to involve overestimating oneself, such as being conceited or narcissistic. Present evidence does not indicate that there is anything wrong with having an accurate appreciation of one's good points and strengths, particularly if this is tempered with some interpersonal humility and with an accurate recognition of one's faults and weaknesses. Some experts conclude from this that there are right and wrong (or "true" and "false") kinds of high self-esteem. To make such a distinction, however, is already to shift the focus away from self-esteem per se (in the sense of thinking well of oneself) and on to the issue of how good a person one can manage to be.

To understand this, suppose there were an effective way to sort "true" from "false" versions of high self-esteem. For example, a team of researchers might identify the students who think they are smart and then give them an IQ test to see which ones are really smart. The ones who are smart and know it have "true" high self-esteem, and the ones who overestimate their intelligence have "false" high self-esteem. Suppose, then, that the researchers find that "true" high self-esteem is associated with success in school, whereas "false" high self-esteem tends to backfire (a likely outcome). Would this show that some forms of self-esteem are better than others? On the contrary, it seems to show that self-esteem is irrelevant. Remember, the students with "true" self-esteem are by definition smarter than those with false high self-esteem, and so it is no surprise that they do better in school. Both groups think they're equally smart, which suggests that the mere fact of thinking oneself smart is irrelevant. What matters is the underlying reality of actually being smart. In other words, perhaps the underlying reality rather than the perception matters most. Self-esteem is merely the perception, not the reality. When perception does matter, the best thing may well be to be accurate—neither overestimating nor underestimating oneself. Those who underestimate their intelligence may avoid challenges or give up too easily. Those who overestimate their intelligence may get in over their heads or may not bother to work hard enough. Either distortion can interfere with learning.

Achieving a balanced, accurate appraisal of oneself is quite difficult. In the mean time, the world might be a better place if more people would forget about trying to boost their self-esteem and concentrate instead on trying to be a better person.

Social Motives

What do people with low self-esteem want? This question has led various theorists to pose a wide assortment of answers. Some have asserted that people with low self-esteem desire to fail or suffer. Some have proposed that they want to confirm their bad opinions of themselves. Some have proposed that they want to gain esteem at all costs. Others have proposed that their motivations are largely the same as those of people with high self-esteem.

After many years of research, some answers have finally emerged. The notion that people with low self-esteem desire to fail or suffer in order to prove how bad they are has not been confirmed. People with low self-esteem want to succeed as much as people with high self-esteem; they are simply less confident that they will be able to do so (McFarlin and Blascovich, 1981).

The broadest motivational pattern associated with low self-esteem seems to be one of self-protection (Baumeister, Tice, and Hutton, 1989). That is, people with low self-esteem worry about failure, rejection, humiliation, and other unpleasant outcomes, and they seem to go through life watching out for such dangers and trying to minimize them. People with high self-esteem, in contrast, seem to spend much less time worrying about failure or protecting themselves from it. They do hate to fail, but in general they do not expect to fail; and so self-protection is not an overriding concern.

To put this in broader perspective, it is helpful to realize that nearly everyone wants to do well—to succeed at work, to make friends, to have good intimate relationships, and so forth. As part of that, nearly everyone wants to be well regarded by others and to be able to respect him- or herself too. The motive to think well of oneself can, however, be subdivided into two motives: self-enhancement, which is the desire to gain esteem, and self-protection, which is the desire to avoid losing esteem. Often, the self-enhancement motive and the self-protection motive operate together, in tandem, such as when someone tries to make the best possible score on an examination.

Other times, however, the two motives are opposed. For example, when you call someone to ask for a date, the two motives are pitted against each other. If the other person accepts the invitation, you may feel a gain in esteem, but if the other person rejects you, you may lose esteem. Asking someone out, therefore, is risky from an esteem point of view. If the self-enhancement motive predominates, and you are mainly concerned with the opportunity to gain esteem, then you may well take the chance. But if the self-protection motive predominates, you would not make the call in order to prevent the possibility of being rejected. Similar arguments apply in many other situations, such as accepting a challenge or undertaking a public performance where there are significant opportunities for both gaining and losing esteem.

In general, people with high self-esteem are oriented toward self-enhancement. They are looking for ways to gain esteem and to do even better than they have done so far. They do not expect to fail or to be rejected, so they do not worry about it much. In contrast, people with low self-esteem give priority to self-protection. They might be happy to gain esteem, but gaining esteem does not dominate their outlook on life. Instead, they look for ways to avoid or minimize possible failures, rejections, and setbacks.

Plasticity

People with low self-esteem tend to be more malleable and gullible than people with high self-esteem (Brockner, 1984). This is a common pattern across many spheres of behavior. People with low self-esteem are more likely to change their attitudes when someone tries to persuade them (Janis, 1954). They may yield or conform to group influence more than others, and they are more willing to take advice. Their behavior changes more from one situation to another.

The malleability may well be connected with the two broad patterns that we have already identified. Because people with low self-esteem lack firm, consistent self-concepts, it is harder for them than for other people to resist situational influences and follow their own inner promptings. And because they are oriented toward self-protection, they may find it safer to go along with the group and do what they are told rather than strike out on their own.

Emotion and Coping

High self-esteem does not produce a great many benefits or successes in life, but it does undoubtedly make one feel better. As a result, some of the most important differences between high and low self-esteem involve emotion. One difference is in the overall positivity of emotion. People with low self-esteem are more likely to suffer unpleasant emotional states. As we have already seen, low self-esteem correlates strongly with anxiety and depression, which are two of the most common and serious patterns of emotional distress. In a recent study in which people kept diaries of their emotions, people with low self-esteem showed more negative emotions of all sorts than people with high self-esteem (Campbell, Chew, and Scratchley, 1991). They had more bad moods and fewer good moods.

Beyond the simple issue of good versus bad emotions, however, there is another emotional difference. People with low self-esteem have higher emotional lability than people with high self-esteem (Campbell, Chew, and Scratchley, 1991; Campbell and Lavallee, 1993). That is, their emotions fluctuate more widely from one day to the next or one hour to the next. High self-esteem apparently helps keep one on an even keel, whereas low self-esteem can contribute one riding an emotional roller-coaster.

Probably the emotional lability of low self-esteem is linked to plasticity. After all, it is hard not to respond to the immediate event or situation if you are having a strong emotional reaction to it. The self-concept confusion may also be connected. If your ideas about yourself are not firmly fixed, then each event can have a bigger impact on the way you think and feel about yourself, which in turn will set off stronger emotional reactions.

Self-esteem can thus be understood as an emotional resource, and this may explain the difference in resiliency in the face of stress, trauma, and setbacks. People with high self-esteem seem to have a stock of positive feelings, possibly associated with all the positive beliefs they hold about themselves. When something goes wrong, they can draw on these beliefs and feelings to help themselves shrug off the misfortune, feel better, and maybe try again (Steele, 1988). In contrast, people with low self-esteem have a much smaller stock of positive beliefs and feelings, so they may feel overwhelmed or devastated when something goes wrong.

Prejudice

On the surface, it seems that people with low self-esteem are more prejudiced than people with high self-esteem. Several studies have shown, for example, that people with low self-esteem give more negative ratings to minority group members and other stereotyped groups. But one must recall that low self-esteem means giving oneself a negative rating. To examine prejudice, one must ask: Do people with low self-esteem rate others worse than themselves?

The answer appears to be no. People with low self-esteem rate themselves, members of their own group, and members of other groups all about the same (Crocker and Schwartz, 1985). All of these ratings tend to be somewhat negative when compared to the ratings given by people with high self-esteem. But the negativity does not reflect any selective prejudice, for it applies to everyone. People with low self-esteem are apparently more critical of everyone—including minority groups and themselves. When one looks at the difference between how one rates oneself and how one

rates members of outgroups, it is people with high self-esteem who emerge as more prejudiced (Crocker and Schwartz, 1985).

Maintaining Self-Esteem

How do people keep up their self-esteem? And why do some people seem unable to form a favorable view of themselves? In principle, one means to achieving high self-esteem would be to succeed at everything. As long as work and social life go well, there is not much danger to one's self-esteem. Unfortunately, life does not usually cooperate, and nearly everyone experiences periodic setbacks, failures, rejections, interpersonal conflicts, and other events that strike painful blows to their sense of self-worth.

Most studies have not found that people with high self-esteem are more talented, intelligent, likable, attractive, or otherwise superior to people with low self-esteem. Indeed, the more common finding among laboratory researchers is that the actual performance of people with high self-esteem is, on average, no different from that of people with low self-esteem. People with high self-esteem believe they are better: they rate their performance better, they consider themselves more beautiful or handsome, and so forth, as compared with people who have low self-esteem. But the difference seems to be mainly one of perception. For example, studies that ask unbiased judges to rate people's attractiveness conclude that people with high and low self-esteem are about equally attractive—but studies that ask people to rate their own physical appearance find that people with high self-esteem consistently rate themselves as being more attractive (for example, Harter, 1993).

Success in life depends on more than ability, however. Two people may have precisely the same amount of talent, but one may succeed better than the other by virtue of choosing more appropriate undertakings. (For example, two equally smart and equally knowledgeable people may get different grades depending on which courses they take.) Remember, people with high self-esteem seem to have superior knowledge about themselves (Campbell, 1990), and this knowledge can prove useful in selecting the optimal courses, jobs, challenges, projects, and dating partners. Experiments have indeed shown that people with high self-esteem are better at choosing the right level of challenge for themselves to ensure maximum success (as long as they are not distracted by an ego threat; Baumeister, Heatherton, and Tice, 1993). This kind of advantage may be what helps people with high self-esteem to perform a little better in school (and elsewhere) without actually being any smarter (Felson, 1993; Hattie and Hansford, 1982).

Thus, it is plausible that some people can sustain higher self-esteem than others by achieving more successes, even without any superior gifts. Undoubtedly, however, the other route to maintaining high self-esteem involves various styles of thinking that boost one's self-appraisal. Many of these techniques involve self-deception, to the extent that people fool themselves in systematic ways to maintain comfortable, flattering illusions about how great they are. A famous article by Anthony Greenwald (1980) compared the self to a totalitarian regime in the way it rewrites history to make itself look good. The major esteem-boosting and self-deception techniques that researchers have identified are as follows (from Baumeister, in press):

First, people systematically take credit for success but deny blame for failure. This self-serving bias has been widely documented in many contexts and studies (Zuckerman, 1979). When something important happens, people are quick to judge whether or not they are responsible, and they make those judgments in a one-sided fashion. People with high self-esteem are especially prone to show this pattern of grabbing the credit but denying the blame (for example, Fitch, 1970).

Second, people happily and uncritically accept information that makes them look good, but when someone criticizes them, they often stop to find faults or flaws in the critic's comments. For example, when people take a test and are then asked whether the test was valid, their answers depend heavily on how well they are told they performed (Pyszczynski, Greenberg, and Holt, 1985; Wyer and Frey, 1983; see also Kunda, 1990). As many instructors know, students who did well on a test think the test was fair and objective, whereas those who did badly are more likely to believe that the test was biased or inappropriate. A variation on this is that people dismiss criticism as motivated by prejudice or personal animosity, and their self-esteem is unaffected even when someone tells them that they have done badly or have undesirable traits (Crocker and Major, 1989; Crocker, Voelkl, Testa, and Major, 1991).

Third, people shift the amount of attention they pay when they receive feedback about their abilities or performances (Baumeister and Cairns, 1992). When people receive positive, flattering feedback, they often linger over it, study it carefully, and let its implications sink in. In contrast, when they hear criticism or unfavorable remarks, they tend to skip over them or pay much less attention.

Fourth, people show biased memory. They recall their successes and good points better than their failures and bad points (Crary, 1966; Kuiper and Derry, 1982; Mischel, Ebbesen, and Zeiss, 1976). Fifth, they have ways of sorting through their memory to prove to themselves that they fit whatever pattern is desirable. Thus, when people are led to believe that being an introvert leads to success, they recall more of their own actions as introverted, and they are quicker to come up with introverted memories, than when they are told that extroversion is associated with success (Sanitioso, Kunda, and Fong, 1990).

Sixth, they compare themselves selectively to targets that make them feel good. In particular, they engage in downward comparison, which means that they identify people who are doing worse than themselves to use as a baseline for evaluating themselves (Wills, 1981). People like to have some contact with people who are less intelligent, less attractive, or fatter than they are, because seeing such individuals makes them feel good about themselves.

Seventh, people distort their perceptions of others so as to furnish a rosy view of their own traits and opinions. With opinions and beliefs, people exhibit a false consensus effect, which means that they overestimate the proportion of people who would agree with them—and which encourages them to think they must be right: "I must be correct, because everybody agrees with me." In contrast, with abilities, people show a false uniqueness effect, which means that they underestimate the proportion of others who have similar abilities. This helps people feel that their abilities are special, because they think hardly anyone could perform as well as they do. The combination of false uniqueness and false consensus effects has been especially linked to high self-esteem, and indeed it seems well designed to give people a comfortable sense of personal superiority (Campbell, 1986; Marks, 1984; Suls and Wan, 1987).

These patterns are fairly common and widespread. This is not to say that everyone always uses them, but most people do show some of them. More to the point, people with high self-esteem use them more than others. We noted earlier that self-esteem seems to be somewhat inflated across the U.S. population today, and these techniques indicate how people give their self-esteem an extra boost, perhaps beyond what is warranted. These are the means, in other words, by which the average person convinces him- or herself that he or she is above average.

・・・

REFERENCES

Baumeister, R. F. (1993). Understanding the inner nature of low self-esteem: Uncertain, fragile, protective, and conflicted. In R. Baumeister (Ed.), *Self-esteem: The puzzle of low self regard* (pp. 201–218). New York: Plenum.

Baumeister, R. F. (1998). The self. In D. T. Gilbert, S. T. Fiske, and G. Lindzey (Eds.), *Handbook of social psychology.* 4th ed. (pp. 680–740). New York McGraw-Hill.

Baumeister, R. F., and Cairns, K. J. (1992). Repression and self-presentation: When audiences interfere with self-deceptive strategies. *Journal of Personality and Social Psychology, 62,* 851–862.

Baumeister, R. F., and Leary, M. R. (1995). The need to belong: Desire for interpersonal attachments as a fundamental human motivation. *Psychological Bulletin, 117,* 497–529.

Baumeister, R. F., Smart, L., and Boden, J. M. (1996). Relation of threatened egotism to violence and aggression: The dark side of high self-esteem. *Psychological Review, 103,* 5–33.

Baumeister, R. F., Tice, D. M., and Hutton, D. G. (1989). Self-presentational motivations and personality differences in self-esteem *Journal of Personality, 57,* 547–579.

Becker, E. (1973). *The denial of death.* New York: Free Press.

Brockner, J. (1984). Low self-esteem and behavioral plasticity: Some implications for personality and social psychology. In L. Wheeler (Ed.), *Review of personality and social psychology.* Vol. 4 (pp. 237–271). Beverly Hills, CA: Sage.

California Task Force to Promote Self-esteem and Personal and Social Responsibility (1990). *Toward a state of self-esteem.* Sacramento California State Department of Education.

Campbell, J. D. (1986) Similarity and uniqueness: The effects of attribute type, relevance, and individual differences in self-esteem and depression, *Journal of Personality and Social Psychology, 50,* 281–294.

Campbell. J. D. (1990). Self-esteem and clarity of the self concept. *Journal of Personality and Social Psychology, 59* 538–549.

Campbell, J. D., Chew, B., and Scratchley, L. S. (1991) Cognitive and emotional reactions to daily events: The effects of self-esteem and self-complexity. *Journal of Personality, 59,* 473–505.

Campbell, J. D., and Lavallee, L. F. (1993). Who am I? The role of self-concept confusion in understanding the behavior of people with low self-esteem. In R. Baumeister (Ed.), *Self-esteem: The puzzle of low self-regard* (pp. 320). New York: Plenum.

Colvin, C. R., Block, J., and Funder, D. C. (1995). Overly positive evaluations and personality: Negative implications for mental health. *Journal of Personality and Social Psychology, 68,* 1152–1162.

Coopersmith, S. (1967). *The antecedents of self-esteem.* San Francisco, CA: Freeman.

Crary, W. G. (1966). Reactions to incongruent self-experiences. *Journal of Consulting Psychology, 30,* 246–252.

Crocker, J., and Major, B. (1989). Social stigma and self-esteem: The self-protective properties of stigma. *Psychological Review, 96,* 608–630.

Crocker, J., and Schwartz, I. (1985). Prejudice and ingroup favoritism in a minimal intergroup situation: Effects of self-esteem. *Personality and Social Psychology Bulletin, 11,* 379–386.

Crocker, J., Voelkl, K., Testa, M., and Major, B. (1991). Social stigma: The affective consequences of attributional ambiguity. *Journal of Personality and Social Psychology, 60,* 218–228.

Pelson, R. B. (1993). The (somewhat) social self: How others affect self-appraisals. In J. Suls (Ed.), *Psychological perspectives on the self.* Vol. 4 (pp. 1–26), Hillsdale, NJ: Erlbaum.

Fitch, G. (1970). Effects of self-esteem, perceived performance, and choice on causal attributions. *Journal of Personality and Social Psychology, 16,* 311–315.

Fleming, J. S. and Courtney, B. E. (1984). The dimensionality of self-esteem: II. Hierarchical facet model for revised measurement scales. *Journal of Personality and Social Psychology, 46,* 404–421.

Greenberg, J., Pyszczynski, T., and Solomon, S. (1986). The causes and consequences of self-esteem: A terror management theory. In R. Baumeister (Ed.), *Public self and private self.* New York: Springer-Verlag.

Greenberg, J., Solomon, S., Pyszczynski, T., Rosenblatt, A., Burling, J., Lyon, D., Simon, L., and Pinel, E. (1992). Why do people need self-esteem? Converging evidence that self-esteem serves an anxiety-buffering function. *Journal of Personality and Social Psychology, 63,* 913–922.

Greenwald, A. G. (1980). The totalitarian ego: Fabrication and revision of personal history. *American Psychologist, 35,* 603–613.

Harter, S. (1993). Causes and consequences of low self-esteem in children and adolescents. In R. Baumeister (Ed.), *Self-esteem: The puzzle of low self-regard* (pp. 87–116). New York: Plenum.

Hattie, J. A., and Hansford, B. C. (1982). Self measures and achievement: Computing a traditional review of literature with meta-analysis. *Australian Journal of Education, 25,* 71–75.

Heatherton, T. F., and Ambady, N. (1993). Self-esteem, self-prediction, and living up to commitments. In R. Baumeister (Ed,), *Self-esteem: The puzzle of low self-regard* (pp. 131–145). New York: Plenum.

Janis, I. L. (1954), Personality correlates of susceptibility to persuasion. *Journal of Personality, 22,* 504–518.

Kuiper, N. A., and Deny, P. A. (1982). Depressed and nondepressed content self-reference in mild depression. *Journal of Personality, 50,* 67–79.

Kunda, Z. (1990). The case for motivated reasoning. *Psychological Bulletin, 108,* 480–498.

Leary, M. R., and Kowalski, R. (1995). *Social anxiety.* New York: Guilford.

Leary, M. R., Tambor, E. S., Terdal, S. K., and Downs, D. L. (1995), Self-esteem as an interpersonal monitor: The sociometer hypothesis. *Journal of Personality and Social Psychology, 68,* 518–530.

Marks, G. (1984). Thinking one's abilities are unique and one's opinions are common. *Personality and Social Psychology Bulletin, 10,* 203–208.

McFarlin, D. B., and Blascovich, J. (1981). Effects of self-esteem and performance feedback on future affective preferences and cognitive expectations. *Journal of Personality and Social Psychology, 40,* 521–531.

Mecca, A. M., Smelser, N. J., and Vasconcellos, J. (Eds.). (1989). *The social importance of self-esteem.* Berkeley: University of California Press.

Mischel, W., Ebbesen, E. B., and Zeiss, A. R. (1976). Determinants of selective memory about the self. *Journal of Consulting and Clinical Psychology, 44,* 92–103.

Pyszczynski, T., Greenberg, J., and Holt, K. (1985). Maintaining consistency between self-serving beliefs and available data: A bias in information processing. *Personality and Social Psychology Bulletin, 11,* 179–190.

Pyszczynski, T., Greenberg, J., and Solomon, S. (In press), Why do we need what we need? A terror management perspective on the roots of human social motivation. *Psychological Inquiry.*

Rosenberg, M. (1965). *Society and the adolescent self-image.* Princeton, NJ: Princeton University Press.

Sanitioso, R., Kunda, Z., and Fong, G. T. (1990). Motivated recruitment of autobiographical memory. *Journal of Personality and Social Psychology, 59,* 229–241.

Schlenker, B. R., and Leary, M. R. (1982). Social anxiety and self presentation: A conceptualization and model. *Psychological Bulletin, 92,* 641–669.

Shrauger, J. S., and Sorman, P. B. (1977). Self-evaluations, initial success and failure, and improvement as determinants of persistence. *Journal of Consulting and Clinical Psychology, 45,* 784–795.

Steele, C. M. (1988). The psychology of self-affirmation. Sustaining the integrity of the self. In L. Berkowitz (Ed.), Advances in experimental social psychology. Vol. 21 (pp. 261–302). New York Academic Press.

Suls, J., and Wan, C. K. (1987). In search of the false uniqueness phenomenon: Fear and estimates of social consensus. *Journal of Personality and Social Psychology, 52,* 211–217.

Taylor, S. E. (1983). Adjustment to threatening events: A theory of cognitive adaptation. *American Psychologist, 38,* 1161–1173.

Taylor, S. E. (1989). *Positive illusions: Creative self-deception and the healthy mind.* New York: Basic Book.

Tennen, H., and Affleck, G. (1993). The puzzles of self-esteem: A clinical perspective. In R. Baumeister (Ed.), *Self-esteem: The puzzle of low self-regard* (pp. 241–262). New York: Plenum.

Wills, T. A. (1981). Downward comparison principles in social psychology. *Psychological Bulletin, 90,* 245–271.

Wyer, R. S., and Frey, D. (1983). The effects of feedback about self and others on the recall and judgments of feedback-relevant information. *Journal of Experimental Social Psychology, 19,* 540–559.

Zuckerman, M. (1979). Attribution of success and failure revisited, or: The motivational bias is alive and well in attribution theory. *Journal of Personality, 47,* 245–287.

ᔐ Questions

1. Is high self-esteem really as beneficial as it appears to be? Is low self-esteem really so bad? Answer by considering current research findings on who is more likely to act out violently, become depressed, or discriminate against others.

2. A popular notion is that the best way to build children's self-esteem is to praise them regularly regardless of whether or not their behavior is good. How does current research on self-esteem compare to that notion? What is the best way to raise children to have healthy self-esteem?

3. If people who are unlikable, unattractive, and incompetent have low self-esteem and are excluded from social groups, what does this suggest about the purpose of self-esteem?

4. How does the average person convince themselves that they are above average?

FEMALE AND MALE PERCEPTIONS OF IDEAL BODY SHAPES

Lawrence D. Cohn, *University of Texas, El Paso*
Nancy E. Adler, *University of California, San Francisco*

ॐ

Why are we obsessed with having an ideal body? Do we think an ideal body will make us more attractive to potential mates, or do we think it's expected of us?

Using body silhouettes, Lawrence Cohn and Nancy Adler asked men and women to select the figures that best fit their current body shape, their ideal body shape, the shape they believed their same-sex peers would want to have, and the shape they believed the opposite sex would find most attractive.

Previous research on body image looked only at the body image that women have and the body image that women believe men find attractive. This study goes a step further to evaluate what both men and women believe is most desirable for themselves, for their same-sex peers, and for their partners. The results suggest that our own peers represent an additional source of pressure influencing our standards of ideal body shape.

The prevalence of eating disorders and dieting behavior among women has increased dramatically during the past 20 years. This shift in behavior has been linked to a steady shift in the cultural definition of feminine beauty, with increasing pressure placed on women to attain thin figures (Mazur, 1986; Silverstein, Peterson & Perdue, 1986). Beauty pageant contestants, for example, have become increasingly slender since the 1960s, and pageant winners tend to be even thinner than other contestants (Garner, Garfinkel, Schwartz and Thompson, 1980). In contrast, the average weight of American women has increased during the past two decades (Striegel-Moore, McAvay and Rodin, 1986).

The pressure towards thinness that women experience is often attributed to male preferences for slender physiques, which may be of particular concern to women in heterosexual relationships. Men are more likely than women to judge the attractiveness of the other sex on the basis of physical attributes rather than personality traits (Mazure, 1986). This gender difference is present as early as ninth grade, where young boys' descriptions of the ideal woman emphasize good looks and related physical characteristics. In contrast, young girls emphasize interpersonal traits such as kindness and honesty in their descriptions of the ideal man (Stiles, Gibbons and Schnellmann, 1990). Females may acquire an early awareness

of male preferences and may then develop their own preference for a slim figure.

Recent studies, however, suggest that women overestimate the extent to which men value thinness. Fallon and Rozin (1985) presented college women with nine female body silhouettes, ranging from thin to heavy. The silhouette that women selected as most attractive to men was significantly thinner than the female silhouette that men actually chose as most attractive. The tendency to exaggerate male preferences for thin figures has also been observed among middle school children (Cohn et al., 1987), mothers of college students (Rozin and Fallon, 1988), and college women with abnormal eating behaviors (Zellner, Harner, and Adler, 1989). Along with the studies on male preferences, these findings suggest that both actual and perceived preferences of males may push women towards the pursuit of slimness.

This analysis may be oversimplified, however, and other forces may also create pressures for slimness among women. Fallon and Rozin (185) found that 20% of the women in their college sample desired body figures that were thinner than the body figures they perceived as most attractive to men . A similar bias characterized the body figure choices of middle-school girls aged 10–15 (Cohn et al., 1987), high school girls (Dwyer, Feldman, Seltzer and Mayer, 1969), and college students with eating disorders (Zellner et al., 1989).

For some women, the anticipated reactions of same-sex peers may be of greater importance in their pursuit of slimness than are the anticipated reactions of male peers

From: Lawrence D. Cohn and Nancy E. Adler, reprinted from *Psychology of Women Quarterly* 16, no. 1 (March 1992), by permission of Sage Publications, Inc.

(Streigel-Moore et al., 1986). Indeed, for many women the pressure to achieve a thin body figure may arise from comparisons of their own figures with the ideal figure held by female peers. The exaggeration by women of male preferences for thin figures has been demonstrated, but no one has examined if women also exaggerate the desirability of thin figures among female peers. The present study addressed this issue, examining female and male perception of ideal body figures for themselves, same-sex peers, and other-sex peers.

❧ METHOD

Participants

Participants were 87 women and 118 men attending liberal arts classes at a small private midwestern college. The majority of participants (78% of the women and 62% of the men) were recruited from classes required of all first-year students; upper level students were recruited from other liberal arts courses. The mean age for women and men was 19.6 and 18.7, respectively. Eighty-six percent of the students were white, 7% Asian, and 5% black.

Measures

Body Figure Ratings

Participants were presented with nine body silhouettes of their own sex ordered from thin to heavy (Stunkard, Sorensen, and Schulsinger, 1983). Each silhouette was approximately 2.5 in. (7 cm) high; the complete set of silhouettes was presented on a single 8.5- x 11-in. sheet of paper. Each drawing corresponded to a value on a 90-point scale (10 = thinnest figure, 90 = heaviest figure) that was located beneath the silhouettes. Using this scale, participants responded to four questions: (a) "Which drawing looks most like your own figure?" (CURRENT), (b) "Which figure do you most want to look like?" (OWN IDEAL), (c) "Which figure do you think most women (men) want to look like or find most attractive" (PEER IDEAL), and (d) "Which figure do you think men (women) find most attractive?" (ATTRACTIVE).[1]

Nine additional body silhouettes of the other sex were also shown to participants. Respondents selected (a) the silhouette they found most attractive (OTHER ATTRACTIVE) and (b) the silhouette they thought that the other sex would most want to look like (OTHER SEX IDEAL).

Self-Reported Body Weight and Body Satisfaction

Single item self-report measures were used to assess current height, current weight, ideal height, and ideal weight. Quetelet's index (current weight/height^2) was used as a measure of body mass (Garrow and Webster, 1985). The validity of self-reported height and weight data has been established

in previous research. Stewart (1982) reported validity coefficients close to unity ($r > .97$) for assessments of self-reported and measured weight obtained from females and males. The correlation between actual and self-reported weight is also high ($r > .97$) among participants who perceived themselves to be overweight. These findings suggest that little distortion was introduced into our assessment procedure by using self-reported weight.

Three single-item self-report measures were used to assess different aspects of body dissatisfaction:

> Weight: "I wish I was (a) a little thinner, (b) a lot thinner, (c) no different (d) a little heavier, (e) a lot heavier."
> Height: "I wish I was: (a) a little shorter, (b) a lot shorter, (c) no different (d) a little taller, (e) a lot taller."
> Physical status: "I am: (a) very skinny, (b) a little skinny, (c) neither skinny nor fat, (d) a little fat, (e) very fat."

Responses to these three scales were examined separately rather than combined into a single measure of body dissatisfaction. For each scale, we examined the proportion of respondents endorsing each of the five response categories. This strategy permitted us to examine the magnitude and direction of weight, height, and physical status dissatisfaction.

Dieting Behavior

A 12-item survey of dieting strategies was used to assess current dieting behavior. Items were chosen from a pool of 25 dieting strategies employed by college-age women and men (Klesges, Mizes, and Klesges, 1987). Items were selected to represent a range of dieting behaviors, from harmless to harmful. Dieting behaviors ranged from reducing sweets and skipping meals to self-induced vomiting and the use of diuretics and laxatives. Respondents indicated which dieting strategies they had used during the 6 months preceding the survey.

Items assessing body weight, body satisfaction (weight, height, and physical status), and dieting behavior were embedded in a longer 39-item questionnaire that was designed to assess recollections of body dissatisfaction during childhood, adolescence, and young adulthood. The reliability and validity of this instrument has not been established, and the results are not used in the present analyses.

Procedures

Questionnaires were administered during regularly scheduled classes. Students were informed that the survey was being conducted to learn more about what people like and dislike about their body figures and how these feelings relate to dieting behavior. Student participation was voluntary, and questionnaires were completed anonymously. Silhouette ratings were completed first, followed by assessments of current weight, ideal weight, and body dissatisfaction.

☙ RESULTS

Validity of Silhouette Ratings

For both sexes, CURRENT ratings were strongly correlated with body mass (women $r[77] = .69$, $p < .001$; men, $r[108] = .75$, $p < .001$) and body weight (women, $r[77] = .65$ $p < .001$, men, $r[113] = .72$ $p < .001$). These findings are comparable to those from a study validating the use of the Stunkard silhouettes as an anthropometric measure of adult body size (Mueller, Joos, and Schull, 1985). For adult participants, correlations between body mass and silhouette choice ranged from .65 to .84 for untrained observers and from .85 to .92 for trained observers. Our college students were about as accurate in their self-ratings as were independent but untrained judges.

An alternate means for assessing validity is the correspondence between self-reported weight dissatisfaction (current weight minus ideal weight) and body image dissatisfaction as measured by body figure ratings (CURRENT minus OWN IDEAL). Here, too, the correspondence between measures is strong: for women, $r(76) = .76$, $p < .001$; for men, $r(110) = .79$, $p < .001$.

Evidence for the external validity of the body figure ratings is found in the association between body dissatisfaction and dieting behavior. Approximately 17% of the women used laxatives, diuretics, or self-induced vomiting as techniques for reducing weight (strategies reported by only 1% of our male sample). As expected, women who employed these strategies expressed significantly greater body dissatisfaction (CURRENT minus OWN IDEAL: $M = 12.3$) than did women who did not use these strategies ($M = 7.1$; $t[83] = 1.97$, $p < .05$).

Body Figure Ratings

A 2 (Sex) $\times$ 6 (Rating Task) repeated measures analysis of variance yielded significant effects for Sex ($F[1, 197] = 45.0$, $P < .0001$), Rating Task ($F[5, 193] = 13.4$, $p < .0001$), and Sex x Rating Task interaction ($F[5, 193] = 43$, $p < .0001$).

Because multiple planned comparisons were conducted (six comparisons within each sex) we used an unweighted Bonferonni adjustment to control for an inflated Type I error rate (Rosenthal and Rubin, 1984). This set individual significance levels at .008, yielding an overall alpha of .05 per set of comparisons.

Female Ratings

The body preferences of women revealed a strong bias towards thinness (CURRENT minus OWN IDEAL: $M = 8.6$, paired $t[86] = 10.3$, $p < .0001$). Approximately half of the

women selected OWN IDEAL and ATTRACTIVE figures that were at least one body silhouette thinner than their own current size.

As predicted, the greatest bias towards thinness was found in women's perceptions of other women's body figure preferences (Figure 1). The silhouettes that women selected as most desired by female peers were significantly thinner than (a) the silhouettes that women actually selected as ideal (OWN IDEAL minus PEER IDEAL: $M = 3.7$, paired $t[86] = 6.1$, $p < .0001$) and (b) the silhouette that women selected as most attractive to men (ATTRACTIVE minus OWN IDEAL: $M = 2.0$, paired $t[86] = 2.7$, $p = .009$).

The belief that "other women" value thin figures was also evident in the greater proportion of women selecting a PEER IDEAL that was thinner than their own ideal size: 50 % of the women identified their peers' ideal figure as thinner than their own ideal size (PEER IDEAL minus OWN IDEAL < 0), whereas only 6% of the women identified their peers' ideal figure as heavier than their own ideal size (PEER IDEAL minus OWN IDEAL > 0).

Consistent with previous findings, women overestimated the extent to which men perceive thin women as attractive (women's ATTRACTIVE minus men's OTHER ATTRACTIVE: $M = -5.4$, $t[202] = 5.7$, $p < .001$). Most notably, 69% of the women regarded the three thinnest silhouettes as most attractive to men, although only 25% of the men selected these figures as most attractive to them.

Figure 1 *Mean body figure ratings of women (top) and men (bottom). Total scale values ranged from 10 to 90. (Adapted from Stunkard et al., 1983.)*

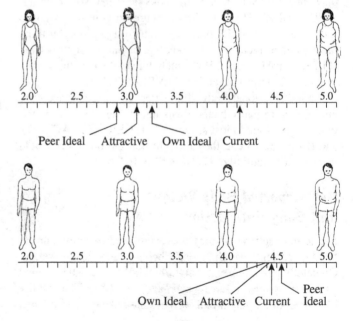

Male Ratings

Men selected a PEER IDEAL that was significantly heavier than the male silhouette that peers actually selected as ideal or attractive to women (PEER IDEAL minus OWN IDEAL: $M = 1.3$, paired $t[117] = 2.1$, $p = .04$; PEER IDEAL minus ATTRACTIVE: $M = 1.4$, paired $t[116] = 2.8$ $p = .005$). Like women, men exaggerated their peers' preferences for a stereotypic body shape; in this case, for a larger physique (and presumably more muscular shape).

Like women, men also misjudged the body size that was most attractive to the other sex, overestimating the extent to which women view large (and presumably muscular) figures as attractive (men's ATTRACTIVE minus women's OTHER ATTRACTIVE: $M = 1.8$, $t[201] = 1.98$, $p < .05$).

Unlike women, men did not reveal a uniform preference for a particular body size; 34% of the men wished to be thinner (OWN IDEAL minus CURRENT < 0), whereas 36% of the men wished to be heavier (OWN IDEAL minus CURRENT > 0). Self-reported weight dissatisfaction revealed a similar pattern of discontent; 41.5% of the men expressed a desire to be either "a little thinner" or "a lot thinner," whereas 38% of the men expressed a desire to be "a little heavier" or "a lot heavier."

Gender Differences in Body Figure Dissatisfaction

Body dissatisfaction in women invariably reflected a desire to be slimmer. Not a single woman selected an ideal figure that was heavier than her own current size. This bias towards slimness was not the product of distorted perceptions of their own body (women erroneously viewing themselves as extremely overweight). Only 6% of the women described themselves as "very fat"; yet 4 times as many women (24%) wished to be "a lot thinner." These findings suggest that although women do not view themselves as very fat, the preference is for much thinner figures.

Unlike women, men were equally divided in their desire for either slimmer or heavier figures. This variability indicates that men express significantly less body dissatisfaction than do women (Figure 1: for women, CURRENT minus OWN IDEAL: M = 8.6, $SD = 7.6$; for men, CURRENT minus IDEAL: $M = 0.7$, $SD = 11.5$; $t[201] = 5.5$, $p < .01$). However, sex differences in body dissatisfaction disappear when we compared the absolute value of CURRENT minus OWN IDEAL discrepancies among men and women (women, $M = 8.6$, $SD = 7.6$; men, $M = 7.0$, $SD = 9.2$; $t[201] = 1.3$, $p < .10$).[2]

✄ DISCUSSION

The current findings are based on our respondents' perceptions of their current body size, ideal body size, and the body ideal attributed to same and other-sex peers. Although individuals may distort estimates of their current body size, this distortion is not likely to have biased our results. We have not sought to assess the actual body parameters of our respondents but rather their perceived size relative to the ideal figure attributed to same and other-sex peers.

Women in our sample shared a common view of an ideal female body size. Although previous research has shown that women hold an inaccurate view of the values of men in relation to body size, the current research shows that this distortion also applies to perceptions of women's values. The college women in our sample overestimated the extent to which thin figures were attractive to men, and women also overestimated the extent to which thin figures were held as ideal by female peers. Although partially accurate, these perceptions exaggerate the extent to which slender female figures are favored by peers of either sex. Women do indeed wish to be thinner than their current size, but in aggregate the ideal size desired by female peers is not as thin as women believe it to be. Similarly, women correctly perceived that men were attracted to body figures that were thinner than the average body size of women in our sample; but men did not prefer figures that were as thin as the figure women deemed most attractive to men.

For many women, the pressure to achieve a thin body figure may arise from comparisons of their own figure with the ideal figure attributed to female peers. Ironically, our findings suggest that women exaggerate the extent to which female peers desire thin figures.

Why do women exaggerate the desirability of thin figures? This bias can be attributed to the social pressures placed on women to pursue thin figures. However, the failure to judge accurately the body preferences of peers is not unique to women. Men in our sample also exaggerated the desirability of achieving the stereotypic ideal male physique, which appears to be heavier (and probably more muscular) than the average male body. These findings suggest a new interpretation of women's tendency to exaggerate male preferences for slender physiques (Cohn et al., 1987; Fallon and Rozin, 1985; Rozin and Fallon, 1988; Zellner et al., 1989). This misperception may not be due to exaggerated weight concerns but, rather, to biases associated with stereotypic judgments.

Previous research has revealed that women react more negatively than men to departures from their ideal body size (Pliner, Chaiken, and Flett, 1990; Rozin and Fallon, 1988). Women, for example, are more likely than men to perceive social penalties attached to being overweight (Tiggemann and Rothblum, 1988). Similarly, women are more likely than men to perceive social benefits associated with achieving their ideal weight (Klesges et al., 1987). Our data suggest that an additional pressure may cause women to react more negatively than men to departures from their ideal weight: Women appear to share a common definition of an ideal figure. Almost all women regarded thin figures as desirable. In contrast, men revealed less consensus in their views of an ideal physique. Some men valued figures that were thinner than their peers' ideal, whereas other men valued figures that were heavier. Thus, when men fail to achieve their ideal size they may not perceive a deviation from a well-established norm thought to be shared by same and other-sex peers. For women, however, the discrepancy between current and ideal figure implies a departure from a standard of attractiveness that they believe is accepted by men and women alike. Deviation from this perceived norm may make women especially self-conscious and may generate additional pressure to lose weight.

Men may display greater consensus in their perceptions of an ideal body shape than the current results suggest. Our assessment of desirable body shapes focused exclusively on a single body dimension, weight. Muscularity, however, is a concern of many males. A study of 10th- and 12th-grade boys revealed that one-half of the respondents desired larger biceps, wrists, shoulders, and chests (Huenemann, Shapiro, Hampton, and Mitchell, 1966). A desire for larger chests and arms has also been observed among college men (Calden, Lundy, and Schlafer, 1959). The body silhouettes employed in the current study only depicted changes in weight status. Future research should test the hypothesis that males display greater variability in their perception of an ideal body shape by including assessments of muscularity as well as weight.

Men's tendency to exaggerate the attractiveness of large physiques may place underweight men at risk for disturbances in body image. In one of the few studies addressing this issue, Harmatz, Gronendyke, and Thomas (1985) found that underweight college men viewed themselves as negatively as overweight college women viewed themselves, although these women are the usual focus of health professionals. As society becomes more fitness conscious, there may be a shift in the cultural definition of an ideal male physique, with greater emphasis placed on adolescent males attaining large and muscular figures. Indeed, a recent survey of 150 high schools revealed that almost 7% of 12th-grade male students had used anabolic steroids to increase their body size (Buckley et al., 1988). This percentage is higher than the estimated incidence of anorexia (Andersen, 1983) and is comparable to the reported incidence of bulimia among female high school students (Mizes, 1985).

Studies of body dissatisfaction have typically employed samples of Caucasian females and males, as did the current research. Future research should examine ethnically diverse samples for the same judgmental biases that have been observed among Caucasians. Such research should help to identify the mechanisms that are responsible for the development of ideal body shapes and the consequences, both for dieting behavior and self-concept, of holding various ideals and perceptions of norms of body size.

ENDNOTES

[1]Thompson and Psaltis (1988) reported that seemingly minor changes in instructions produced significant differences in the CURRENT silhouettes chosen by respondents. Respondents in their study were more likely to chose larger CURRENT figures when asked to select on the basis of how they felt they looked rather than how they thought they looked. The present study instructed subjects to select silhouettes based on how they thought they looked.

[2]Sex differences in current minus ideal weight discrepancies also disappear when examining absolute values (CURRENT WEIGHT minus IDEAL WEIGHT: women, $M = 12.4$, $SD = 12.3$; men, $M = 10.9$, $SD = 8.6$; $t[201] = 1.0$, $p = .17$).

REFERENCES

Andersen, A. E. (1983). Anorexia nervosa and bulimia: A spectrum of eating disorders. *Journal of Adolescent Health Care, 4,* 15–21.

Buckley, W. E., Yesalis, C. E., Friedl, K. E., Anderson, W. A., Streit, A. L., and Wright, J. E. (1988). Estimated prevalence of anabolic steroid use among male high school seniors. *Journal of the American Medical Association, 260,* 3441–3445.

Calden, G., Lundy, R. M., and Schlafer, R. J. (1959). Sex differences in body concepts. *Journal of Consulting Psychology, 23,* 378.

Cohn, L. D., Adler, N. E., Irwin, C. E., Jr., Millstein, S. G., Kegeles, S. M., and Stone, G. (1987). Body-figure preferences in male and female adolescents. *Journal of Abnormal Psychology, 96,* 276–279.

Dwyer, J. T., Feldman, J. J., Selzer, C. C., and Mayer, J. (1969). Adolescent attitudes toward weight and appearance. *Journal of Nutrition Education, 1,* 14–19.

Fallon, A. E., and Rozin, P. (1985), Sex differences in perceptions of desirable body shape. *Journal of Abnormal Psychology, 94,* 102–105.

Garner, D. M., and Garfinkel, P. E., Schwartz, D., and Thompson, M. (1980). Cultural expectations of thinness in women. *Psychological Reports, 47,* 483–491.

Garrow, J. S., and Webster, J. (1985). Quetelet's index (W/H²) as a measure of fatness. *International Journal of Obesity, 9,* 147–153.

Harmatz, M. G., Gronendyke, J., and Thomas, T. (1985). The underweight male: The unrecognized problem group of body image research. *Journal of Obesity and Weight Regulation, 41,* 258–267.

Huenemann, R. L., Shapiro, L. R., Hampton, M. C., and Mitchell, B. W. (1966). A longitudinal study of gross body composition and body conformation and their association with food and activity in a teen-age population. *American Journal of Clinical Nutrition, 18,* 325–338.

Klesges, L. M., Mizes, J. S., and Klesges, R. C. (1987). Self-help dieting strategies in college males and females. *International Journal of Eating Disorders, 6,* 409–417.

Mazur, A. (1986). U.S. trends in feminine beauty and overadaptation. *Journal of Sex Research, 22,* 281–303.

Mizes, J. S. (1985). Bulimia: A review of its symptomatology and treatment. *Advances in Behavioral Research Therapy, 7,* 91–142.

Mueller, W. H., Joos, S. K., and Schull, W. J. (1985). Alternative measurements of obesity; Accuracy of body silhouettes and reported weights and heights in a Mexican-American sample. *International Journal of Obesity, 9,* 193–200.

Pliner, P., Chaiken, S., and Flett, G. L. (1990). Gender differences in concern with body weight and physical appearance over the life span. *Personality and Social Psychology Bulletin, 16,* 263–273.

Rosenthal, R., and Rubin, D. B. (1984). Multiple contrasts and ordered Bonferroni procedures. *Journal of Educational Psychology, 76,* 1028–1034.

Rozin, R., and Fallon, A. E. (1988). Body image, attitudes to weight and misperceptions of figure preferences of the opposite sex: A comparison of men and women in two generations. *Journal of Abnormal Psychology, 97,* 342–345.

Silverstein, B., Peterson, B., and Perdue, L. (1986). Some correlates of the thin standard of bodily attractiveness for women. *International Journal of Eating Disorders, 5,* 895–905.

Stewart, A. I. (1982). The reliability and validity of self-reported weight. *Journal of Chronic Diseases, 35,* 295–309.

Stiles, D. A., Gibbons, J. L., and Schnellmann, J. (1990). Opposite-sex ideal in the U.S.A. and Mexico as perceived by young adolescents. *Journal of Cross-Cultural Psychology, 21,* 180–199.

Striegel-Moore, R. H., McAvay, G., and Rodin, J. (1986). Psychological and behavioral correlates of feeling fat in women. *International Journal of Eating Disorders, 5,* 937–947.

Stunkard, A. J., Sorensen, T., and Schulsinger, F. (1983). Use of the Danish adoption register for the study of obesity and thinness. In S. Kety (Ed.), *The genetics of neurological and psychiatric disorders* (pp. 115–120). New York: Raven Press.

Thompson, M., and Psaltis, B. A. (1988). A replication and extension of Fallon and Rozin (1985). *International Journal of Eating Disorders, 7,* 813–817.

Tiggemann, M., and Rothblum, E. D. (1988). Gender difference in social consequences of perceived overweight in the United States and Australia. *Sex Roles, 18,* 75–86.

Zellner, D. A., Harner, D. E., and Adler, R. L. (1989). Effects of eating abnormalities and gender on perceptions of desirable body shape. *Journal of Abnormal Psychology, 98,* 93–96.

ℰ Questions

1. What are the implications of the finding that women believe an ideal woman's body in the eye of their peers is thinner than what men find most attractive? What are the consequences of this misperception?

2. According to the results presented here, who is more dissatisfied with their current body shapes—men or women—or are they equally dissatisfied? Is anybody satisfied with his or her body? What does it say about the power of social norms if everybody is dissatisfied with his or her body shape?

3. When it comes to today's standards of ideal body shapes, are young women more influenced by what they think men want, what they think other women value, or by sources not mentioned in the article? What might these other sources be?

4. In the more than ten years since this research was conducted, have cultural pressures young men feel to maintain an ideal body shape changed? How do these pressures affect men? How are they different from pressures that women feel?

Chapter 5:
Personality

Personality

Marsha Hatcher/SuperStock

Prologue

Identical Twins Raised Apart

The identical twin boys were separated at the age of 37 days and were adopted by two different working-class families. Coincidentally, both were named Jim by their adoptive families. They did not meet each other again until they were 39 years old. Both Jims liked math in school, but neither liked spelling. At 10 years of age, they both developed sinus headaches; a few years later, they both developed migraine headaches. They both used the same words to describe their head pain. The twins had identical pulse rates and blood pressures, and both put on 10 pounds of weight at the same time in their lives. Both Jims were clerical workers who enjoyed woodworking, served as volunteers for police agencies, enjoyed spending their vacations in the tropics, had married and divorced women named Linda, chewed their nails, owned dogs named Toy, and drove Chevrolets.

Bridget and Dorothy, also identical twins, were 39 years old when they were reunited. Each came to their meeting wearing seven rings on her fingers, two bracelets on one wrist, and a watch and a bracelet on the other. Although the two women were raised by families of widely different socioeconomic levels, their personalities were very similar. The most striking difference between them was that the twin raised by the family of modest means had problems with her teeth.

Oskar and Jack were born in Trinidad. Their mother, a German, took Oskar back to Germany, where he was raised as a Catholic. He became a member of a Nazi youth group. Jack was raised by his father in the Caribbean as a Jew. He spent part of his adolescence on a kibbutz in Israel. At the time of their reunion, Oskar lived in Germany, and Jack, in southern California. When the twins met at the airport, both were wearing wire-rimmed glasses and two-pocket shirts with epaulets. Both had moustaches. They both liked spicy foods and sweet liqueurs, tended to fall asleep while watching television, kept rubber bands on their wrists, thought it funny to sneeze in a crowd of people, flushed the toilet before using it, and read magazines from back to front. Although their backgrounds were

D. Gorton

The reunion of this pair of twins, the Jims, prompted Dr. Thomas Bouchard to initiate the Minnesota Study of Twins Reared Apart.

very different, their scores on a widely used personality test were similar.

These striking cases of identical twins reunited in adulthood suggest that heredity plays an important role in shaping personality. However, like all pieces of anecdotal evidence, such case histories must be regarded as clues, subject to confirmation by careful scientific evaluation. The Minnesota Study of Twins Reared Apart is one of several research projects designed to determine the roles of heredity and environment in the development of personality. ■

Common experience tells us that no one else is just like us, but how do we describe these differences? If you were asked "How does your best friend differ from you?" you would probably use descriptions that generalize that person's behaviors, such as "He tends to see only the good in people, whereas I'm more realistic." or "She's a bit of a neat-freak compared with me." We try to convey something about our friend that covers more than just the here and now.

Everyday observations like these provide a starting point for psychology's study of personality. But psychology's approach to studying personality is more than informal generalizations. To psychologists, the concept generally has a much more specific definition: **Personality** is a particular pattern of behavior and thinking that prevails across time and situations and differentiates one person from another. The goal of psychologists who study personality is to discover the causes of individual differences in behavior.

What types of research efforts are necessary to study personality? Some psychologists devote their efforts to the development of tests that can reliably measure differences in personality. Others try to identify the events—biological and environmental—that cause people to behave as they do. Thus, research on human personality requires two kinds of effort: identifying personality characteristics and determining the variables that produce and control them (Buss, 1995). Keep in mind that in the study of personality, we must be careful to avoid the nominal fallacy, is the false belief that the causes of an event are explained by simply naming and identifying them. Merely *identifying* and *describing* a personality characteristic is not the same as *explaining* it.

---

personality   A particular pattern of behavior and thinking prevailing across time and situations that differentiates one person from another.

personality types   Different categories into which personality characteristics can be assigned based on factors such as developmental experiences or physical characteristics.

personality trait   An enduring personal characteristic that reveals itself in a particular pattern of behavior in a variety of situations.

Trait Theories of Personality

Among the first categorizations of personality was one based on the concept of personality traits. Personality theorists who study traits use the term much in the way we often think of personality in everyday life—to denote a set of personal characteristics that determine the different ways we act and react in a variety of situations (Sneed, McCrae, & Funder, 1998). However, as you will see, trait theorists do not all agree on exactly which characteristics to include. Let's begin by differentiating personality *types* from personality *traits*.

Personality Types and Traits

The earliest known explanation for individual differences in personality was proposed by the Greek physician Hippocrates in the fourth century BC and refined by his successor Galen in the second century AD. The theory was based on then-common medical beliefs that originated with the ancient Greeks. The body was thought to contain four humors, or fluids: yellow bile, black bile, phlegm, and blood. People were classified according to the disposition supposedly produced by the predominance of one of these humors in their systems. Choleric people, who had an excess of yellow bile, were bad-tempered and irritable. Melancholic people, who had an excess of black bile, had gloomy and pessimistic temperaments. Phlegmatic people, whose bodies contained an excessive amount of phlegm, were sluggish, calm, and unexcitable. Sanguine people had a preponderance of blood (*sanguis*), which made them cheerful and passionate. (See FIGURE 1.)

Later biological investigations, of course, discredited the humoral theory. However, the notion that people could be divided into different **personality types**—different categories into which personality characteristics can be assigned based on factors such as developmental experiences—persisted long afterward. After identifying and defining personality types, theorists must determine whether these types actually exist and whether knowing an individual's personality type can lead to valid predictions about his or her behavior in different situations.

Most investigators today reject the idea that people can be assigned to discrete categories. Instead, they generally conceive of individual differences in personality as being differences in degree, not kind. Rather than focusing on types, many current investigators prefer to measure the degree to which an individual expresses a particular personality trait. A **personality trait** is an enduring personal characteristic that reveals itself in a particular pattern of behavior in different situations. A simple example illustrates the difference between types and traits. We could classify people into two different *types*: tall people and short people. Note that this is an either/or categorization. We do use these categorical terms in everyday language, but we all recognize that height is best conceived of as a *trait*—a dimension on which people differ along a wide range of values. If we measure the height of a

[**FIGURE 1**] Characteristics of the four humors, according to a medieval artist: (a) *choleric*—violent and aggressive temperament; (b) *melancholic*—gloomy and pessimistic temperament; (c) *phlegmatic*—sluggish, relaxed, and dull temperament; and (d) *sanguine*— outgoing, passionate, and fun-loving temperament.

Illustrations © Bettmann/CORBIS.

(a)   (b)   (c)   (d)

large sample of people, we will find instances all along the distribution, from very short to very tall, with most people falling in between the extremes. (See FIGURE 2.) It is not that people are only either tall or short (analogous to personality types) but that people vary in the extent to which they show tallness or shortness (analogous to personality traits).

We've all had experiences with people who behave in different characteristic ways: Some are friendly, some are mean, some are lazy, some are timid, and some are reckless. Trait theories of personality fit this commonsense view. However, personality traits are not the same as patterns of behavior: They are factors that underlie these patterns and are responsible for them; they produce physical or material states that are the causes of our behaviors. This does not mean that the acquisition of personality traits is strictly biological and that learning is not involved. However, if our personality traits are changed through learning, those changes must have a neurological basis in the brain. In other words, we carry our personality traits around with us in our heads—or, more exactly, in our brains.

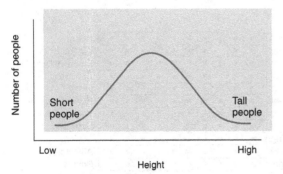

[**FIGURE 2**] The distribution of height. We can measure people's heights, a trait, on a continuous scale. We can also look at the extremes and divide people into the categories of short and tall types.

Identification of Personality Traits

Trait theorists are still in the process of discovering, describing, and naming the regular behavior patterns that people exhibit. In this section, we introduce several influential trait-categorization models: the theories of Gordon Allport, Raymond Cattell, and Hans Eysenck, as well as the five-factor model and related frameworks proposed by other trait psychologists.

Allport's Search for Traits Gordon Allport (1897–1967) was one of the first psychologists to search systematically for a basic core of personality traits. He began his work by identifying all words in an unabridged dictionary of the English language that described aspects of personality (Allport & Odbert, 1936); he found approximately 18,000 such entries. Allport then conducted analyses that identified those words that described only stable personality characteristics. He eliminated words that represented temporary states, such as *flustered,* or evaluations, such as *admirable.*

Why did Allport undertake this exercise? He believed that the considerable extent to which trait labels appear in human languages attests to the importance of traits in how people think about themselves and others. Indirectly, then, the wealth of trait terms in English helped confirm his belief that a well-developed trait theory would have value in understanding human functioning. Allport believed that traits are neuropsychological properties that lead to behavioral consistency over time and contexts by producing functional similarity in the way each of us interprets and experiences events. That is, people with a particular trait react similarly across situations, because they experience a unique sense of similarity across those situations that guides their feelings, thoughts, and behavior. Evidence suggests that some traits persist over time. In a 44-year longitudinal study, researchers found that creativity and some aspects of personality remained consistent over time (Feist & Barron, 2003).

According to Allport, some traits have greater influence on their possessors than others. The most powerful of all are those he termed *cardinal traits.* Cardinal traits exercise a strong unifying influence on a person's behavior. Allport believed that these traits are rare, but that people characterized by them clearly stand out from the crowd. Examples include Adolf Hitler and his relentless exercise of oppressive power, Nelson Mandela's commitment to justice, and Mother Teresa's selfless devotion. In contrast, *central traits* are less singular in their influence than cardinal traits but capture important characteristics of an individual. When we say that someone is honest and warm to distinguish that person from others, we capture Allport's meaning of central traits. Finally, Allport's category of *secondary traits* includes characteristics that have only a minor influence on the consistency of individual behavior. An example would be a person's tendency to change jobs frequently.

Allport's research stimulated other psychologists to think about personality in terms of traits or dispositions. Most modern trait theories can be traced to Allport's earlier theoretical work. Like Allport, modern trait theorists maintain that only when we know how to describe an individual's personality will we be able to explain it.

Cattell: Sixteen Personality Factors

Raymond Cattell (1905–1998) used Allport's list of 18,000 trait words as a starting point for his own theory of traits. Cattell winnowed this large word set down to 171 adjectives that he believed made up a relatively complete set of distinct *surface traits* (those that are apparent in observable behaviors). He then used the process of factor analysis to identify clusters of these traits that he believed in turn represented underlying traits. Cattell analyzed questionnaire responses from thousands of people in this manner; eventually he identified the 16 key personality

---

extroversion The tendency to seek the company of other people, to engage in conversation and other social behaviors with them, and to be spontaneous.

introversion The tendency to avoid the company of other people, to be inhibited and cautious; shyness.

neuroticism The tendency to be anxious, worried, and full of guilt.

Surface traits, such as friendliness, are those traits that are obvious to others.

Jose Luis Pelaez, Inc./Corbis

factors shown in FIGURE 3. He referred to these 16 traits as *source traits,* because in his view, they were the cornerstones on which personality is built. These 16 traits group the surface traits together into different independent contributions to an individual's personality. Figure 3 illustrates a personality profile of a hypothetical individual rated on Cattell's 16 factors. Think of someone you know well. Do you think you would be able to predict how they would score on these factors? Do you think these factors would help you predict the behavior of someone you did not know?

Eysenck: Three Factors

Hans Eysenck (1916–1997) also used factor analysis to devise a theory of personality (Eysenck, 1970; Eysenck & Eysenck, 1985). His research identified three important factors: extroversion, neuroticism, and psychoticism. These factors are bipolar dimensions. That is, extroversion is the opposite of introversion, neuroticism is the opposite of emotional stability, and psychoticism is the opposite of self-control. Individuals are rated on a continuum between the poles of these factors. People high in **extroversion** have an outgoing nature and a high level of activity. In general, extroverts like people and socializing, are spontaneous, and take risks. **Introversion** is at the opposite end of the scale: Introverts are shy, reserved, and careful. People at the high end of **neuroticism** are fraught with worry and guilt and are moody and unstable. Those who score

---

[**FIGURE 3**] A hypothetical personality profile using Cattell's 16 personality factors.

(Adapted from the 16PF® Practitioner Report. Copyright © 2005 by the Institute for Personality and Ability Testing, Inc., Champaign, Illinois, USA. Reproduced with permission. All rights reserved.)

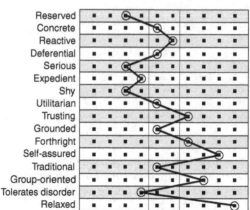

low on neuroticism are even-tempered and are characterized by **emotional stability.** **Psychoticism** involves an aggressive, egocentric, and antisocial nature; in contrast, a person with **self-control** has a kind and considerate nature and is obedient of rules and laws. Note that Eysenck's use of the term "psychoticism" is different from its use by most clinical psychologists; his term refers to antisocial tendencies, not to a mental illness. A person at the extreme end of the distribution of psychoticism in Eysenck's model would receive the diagnosis of antisocial personality disorder.

TABLE 1 lists some questions that have high correlations or factor *loadings* on Eysenck's three dimensions. The best way to understand the meaning of these traits is to read the questions and to imagine the kinds of people who would answer yes or no to each group. If a factor loading is preceded by a minus sign, it means that people who say no receive high scores on the trait; otherwise, high scores are obtained by those who answer yes.

Eysenck argued that the most important aspects of a person's personality are determined by the combination of that person's positions on the three dimensions of extroversion, neuroticism, and psychoticism—just as colors are produced by the combinations of the three dimensions of hue, saturation, and brightness. FIGURE 4 illustrates the effects of various combinations of the first two of these dimensions—extroversion and neuroticism—and relates them to the four dispositions described by Hippocrates and Galen.

[**FIGURE 4**] Eysenck's theory illustrated for two factors. According to Eysenck, the two dimensions of neuroticism (labeled here as stable versus unstable) and introversion–extroversion combine to form a variety of personality characteristics. The four personality types based on the Greek theory of humors are shown in the center.

(From Eysenck, H. J. (1973). *The inequality of man.* London: Temple Smith. Reprinted with permission from the H. J. Eysenck Memorial Fund.)

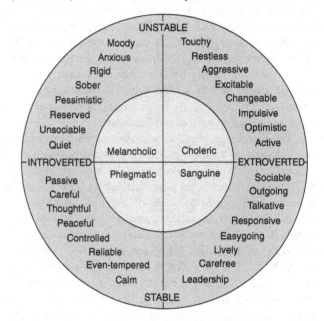

Eysenck's theory has received considerable support, especially from his own laboratory, which was highly productive. Most trait theorists accept the existence of his three factors, because they have emerged in factor analyses performed by many different researchers.

The Five-Factor Model Recall that Allport attempted to discover personality traits through an analysis of the words we use in everyday language to talk about personality. Languages reflect the observations of members of a culture; that is, people invent words to describe distinctions they notice. An analysis of such distinctions by Tupes and Christal (1961), replicated by Norman (1963), has led to the five-factor model (Costa & McCrae, 1998a; McCrae & Costa, 1997, 1999, 2004). The **five-factor model** proposes that personality is composed of five primary dimensions: neuroticism, extroversion, openness, agreeableness, and conscientiousness. These factors are

[**TABLE 1**] Some Items from Eysenck's Tests of Extroversion, Neuroticism, and Psychoticism

Factor	Loading
Extroversion	
Do you like mixing with people?	.70
Do you like plenty of bustle and excitement around you?	.65
Are you rather lively?	.63
Neuroticism	
Do you often feel "fed up"?	.67
Do you often feel lonely?	.60
Does your mood often go up and down?	.59
Psychoticism	
Do good manners and cleanliness matter much to you?	−.55
Does it worry you if you know there are mistakes in your work?	−.53
Do you like taking risks for fun?	.51

Source: Adapted from Eysenck, H. J., & Eysenck, M. W. (1985). *Personality and individual differences: A natural science approach.* New York: Plenum Press. Reprinted with kind permission from Springer Science and Business Media and from the H. J. Eysenck Memorial Fund.

emotional stability The tendency to be relaxed and at peace with oneself.

psychoticism The tendency to be aggressive, egocentric, and antisocial.

self-control Behavior that produces a larger, long-term reward when people are faced with the choice between it and a smaller, short-term reward; also the tendency to be kind, considerate, and obedient of laws and rules.

five-factor model A theory stating that personality is composed of five primary dimensions: neuroticism, extroversion, openness, agreeableness, and conscientiousness. This theory was developed using factor analyses of ratings of the words people use to describe personality characteristics.

measured by the **Neuroticism, Extroversion, and Openness Personality Inventory or (NEO-PI-R).** (The name was chosen before the factors of agreeableness and conscientiousness were added, and the "R" stands for "revised." If you want a more useful mnemonic to remember the dimensions, think of the acronym OCEAN for openness, conscientiousness, extroversion, agreeableness, and neuroticism.)

The NEO-PI-R consists of 240 items that can potentially be used to describe the person being evaluated. The test items can be answered by the participant or by someone he or she knows well (Costa & McCrae, 1998b). The test items are brief sentences, such as "I really like most people I meet" or (for ratings by someone else) "She has a very active imagination." The person completing the test rates the accuracy of each item on a scale of 1 to 5, from *strong disagreement* to *strong agreement.* The sums of the answers to different sets of items represent scores on each of the five factors.

The five-factor model is regarded by many personality psychologists as a robust model of personality (Wiggins & Trapnell, 1997; Wiggins & Pincus, 2002; Paunonen, 2003). Although it originated in the factor analysis tradition of Cattell, it seems to incorporate some of the traits suggested by Eysenck, especially neuroticism and extroversion (Goldberg, 1993). It has considerable cross-cultural applicability (e.g., McCrae et al., 1998; Allik & McCrae, 2002, 2004). Self-ratings on the NEO-PI-R agree closely with ratings by family members (García, et al., 2007). Furthermore, it predicts other aspects that seem related to personality. DeNeve and Cooper (1998) showed that the five factors can be used to predict subjective well-being, and Vollrath (2000) found moderate predictability for responses to "daily hassles" experienced by college students. Barrick, Mount, and Judge (2001) reported a meta-analysis of studies measuring job performance relative to the five personality dimensions. Generally speaking, extroversion seems to predict success in jobs that require leadership (managerial positions) or in jobs demanding the ability to improvise to reach goals (sales positions). Not surprisingly, conscientiousness predicts success across job classifications.

Is there a biological basis for these five factors? A rapidly accumulating body of evidence points to a very strong degree of heritability (Jang, Livesley, & Vernon, 1996; Loehlin, et al., 1998; McCrae et al., 2000; Livesley, Jang, & Vernon, 2003). Correlations in traits are higher within monozygotic twins than dizygotic twins (Vernon, et al., 2008). The data suggest that environmental factors pale beside genetic influences.

Neuroticism, Extroversion, and Openness Personality Inventory (NEO-PI-R)   The instrument used to measure the elements described in the five-factor model (neuroticism, extroversion, openness, agreeableness, and conscientiousness).

Machiavellianism   A personality trait measuring skill at manipulating other people for one's own ends.

psychopathy   A personality trait measuring impulsivity and lack of empathy or remorse for harm caused by one's actions.

narcissism   A personality trait measuring grandiosity and feelings of superiority.

Finally, five is not necessarily the final number of fundamental personality dimensions. Jackson (Jackson & Tremblay, 2002) argued that a six-factor model may be more appropriate. According to Jackson, the conscientiousness factor in the traditional five-factor model actually represents two distinct dimensions. One of these component dimensions, *methodicalness,* reflects planfulness and a need for orderliness. The other, *industriousness,* is characterized by perseverance and achievement orientation.

The Dark Triad Some personality psychologists have suggested that a special cluster of traits may underlie socially offensive personalities. For example, it has been noted that habitual criminals sometimes exhibit great skill in manipulating individuals, while exhibiting little sign of the regret that most people feel when their actions harm or offend others. The skill at manipulation has been called **Machiavellianism** after the Italian writer of the Renaissance classic on politics, *The Prince.* A pronounced lack of empathy and a high degree of impulsivity has been identified with a trait known as **psychopathy.** Paulhus and Williams (2002) suggested that these two traits, together with a trait called **narcissism,** which leads to grandiosity and feelings of superiority, formed a "Dark Triad" of overlapping negative traits. The Dark Triad is considered distinct from the Big Five, although low to moderate correlations are found between them (Jakobwitz & Egan, 2006; Egan & McCorkindale, 2007). Male subjects tend to score higher on tests that measure Dark Triad traits, although the intercorrelations between the traits are similar across the sexes. So, although women may not exhibit Dark Triad traits as much as men, women who have this personality manifest it in the same general way that men would. Vernon, et al. (2008) also measured the correlation of Dark Triad traits between twins, and find considerable genetic influence on these traits.

At their extreme, the Dark Triad personality seems to epitomize the notion of a cold, calculating, domineering, and remorseless criminal. It may be that this represents a "criminal personality type." However, it's probably a mistake to label these traits intrinsically maladaptive. Traits are collective descriptions for certain behaviors, and behaviors are adaptive or not, depending on the context. The increasing social isolation of the modern world may reward many of the milder aspects of the Dark Triad.

Traits across Cultures Any comprehensive theory of personality must be able to encompass all cultures, countries, and languages. If personality comprises a standard set of factors, which we all exhibit to a lesser or greater extent, then these factors should be exhibited or reported cross-culturally. If not, then the theory is culture specific and describes only personality within a limited number of cultures.

In personality, problems in demonstrating universality lie in taxonomy. Do the same words mean the same thing across cultures? For example, various cultures attribute different meanings to factor 5 (conscientiousness) of the Big Five model

(Caprara and Perugini, 1994). It means something different to the Dutch, Hungarians, and Italians, and to the Americans, Germans, Czechs, and Poles. In a review of the evidence for the universality of a collection of basic personality traits, Boele de Raad, from the University of Groningen in The Netherlands, suggested that the best one can do is to find acceptable counterparts of the Big Five in all cultures; the first three factors of the model can be found in most cultures, but the cross-cultural validity of others may be questionable (De Raad, 1998).

McCrae and Terracciano (2005) asked college students from 50 cultures, including Arabic and Black African cultures, to identify a man or woman they knew well and rate him or her by using the third-person version of the Revised NEO Personality Inventory. The Big Five structure was replicated in almost all cultures (Morocco and Nigeria were two of the half dozen or so not to show this pattern). Women were more positive than men in rating others, especially when rating other women.

In a separate study of the geography of personality traits, Allik & Mcrae (2004) examined whether respondents from 36 cultures differed according to the Big Five personality dimension. They found that the culture's temperature or its distance from the equator was not related to personality. However, cultures that were geographically close appeared to share similar personality traits: the greatest geographical distinction was between European and American cultures, and Asian and African cultures. Americans and Europeans were significantly more extraverted and open to experience but less agreeable than peoples from other cultures. Why?

The authors suggest that the results may be due to shared gene pools (China and Korea, for example, share genetic ancestry) or to features of those cultures. Studying the process of acculturation—the assimilation of a person's behavior with that person's culture—might help identify which is correct. For example, a study of Chinese people who emigrated to Canada found that differences between these people and European Canadians was attenuated the longer the Chinese lived in Canada (McCrae et al., 1998). Openness and agreeableness, in particular, increased in the immigrant group, but introversion remained stable and did not match levels seen in European Canadians. These data suggest that some personality traits might be adopted or enhanced by acculturation, but others may not.

Can cultures also differ according to what they believe about personality? Implicit trait theories describe whether people ascribed differences in personality to stable traits or, instead, to the immediate context or situation of an individual. In a later section of this chapter, we look at how personality theorists approach this question. Here, we consider what the layperson believes. Church et al. (2005) investigated cross-cultural beliefs about personality in what they called two individualistic cultures—America and Australia—and two collectivistic cultures—Mexico and the Philippines. They hypothesized that the more individualistic the culture, the greater or stronger the culture's beliefs in traits, rather than in situations, as determinants of behavior. Trait beliefs were stronger in Americans than in Mexicans or Philippinos, but contextual beliefs were weaker.

Gavin Hellier/Robert Harding World Imagery/Getty Images

Alistair Berg/Getty Images Royalty Free

Individuals within cultures that are geographically close appear to share similar Big Five personality traits.

QUESTIONS TO CONSIDER

1. Think of one personality trait that you are sure you possess. How did you come to possess this trait? To what extent does possessing this trait explain the kind of person you are?

2. Consider the culture you have been raised in. Are some of the traits we've discussed more valued than others within your culture? Do you think this might have an impact on the likelihood that you would show such traits?

3. Make a list of all of the personality traits that you feel describe you. Which approach to personality—Cattell's, Eysenck's, or the five-factor model—do you think best represents the personality traits you possess? What are the reasons for your answer?

Psychobiological Approaches

The statistical evidence from factor analysis provides a description of consistent patterns of behaviors that we can identify as traits. At the beginning of the chapter, it was noted that we carry our personality traits around in our brains. That is, personality traits are the result of actions of the brain. Although we are far from understanding the psychobiology of personality, some progress has been made.

Jim Craigmyle/Corbis

Research into the genetic basis of personality suggests that traits such as extroversion may be inherited.

Heritability of Personality Traits

Cattell and Eysenck, among other trait theorists, asserted that a person's genetic history has a strong influence on his or her personality. Many studies have shown that some personality traits are strongly heritable (e.g., Bouchard & Hur, 1998; Krueger, Markon, & Bouchard, 2003).

Psychologists assess the heritability of a trait by comparing identical and fraternal twins, comparing twins raised together and twins raised apart, and comparing twins raised by biological and adoptive relatives. Many studies have found that identical twins are more similar to each other on a variety of personality measures than are fraternal twins, which indicates that these characteristics are heritable (e.g., McCrae et al., 2000; Jang et al., 2002; Livesley, Jang, & Vernon, 2003; Vernon, et al., 2008). FIGURE 5 shows correlations for "big five" personality traits between members of identical and fraternal twin pairs. Identical twins' personality traits correlate much more than do those of fraternal twins. Bouchard (1997) found that identical twins' personality traits generally correlated nearly twice as much as those of fraternal twins. The similarities shown by the identical twins in the prologue—Jim and Jim, who were separated early in life and united many years later—attest to the strength of genetic factors in influencing personality.

Zuckerman (1991) compiled the results of 11 studies using various tests of Eysenck's personality factors of extroversion, neuroticism, and psychoticism. Every study found that identical twins were more similar than fraternal twins on every measure. According to Zuckerman's calculations, the best estimates of the heritability of these three traits are, for extroversion, 70%; for psychoticism, 59%; and for neuroticism, 48%. The results of these studies suggest that heredity is responsible for 50 to 70% of the variability in these three personality traits. Thus, it might appear that the remaining 30 to 50% of the variability would be caused by differences in environment. In other words, some family environments should tend to produce extroverts, others should tend to produce introverts, and so on.

Research indicates, however, that the matter is not so simple. If family environment has a significant effect on personality characteristics, then identical twins raised together should be more similar than those raised apart. In the studies reviewed by Zuckerman (1991), they were not. Several of those studies measured the correlation in personality traits of pairs of identical twins raised together and apart. Taken as a group, these studies found no differences—indicating that differences in family environment seem to account for none of the variability of personality traits in the twins who were tested. Researchers are now developing more sensitive measures of family environment variables (e.g., Vernon, et al., 1997; Keltikangas-Järvinen & Heinonen, 2003). As these techniques evolve, we should be better able to examine the relative contributions of genetics and experience to personality.

Heredity and environment do interact. The major source of the interaction seems to be the effect that people's heredity has on their family environments (Plomin & Bergeman, 1991; Plomin & Asbury, 2001). That is, a person's genetic endowment plays an important role in determining how family members interact with him or her. Two possible explanations exist for these results: The family environments could have been more similar for identical

[**FIGURE 5**] Correspondence between personality traits of identical and fraternal twins. These data show the degree to which the scores of identical and fraternal twins are correlated on each of the "big five" personality traits. The correlations for identical twins are more than double those of fraternal twins on each trait. This indicates that genes we receive from our parents do influence personality structure.

(Adapted from Bouchard, T. J. Jr. (1997). *The genetics of personality.* In K. Blum & E.P. Noble (Eds.), *The handbook of psychiatric genetics* (pp. 273–296). Boca Raton, FL: CRC Press Inc. Reproduced by permission of the Routledge/ Taylor & Francis Group, LLC, and T. J. Bouchard.)

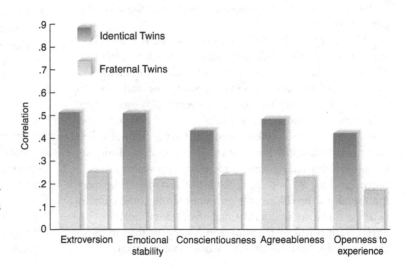

twins than for fraternal twins, or the family environments could have really been the same in all cases but simply have been *perceived* as different by the fraternal twins. Evidence suggests that the first possibility is correct. That is, the family environments really were more similar for identical twins (Loehlin, 1992).

How can this be? One might think that each family has a certain environment and that everyone in the household would come equally under its influence. Even within a family, each member experiences different social interactions. Although aspects of a family are shared by the entire household, the factors that play the largest role in shaping personality development appear to come from unique social interactions between an individual and other family members. Because of hereditary differences, one child may be more sociable; this child will be the recipient of more social interactions. Another child may be abrasive and disagreeable; this child will be treated more coldly. In the case of identical twins, who have no hereditary differences, the amount and style of social interaction with each twin is likely to be similar. Thus, although a child's environment plays an important part in his or her personality development, hereditary factors play a large role in determining the nature of this environment.

One caution about this interpretation is in order. Although the studies cited have been replicated in several cultures, none of them has investigated the effects of the full range of cultural differences in family lives. That is, when comparisons have been made between twins raised together and those raised apart, almost all have involved family environments *within* the same culture. It is possible that cultural differences in family environments could be even more important than the differences produced by a person's heredity. Hur (2005) found that the shared environment of Korean families affected aspects of self-perception more than it did in American families.

Should we assume that all personality traits are a product, direct or indirect, of a person's heredity? The answer is no. Some attributes and attitudes show a strong effect of shared environment but almost no effect of genetics. For example, twin studies have found a strong influence of family environment, but not of heredity, on involvement in religion, masculinity/femininity, attitudes toward racial integration, and intellectual interests (Loehlin & Nichols, 1976; Rose, 1995). Thus, people tend to *learn* from their family environments some important social attitudes associated with their personalities.

Another way of examining the question of heredity is to look at personality early in life, in infancy. The NEO-PI-R was not designed to be administered to infants, but psychologists use a related concept to describe the behaviors of infants—**temperament,** or each infant's individual pattern of behaviors and emotional reactions. Parents often will characterize their infant children in terms of temperament (as when your mother recalls you as a "fussy" or "quiet" baby), and several scales exist for measuring temperaments in infants and preschool children. For example, in one assessment questionnaire,

caregivers are asked a variety of questions, such as "When your child was being approached by an unfamiliar adult while shopping or out walking, how often did your child show distress or cry?" Unlike the case with personality, as yet no commonly agreed-on description of temperament exists; however, one measure, the Toddler Behavior Assessment Questionnaire, proposes that temperament can be measured with respect to five dimensions: activity level, pleasure, social fearfulness, anger proneness, and interest/persistence.

The environmental factors of the family that affect temperament seem to be the unique social influences we just discussed. Correlations between infant siblings who are adopted and not related are very low (Saudino, 2005). The different temperaments of children within a family seem to be based on their individual interactions with other family members. As children develop, their temperaments show some change. Generally, the changed aspects of temperament seem to be the result of environmental factors, whereas the stable aspects are controlled by genetics (Saudino, 2005).

Brain Mechanisms in Personality

Patients with damage to the front of the brain, the orbitofrontal cortex, behave differently from those with damage to other areas of brain; they are more impulsive, engage in more inappropriate behavior, and report more anger and less happiness (Berlin, Rolls, & Kischika, 2004). Traumatic brain injury to the frontal lobe in children as young as 5 or as old as 14 is associated with personality changes seen 6 and 12 months after injury (Max et al., 2006). Curiously, given the marked changes in "personality" observed in frontal lobe patients, Berlin, Rolls, & Kischika (2004) found no significant differences between the groups on a standard measure of personality (the Big Five). Where, if anywhere, do the neural correlates of personality reside?

Studies of healthy individuals have provided more-specific but complex data. Canli et al. (2001) predicted that extraversion would be correlated with greater brain activation when people watch pleasant images, whereas neuroticism would be correlated with greater brain activation when participants watch unpleasant images. Their hypothesis was based on the assumption that extroverts would be more positively disposed and would respond enthusiastically to pleasant stimuli, whereas neurotic participants would react intensely to negative stimuli. This pattern was found in an *f*MRI study of 14 women.

The amygdala is activated when participants see fearful faces, especially ones that increase in intensity. Canli et al. (2002), however, also found that personality type—specifically, extraversion—is associated with amygdala activation when participants watch happy faces. The more extrovert the individual, the greater the activation in this structure. No other interaction between emotion and personality was found.

---

temperament An individual's pattern of behaviors and emotional reactions.

Zuckerman (1991) suggests that extroversion, neuroticism, and psychoticism are determined by the neural systems responsible for reinforcement, punishment, and arousal. People who score high on extroversion are particularly sensitive to reinforcement—perhaps their neural reinforcement systems are especially active. People who score high on neuroticism are anxious and fearful. If they also score high on psychoticism, they are hostile as well. People who score high on psychoticism have difficulty learning when not to do something. As Zuckerman suggested, they have a low sensitivity to punishment. They also have a high tolerance for arousal and excitation; in other words, we could say that their optimal level of arousal is abnormally high. TABLE 2 summarizes Zuckerman's hypothetical explanations for the three major personality dimensions.

Few studies have directly tested the hypothesis that personality differences can be accounted for by biological differences. However, research using laboratory animals has provided support for Zuckerman's suggestions concerning neuroticism. A neurotic person avoids unfamiliar situations because he or she fears encountering aversive stimuli, whereas an emotionally stable person is likely to investigate unfamiliar situations to see whether anything interesting will happen. The same is true for other species. For example, about 15% of kittens avoid novel objects, and this tendency persists when they become adults; some adult cats are timid, whereas others are bold. When a timid cat encounters a novel stimulus (such as a rat), the neural circuits in its amygdala responsible for defensive responses become more active (Adamec & Stark-Adamec, 1986). (Yes, some cats are afraid of rats.)

Biological Basis for Shyness

Kagan, Reznick, and Snidman (1988) investigated the possibility that timidity in social situations (shyness) has a biological basis in humans. They noted that about 10 to 15% of normal children between the ages of 2 and 3 become quiet, watchful, and subdued when they encounter an unfamiliar situation. In other words, like the kittens, they are shy and cautious in approaching novel stimuli. Childhood shyness seems to be related to two personality dimensions: a low level of extroversion and a high level of neuroticism (Briggs, 1988).

Kagan and his colleagues (1988) selected two groups of 21-month-old and 31-month-old children according to their reactions to unfamiliar people and situations. The shy group consisted of children who showed signs of inhibition, such as clinging to their mothers or remaining close to them, remaining silent, and failing to approach strangers or other novel stimuli. The children in the non-shy group showed no such inhibition; these children approached the strangers and explored the novel environment. The children were similarly tested for shyness several more times, up to the age of 7.5 years.

The investigators found shyness to be an enduring trait: Children who were shy at the ages of 21 or 31 months continued to be shy at the age of 7.5 years. In addition, the two groups of children showed differences in their physiological reactions to the test situation. Shy children were more likely to show increases in heart rate, their pupils tended to be more dilated, their urine contained more norepinephrine, and their saliva contained more cortisol. (Norepinephrine and cortisol are two hormones secreted during times of stress. Furthermore, their secretion in fear-provoking situations is controlled by the amygdala.) Obviously, the shy

[**FIGURE 6**] Two regions of the brain that are activated by viewing facial stimuli: the amygdala (Amy) and the ocipito-temporal cortex (OTC). People who, as two year olds, were inhibited in their reactions showed greater activation in the Amy region when, as adults, they saw novel faces, compared to people who were uninhibited as children. (Photograph from Schwartz, C.E., Wright, C.I., Shin, L.M., Kagan, J., & Rauch, S.L. (2003). Inhibited and uninhibited infants "grown up": Adult amygdalar response to novelty. *Science, 300,* 1952–1953.)

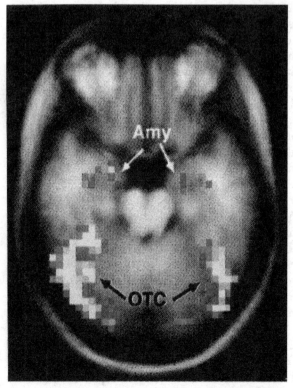

Courtesy of Carl Schwartz

[**TABLE 2**] Zuckerman's (1991) Hypothetical Biological Characteristics That Correspond to Personality Dimensions

Personality Trait	Biological Characteristics
Extroversion	High sensitivity to reinforcement
Neuroticism	High sensitivity to punishment
Psychoticism	Low sensitivity to punishment; high optimum level of arousal

children found the situation stressful, whereas the non-shy children did not.

This study suggests that the biological basis of an important personality characteristic during childhood—shyness—may be the excitability of neural circuits that control avoidance behaviors. When Kagan and his colleagues first raised this possibility, the methods of functional brain imaging were not available, but 20 years later, they had a chance to test, as adults, some of the children who had been classified as either shy or not at the age of 2 years. People who had shown signs of inhibition and shyness as 2-year-olds showed greater activity in the amygdala when they viewed pictures of unfamiliar faces than when they saw familiar faces. (See FIGURE 6.) Adults who had not shown inhibition as infants did not exhibit this difference (Schwartz et al., 2003).

focus On

Gender Differences in Personality

From a very early age, people in all cultures learn that boys and girls and men and women are different in at least two ways—physically and psychologically. The psychological differences often are more difficult to detect than the physical differences, but nonetheless, males and females tend not only to perceive aspects of their environments differently, but also to behave differently under some circumstances. Usually these cultures hold certain beliefs, called stereotypes, about differences between males and females. In general, stereotypes about men are more flattering than are those about women: Men are stereotyped as being more competent, independent, decisive, and logical. Women are stereotyped as being less competent, competitive, ambitious, independent, and active (Broverman et al., 1972).

For example, consider how males and females in three different Papua New Guinea tribes are expected to act (Harris, 1991). Among the Arapesh, both men and women are expected to be cooperative and sympathetic, much as Western cultures expect the ideal "mom" to be. Among the Mundugumor, both men and women are expected to be fierce and aggressive, similar to what we might expect of the men in our culture whom we call "macho." Finally, among the Tchambuli, women shave their heads, are boisterous, and provide food; the men tend to focus on art, their hairstyles, and gossiping about women.

These stereotypes are social constructions based on cultural expectations of how a man or a woman should behave. Are there differences between genders with respect to the Big Five traits? General sex differences were reported in a 55-culture study by Schmitt et al. (2008). In a sample of just over 17.5 thousand participants, they found that women reported higher levels of neuroticism, extraversion, agreeableness, and conscientiousness than did men and that these differences were much more pronounced in

cultures that are healthy, prosperous, and more egalitarian. Chapman et al. (2007) likewise found that women showed moderately higher measures of Neuroticism and Agreeableness. The gender difference in Agreeableness suggests a link to social behavior.

A social behavior that shows large gender differences is aggression. During play, young boys react to provocation with greater anger than do young girls (Fabes et al., 1996). In a longitudinal study of elementary and high school students, boys were shown to be more aggressive than girls, and patterns of aggression were found to be less stable for boys than for girls (Woodall & Matthews, 1993).

Even so, gender differences in aggression may vary in different cultures. In one study of preschoolers, for example, American and Israeli girls were shown to start fewer fights than did their respective male counterparts, but Israeli girls started more fights than did American boys (Lauer, cited in Bower, 1991). The higher levels of aggression among Israeli children may be due in part to their country's constant preparation for and frequent participation in military conflicts.

Several other gender differences related to personality and social behavior have been documented. Males tend to emerge as leaders when the groups to which they belong need to accomplish a specific task. Females tend to emerge

To a large extent, the specific culture in which people live influences the gender-linked behavioral tendencies and personality traits of males and females.

as leaders when the groups to which they belong stress interpersonal relationships (Eagly & Karau, 1991). Males tend to report higher thresholds for pain than do females, and females on average report a greater willingness to report pain than does the typical male (Wise et al., 2002). Females tend to be more empathetic and tend to offer assistance to others when the situation demands comforting others. Men are more likely to offer assistance when the situation demands physical aid (Eisenberg et al., 1991). Likewise, males tend to be less intimate, whereas females tend to be more empathetic and expressive in their relationships (Buss, 1995).

QUESTIONS TO CONSIDER

1. Of identical twin boys, one is much more outgoing than the other. If personality traits are heritable, how would you explain this difference—how can twins share 100% of their genes yet have different "personalities"?

2. Are you a thrill seeker? To what extent do you seek out situations that might be considered risky or at least mildly exciting? Depending on your answers to these questions, what might Zuckerman say about your personality (in terms of psychoticism)?

Social Cognitive Approaches

Some psychologists view personality as the result of a behavioral learning process in which environmental variables act on the individual to produce behaviors. We might interpret certain behaviors in terms of traits like "extroversion," but the key question is why "extrovert behaviors" are frequently demonstrated by a particular person, and why that person might use them in one situation but not in another.

Models that interpret personality as behavior stem partially from B. F. Skinner's experimental analysis of behavior. Although Skinner's work has influenced contemporary personality theory, he should not be mistaken for a personality theorist. Personality was definitely not Skinner's focus, but his ideas have relevance when we consider personality as a description for a certain set of behaviors.

Skinner believed that the consequences of behavior were important causal factors. Environmental variables are those that define the contingencies between stimuli, behaviors, and outcomes. Behavior is consistent from one situation to the next if it is maintained by similar kinds of consequences across those situations. Behavior changes only when the consequences change.

Behaviorists influenced by Skinner's approach have attempted to apply the experimental analysis of behavior to social contingencies and social behaviors. However, many choose to apply a behavioral approach by blending it with cognitive theory. The result is **social cognitive theory,** which embodies the idea that both the consequences of behavior and an individual's beliefs about those consequences determine personality. Because many of the consequences we receive for our behaviors come from others, social behaviors are important sources for the behaviors and thoughts that distinguish us as individuals. One such researcher is Albert Bandura (b. 1925) who combined elements of learning theory with cognitive concepts to explain social behavior.

Expectancies and Observational Learning

Bandura's theory is based on **observational learning,** which is learning through observation of the consequences that others (usually called *models*) experience as a result of their behaviors. Observational learning is undoubtedly important in animal species whose young must learn a behavior before they are physically able to perform it. Your own experience is no doubt filled with examples of observational learning—it is partly through observation that we learn to dance, to make a paper airplane, to write in cursive, and to engage in many other activities. The more complex the behavior, *the more times we must observe it being executed, and practice what we have observed,* before we can learn it well. Learning to tie a shoelace requires more attention to details than learning to roll a ball across the floor.

Observational learning is more than just imitation. It also depends on reinforcement, as in other forms of learning. The nature of the reinforcement differs, however, in that it is the model who is reinforced. In other words, reinforcement is *vicarious,* and not directly experienced by the observer.

At the heart of the social learning theory account of personality is the idea that personality develops as we observe and imitate the actions of others. Our observation of a model performing a behavior leads to an expectancy that our performance of the same behavior will produce a favorable result.

Mark Richards/PhotoEdit Inc.

---

social cognitive theory   The idea that both consequences of behavior and an individual's beliefs about those consequences determine personality.

observational learning   Learning that takes place when we see the kinds of consequences others (called models) experience as a result of their behavior.

The vicarious nature of some learning experiences is obvious in children as they imitate the actions of others. A 3-year-old who applies deodorant to herself does so not because this behavior has been reinforced in the past, but rather because after watching her mother do it, she expects it would be "fun" for her to do so, too.

Vicarious reinforcement is made possible, in Bandura's theory, through cognition (Bandura, 1986, 1995, 2002; Bandura & Locke, 2003). In particular, individuals can form an expectancy based on their behaviors. An **expectancy** is an individual's belief that a specific consequence will follow a specific action. To put it another way, expectancy has to do with how someone perceives the contingencies of reinforcement for his or her own behavior. If a person does something, it may be because he or she expects to be rewarded or punished. In different situations, expectancies may vary. For example, a young boy may learn that he can get what he wants from his younger sister by hitting her. However, on one occasion, his parents may catch him hitting his sister and punish him. His expectancy may now change: He may still get what he wants by behaving aggressively, but if he is caught, he'll be punished. This new expectancy may influence how he behaves toward his sister in the future, especially when his parents are present.

Reciprocal Determinism and Self-Efficacy

Bandura, unlike many other theorists, does not believe that either personal characteristics (traits) or the environment alone determines personality (Bandura, 1978). Rather, he argued for **reciprocal determinism**—the idea that behavior, environmental variables, and cognitive variables interact to determine personality. (See FIGURE 7.) We know that our actions can affect the environment. We also know that the environment can affect our behavior. Likewise, our perceptions may affect the ways in which we behave to change the environment, and in turn, those changes can influence our perceptions. For example, when our acts of kindness are met with kindness in return, we perceive the environment as friendly and are apt to show kindness under other, similar circumstances. Likewise, when we are treated rudely, we perceive the environment as unfriendly (perhaps hostile) and will likely attempt to avoid or change similar environments in the future.

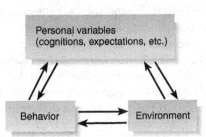

[**FIGURE 7**] Patterns of interaction in reciprocal determinism. According to Bandura, behavior, environment, and cognitive variables, such as expectations and perceptions, interact to determine personality.

The term **self-efficacy** refers to a person's beliefs about his or her ability to act as required in a particular situation to experience satisfying outcomes (Bandura, 1982, 1997). According to Bandura, our degree of self-efficacy is an important determinant of whether we will attempt to make changes in our environment. Each day we make many decisions based on our perceptions of the extent to which our actions will produce reinforcement. Our actions are based on our evaluation of our competency. Moreover, self-efficacy not only determines whether we will engage in a particular behavior; it also determines the extent to which we will maintain that behavior in the face of adversity. For example, if you believe that you are underqualified for a job as ski instructor at a fancy ski resort, even though you really want the job, you are not apt to apply for an interview—you expect that nothing good could come of the effort. However, if you are confident of your qualifications, you will surely attempt to get an interview. Even if you are turned down for that job, you may interview for a position at another resort, because you are sure of your abilities. Eventually your abilities will produce the outcome you want. Low self-efficacy can hamper both the frequency and the quality of behavior–environment interactions, whereas high self-efficacy can facilitate both.

Personality across Time

Earlier we saw that trait theorists seek to explain two aspects of personality: the distinctiveness of any one individual, and the aspects of personality that stay the same within that individual. Is this second objective reasonable? Does stability to personality exist? Can the introverted high school student become a social star in college?

One extreme position, consistent with the behavior approach, is to assume that the behaviors that make up our personality are specific to a given situation and are not the result of any persevering traits. This position is known as **situationism.** Discriminative stimuli can control behaviors; perhaps personality is likewise dependent on the stimuli can that control behaviors. Would a person high in conscientiousness stop at a red light at 3:00 in the morning with no one around and no chance of being caught? If you think the answer is "no," then you probably see the point.

This question is amenable to empirical test and has been the subject of much research (see the *Focus On* feature later in this section). In response to this research, some personality psychologists have argued for theories that represent the

expectancy The belief that a certain consequence will follow a certain action.

reciprocal determinism The idea that behavior, environment, and person variables interact to determine personality.

self-efficacy People's beliefs about how well or badly will perform tasks.

situationism The view that the behaviors defining a certain personality are determined solely by the current situation rather than by any persevering traits.

situation as part of the rules that govern behavior. Stability in personality, in this view, is a consequence of stability in the underlying rules. Variation results from the way the situation activates those rules. For example, social cognitive theory might say that your use of swear words in your verbal behavior would be affected by whom you were talking to. Perhaps your parents are stricter about swearing than your friends. Consequently, your speech would be more conservative when you talk to your parents than when you talk to your friends. If you're often with your friends, your personality might be seen as "tougher."

One possible scheme that makes these factors explicit is the model proposed by Walter Mischel, whose early work was strongly based on situationism, but who has modified that position since. Mischel, like Bandura, believes that much of personality is learned through interaction with the environment. Also like Bandura, Mischel emphasizes the role of cognition in determining how people learn the relationship between their behavior and its consequences. In addition, though, Mischel argues that individual differences in cognition, or **person variables,** as he calls them, account for differences in personality. Five person variables, as follows, figure prominently in this version of social cognitive theory (Mischel, 1990, 2003; Mischel, Cantor, & Feldman, 1996):

- *Competencies.* We each have different skills, abilities, and capacities. What we know and the kinds of behaviors that have been reinforced in the past influence the kinds of actions in which we will likely engage in the future.

- *Encoding strategies and personal constructs.* We also differ in our ability to process information. The way we process information determines how we perceive different situations. One person may perceive going on a date as fun, and so may look forward to it; another person may perceive going on a date as potentially boring, and so may dread it.

- *Expectancies.* On the basis of our past behavior and our knowledge of current situations, we form expectancies about the effects of our behavior on the environment. Expecting our behavior to affect the environment positively leads to one action; expecting our behavior to affect it negatively leads to another.

- *Subjective values.* The degree to which we value certain reinforcers over others influences our behavior. We seek those outcomes that we value most.

- *Self-regulatory systems and plans.* We monitor our progress toward achieving goals and subject ourselves to either self-punishment or self-reinforcement, depending on our progress. We also modify and formulate plans regarding how we think a goal can best be achieved.

---

person variables   Individual differences in cognition, which, according to Mischel, include competencies, encoding strategies and personal constructs, expectancies, subjective values, and self-regulatory systems and plans.

Mischel's is a dynamic view; it envisions people's thoughts and behaviors undergoing constant change as they interact with the environment. New plans are made, and old ones are reformulated; people adjust their actions in accordance with their competencies, subjective values, and expectancies of behavior–environment interactions. Between these periods of change, however, person variables provide stable rules for behavior akin to those described by trait theories.

focus On

Traits versus Situations as Predictors of Behavior

Social cognitive theorists stress the importance of the environment as an influence on behavior and tend to place less emphasis on the role of enduring personal traits. They argue that the situation often plays a strong role in determining behavior. In contrast, trait theorists argue that personality traits are stable characteristics of individuals and that knowing something about these traits permits us to predict an individual's behavior in a variety of situations. What evidence exists for both positions?

The Case for Situationism

Mischel (1968, 1976) suggested that stable personality traits do not exist—or that if they do, they are of little importance. Situations, not traits, best predict behavior, Mischel argued. He asks us to consider two situations: (1) a party to celebrate someone's winning a large sum of money in a lottery, and (2) a funeral. People will be much more talkative, cheerful, and outgoing at the party than at the funeral. In this case, knowing the situation has much more predictive value for behavior than knowing the test score someone might receive on a test of introversion–extroversion.

Mischel can cite a wealth of empirical research evidence for his position. One of the first of these studies was performed in the 1920s. Hartshorne and May (1928) designed a set of behavioral tests to measure the traits of honesty and self-control and administered them to more than 10,000 students in elementary and high schools. The tests gave the children the opportunity to be dishonest—for example, to cheat on a test, lie about the amount of homework they had done, or keep money with which they had been entrusted. In all cases, the researchers had access to what the children actually did. They found that a child who acted honestly (or dishonestly) in one situation did not necessarily act the same way in a different situation.

Mischel (1968) reviewed evidence from research performed after the Hartshorne and May study and found that most personal characteristics showed the same low cross-situational consistency—0.30 or lower. He concluded that the concept of personality trait was not very useful.

The Case for Personality Traits

Other psychologists disagree with Mischel. For example, Epstein (1979, 1986) claimed that personality traits are more stable than some of the studies had suggested. He noted that assessments of cross-situational consistency usually test a group of people on two occasions and correlate their behavior in one situation with their behavior in the other. Epstein showed that repeated measurements across several days yielded much higher correlations. In a study of his own, a group of 28 undergraduates kept daily records of their most pleasant and most unpleasant experiences for a month. For each experience, they recorded the emotions they felt, their impulses to action, and their actual behavior. The correlation between a given participant's emotions, impulses, or behavior on any 2 days was rather low—on the order of 0.30. However, when Epstein grouped measurements (that is, correlated the ratings obtained on odd-numbered days with those obtained on even-numbered days), the correlation rose dramatically—to around 0.80. That is, the correlation became much higher when the records of a group of days were compared with those of a different group of days than when a single day was compared with another single day.

A Reconciliation?

Mischel and Shoda (1995, 1998) proposed a move toward reconciliation of the trait and situations approaches in the form of what they call the cognitive–affective processing system approach (CAPS). The CAPS approach recognizes the multiple influences of biology, affect, cognition, and learning. An individual's personality is a network of relatively stable components, such as expectations, beliefs, memories, and feelings. However, the specific components that are active at a specific time depends on the interaction that occurs with the environment and among the components themselves. As an example, Shoda and Smith (2004) point to Shakespeare's classic play, *Hamlet*. Hamlet's uncle, Claudius, is a cold and treacherous killer who, if he had been real rather than fictitious, would probably have scored high on the Dark Triad traits. Nevertheless, he manages to hide his nature and his crime from Hamlet through most of the play. It is only when Hamlet stages a play recreating the crime that the specific feelings and memories of his past cause Claudius, through his behavior, to reveal his guilt.

Through their CAPS framework, Mischel and Shoda appear to extend an olive branch to traditional trait theory. However, this acknowledgment that both traits and situation can interact leaves unresolved the question of how each should be studied. Funder (2006) suggested that future research in personality theory will need to grapple with issues such as what makes a situation similar or different, and what is the source of behavioral variation.

Locus of Control

With the growth of the Internet, email has become a widespread means of communication. For many people, email is a convenient way to keep in touch and to conduct business, but it has no special urgency. In contrast, others view email messages as much more pressing matters; they feel compelled to respond to each message as quickly as possible. Hair, Renaud, and Ramsay (2007) found that among this latter type of user were people who viewed the rapid nature of email as a positive and helpful aspect; for others, though, it was considered a source of considerable stress.

What could account for this difference? If you think about how email affects your own life, one aspect about it is undeniable: it can be a considerable source of distraction. If you yourself find the pace of electronic communication stressful, it could be because you regard it and other external distractions as unavoidable influences on your life that you cannot control. Lack of control could be the source of your stress.

Social cognitive theorist Julian Rotter (1966, 1990) focused on the extent to which people perceive themselves to be in control of the consequences of their behavior. Theories of **locus of control** (plural: loci of control) focus on whether people believe that the consequences of their actions are controlled by internal person variables or by external environmental variables. A person who expects to control his or her own fate—or, more technically, who perceives that rewards are dependent on his or her own behavior—has an *internal locus of control*. A person who sees his or her life as being controlled by external forces unaffected by his or her own behavior has an *external locus of control*. (See FIGURE 8.)

Rotter developed the *I-E Scale*, which assesses the degree to which people perceive the consequences of their behavior to be under the control of internal or external variables. The I-E Scale contains 29 pairs of statements with which a person indicates his or her degree of agreement. A typical item on the scale might look something like this:

> The grades that I get depend on my abilities and how hard I work to get them.
>
> The grades that I get depend mostly on my teacher and his or her tests.

Researchers score the scale by counting the number of choices consistent with either the internal or the external locus of control orientation. Scores may range from 0 to 23, with lower scores indicative of greater internal locus of control. The highest possible score is 23, because six of the choice pairs are nonscored "filler" items. Of all the populations Rotter has assessed with the I-E Scale, a group of U.S. Peace Corps volunteers showed the highest level of internal locus of control (Rotter, 1966).

----

locus of control An individual's beliefs that the consequences of his or her actions are controlled by internal, person variables or by external, environmental variables.

[FIGURE 8] Internal and external loci of control. People having internal loci of control perceive themselves as able to determine the outcomes of the events in their lives. People having external loci of control perceive the events in their lives as determined by environmental variables.

When Rotter published his work on the I-E Scale in 1966, the concept captured the imaginations of researchers; it seemed to be an antidote to what was perceived in the 1960s as an overemphasis on drive and motivational concepts (Lefcourt, 1992). The attraction has been long lived, and the scale has been used in hundreds if not thousands of studies of social behavior in a wide variety of situations. Consider some of the findings obtained from research using the I-E Scale (Lefcourt, 1966, 1992):

- People with an internal locus-of-control orientation believe that achievement of their goals depends on their personal efforts toward accomplishing those goals.

- People having an internal locus-of-control orientation will work harder to obtain a goal if they believe that they can control the outcome in a specific situation. Even when people with external orientations are told that a goal can be obtained with their own skill and effort, they tend not to try as hard as those having internal orientations.

- People having internal orientations also are more likely to be aware of and to engage in good health practices. They are more apt to take preventive medicines, to exercise regularly, to diet when appropriate, and to quit smoking than are people having external orientations.

- People having high internal locus of control tend to have strong academic achievement goals and to do well in school. They are, however, also likely to blame themselves when they fail, even when failure is not their fault. People with an external locus of control tend to blame others for their failures.

Whether theories of locus of control can explain our modern angst about email and the speed of modern communication is a bit less clear. Hair, Renaud, and Ramsay (2007) found that people with external locus of control also reported more difficulty handling distractions and extraneous interruptions. This is consistent with the view that external locus of control is related to seeing one's life as controlled by outside influences. However, scores on the I-E scale did not correlate well with reported stress from email, suggesting that something else about the medium makes it such a modern burden.

A person's belief about his or her locus of control is fundamentally a belief about the source of controlling influences; what is the source of this belief? Is locus of control determined by experience, or is it more like a trait? Either of these two possibilities is consistent with the concept of locus of control. Johansson et al. (2001) found that individual differences between twins in their beliefs about how chance affected their health (an external belief) was attributable to shared family environment rather than genetic sources. This implies that beliefs about locus of control may be determined by one's experiences.

People having internal orientations are more likely to engage in good health practices.

Positive Psychology

Psychology has for many years concerned itself with improving human welfare and with healing mental disorders. In the course of that history, psychologists have often looked to those instances in which personality factors have impeded or limited the potential of an individual. Negative factors are often stronger than positive ones (e.g., Rozin & Royzman, 2001), so in this respect, psychologists may be repeating an inherent bias for negativity.

Martin Seligman suggested that psychology should concern itself with the beneficial aspects of personality that make life rewarding and fulfilling (e.g., Seligman and Csikszentmihalyi, 2000). **Positive psychology** is a psychological program that examines optimal human functioning (Linley et al., 2006). It is an agenda that many psychologists have adopted to study the origins, processes, and mechanisms that lead to psychological well-being, satisfaction, and fulfillment. Like humanistic psychology, which is discussed later in the chapter, positive psychology concerns the valued aspects of personality. It is, however, more closely identified with the scientific methods of biological, behavioral, cognitive, and social research.

As one example of positive psychology, Fincham and Beach (2007) looked at forgiveness as a factor in the quality of a marriage. Forgiveness is an active process by which an individual voluntarily reduces the negative emotions felt toward a transgressor. Married life (or any close partnered relationship, for that matter) produces many opportunities for forgiveness. Fincham and Beach asked married individuals to consider an instance in which their partner had said or done something to hurt them. They then looked at whether a tendency to forgive that act was correlated with the quality and happiness of marriage, either at the time, or 12 months later. It turned out that, for both husbands and wives, a tendency to forgive was correlated with the quality of the marriage at the time. (Interestingly, wives' tendency to forgive their husbands did not correlate with their husbands' tendency to forgive them.)

It's worth noting that the social roles for women place a strong emphasis on social skills, and this may encourage them to see forgiveness as an active strategy to maintain a strong marital bond. Positive psychology would seek to understand this interplay between personality variables that promote a valued relationship. The cognitive and behavioral approaches of this section would be helpful to this understanding.

QUESTIONS TO CONSIDER

1. Think of a situation in which you modeled your behavior after someone else's. What factors led you to imitate this behavior? To what extent did you form an expectancy that imitating this behavior would lead to a particular consequence?
2. Provide a personal example of reciprocal determinism. Explain the interaction of behavior, environmental variables, and cognitive variables in this example.
3. Do you believe that you have an internal or an external locus of control? Give an example of a recent decision that you made or a social interaction that you had. How would your life be different if you adopted the opposite locus-of-control orientation?

The Psychodynamic Approach

For many people, the name Sigmund Freud is synonymous with psychology. Indeed, his work has had profound and lasting effects on Western culture. Terms such as *ego, libido, repression, rationalization,* and *fixation* are as familiar to many laypeople as to clinicians. Before Freud formulated his theory, people believed that most behavior was determined by rational, conscious processes. Freud was the first to claim that what we do is often irrational and that the reasons for our behavior are seldom conscious. The mind, to Freud, was a battleground for the warring factions of instinct, reason, and conscience; the term **psychodynamic** refers to this struggle. As you will soon see, although Freud's work began with the clinical treatment of patients with psychological problems, it later provided a framework for explaining how psychodynamic factors determine personality.

The Development of Freud's Theory

Sigmund Freud (1856–1939) was a Viennese physician who acquired his early training in neurology in the laboratory of Ernst Wilhelm von Brücke, an eminent physiologist and neuroanatomist. Freud's work in the laboratory consisted mostly of careful anatomical observation rather than experimentation. Careful observation also characterized his later work with human behavior; he made detailed observations of individual patients and drew inferences about the structure of the human mind from these cases.

Freud, after studying in Paris with Jean Martin Charcot, who was investigating the usefulness of hypnosis as a treatment for hysteria, opened his own medical practice in Vienna. He began an association with the prominent physician Josef Breuer. They published a seminal book called *Studies on Hysteria,* and one of the cases cited in it, that of Anna O., provided the evidence that led to some of the most important tenets of Freud's theory. Anna O. had a staggering number of symptoms, including loss of speech, disturbances in vision, headaches, and paralysis and loss of feeling in her right arm. Under hypnosis, Anna was asked to think about the time when her symptoms had started. Each of her symptoms appeared to have begun just when she was unable to express a strongly felt emotion. While under hypnosis she experienced

---

positive psychology A program of psychology that examines the basis of optimal human functioning, with emphasis on the origins, processes, and mechanisms of human well-being.

psychodynamic Characterized by conflict among instincts, reason, and conscience; describes the mental processes envisioned in Freudian theory.

these emotions again, and the experience gave her relief from her symptoms. It was as if the emotions had been bottled up, and reliving the original experiences uncorked them. This release of energy (which Breuer and Freud called *catharsis*) presumably eliminated her symptoms.

Apparently, the woman was not cured, however. Ellenberger (1972) discovered hospital records indicating that Anna O. continued to take morphine for the distress caused by the disorders Breuer had supposedly cured. Freud appears to have eventually learned the truth, but this fact did not become generally known until recently. Breuer's failure to help Anna O. with her problems does not really undermine Freud's approach, however. The Freudian theory of personality must stand or fall on its own merits, despite the fact that one of its prime teaching examples appears to be largely fiction.

Freud concluded from his observations of patients that all human behavior is motivated by instinctual drives, which, when activated, supply "psychic energy." According to Freud, if something prevents the psychic energy caused by activation of a drive from being discharged, psychological disturbances will result.

Freud believed that instinctual drives are triggered by events in a person's life. Traumatic events may seriously threaten the desired state of psychic energy equilibrium. During a traumatic event, a person may try to deny or hide a strong emotional reaction rather than express it. Indeed, sometimes we must hide and not act on strong emotions, according to Freud. But there is a cost to hiding emotional reactions and suppressing the psychic energy that fuels them: The emotion may be expressed neurotically—that is, with excessive anxiety. The individual will not be able to recall the extreme emotional reactions, because they will be embedded in the **unconscious,** the inaccessible part of the mind. Unconscious emotions, however, still exert control over conscious thoughts and actions. As we will see later, according to Freud, the ways in which those emotions eventually find a degree of release will help define our unique personalities.

Freud also believed that the mind actively prevents unconscious memories of traumatic events from reaching conscious awareness. That is, the mind *represses* the memories of anxiety-provoking traumatic events from being consciously discovered. Freud used the metaphor of an iceberg to describe the mind. Only the tip of an iceberg is visible above

water; the much larger and more important part is submerged. Likewise, the conscious mind hides a larger and more important part of the mind—the unconscious. To understand someone's personality, we must tap into that individual's unconscious.

Structures of the Mind: Id, Ego, and Superego

Freud was struck by the fact that psychological disturbances could stem from events that a person apparently could no longer consciously recall, although the events could be revealed during hypnosis. This phenomenon led him to conclude that the mind consists of unconscious, preconscious, and conscious elements. The *unconscious* includes mental events of which we are not aware; the *conscious* entails mental events of which we are aware; and the *preconscious* involves mental events that may become conscious through effort.

Freud divided the mind into three structures: the id, the ego, and the superego. (See FIGURE 9.) The operations of the **id** are completely unconscious. The id contains the **libido,** which is the primary source of instinctual motivation for all psychic forces. The id obeys only one rule—to obtain immediate gratification in whatever form it may take—called the **pleasure principle.** If you are hungry, the id compels you to eat; if you are angry, the id prompts you to strike out or to seek revenge or to destroy something; if you are sexually aroused, the id presses for immediate sexual gratification. It is important to understand that for Freud, the id was a source of unrestrained, uncivilized, and ultimately harmful behavior.

The **ego** is the thinking, planning, and protective self; it controls and integrates behavior. It acts as a mediator, negotiating a

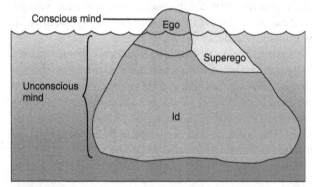

[**FIGURE 9**] Freud's conception of the structure of the mind. Freud compared the conscious portion of the mind to the tip of an iceberg and the unconscious portion to the larger part of the iceberg below the water's surface. The id is completely unconscious, but both the ego and the superego may be partially conscious and partially unconscious. In addition, Freud argued that part of the mind is preconscious (not shown in this figure), containing information that may be brought into consciousness through effort.

---

unconscious   The inaccessible part of the mind.

id   The unconscious reservoir of libido, the psychic energy that fuels instincts and psychic processes.

libido   An insistent, instinctual force that is unresponsive to the demands of reality; the primary source of motivation.

pleasure principle   The rule that the id obeys: Obtain immediate gratification, whatever form it may take.

ego   The general manager of personality, making decisions balancing the pleasures that will be pursued at the id's demand against the person's safety requirements and the moral dictates of the superego.

[**TABLE 3**] Freudian Defense Mechanisms

Defense Mechanism	Description	Example
Repression	Unconsciously barring memories of traumatic experiences from reaching conscious awareness.	Being unable to remember traumatic childhood sexual abuse or other traumatic events that occurred earlier in life.
Reaction Formation	Replacing an anxiety-provoking idea with its opposite.	Having intense feelings of dislike for a person but acting friendly and kind toward him or her.
Projection	Denying your unacceptable feelings and desires and finding them in others.	Denying your hostility toward a person but believing that that person is hostile toward you.
Sublimation	Channeling psychic energy from an unacceptable drive into a more acceptable one.	Diverting energy from the sex drive to produce a work of art.
Rationalization	Creating an acceptable reason for a behavior that is actually performed for a less acceptable reason.	Asserting that you enjoy a wrestling match as an athletic contest when in fact you enjoy the vicarious violence.
Denial	Negating or dismissing the reality of an unpleasant truth.	Asserting that a loved one is not dead but is missing in action and unable to communicate.

This table shows several of the most frequently used defense mechanisms.

compromise among the pressures of the id, the counterpressures of the superego (described next), and the demands of reality. The ego's functions of perception, cognition, and memory perform this mediation. The ego is driven by the **reality principle**—the tendency to satisfy the id's demands realistically, which almost always involves compromising the demands of the id and the superego. Adherence to the reality principle involves delaying gratification of a drive until an appropriate goal is located. To ward off the demands of the id when these demands cannot be gratified, the ego uses defense mechanisms (described later). Some of the functions of the ego are unconscious.

The **superego** is subdivided into the conscience and the ego-ideal. The **conscience** is the internalization of the rules and restrictions of society. It determines which behaviors are permissible and punishes wrongdoing with feelings of guilt. The **ego-ideal** is the internalization of what society values and what the person will strive to achieve.

Freud believed the mind to be full of conflicts. A conflict may begin when one of the two primary drives, the sexual instinctual drive or the aggressive instinctual drive, is aroused. The id demands gratification of these drives but often is held in check by the superego's internalized prohibitions against the behaviors that the drives tend to produce. *Internalized prohibitions* are rules of behavior learned in childhood that protect the person from the guilt he or she would feel if the instinctual drives were allowed to express themselves. The result of the conflict is *compromise formation,* in which a compromise is reached between the demands of the id and the suppressive effects of the superego. According to Freud, phenomena such as dreams, artistic creations, and slips of the tongue (we now call them Freudian slips) are examples of compromise formation.

Defense Mechanisms

According to Freud, the ego contains **defense mechanisms**—mental systems that become active whenever the id's unconscious instinctual drives come into conflict with the superego's internalized prohibitions. The signal for the ego to use one of its defenses is the state of anxiety produced by an intrapsychic conflict, which motivates the ego to apply a defense mechanism and thus reduce the anxiety. TABLE 3 presents six important defense mechanisms along with examples.

Interestingly, researchers have found that the use of defense mechanisms predicts personality changes in later adulthood (Cramer, 2003). The investigators measured participants' personality traits over a 24-year period by using the five-factor model. Although most personality traits remained reasonably stable, the use of defense mechanisms such as denial and projection correlated with an increased neuroticism, decreased extroversion, and decreased agreeableness among some study participants in later adulthood. The use of these defense mechanisms was not found to be negative in all cases, though. Among

---

reality principle   The tendency to satisfy the id's demands realistically, which almost always involves compromising the demands of the id and superego.

superego   The repository of an individual's moral values, divided into the conscience—the internalization of society's rules and regulations—and the ego-ideal—the internalization of the individual's goals.

conscience   The internalization of the rules and restrictions of society; it determines which behaviors are permissible and punishes wrongdoing with feelings of guilt.

ego-ideal   The internalization of what a person would like to be—his or her goals and ambitions.

defense mechanisms   Mental systems that become active whenever unconscious instinctual drives of the id come into conflict with internalized prohibitions of the superego.

Jim Arbogast/Photodisc/Getty Images Royalty Free

Freud argued that creativity was often the result of sublimation—the redirection of psychic energy from unacceptable actions, such as unrestrained sexual behavior, to acceptable actions, such as the jointly sensual and creative work shown here.

participants who used defense mechanisms, low scores on IQ tests were found to correlate with positive personality traits.

Freud's Psychosexual Theory of Personality Development

Freud believed that personality development involves passing through several *psychosexual stages* of development—stages in which the individual seeks pleasure from specific parts of the body called *erogenous zones*. As we will see, each stage of personality development involves deriving physical pleasure from a different erogenous zone. (Freud used the term "sexual" to refer to physical pleasures and to the many ways an individual might seek to gratify an urge for such pleasure. When referring to children, he did not use the term to refer to adult sexual feelings or orgasmic pleasure.)

Freud's theory of personality development has been extremely influential because of its ability to explain personality disorders in terms of whole or partial **fixation**—arrested

---

fixation   A brief interval between saccadic eye movements during which the eye does not move; the brain accesses visual information during this time. Also, in Freudian theory, the continued attachment of psychic energy to an erogenous zone due to incomplete passage through one of the psychosexual stages.

oral stage   The first of Freud's psychosexual stages, during which the mouth is the major erogenous zone because it appeases the hunger drive.

anal stage   The second of Freud's psychosexual stages, during which the primary erogenous zone is the anus because of the pleasure derived from vacating a full bowel.

phallic stage   The third of Freud's psychosexual stages during which the primary erogenous zone is the genital area and pleasure derives from both direct genital stimulation and general physical contact.

---

development due to a person's failure to pass completely through a given stage of development. Freud believed that a person becomes fixated at a particular stage of development when he or she becomes strongly attached to the erogenous zone involved in that stage.

For Freud, personality development begins in infancy. Because newborn babies can do little more than suck and swallow, their sexual instinctual drive finds an outlet in these activities. We can think of infants at this stage as being dominated by the id. Over- or undergratification of the hunger drive during this **oral stage** can result in fixation. Undergratification might result from early weaning, and overgratification, from too zealous attempts by parents to feed the infant. According to Freud, too little gratification during the oral stage will set in motion the development of personality traits related to dependency—what we commonly refer to as "clinging vine" characteristics. Too much gratification, or overstimulation, will lay the groundwork for the development of aggressive personality characteristics. Other oral-stage fixation activities include habits such as smoking, hoarding, and excessive eating.

The **anal stage** of personality development begins during the second year of life. According to Freud, sensual pleasure derives from emptying the bowels. Around this time, most parents place demands on their toddlers to control their bowels, to delay their gratification, through toilet training. The stage is set for the early development of ego functions—the deliberate management of id impulses (in this case, the desire to vacate the bowels as soon as the urge arises). The way that parents toilet train their infants will again have a stage-setting effect on later personality development. Harsh toilet training characterized by punishment when a child fails to reach the toilet may lead to fixation at this stage. The personality characteristics that start to develop will center on orderliness and a need for control. In their adult form, we would refer to these characteristics as compulsiveness and, at an extreme, megalomania (a single-minded need for power and control). Mild toilet training, the preferred method, involves encouraging and praising the infant for successfully producing the bowel movement at the right place and time. The stage is set for pride in the expression of id needs coupled with appropriate ego control. Personality characteristics that should evolve include creativity and emotional expressiveness.

At around age 3 years, a child discovers that it is pleasurable to play with his penis or her clitoris (again, an immature sexuality), and enters the **phallic stage.** (*Phallus* means "penis," but Freud used the term "phallic stage" for children of both genders.) Children during this stage form strong immature sexual attachments to the parent of the opposite sex. This occurs, according to Freud, because mothers predominantly nurture male children and fathers predominantly nurture female children. In other words, opposite-sex parents become the focus of sensual pleasure for children during this stage. According to Freud, children experience jealousy of their same-sex parent's close relationship with the opposite-sex parent—the parent that children want exclusively for themselves.

The process diverges for boys and girls beyond this point. A boy's love of his mother is mixed with hostility

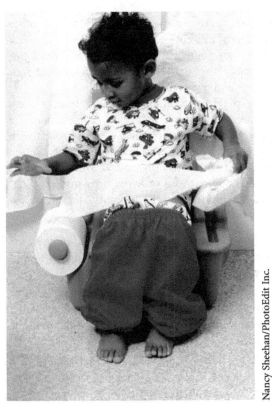

Does toilet training affect personality development? Freud thought so: He asserted that improper toilet training caused personality development to become fixated during the anal stage of psychosexual development.

toward and, importantly, fear of his rival father. Freud believed that boys unconsciously fear being punished by their fathers for their desire for their mothers, including the ultimate punishment—castration. These elements constitute the *Oedipus complex* (after the king of Greek mythology who unknowingly married his mother after killing his father). This rich mix of emotions demands resolution.

A girl's love of her father and envy of her mother, Freud said, is complicated by her discovery that she does not have a penis. This discovery, Freud theorized, leads to *penis envy* and girls' magical belief that they can acquire a penis through their attachment to their father. They then gravitate even more strongly toward their fathers, who have the organ they do not, to associate with power and compensate for their self-perceived weakness. These powerful emotions are what Freud called the *Electra complex*. (In Greek mythology, Electra, aided by her brother, killed her mother and her mother's lover to avenge her father's death.)

The conflict for both girls and boys is resolved through a process called *identification*. According to Freud, children of both sexes turn their attention to their same-sex parent—the father for boys and the mother for girls. They begin to imitate their same-sex parent in many ways and in a sense to idolize them. The effect of this imitation is to build a strong bond between the flattered and approving parent and the

attentive, hero-worshipping son or heroine-worshipping daughter. Fear and envy are resolved. Gender roles are learned, and anxiety over the genitals is resolved. This process of identification is also the initial source of *superego* development. Through their admiration and imitation of the same-sex parent, children learn society's fundamental principles of right and wrong (as interpreted by the parents, of course).

After the phallic stage comes a **latency period** of several years, during which the child's sexual instinctual drive is mostly submerged. After this period is the onset of puberty. The child, now an adolescent, begins to form adult sexual attachments to young people of the other sex. Because the sexual instinctual drive now finds its outlet in heterosexual genital contact, this stage is known as the **genital stage.**

According to Freud, the results of psychosexual development amount to the building blocks of personality and general psychological functioning. Children develop basic ego and superego functions and gender role identities. Their own special mixes of fixations will follow them through life and manifest themselves as distinctive personality traits.

Further Development of Freud's Theory: The Neo-Freudians

As you might imagine, Freud's theory created quite a controversy in the Victorian era when it was unveiled. Its emphasis on childhood sexuality and on seething internal conflicts seemed preposterous and offensive to many. Yet the theory's proposal that adults' thoughts and behavior stem from unconscious forces as well as from early childhood experiences was revolutionary and was recognized by many scholars as a genuinely original idea. Freud attracted many followers who studied his work closely but did not accept it completely. Each of these people agreed with Freud's view on the dynamic forces operating within the psyche. Each of them disagreed with Freud, though, on how much importance to place on the role of unconscious sexual and aggressive instincts in shaping personality.

Carl Jung Many scholars and physicians of the early twentieth century were influenced by Freud's psychodynamic theory and studied with him. One of these people was Carl Jung (1875–1961). Freud called Jung "his adopted eldest son, his crown prince and successor" (Hall & Nordby, 1973, p. 23). However, Jung developed his own version of psychodynamic theory, in which he deemphasized the importance of sexuality. He also disagreed with his mentor on the structure of the unconscious. Freud had little tolerance, and often much sarcasm, for those who disagreed with him. After 1913, he and Jung never saw each other again. Jung continued to develop his theory after the split, drawing ideas from mythology, anthropology,

latency period In Freudian theory, the period between the phallic stage and the genital stage, during which sexual urges are submerged.

genital stage The final of Freud's psychosexual stages (from puberty through adolescence). During this stage the adolescent develops adult sexual desires.

history, and religion, as well as from an active clinical practice in which he saw people with psychological disorders.

One of Jung's more important contributions to psychodynamic theory was his idea of the **collective unconscious,** which contains shared ("collective") memories and ideas inherited from our ancestors. Stored in the collective unconscious are **archetypes,** inherited and universal thought forms and patterns that allow us to notice particular aspects of our world. From the dawn of our species, all humans have had roughly similar experiences with things such as mothers, evil, masculinity, and femininity. Each one of these is represented by an archetype. For example, the *shadow* is the archetype containing basic instincts that allow us to recognize aspects of the world such as evil, sin, and carnality. Archetypes are not stored images or ideas—we are not born with a picture of evil stored somewhere in our brains—but inherited dispositions to behave, perceive, and think in certain ways.

Alfred Adler

Alfred Adler (1870–1937), like Jung, studied with Freud. Also like Jung, Adler believed that Freud had overemphasized sexuality. Adler argued that feelings of inferiority play the key role in personality development. At birth, we are dependent on others for survival. Early in our development, we encounter mostly older, more experienced people who are more capable than we are in almost every aspect of life. The inferiority we feel may be social, intellectual, physical, or athletic. These feelings create tension that motivates us to compensate for the deficiency. Emerging from this need to compensate is a **striving for superiority,** which Adler believed to be the major motivational force in life. In Adler's theory, superiority connotes a "personal best" approach rather than defining achievement merely in terms of outperforming others. Our unique experiences with inferiority, and our consequent strivings for superiority, become organizing principles in our lives and therefore define our personalities.

According to Adler (1939), an individual's striving for superiority is affected by another force, *social interest,* which is an innate desire to contribute to society. So although individuals have a need to seek personal superiority, they have a greater desire to sacrifice for causes that benefit the society as a whole. Thus, whereas Freud believed that people act in their own self-interests, motivated by the id, Adler believed that people desire to help others, directed by social interest. In asserting that positive rather than negative motives direct personality, Adler's ideas represented a sea change in psychodynamic theory.

---

collective unconscious According to Jung, the shared unconscious memories and ideas inherited from our ancestors over the course of human evolution.

archetypes Universal thought forms and patterns that Jung believed resided in the collective unconscious.

striving for superiority Our motivation to achieve our full potential. Adler argued that striving for superiority is born from our need to compensate for our inferiority.

basic orientations Horney's sets of personality characteristics that correspond to the strategies of moving toward others, moving against others, and moving away from others.

Karen Horney

Karen Horney (1885–1952), like other Freudian dissenters, did not believe that sex and aggression are the primary determinants of personality. She did agree with Freud, though, that anxiety is a basic problem that people must address and overcome.

According to Horney, individuals have basic anxiety caused by insecurities in relationships. People often feel alone, helpless, or uncomfortable in their interactions with others. For example, a person who begins a new job is often unsure of how to perform his or her duties, whom to ask for help, and how to approach his or her new co-workers. Horney theorized that to deal with basic anxiety, the individual has three options (Horney, 1950):

- *Moving toward others.* Accept the situation, and become dependent on others. This strategy may entail an exaggerated desire for approval or affection.

- *Moving against others.* Resist the situation, and become aggressive. This strategy may involve an exaggerated need for power, exploitation of others, recognition, or achievement.

- *Moving away from others.* Withdraw from others, and become isolated. This strategy may involve an exaggerated need for self-sufficiency, privacy, or independence.

Horney believed that these three strategies corresponded to three basic orientations with which people approach their lives. These **basic orientations** reflect different personality characteristics. The *self-effacing solution* corresponds to the moving-toward-others strategy and involves the desire to be loved. The *self-expansive solution* corresponds to the moving-against-others strategy and involves the desire to master oneself. The *resignation solution* corresponds to the moving-away-from-others strategy and involves striving to be independent of others. For Horney, personality is a mixture of these three strategies and basic orientations. As the source of anxiety varies from one situation to the next, so may the strategy and basic orientation used to cope with it.

Erik Erikson

Erik Erikson (1902–1994) studied with Anna Freud, Sigmund Freud's daughter. Erikson emphasized social aspects of personality development rather than biological factors. He also differed with Freud about the timing of personality development. For Freud, the most important development occurs during early childhood. Erikson emphasized the ongoing process of development throughout the life span. Erikson proposed that people's personality traits develop as a result of a series of crises they encounter in their social relations with other people. Because these crises continue throughout life, psychosocial development does not end when people become adults. Erikson's theory of lifelong development has been very influential, and his term "identity crisis" has become a familiar, although possibly overextended household term.

Melanie Klein and Object-Relations Theory Yet another dissenter from Freud's ideas was Melanie Klein (1882–1960). Klein thought that the psychodynamic battleground that Freud proposed occurs very early in life, during infancy. Furthermore, its origins are different from the basis Freud proposed. An infant begins life utterly dependent on another. That other person, of course, is the infant's mother. The interactions between infant and mother are so deep and intense that they form the focus of the infant's structure of drives. Some of these interactions provoke anger and frustration (as when the mother withdraws the feeding infant from her breast); others provoke strong emotions of dependence as the child begins to recognize that the mother is more than a breast to feed from. These reactions threaten to overwhelm the individuality of the infant. The way in which the infant resolves the conflict, Klein believed, is reflected in the adult's personality (Gomez, 1997).

Klein's work stimulated a contrasting school of psychodynamic theory called **object-relations theory.** According to object-relations theory, adult personality reflects the relationships that the individual establishes with others when the individual is an infant. The term "object" is not confined to inanimate things; rather, it includes the people, especially the mother, that the infant must relate to. For object-relations theorists, relationships are the key to personality development. An individual forms a mental representation of his or her self, of others, and of the relationships that tie them together. For many object-relations theorists, the need that drives the development of personality is not sexual gratification, as Freud believed, but rather the need for other human beings (Westen, 1998).

Some Observations on Psychodynamic Theory and Research

Sigmund Freud's theory has profoundly affected psychological theory, psychotherapy, and literature. His ideas have provided many people with food for thought. However, his theory has received little empirical support, mainly because he used concepts that are difficult to operationalize. How can anyone study the ego, the superego, or the id? How can a researcher prove (or disprove) through experimentation that an artist's creativity is the result of a displaced aggressive or sexual instinctual drive? Although the theories of Jung, Adler, Horney, Erikson, and Klein have their followers, they have not led to much in the way of scientific research. Conversely, some of Freud's fundamental concepts are alive and well today. In later chapters, you will read about evidence for unconscious processing of social information and about the impact on well-being of discussing traumatic events.

QUESTIONS TO CONSIDER

1. Have you ever found yourself using any of the Freudian defense mechanisms discussed in this chapter? If so, under what circumstances do you tend to use them, and

what unconscious conflict do you suppose you might be protecting yourself from?

2. Do you possess any behaviors that might represent fixations? If so, what are they, and what fixations do they represent?

3. Which neo-Freudian view on personality development makes the most sense to you? Why do you feel this way—what is your rationale for concluding that one view is more sensible than the others? Which of the theories best explains your own personality development? Provide an example.

The Humanistic Approach

The **humanistic approach** to the study of personality emphasizes the positive, fulfilling elements of life. Humanistic psychologists are interested in nurturing personal growth, life satisfaction, and positive human values. These theorists believe that people are innately good and that each of us has an internal drive for **self-actualization**—the realization of our true intellectual and emotional potential. The two most influential humanistic theorists have been Abraham Maslow and Carl Rogers.

Maslow and Self-Actualization

For Abraham Maslow (1908–1970), human motivation is based on a hierarchy of needs. Our motivation for different activities passes through several levels, with entrance to subsequent levels dependent on our first satisfying needs in previous levels. (See FIGURE 10.) If an individual's needs are not met, he or she cannot scale the hierarchy and so will fail to attain his or her true potential.

In Maslow's view, understanding personality requires understanding this hierarchy. Our most basic needs are *physiological needs,* including needs for food, water, oxygen, rest, and so on. Until these needs are met, we cannot be motivated by needs found in the next level (or any other level). If our physiological needs are met, we find ourselves motivated by *safety needs,* including needs for security and comfort as well as for peace and freedom from fear. Once the basic survival and safety needs are met, we can become motivated by *attachment needs,* the need to love and to be loved, to have friends and to be a friend. Next, we seek to satisfy *esteem needs*—to be competent and recognized as such. You are probably beginning to get the picture: We are motivated to achieve needs higher in the hierarchy only after first satisfying lower needs. If we are able to lead a life

---

object-relations theory   The theory that personality is the reflection of relationships that the individual establishes with others as an infant.

humanistic approach   An approach to the study of personality that emphasizes the positive, fulfilling aspects of life.

self-actualization   The realization of our true intellectual and emotional potential.

[FIGURE 10] Maslow's hierarchy of needs. According to Maslow, every person's goal is to become self-actualized. In order to achieve this goal, individuals must first satisfy several basic needs.

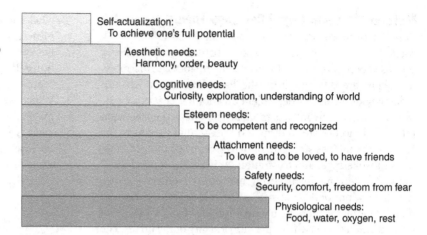

Self-actualization:
To achieve one's full potential

Aesthetic needs:
Harmony, order, beauty

Cognitive needs:
Curiosity, exploration, understanding of world

Esteem needs:
To be competent and recognized

Attachment needs:
To love and to be loved, to have friends

Safety needs:
Security, comfort, freedom from fear

Physiological needs:
Food, water, oxygen, rest

in which we possess food, shelter, love, esteem, intellectual stimulation, and beauty, then we are free to pursue self-actualization.

Maslow based his theory partially on his own assumptions about human potential and partially on his case studies of historical figures whom he believed to be self-actualized, including Albert Einstein, Eleanor Roosevelt, and Frederick Douglass. Maslow examined the lives of each of these people to assess the common qualities that led each to become self-actualized. In general, he found that these individuals were very accepting of themselves and of their life circumstances; were focused on finding solutions to pressing cultural problems rather than to personal problems; were open to others' opinions and ideas; were spontaneous in their emotional reactions to events in their lives; had strong senses of privacy, autonomy, human

values, and appreciation of life; and had a few very close, intimate friendships rather than many superficial ones.

Maslow (1964) believed that the innate drive for self-actualization is not specific to any particular culture. He viewed it as a fundamental part of human nature. In his words, "Man has a higher and transcendent nature, and this is part of his essence . . . his biological nature of a species which has evolved" (p. xvi).

Rogers and Conditions of Worth

Carl Rogers (1902–1987) also believed that people are motivated to grow psychologically, aspiring to higher levels of fulfillment as they progress toward self-actualization (Rogers, 1961). Like Maslow, Rogers believed that people are inherently good and have an innate desire to become better. Rogers, though, did not view personality development in terms of satisfying a hierarchy of needs. Instead, he believed that personality development centers on our *self-concept*, or our opinion of ourself, and on the way we are treated by others.

Rogers argued that all people have a need for *positive regard*, or approval, warmth, love, respect, and affection flowing from others. Young children, in particular, show this need when they seek approval for their actions from parents and siblings. The key to developing a psychologically healthy personality is for us to develop a positive self-concept or image of ourself. How do we do this? Rogers's answer is that we are happy if we feel that others are happy with us. Likewise, we also are unhappy with ourselves when others are disappointed in or unsatisfied with us. Thus, our feelings toward ourselves depend to a large extent on what others think of us. As children, we learn that certain conditions or criteria must be met before others give us positive regard. Rogers called these criteria **conditions of worth.**

Positive regard is often conditional. For example, parents may act approvingly toward their young son when he helps in the kitchen or in the yard but not when he pinches his younger sister or tells a fib about how many cookies he has taken from the cookie jar. The boy learns that what others

Abraham Maslow considered Albert Einstein to possess qualities representative of self-actualization, including self-acceptance, a focus on finding solutions to cultural problems, open-mindedness, and spontaneity.

conditions of worth Conditions that others place on us for receiving their positive regard.

think of him depends on his actions. Soon, too, he may come to view himself as others view him and his behavior: "People like me when I do something good, and they don't like me when I do something bad."

Although conditions of worth are a necessary part of the socialization process, they can have negative effects on personality development if satisfying them becomes the individual's major ambition. In Rogers's view, children often want others to like them to the extent that gaining positive regard is a major focus of their lives. So long as any individual focuses chiefly on seeking positive regard from others, he or she may ignore other aspects of life, especially those that lead to positive personality growth. In Rogers's view, then, conditions of worth may stand in the way of self-actualization. According to Rogers, the solution to this problem is **unconditional positive regard,** or love and acceptance that has no strings attached. In a family setting, this means that parents may establish rules and expect their children to obey them, but not through methods that compromise the children's feelings of worth and self-respect. For example, if a child misbehaves, the parents should focus on the child's behavior and not on the child. The parent is free to stop destructive behavior but should not implicitly undermine the child's self-concept through negative labeling ("What a stupid thing to do;" "You're such a bad girl;" "You must want to hurt Mommy"). Implementing unconditional regard in this way permits children to explore life within reasonable bounds and thereby to realize their inherent potential. Rogers would

SW Productions/Brain X Pictures/Jupiter Images Royalty Free

According to Rogers, all people have a basic need for approval, warmth, and love from others. This need is best met through unconditional positive regard: love and acceptance with no strings attached.

say that parents need to understand and believe that their children are intrinsically good. Bad behavior, in his view, results only when the child's positive potential is being undermined or constrained by the social environment.

In developing his theory, Rogers used unstructured interviews in which the client, not the therapist, directed the course of the conversation. Rogers believed that if the therapist provides an atmosphere of unconditional positive regard, clients will eventually reveal their *true selves,* the kind of people they now are, as well as their *ideal selves,* the kind of people they would like to become.

Some Observations on the Humanistic Approach

The humanistic approach is impressive because of its emphasis on individuals' quest for a healthy and positive life for themselves and others. Indeed, the approach has wide appeal to those who seek an alternative to the more mechanistic biologically or environmentally determined views of human nature. However, critics point out two closely related problems with the humanists' approach.

First, many of the concepts used by humanistic psychologists are defined subjectively and so are difficult to test empirically. For example, how might we empirically examine the nature of self-actualization? Few published studies have even attempted to answer this question. By now you know the hallmark of a good scientific theory—the amount of research it generates. On this count, the humanistic approach comes up short by scientific standards. Keep in mind, though, that humanistic theorists are aware that the structure of their theories hinders the use of scientific research methods. Maslow, for instance, simply did not care—he believed that the scientific method was a hindrance to the development of psychology. Many humanistic psychologists believe that a deeper understanding of human nature can be achieved without the scientific method.

A second criticism of the humanistic approach is that it cannot account for the origins of personality. It is subject to the nominal fallacy; it describes personality, but it does not explain it. Humanistic psychologists believe that the impulse toward self-actualization is an innate tendency, but no research shows this to be so. Conditions of worth are said to hamper a child's quest for self-actualization and thus to alter the course of personality development away from positive psychological growth. However, the humanistic approach provides no objective explanation of this process.

Before moving on to the next section, take a few moments to examine TABLE 4, which reviews each of the major theories of personality discussed.

---

unconditional positive regard In Rogers's approach, the therapist's assertion that a client's worth as a human being is not dependent on anything that he or she thinks, does, or feels; love and acceptance of an individual with no strings attached.

[TABLE 4] A Summary of the Major Personality Theories

Theory	Primary Figures	Primary Emphases	Primary Strengths	Primary Limitations
Trait	Allport, Cattell, Eysenck, McCrae, Costa	An individual's traits determine personality.	Focuses on stability of behavior over long periods; attempts to measure traits objectively.	Largely descriptive; ignores situational variables that may affect behavior.
Psychobiological	Zuckerman, Plomin, Kagan	Genetics and the brain and nervous system play important roles in personality development.	Emphasizes the interaction of biology and environment in determining personality; uses rigorous empirical approach.	Relies on correlational methods in determining the role of genetics in personality.
Social Learning	Bandura, Mischel, Rotter	Personality is determined by both the consequences of behavior and our perception of those consequences.	Focuses on direct study of behavior and stresses rigorous experimentation.	Ignores biological influences on personality development; often more descriptive than explanatory.
Psychodynamic	Freud, Jung, Adler, Horney, Erikson, Klein	Personality is shaped by unconscious psychic conflicts and the repression of anxiety-provoking ideas and desires.	Argues that behavior may be influenced by forces outside conscious awareness.	Built on basic concepts that are not empirically testable.
Humanistic	Maslow, Rogers	Positive aspects of human nature and the quest to become a better person are central to personality.	Proves useful in therapeutic settings.	Contains untestable concepts; primarily descriptive.

QUESTIONS TO CONSIDER

1. Are you a self-actualized person? If not, what obstacles might be standing in the way of your reaching your true potential?
2. Describe some of the conditions of worth that others have imposed on you as you have developed into an adult. Explain how your experience confirms or disconfirms Rogers's idea that conditions of worth are impediments to personal growth and to the development of a healthy self-concept.

Assessment of Personality

One of the best ways to get to know people—what they are like and how they react in certain situations—is to spend time with them. Obviously, psychologists do not have the luxury of spending large amounts of time with people to learn about their personalities. Generally, they have only a short period to accomplish this goal. From this necessity, personality tests were first developed. The underlying assumption of any personality test is that personality charac-

teristics can be measured. This final section of the chapter describes the two primary types of personality tests—objective tests and projective tests—and discusses the three tests most frequently used by clinical psychologists (Watkins, et al., 1995).

Objective Tests of Personality

Objective personality tests are similar in structure to classroom tests. Most contain multiple-choice and true/false items, although some allow test takers to indicate the extent to which they agree or disagree with an item. The responses that participants can make on objective tests are constrained by the test design. The questions asked are unambiguous, and explicit rules for scoring the participants' responses can be specified in advance.

One of the oldest and most widely used objective tests of personality is the **Minnesota Multiphasic Personality Inventory (MMPI),** originally devised in 1939. The purpose for developing the test was to produce an objective, reliable method for identifying various personality traits that were related to mental health. The developers believed that this test would be valuable in assessing people for a variety of purposes. For instance, it would provide a specific means of determining how effective psychotherapy was. Improvement in people's scores over the course of treatment would indicate that the treatment was successful. The test was developed by administering several hundred true/false items to several groups of people in mental institutions in Minnesota who had been diagnosed as having certain psychological disorders. Clinicians had ar-

---

objective personality tests Tests for measuring personality that can be scored objectively, such as a multiple-choice or true/false test.

Minnesota Multiphasic Personality Inventory (MMPI) An objective test originally designed to distinguish individuals with psychological problems from normal individuals. The MMPI has since become popular as a means of attempting to identify personality characteristics of people in many everyday settings.

rived at these diagnoses through psychiatric interviews with the patients. The control group consisted of relatives and friends of the patients, who were tested when they came to visit them. (Whether these people constituted the best possible group of normal participants is questionable.)

The current, revised version of this test, the MMPI-2, has norms based on a sample of people that is much more representative ethnically and geographically than the original sample was (Graham, 1990; see also Butcher, 2000). It includes 567 questions, grouped into 10 *clinical scales* and several *validity scales*. A particular item can be used on more than one scale. For example, both people who are depressed and people who are hypochondriacal tend to agree that they have gastrointestinal problems. The clinical scales include terms traditionally used to label psychiatric patients, such as hypochondriasis, depression, and paranoia.

Four validity scales were devised to provide the tester with some assurance that participants are answering questions reliably and accurately and that they can read the questions and pay attention to them. The ? scale ("cannot say") is simply the number of questions not answered. A high score on this scale indicates either that the person finds some questions irrelevant or that the person is evading issues he or she finds painful.

The L scale ("lie") contains items such as "I do not read every editorial in the newspaper every day" and "My table manners are not quite as good at home as when I am out in company." A person who disagrees with questions like these is almost certainly not telling the truth. A high score on the L scale suggests the need for caution in interpreting other scales and also reveals something about the participant's personality.

The F scale ("frequency") consists of items that are answered one way by at least 90% of the normal population. The usual responses are "false" to items such as "I can easily make other people afraid of me, and sometimes do it for the fun of it" and "true" to items such as "I am liked by most people who know me." A high score on this scale indicates carelessness, poor reading ability, or very unusual personality traits.

The K scale ("defensiveness") was devised to identify people who are trying to hide their feelings to guard against internal conflicts that might cause them emotional distress. A person receives a high value on the K scale by answering "false" to statements such as "Criticism or scolding hurts me terribly" and "At times, my mind seems to work more slowly than usual."

As well as being used in clinical assessment, the MMPI has been used extensively in personality research, and several other tests, including the California Psychological Inventory and the Taylor Manifest Anxiety Scale, are based on it. However, the MMPI was developed as a way of assessing clinical states. A clinical psychologist is faced with a very different task from that of a personality theorist describing general traits of personality. Thus, the factors that might be important to the Five Factor explanation of behavior may not be relevant to questions of therapy or the classification of mental disorders.

A recent development in personality assessment has been a movement to produce an "open source" set of personality tests that can be used by researchers around the world. One such project is the International Personality Item Pool. The items included in this set are specifically designed to be readily translated into other languages, facilitating cross-cultural comparisons. The project is still under development, but does promise to have a large impact on personality research (Goldberg, et al., 2006). You can examine the current status of this project at www.ipip.ori.org.

Projective Tests of Personality

Projective tests of personality are different in form from objective ones and are derived from psychodynamic theories of personality. Psychoanalytically oriented psychologists believe that behavior is determined more by unconscious processes than by conscious thoughts or feelings. Thus, they believe that a test that asks straightforward questions is unlikely to tap the real roots of an individual's personality characteristics. **Projective tests** are designed to be ambiguous; the hope is that test-takers' answers will be more revealing than simple agreement or disagreement with statements provided by objective tests. The assumption of projective tests is that individuals will "project" their personalities into the ambiguous situations and thus will make responses that give clues to their personalities. To someone trained in the interpretation of projective tests, these clues can provide insight into the individual's personality. In addition, the ambiguity of the tests makes it unlikely that participants will have preconceived notions about which answers are socially desirable. Thus, it will be difficult for participants to give biased answers in an attempt to look better (or worse) than they actually are.

The Rorschach Inkblot Test   One of the oldest projective tests of personality is the Rorschach Inkblot Test, published in 1921 by Hermann Rorschach, a Swiss psychiatrist. The **Rorschach Inkblot Test** consists of 10 pictures of inkblots. Rorschach published these pictures from images made by spilling ink on a piece of paper and then folding the paper in half, producing blots that were symmetrical in relation to the line of the fold. Five of the inkblots in the test are black and white, and five are colored. (See FIGURE 11.) The participant is shown each card and asked to describe what it looks like. Then the cards are shown again, and the participant is asked to point out the features he or she used to de-

---

projective tests   Unstructured personality measures in which a person is shown a series of ambiguous stimuli, such as pictures, inkblots, or incomplete drawings. The person is asked to describe what he or she "sees" in each stimulus or to create stories that reflect the theme of the drawing or picture.

Rorschach Inkblot Test   A projective test in which a person is shown a series of symmetrical inkblots and asked to describe what he or she thinks they represent.

[**FIGURE 11**] An inkblot similar to one of the blots that appear in the Rorschach Inkblot Test.

termine what was seen. The responses and the nature of the features the participant uses to make them are scored on several dimensions.

In the following example described by Pervin (1975), a person's response to a particular inkblot (not the example shown in Figure 11) might be "Two bears with their paws touching one another playing pattycake, or could be they are fighting, and the red is the blood from the fighting." The classification of this response, also described by Pervin, would be: Large detail of the blot was used, good form was used, movement was noted, color was used in the response about blood, an animal was seen, and a popular response (two bears) was made. A possible interpretation of the response might be:

> Subject starts off with popular response and animals expressing playful, "childish" behavior. Response is then given in terms of hostile act with accompanying inquiry. Pure color response and blood content suggest he may have difficulty controlling his response to the environment. Is a playful, childlike exterior used by him to disguise hostile, destructive feelings that threaten to break out in his dealings with the environment? (Pervin, 1975, p. 37)

Although the interpretation of people's responses to the Rorschach Inkblot Test was originally based on psychoanalytical theory, many investigators have used it in an empirical fashion. That is, a variety of different scoring methods have been devised, and the scores obtained by these methods have been correlated with clinical diagnoses, just as investigators have done with people's scores on the MMPI. When this test is used empirically, the style and content of the responses are not interpreted in terms of a theory (as Rorschach interpreted them) but are simply correlated with other measures of personality.

Thematic Apperception Test (TAT) A projective test in which a person is shown a series of ambiguous pictures that involve people. The person is asked to make up a story about what the people are doing or thinking. The person's responses are believed to reflect aspects of his or her personality.

The Thematic Apperception Test Another popular projective test, the **Thematic Apperception Test (TAT)**, was developed in 1938 by psychologists Henry Murray and C. D. Morgan to measure various psychological needs. People are shown a picture of a very ambiguous situation and asked to tell a story about what is happening in the picture—to explain the situation, what led up to it, what the characters are thinking and saying, and what the final outcome will be. The idea is that test takers will "project" themselves into the scene and that their stories will therefore reflect their own needs.

As you might imagine, scoring is difficult and requires a great deal of practice and skill. The tester attempts to infer the psychological needs expressed in the stories. Consider the responses of one woman to several TAT cards, along with a clinician's interpretation of these responses (Phares, 1979). The questions asked by the examiner are in parentheses.

> Card 3BM. Looks like a little boy crying for something he can't have. (Why is he crying?) Probably because he can't go somewhere. (How will it turn out?) Probably sit there and sob hisself to sleep. Card 3GF. Looks like her boyfriend might have let her down. She hurt his feelings. He's closed the door on her. (What did he say?) I don't know. Card 10. Looks like there's sorrow here. Grieving about something. (About what?) Looks like maybe one of the children's passed away. Interpretation: The TAT produced responses that were uniformly indicative of unhappiness, threat, misfortune, a lack of control over environmental forces. None of the test responses were indicative of satisfaction, happy endings, etc. . . . In summary, the test results point to an individual who is anxious and, at the same time, depressed. (Phares, 1979, p. 273)

The pattern of responses in this case is quite consistent; few people would disagree with the conclusion that the woman is sad and depressed. However, not all people provide such clear-cut responses, and interpreting differences in the stories of people who are relatively well adjusted is much more difficult. As a result, distinguishing among people with different but normal personality traits is hard.

Evaluation of Projective Tests

Most empirical studies have found that projective tests such as the Rorschach Inkblot Test and the TAT have poor reliability and little validity. For example, Eron (1950) found no differences between the scores of people in mental hospitals and the scores of college students. (You can supply your own joke about that.) Entwisle (1972) reported that "recent studies . . . yield few positive relationships between need achievement [measured by the TAT] and other variables" (p. 179). Lundy (1988) suggests that in many of the situations used to validate the TAT, test takers are likely to realize that they are talking about themselves when they tell a story about the cards and may be careful about what they say.

Even if people taking the TAT are not on their guard, their scores are especially sensitive to their moods (Masling, 1960, 1998). Therefore, the scores they receive on one day are often very different from those they receive on another day, but a test of personality is supposed to measure enduring traits that persist over time and in a variety of situations. The TAT also has been criticized for potential gender bias, mostly because of male-dominated themes, such as power, ambition, and status, used to score the test (Worchel, Aaron, & Yates, 1990).

The reliability and validity of the Rorschach Inkblot Test also are rather low. One study that used the most reliable scoring method found little or no correlation between participants' scores on the Rorschach and their scores on six objective tests of personality (Greenwald, 1990, 1999).

If projective tests such as the Rorschach and the TAT have been found to be of low reliability and validity, why do many clinical psychologists and psychiatrists continue to use them? The primary reason seems to be tradition. The use of these tests has a long history, and the rationale for the tests is consistent with psychodynamic explanations of personality. Many psychodynamic and clinical psychologists still argue that the tests provide them with valuable tools for discovering and evaluating inner determinants of personality (Watkins, 2000).

QUESTIONS TO CONSIDER

1. Which kind of personality inventory—objective tests or projective tests—do you suppose would be more effective in revealing important aspects of your personality? Why?
2. If your results on a personality inventory revealed that you possess a personality trait that you didn't think you had (especially if it is a negative trait), how would you react? Would you tend to disparage the test, or would you admit that in fact this trait is part of your personality?
3. What kinds of personality differences between men and women have you noticed? Are these differences genuine, or do your observations reflect the stereotypes you hold of the sexes? How do you know?

Epilogue

Identical Twins Raised Together

The similarity shown by some cases of identical twins raised apart, such as the two Jims, Bridget and Dorothy, and Oskar and Jack, is impressive. Oskar and Jack, for example, were raised in very different countries and were brought up to identify with remarkably dissimilar cultures. Yet they showed parallels in many behaviors–such as choice of shirt style and type of eyeglasses. What could explain the odd quirks like wearing rubber bands on their wrists?

Although the twins in this prologue share identical genomes, it's obviously a stretch to say that genes control behavior to this level of detail. One of the values of personality theory to psychology is that it provides a higher-level description of behaviors. The study of personality helps us understand which of the similarities and differences are important. Knowing how to group behaviors together helps us analyze the causal factors behind them.

As a concrete example, consider two women, born as identical twins, interviewed by Kaminsky and his colleagues (Kaminsky et al., 2008). When these twins were young, their parents dressed them identically, making them physically indistinguishable. As girls, they were the best of friends and, as adults, they remain emotionally close. Yet they followed very different paths in life: One twin left home when she was 17, traveled, learned languages, and eventually became a war correspondent. She covered many of the world's hotspots, saw people killed, and married, in her forties, a cameraman who also worked on war assignments. They have no children. Her twin, who had no interest in learning a language, stayed home, married while young to a lawyer, had two children, and now works in a law office. When tested on various personality measures, such as the MMPI, they showed many differences. For example, the second twin, working in the law office, showed traits reflecting anxiety, tension, and discomfort, whereas the war correspondent did not. Basically, in several measures, the war correspondent showed traits that seemed risk seeking, whereas her twin sister seemed risk averse.

The twins in this study are the other side of the twin question: They were raised together, but show strong differences in the careers they chose and the way they lived their lives. The source of these differences has been difficult to identify; Kaminsky and his colleagues found some clues in the epigenetic changes. These clues concerned a region of the twins' genome that has been linked to the ability to handle stress—an obvious link to their different tolerance for risk. If clues like these can be confirmed, it may be that the information supplied by tests such as the MMPI will be linked to specific regions on the genome.

CHAPTER SUMMARY

Trait Theories of Personality

We can conceive of personality characteristics as types or traits. The earliest theory of personality classified people into types according to their predominant humor, or body fluid. Today most psychologists conceive of personality differences as being matters of degree, not of kind.

The search for core personality traits began with Allport, who studied how everyday words are used to describe personality characteristics. Although Allport never isolated a core set of traits, his work inspired others to continue the search for such traits. Several researchers developed their trait theories through factor analysis. Cattell's analyses indicated the existence of 16 personality factors. Eysenck's research suggested that personality is determined by three dimensions: extroversion (versus introversion), neuroticism (versus emotional stability), and psychoticism (versus self-control). McCrae and Costa's five-factor model, based on an analysis of words used to describe people's behavioral traits, includes neuroticism, extroversion, openness, agreeableness, and conscientiousness. Ongoing research may identify additional fundamental personality dimensions including socially negative traits such as the "Dark Triad" of Machiavellianism, narcissism, and psychopathy. Studies of similarities in traits across different cultures have found that the first three traits of the five-factor model can be found in most cultures, and that when people describe someone known to them, they generally use traits from the five-factor model. Some differences exist between cultures, however, and people who immigrate into another culture exhibit changes in some specific traits.

Psychobiological Approaches

Studies of twins indicate that personality factors, especially extroversion, neuroticism, and psychoticism, are affected strongly by genetic factors. However, little evidence is found for an effect of common family environment, largely because each individual's family environment is strongly affected by hereditary factors, such as personality and physical attributes. Family environment does have an influence on social attitudes. Study of infants' temperaments suggests that activity level, social fearfulness, anger proneness, and interest have a genetic component; genetic similarity, however, was less predictive of similarity in expressing happiness.

Important personality traits are likely to be the products of neural systems responsible for reinforcement, punishment, and arousal. Zuckerman believes that extroversion is determined by a sensitive reinforcement system, neuroticism by a sensitive punishment system (which includes the amygdala), and psychoticism by the combination of a deficient punishment system and an abnormally high optimal level of arousal.

Research on shyness indicates that childhood shyness is a relatively stable trait that can be seen in the way children react to strangers and strange situations. The differences between shy and non-shy children manifest themselves in physiological responses controlled by the amygdala that indicate the presence of stress. This pattern of amygdala reactivity persists into adulthood.

Social Cognitive Approaches

Social cognitive theory blends Skinner's notion of reinforcement or other approaches to learning with cognitive concepts, such as expectancy, to explain social interaction and personality. According to Bandura, people learn the relation between their behavior and its consequences by observing how others' behavior is rewarded and punished. Bandura also believes that personality is the result of reciprocal determinism—the interaction of behavior, environment, and cognitive variables. The extent to which a person is likely to attempt to change his or her environment is related to self-efficacy, the expectation that the individual will be successful in producing the change. People with low self-efficacy tend not to try to alter their environments; just the opposite is true for people with high self-efficacy. Mischel has argued that personality differences are due largely to individual differences in cognition. These variables include competencies, encoding strategies and personal constructs, expectancies, subjective values, and self-regulatory systems and plans.

In the past, psychologists disagreed about the relative importance of situations and personality traits in determining a person's behavior. It now appears that personality traits are correlated with behavior, especially when multiple observations of particular behaviors are made. In addition, some situations (such as a funeral or a stoplight) are more powerful than others, exerting more control on people's behavior. Traits and situations interact: Some people may be affected more than others by a particular situation, and people tend to choose the types of situations in which they find themselves. Rotter's research has shown that locus of control—the extent to which people believe that their behavior is controlled by person variables or by environmental variables—is also an important determinant of personality. Positive psychology seeks to integrate knowledge of social and cognitive psychology to explain valued aspects of life, such as happiness and satisfaction.

The Psychodynamic Approach

Freud proposed that the mind is full of conflicts between the primitive urges of the id, the practical concerns of the ego, and the internalized prohibitions of the superego. According to Freud, these conflicts tend to be resolved through compromise formation and through ego defenses such as repression, sublimation, and rationalization. Freud's theory of psychosexual development, a progression through the oral, anal, phallic, and genital stages, provided the basis for a theory of personality and personality disorders.

Freud's followers—most notably Jung, Adler, Horney, Erikson, and Klein—embraced different aspects of Freud's theory, disagreed with other aspects of it, and embellished still other aspects. Jung disagreed with Freud about the structure of the unconscious and the role of sexuality in personality development, and he saw libido as a positive life force. Adler also disagreed with Freud on the importance of sexuality; instead, he emphasized our need to compensate for our inferiority and our innate desire to help others as the major forces in personality development. Horney argued that personality is the result of the strategies and behaviors people use to cope with anxiety, which she believed is the fundamental problem that all people must overcome in the course of normal personality development. Erikson maintained that personality development is more a matter of psychosocial processes than of psychosexual processes. He viewed personality development as involving eight stages, each of which requires resolution of a major conflict or crisis. Resolving the conflict allows the person to pass to the next stage; failing to resolve it inhibits normal personality development. Klein suggested that psychodynamic conflict occurs early in infancy and centers on the relation between the infant and the mother. Her work formed the basis for object-relations theory, which posits that relationships with others constitute the fundamental basis of personality.

The Humanistic Approach

The humanistic approach attempts to understand personality and its development by focusing on the positive side of human nature and on self-actualization, or people's attempts to reach their full potential.

Maslow argued that self-actualization is achieved only after the satisfaction of several other important but lower-level needs; for example, physiological, safety, and attachment needs. Maslow's case study analyses of people whom he believed to be self-actualized revealed several common personality characteristics, including self-acceptance, a focus on addressing cultural rather than personal problems, spontaneity, preservation of privacy, an appreciation for life, and possession of a few intimate friendships.

According to Rogers, the key to becoming self-actualized is developing a healthy self-concept. The primary roadblocks in this quest are conditions of worth—criteria that we must meet to win the positive regard of others. Rogers maintained that too often people value themselves only to the extent that they believe other people do. As a result, they spend their lives seeking the acceptance of others instead of striving to become self-actualized. Rogers proposed that only by treating others with unconditional positive regard can we help people to realize their true potentials.

Although the humanistic approach emphasizes the positive dimensions of human experience and the potential that each of us has for personal growth, it has been faulted for being unscientific. Critics argue that its concepts are vague and untestable and that it is more descriptive than explanatory.

Assessment of Personality

Objective tests contain items that can be answered and scored objectively, such as true/false or multiple-choice questions. One of the most important objective personality tests is the Minnesota Multiphasic Personality Inventory (MMPI), which was devised in 1939 to discriminate empirically among people who had been assigned various psychiatric diagnoses. The MMPI has been used widely in research on personality. More recently, researchers interested in personality have turned to tests not based on people with mental disorders, such as the NEO-PI-R.

Projective tests, such as the Rorschach Inkblot Test and the Thematic Apperception Test, contain ambiguous items that elicit answers that supposedly reveal aspects of personality. Because answers on these tests can vary widely, test administrators must receive special training to interpret them. Unfortunately, evidence suggests that the reliability and validity of projective tests are not particularly high.

succeed with mypsychlab

Visit MyPsychLab for practice quizzes, flashcards, and dozens of videos and animated tutorials, including the following items you can find in the "Multimedia Library":

The Five Factor Model
The Id, Ego, and Superego
Defense Mechanisms
Personality Assessment

KEY TERMS

anal stage
archetypes
basic orientations
collective unconscious
conditions of worth
conscience
defense mechanisms
ego
ego-ideal
emotional stability
expectancy
extroversion
five-factor model
fixation
genital stage
humanistic approach
id
introversion
latency period
libido
locus of control
Machiavellianism
Minnesota Multiphasic-
    Personality Inventory
    (MMPI)
narcissism
neuroticism
Neuroticism, Extroversion,
    and Openness Personality
    Inventory (NEO-PI-R)
object-relations theory
objective personality tests

observational learning
oral stage
person variables
personality
personality trait
personality types
phallic stage
pleasure principle
positive psychology
projective tests
psychodynamic
psychoticism
psychopathy
reality principle
reciprocal determinism
Rorschach Inkblot Test
self-actualization
self-control
self-efficacy
situationism
social cognitive theory
striving for superiority
superego
temperament
Thematic Apperception Test
    (TAT)
unconditional positive
    regard
unconscious

SUGGESTED READING

Carver, C. S., & Scheier, M. F. (2003). *Perspectives on personality* (5th ed.). Boston: Allyn & Bacon.

Wiggins, J. S. (Ed.). (1996). *The five-factor model of personality: Theoretical perspectives.* New York: Guilford Press.

Theories of personality, personality testing, and research on the determinants of personality receive thorough coverage in these two texts.

Bandura, A. (1986). *Social foundations of thought and action: A social cognitive theory.* Englewood Cliffs, NJ: Prentice-Hall.

In this book, Bandura presents his account of social cognition and social behavior, which is derived from the behaviorist tradition and cognitive psychology.

Freud, S. (1957). *General introduction to psychoanalysis* (J. Riviere, Trans.). New York: Permabooks.

Jones, E. (1953). *The life and work of Sigmund Freud.* New York: Basic Books.

The best resource on Freud's theories of personality is Freud himself. Jones provides an interesting discussion of Freud's life as well as of his writings.

References

Adamec, R. E., & Stark-Adamec, C. (1986). Limbic hyperfunction, limbic epilepsy, and interictal behavior: Models and methods of detection. In B. K. Doane & K. E. Livingston (Eds.), *The limbic system* (pp. 129–145). New York: Raven Press.

Allik, J., & McCrae, R. R. (2002). A five-factor theory perspective. In R. R. McCrae & J. Allik (Eds.), *The five-factor model of personality across cultures* (pp. 303–321).

Allik, J., & McCrae, R. R. (2004). Toward a geography of personality traits: Patterns of profiles across 36 cultures. *Journal of Cross-Cultural Psychology, 35*(1), 13–28.

Allport, G. W., & Odbert, H. S. (1936). Trait-names: A psycholexical study. *Psychological Monographs, 47* (1, Whole No. 211).

Bandura, A. (1978). The self system in reciprocal determinism. *American Psychologist, 33,* 344–358.

Bandura, A. (1982). Self-efficacy mechanism in human agency. *American Psychologist, 37,* 122–147.

Bandura, A. (1986). *Social foundations of thought and action: A social-cognitive theory.* Englewood Cliffs, NJ: Prentice-Hall.

Bandura, A. (1995). Exercise of personal and collective efficacy in changing societies. In A. Bandura (Ed.), *Self-efficacy in changing societies.* New York: Cambridge University Press.

Bandura, A. (1997). *Self-efficacy: The exercise of control.* New York: W. H. Freeman.

Bandura, A. (2002). Social cognitive theory in cultural context. *Applied Psychology, 51*(2), 269–290.

Bandura, A., & Locke, E. A. (2003). Negative self-efficacy and goal effects revisited. *Journal of Applied Psychology, 88*(1), 87–99.

Barrick, M. R., Mount, M. K., & Judge, T. A. (2001). Personality and performance at the beginning of the new millennium: What do we know and where do we go next? *International Journal of Selection & Assessment, 9*(1–2), 9–30.

Berlin, H. A., Rolls, E. T., & Kischika, U. (2004). Impulsivity, time perception, emotion and reinforcement sensitivity in patients with orbitofrontal cortex lesions. *Brain, 127,* 1108–1126.

Bouchard, T. J., Jr. (1997). The genetics of personality. In K. Blum & E. P. Noble (Eds.), *The handbook of psychiatric genetics* (pp. 273–296). Boca Raton, FL: CRC Press Inc.

Bouchard, T. J., Jr., & Hur, Y.-M. (1998). Genetic and environmental influences on the continuous scales of the Myers-Briggs Type Indicator: An analysis based on twins reared apart. *Journal of Personality, 66,* 135–149.

Bower, M. (1991). Classification of disciplinary events and choices as a function of childhood history. Unpublished manuscript. University of Iowa, Iowa City, IA.

Briggs, S. R. (1988). Shyness: Introversion or neuroticism? *Journal of Research in Personality, 22,* 290–307.

Broverman, I. K., Vogel, S. R., Broverman, D. M., Clarkson, F. E., & Rosenkrantz, P. S. (1972). Sex-role stereotypes: A current appraisal. *Journal of Social Issues, 28,* 59–78.

Buss, A. H. (1995). *Personality: Temperament, social behavior, and the self.* Boston: Allyn & Bacon.

Butcher, J. N. (Ed.). (2000). *Basic sources on the MMPI-2.* Minneapolis: University of Minneapolis Press.

Canli, T., Sivers, H., Whitfield, S. L., Gotlib, I. H., & Gabrieli, J. D. E. (2002). Amygdala response to happy faces as a function of extraversion. *Science, 296,* 2191.

Canli, T., Zhao, Z., Desmond, J. E., Kang, E., Gross, J., & Gabrieli, J. D. E. (2001). An fMRI study of personality influences on brain reactivity to emotional stimuli. *Behavioral Neuroscience, 115,* 33–42.

Caprara, G.V., & Perugini, M. (1994). Personality described by adjectives: Generalizability of the Big Five to the Italian lexical context. *European Journal of Personality, 8,* 357–369.

Chapman, B. P., Duberstein, P. R., Sörensen, S., & Lyness, J. M. (2007). Gender differences in Five Factor Model personality traits in an elderly cohort. *Personality and Individual Differences, 43,* 1594–1603.

Church, A. T., Katigbak, M. S., Ortiz, F. A., del Prado, A. M., Vargas-Flores, J., Ibanez-Reyes, J., Reyes, J. A. S., Pe-Pua, R. & Cabrera, H. F. (2005). Investigating implicit trait theories across cultures. *Journal of Cross-Cultural Psychology, 36,* 476–496.

Costa, P. T., Jr., & McCrae, R. R. (1998a). Trait theories of personality. In D. F. Barone & M. Hersen (Eds.), *Advanced personality* (pp. 103–121). New York: Plenum Press.

Costa, P. T., Jr., & McCrae, R. R. (1998b). The Revised NEO Personality Inventory (NEO-P-R). In S. R. Briggs, J. M. Cheek, & E. M. Donahue (Eds.), *Handbook of adult personality inventories* (pp. 1–29). New York: Plenum.

Cramer, P. (2003). Personality change in later adulthood is predicted by defense mechanism use in early adulthood. *Journal of Research in Personality, 37,* 76–104.

De Raad, B. (1998). Five big, Big-Five issues: rationale, content, structure, status and cross-cultural assessment. *European Psychologist, 3,* 113–124.

DeNeve, K. M., & Cooper, H. (1998). The happy personality: A meta-analysis of 137 personality traits and subjective well-being. *Psychological Bulletin, 124,* 197–229.

Eagly, A. H., & Karau, S. J. (1991). Gender and the emergence of leaders: A meta-analysis. *Journal of Personality and Social Psychology, 60,* 685–710.

Egan, W., & McCorkindale, C. (2007). Narcissism, vanity, personality and mating effort. *Personality and Individual Differences, 43,* 2105–2115.

Eisenberg, N., Fabes, R. A., Schaller, M., Miller, P., Carlo, G., Poulin, R., Shea, C., & Shell, R. (1991). Personality and socialization: Correlates of vicarious emotional responding. *Journal of Personality and Social Psychology, 61,* 459–470.

Ellenberger, H. F. (1972). The story of "Anna O": A critical review with new data. *Journal of the History of the Behavioral Sciences, 8,* 267–279.

Entwisle, D. (1972). To dispel fantasies about fantasy-based measures of achievement motivation. *Psychological Bulletin, 77,* 377–391.

Epstein, S. (1979). The stability of behavior. I. On predicting most of the people much of the time. *Journal of Personality and Social Psychology, 37,* 1097–1126.

Epstein, S. P. (1986). Does aggregation produce spuriously high estimates of behavior stability? *Journal of Personality and Social Psychology, 50,* 1199–1210.

Eron, L. D. (1950). A normative study of the thematic apperception test. *Psychological Monographs, 64,* Whole No. 315.

Eysenck, H. J. (1970). *The structure of human personality* (3rd ed.). London: Methuen.

Eysenck, H. J., & Eysenck, M. W. (1985). *Personality and individual differences: A natural science approach.* New York: Plenum Press, 1985.

Fabes, R. A., Eisenberg, N., Smith, M. C., & Murphy, B. C. (1996). Getting angry at peers: Associations with liking of provocateur. *Child Development, 67,* 942–956.

Feist, G. J., & Barron, F. X. (2003). Predicting creativity from early to late adulthood: Intellect, potential, and personality. *Journal of Research in Personality, 37,* 62–88.

Fincham, F., & Beach, S. R. H. (2007). Forgiveness and marital quality: Precursor or consequence in well-established relationships? *Journal of Positive Psychology, 2,* 260–268.

Funder, D.C. (2006). Towards a resolution of the personality triad: Persons, situations, and behaviors. *Journal of Research in Personality, 40,* 21–34.

García, L. F., Antón, A., García, Ó, & Colom, R. (2007). Do parents and children know each other? A study about agreement on personality within families. *Psicothema, 19,* 120–123.

Goldberg, L. R. (1993). The structure of phenotypic personality traits. *American Psychologist, 48,* 26–34.

Goldberg, L. R., Johnson, J. A., Eber, H. W., Hogan, R., Ashton, M. C., Cloninger, C. R., & Gough, H. G. (2006). The international personality item pool and the future of public-domain personality measures. *Journal of Research in Personality, 40,* 84–96.

Gomez, L. (1997). *An introduction to object relations.* New York: New York University Press.

Graham, J. R. (1990). *MMPI-2: Assessing personality and psychopathology.* New York: Oxford University Press.

Greenwald, D. F. (1990). An external construct validity study of Rorschach personality variables. *Journal of Personality Assessment, 55,* 768–780.

Greenwald, D. F. (1999). Relationships between the Rorschach and the NEO-Five Factor Inventory. *Psychological Reports, 85(2),* 519–527.

Hair, M., Renaud, K. V., & Ramsay, J. (2007). The influence of self-esteem and locus of control on perceived email-related stress. *Computers in Human Behavior, 23,* 2701–2803.

Hall, C. S., & Nordby, V. J. (1973). *A primer of Jungian psychology.* New York: New American Library.

Harris, M. (1991). *Cultural anthropology* (3rd ed.). New York: HarperCollins.

Hartshorne, H., & May, M. A. (1928). *Studies in deceit.* New York: Macmillan.

Hur, Y.-M. (2005). Genetic and environmental influences on self-concept in female preadolescent twins: Comparison of Minnesota and Seoul data. *Twin Research and Human Genetics, 8,* 291–299.

Jackson, D. N., & Tremblay, P. F. (2002). The six-factor personality questionnaire. In B. de Raad (Ed.), *Big five assessment* (pp. 353–375). Ashland, OH: Hogrefe & Huber Publishers.

Jakobwitz, S., & Egan, V. (2006). The dark triad and normal personality traits. *Personality and Individual Differences, 40,* 331–339.

Jang, K. L., Livesley, W. J., & Vernon, P. A. (1996). Heritability of the Big Five personality dimensions and their facets: A twin study. *Journal of Personality, 64,* 577–591.

Jang, K. L., Livesley, W. J., Angleitner, A., Riemann, R., & Vernon, P. (2002). Genetic and environmental influences on the covariance of facets defining the domains of the five-factor model of personality. *Personality & Individual Differences, 33(1),* 83–101.

Johansson, B., Grant, J. D., Plomin, R., Pedersen, N. L., Ahern, F., Berg, S., McClearn, G. E. (2001). Health locus of control in late life: A study of genetic and environmental influences in twins aged 80 years and older. *Health Psychology, 20,* 33–40.

Kagan, J., Reznick, J. S., & Snidman, N. (1988). Biological bases of childhood shyness. *Science, 240,* 167–171.

Kaminsky, Z., Petronis, A., Wang, S.-C., Levine, B., Ghaffar, O., Floden, D., & Feinstein, A. (2008). Epigenetics of personality traits: An illustrative study of identical twins discordant for risk-taking behavior. *Twin Research and Human Genetics, 11,* 1–11.

Keltikangas-Järvinen, L., & Heinonen, K. (2003). Childhood roots of adult hostility: Family factors as predictors of cognitive and affective hostility. *Child Development, 74,* 1751–1768.

Krueger, R. F., Markon, D. E., & Bouchard, T. J., Jr. (2003). The extended genotype: The heritability of personality accounts for the heritability of recalled family environments in twins reared apart. *Journal of Personality, 71(5),* 809–833.

Lefcourt, H. M. (1966). Internal versus external control of reinforcement: A review. *Psychological Bulletin, 65,* 206–220.

Lefcourt, H. M. (1992). Durability and impact of the locus of control construct. *Psychological Bulletin, 112,* 411–414.

Linley, P. A., Joseph, S., Harrington, S., & Wood, A. M. (2006). Positive psychology: Past, present, and (possible) future. *Journal of Positive Psychology, 1,* 3–16.

Livesley, W. J., Jang, K. L., & Vernon, P. A. (2003). Genetic basis of personality structure. In T. Millon & M. J. Lerner (Eds.), *Handbook of psychology: Personality and social psychology, Vol. 5* (pp. 59–83). New York: John Wiley & Sons, Inc.

Loehlin, J. C. (1992). *Genes and environment in personality development.* London: Sage Publications.

Loehlin, J. C., & Nichols, R. C. (1976). *Heredity, environment, and personality.* Austin: University of Texas Press.

Loehlin, J. C., McCrae, R. R., Costa, P. T., & John, O. P. (1998). Heritabilities of common and measure-specific components of the Big Five personality factors. *Journal of Research in Personality, 32,* 431–453.

Lundy, A. C. (1988). Instructional set and thematic apperception test validity. *Journal of Personality Assessment, 52,* 309–320.

Masling, J. (1960). The influence of situational and interpersonal variables in projective testing. *Psychological Bulletin, 57,* 65–85.

Maslow, A. H. (1964). *Religions, values, and peak-experiences.* New York: Viking Press.

Max, J. E., Levin, H., Schachar, R. J., Landis, J., Saunders, A. E., Ewing-Cobbs, L., Chapman, S. B., & Dennis, M. (2006). Predictors of personality change due to traumatic brain injury in children and adolescents six to twenty four months after injury. *Journal of Neuropsychiatry and Clinical Neuroscience, 18,* 21–32.

McCrae, R. R., & Costa, P. T. (1997). Personality trait structure as a human universal. *American Psychologist, 52,* 509–516.

McCrae, R. R., & Costa, P. T., Jr. (1999). A five-factor theory of personality. In L. A. Pervin and O. P. John (Eds.), *Handbook of personality: Theory and research.* (2nd ed.) (pp. 139–153). New York: The Guilford Press.

McCrae, R. R., & Costa, P. T., Jr. (2004). A contemplated revision of the NEO Five-Factor Inventory. *Personality & Individual Differences, 36(3),* 587–596.

McCrae, R. R., & Terracciano, A. (2005). Universal features of personality traits from the observer's perspective: Data from 50 cultures. *Journal of Personality and Social Psychology, 88,* 547–561.

McCrae, R. R., Costa, P. T., Jr., Del Pilar, G. H., Rolland, J. P., & Parker, W. D. (1998). Cross-cultural assessment of the five-factor model: The revised NEO personality inventory. *Journal of Cross-Cultural Psychology, 29,* 171–188.

McCrae, R. R., Costa, P. T., Jr., Ostendorf, F., Angleitner, A., Hrebickova, M., Avia, M. D.,

Sanz, J., Sanchez-Bernardos, M. L., Kusdil, M. E., Woodfield, R., Saunders, P. R., & Smith, P. B. (2000). Nature over nurture: Temperament, personality, and life span development. *Journal of Personality and Social Psychology, 78,* 173–186.

Mischel, W. (1968). *Personality and assessment.* New York: John Wiley & Sons.

Mischel, W. (1976). *Introduction to personality* (2nd ed.). New York: Holt, Rinehart & Winston.

Mischel, W. (1990). Personality dispositions revisited and revised: A view after three decades. In L. Pervin (Ed.), *Handbook of personality: Theory and research* (pp. 111–134). New York: Guilford Press.

Mischel, W. (2003). Challenging the traditional personality psychology paradigm. In R. J. Sternberg (Ed.), *Psychologists defying the crowd: Stories of those who battled the establishment and won* (pp. 139–156). Washington, DC: American Psychological Association.

Mischel, W., & Shoda, Y. (1995). A cognitive-affective system theory of personality: Reconceptualizing situations, dispositions, dynamics, and invariance in personality. *Psychological Review, 102,* 246–268.

Mischel, W., & Shoda, Y. (1998). Reconciling processing dynamics and personality dispositions. *Annual Review of Psychology, 49,* 229–258.

Mischel, W., Cantor, N., & Feldman, S. (1996). Principles of self-regulation: The nature of willpower and self-control. In E. T. Higgins & A. W. Kruglanski (Eds.), *Social psychology: Handbook of basic principles* (pp. 329–360). New York: Guilford Press.

Mischel, W., Shoda, Y., & Rodriguez, M. L. (1989). Delay of gratification in children. *Science, 244,* 933–938.

Paulhus, D. L., & Williams, K. M. (2002). The Dark Triad of personality: Narcissism, machiavellianism, and psychopathy. *Journal of Research in Personality, 36,* 556–563.

Paunonen, S. V. (2003). Big Five factors of personality and replicated predictions of behavior. *Journal of Personality & Social Psychology, 84(2),* 411–422.

Plomin, R., & Asbury, K. (2001). Nature and nurture in the family. *Marriage & Family Review, 33(2–3),* 273–281.

Plomin, R., & Bergeman, C. S. (1991). The nature of nurture: Genetic influence on "environmental" measures. *Behavioral and Brain Sciences, 14,* 373–427.

Rogers, C. R. (1961). *On becoming a person.* Boston: Houghton Mifflin.

Rose, R. J. (1995). Genes and human behavior. *Annual Review of Psychology, 46,* 625–654.

Rotter, J. B. (1966). Generalized expectancies for internal versus external control of reinforcement. *Psychological Monographs, 80(1, Whole No. 609).*

Rotter, J. B. (1990). Internal versus external control of reinforcement: A case history of a variable. *American Psychologist, 45,* 489–493.

Rozin, P., & Royzman, E. B. (2001). Negativity bias, negativity dominance, and contagion. *Personality and Social Psychology Review, 5,* 296–320.

Saudino, K. J. (2005). Behavioral genetics and child temperament. *Developmental and Behavioral Pediatrics, 26,* 214–223.

Schmitt, D. P., Realo, A., Voracek, M., & Allik, J. (2008). Why can't a man be more like a woman? Sex differences in Big Five personality traits across 55 cultures. *Journal of Personality and Social Psychology, 94(1),* 168–182.

Schwartz, C. E., Wright, C.I., Shin, L. M., Kagan, J., & Rauch, S. L. (2003). Inhibited and uninhibited infants "grown up": Adult amygdalar response to novelty. *Science, 300,* 1952–1953.

Seligman, M. E. P., & Csikszentmihalyi, M. (2000). Positive psychology. *American Psychologist, 55,* 5–14.

Shoda, Y., & Smith, R. E. (2004). Conceptualizing personality as a cognitive-affective processing system: A framework for models of maladaptive behavior patterns and change. *Behavior Therapy, 35,* 147–165.

Sneed, C. D., McCrae, R. R., & Funder, D. C. (1998). Lay conceptions of the five-factor model and its indicators. *Personality and Social Psychology Bulletin, 24,* 115–126.

Tupes, E. C., & Christal, R. E. (1961). Recurrent personality factors based on trait ratings. *USAF ASD Technical Report,* 61–97.

Vernon, P. A., Jang, K. L., Harris, J. A., & McCarthy, J. M. (1997). Environmental predictors of personality differences: A twin and sibling study. *Journal of Personality and Social Psychology, 72,* 177–183.

Vernon, P. A., Villani, V. C., Vickers, L. C., & Harris, J. A. (2008). A behavioral genetic investigation of the dark triad and the big 5. *Personality and Individual Differences, 44,* 445–452.

Vollrath, M. (2000). Personality and hassles among university students: A three-year longitudinal study. *European Journal of Personality, 14,* 199–215.

Watkins, C. E., Campbell, V. L., Nieberding, R., & Hallmark, R. (1995). Contemporary practice of psychological assessment by clinical psychologists. *Professional Psychological Research and Practice, 26,* 54–60.

Watkins, C. E., Jr. (2000). Some final thoughts about using tests and assessment procedures in counseling. In Watkins, C. E., Campbell, V. L., Nieberding, R., & Hallmark, R. (1995). Contemporary practice of psychological assessment by clinical psychologists. *Professional Psychological Research and Practice, 26,* 54–60.

Westen, D. (1998). The scientific legacy of Sigmund Freud: Toward a psychodynamically informed psychological science. *Psychological Bulletin, 124,* 333–371.

Wiggins, J. S., & Pincus, A. L. (2002). Personality structure and the structure of personality disorders. In P. T. Costa, Jr., & T. A. Widiger (Eds.), *Personality disorders and the five-factor model of personality* (2nd ed.) (pp. 73–93). Washington, DC: American Psychological Association.

Wiggins, J. S., & Trapnell, P. D. (1997). Personality structure: The return of the Big Five. In R. Hogan, J. A. Johnson, & S. Briggs (Eds.), *Handbook of personality psychology* (pp. 737–765). San Diego: Academic Press.

Wise, E. A., Price, D. D., Myers, C. D., Heft, M. W., & Robinson, M. E. (2002). Gender role expectations of pain: Relationship to experimental pain perception. *Pain, 96(3),* 335–342.

Woodall, K. L., & Matthews, K. A. (1993). Changes in and stability of hostile characteristics: Results from a 4-year longitudinal study of children. *Journal of Personality and Social Psychology, 63,* 491–499.

Worchel, F. F., Aaron, L. L., & Yates, D. F. (1990). Gender bias on the Thematic Apperception Test. *Journal of Personality Assessment, 55,* 593–602.

Zuckerman, M. (1991). *Psychobiology of personality.* Cambridge: Cambridge University Press.

Chapter 6: Interpersonal Attraction and Bonding

Psychologists and sociologists both study social relationships, albeit using different theories and, in some cases, different methods. In the *Handbook of Social Psychology*, a book that reviews the top research in the field today, Terri Orbuch and Susan Sprecher (2006) indicate that much of the early research in this field of interpersonal relationships focused on attraction processes, or what causes people to be attracted to each other in the first place, and much of this work comes from the field of psychology. Some of the dominant theories in this field include reinforcement-affect theory, social exchange theory, balance theory, and excitation-transfer theory.

Applied research on attraction has shown that factors such as physical proximity, similarity with others, physical attractiveness of the other, and reciprocal liking to be relatively consistent predictors of attraction between individuals. More recent research shows that these factors may vary by social context and position—that general predictors of attraction may be different for men and women, as well as across other demographic categories. Men, for instance, appear to be more influenced by physical appearance than are women, while women are more affected than men by the quality of communication.

Sociologists have expanded relationship research in many ways over the years. Employing the symbolic interaction perspective, for instance, sociologists examine the use of narratives in how partners construct the meanings of relationships (see Chapter 2 about narratives). These stories may help to elicit unconscious motives and meanings in relationships that are predictive of real relationship outcomes. In other words, how we construct our beliefs about a relationship—and whether our partner concurs with our stories—can impact the quality of that relationship. From a social structure and personality perspective, many sociologists examine how our structural positions (i.e., race, class, and gender) impact relationship formation and quality. Why do some racial and ethnic groups have higher or lower marriage and divorce rates than others? How are marital (and other) relationships different for those in different social classes or ethnic groups?

Group-processes researchers have applied social exchange theory to study attraction processes. Here, attraction is based on principles of exchange: what people want from another person (e.g., companionship, money, personality, or looks) and what they have to exchange for those things. In addition, we must consider the alternatives to the object of our desire: do they have something that many people want? If so, they are in a stronger position in the relationship market because they have more relationship alternatives than other people do.

Sociologists also contribute to relationship research by employing sociological social psychology perspectives and methods. For instance, the life-course paradigm (see Chapter 6) is particularly well suited to understanding how relationships change over time, and how they intersect with partners' careers (e.g., Becker and Moen 1999). In addition, observational research and in-depth interviews (Chapter 3) may help to elicit the narratives individuals use to create memories and meanings in relationships. Employing such theories and techniques contributes to our understanding of how society impacts our most personal wants and desires.

From: *Social Psychology: Sociological Perspectives*, Second Edition by David E. Rohall, Melissa A. Milkie, and Jeffrey W. Lucas.

Close Quarters:

Why We Fall in Love with the One Nearby

Familiarity may breed contempt, but it also breeds children. That seemingly special charm of your cubicle-mate, next-door neighbor or fellow Peace Corps volunteer may be merely a function of their being nearby and responsive to you.

Since the mid-1980s, Cindy Hazan, an associate professor of human development at Cornell University in Ithaca, New York, has been looking into why we pair up the way we do. It turns out we long to be close to those close by.

Just as an infant forms a special attachment to his mother or caregiver, adult mates become attached to each other through a similar mechanism, Hazan and her colleagues believe. Attachment helps to secure an infant's survival; the bond between adults, while not quite so vital, provides the security and reliability they need to thrive.

Whether it's Mom or your wife-to-be, the presence of your beloved triggers the release of oxytocin, a hormone that induces a state of contentment and stimulates a desire for continued close physical contact. "Proximity is really the core of attachment. Familiar people have a calming, soothing effect on us," says Hazan. Zookeeper's logic applies here: Put two members of any species in the same cage, and they are bound to mate.

This scenario is often played out in the cage that is the workplace, where like-minded humans of both sexes are locked up for eight-to-10 hour days. "When you ask someone why he got together with someone else," Hazan says, "he will never say. 'Well, she was just hanging around.' But propinquity is a big factor. When you have repeated contact with someone, your attraction to them increases. If we have evolved to reproduce, then we shouldn't have to wander around the earth searching for an ideal partner."

What about fate bringing you and your soul mate together, no matter how many miles or office complexes away? "I'm reluctant to pooh-pooh the idea of true love, because it's such a treasured view in our culture," says Hazan. "But there is no empirical evidence to support it. First of all, anyone who has been infatuated more than once and has felt each time, 'This is the person for me!' knows it's wrong. From an evolutionary perspective, it makes zero sense."

We might declare, "I wouldn't date Bob is he were the last man on earth!" But Hazan thinks Bob would grow on us, and that a slow burn over time could boil into a full-blown romance.

Along with proximity, the attachment machine is fueled by stress. In 1973, four Swedes held in a bank vault for six days became enamored of their captors; the incident gave rise to the term "Stockholm syndrome." When 19-year-old publishing heiress Patty Hearst was kidnapped by the Symbionese Liberation Army in 1974, she was soon toting a gun, calling herself Tania and extorting money from her own family.

Hazan says that people nearby are likely partners in stressful situations, because of our natural tendency to seek comfort. "Any port in a storm will do," she says. On September 11, 2011, some strangers who were forced to walk across the Brooklyn Bridge together, or who were trapped in small spaces, reportedly clung tightly to their serendipitous "dates."

The third, and perhaps best, facilitator of attachment is repeated sexual contact. The success of arranged marriage demonstrates this phenomenon. There is no research on whether or not people in arranged marriages experience infatuation, says Hazan, but there is good evidence that they get emotionally attached. An estimated 60 percent of the world's weddings are arranged by family members or religious leaders. And the remaining 40 percent of couples shouldn't be surprised to find themselves cozying up to someone who was right there all along.

—Carlin Flora

The Small-World Problem

STANLEY MILGRAM

Do you personally know Bill Gates, the former CEO of Microsoft? Even if you do not, you might be surprised to discover that on average, it would take only five intermediate acquaintance links to pass a personal message from you to Mr. Gates. This is known as the small-world problem. Because social psychologist Stanley Milgram was interested in these sorts of social links, he devised a creative way to test his ideas about personal communication structure. He discovered that we are all bound together by the social fabric in rather surprising ways.

Almost all of us have had the experience of encountering someone far from home, who, to our surprise, turns out to share a mutual acquaintance with us. This kind of experience occurs with sufficient frequency so that our language even provides a cliché to be uttered at the appropriate moment of recognizing mutual acquaintances.

We say, "My it's a small world."

The simplest way of formulating the small-world problem is: Starting with any two people in the world, what is the probability that they will know each other? A somewhat more sophisticated formulation, however, takes account of the fact that while persons X and Z may not know each other directly, they may share a mutual acquaintance—that is, a person who knows both of them. One can then think of an acquaintance chain with X knowing Y and Y knowing Z.

Moreover, one can imagine circumstances in which X is linked to Z not by a single link, but by a series of links, X-*a*-*b*-*c*-*d* . . . *y*-Z. That is to say, person X knows person *a* who in turn knows person *b*, who knows *c* . . . who knows *y*, who knows Z.

Therefore, another question one may ask is: Given any two people in the world, person X and person Z, how many intermediate acquaintance links are needed before X and Z are connected?

Concern with the small-world problem is not new, nor is it limited to social psychologists like myself. Historians, political scientists, and communication specialists share an interest in the problem. Jane Jacobs, who is concerned with city planning, describes an acquaintance chain in terms of a children's game:

> When my sister and I first came to New York from a small city, we used to amuse ourselves with a game we called Messages. I suppose we were trying, in a dim way, to get a grip on the great, bewildering world into which we had come from our cocoon. The idea was to pick two wildly dissimilar individuals—say a head hunter in the Solomon Islands and a cobbler in Rock Island, Illinois—and assume that one had to get a message to the other by word of mouth; then we would each silently figure out a plausible, or at least possible, chain of persons through which the message could go. The one who could make the shortest plausible chain of messengers won. The head hunter would speak to the head man of his village, who would speak to the trader who came to buy copra, who would speak to the Australian patrol officer when he came through, who would tell the man who was next slated to go to Melbourne on leave, etc. Down at the other end, the cobbler would hear from his priest, who got it from the mayor, who got it from a state senator, who got it from the governor, etc. We soon had these close-to-home messengers down to a routine for almost everybody we could conjure up . . .

The importance of the problem does not lie in these entertaining aspects, but in the fact that it brings under discussion a certain mathematical structure in society, a structure that often plays a part, whether recognized or not, in many discussions of history, sociology, and other disciplines. For example, Henri Pirenne and George Duby, important historians, make the point that in the Dark Ages communication broke down between cities of western Europe. They became isolated and simply did not have contact with each other. The network of acquaintances of individuals became constricted. The disintegration of society was expressed in the growing isolation of communities, and the infrequent contact with those living outside a person's immediate place of residence.

There are two general philosophical views of the small-world problem. One view holds that any two people in the world, no matter how remote from each other, can be linked in terms of intermediate acquaintances, and that the number of such intermediate links is relatively small. This view sees acquaintances in terms of an infinitely intersecting arrangement that permits movement from any social group to another through a series of connecting links.

The second view holds that there are unbridgeable gaps between various groups and that therefore, given any two people in the world, they will never link up because people have circles of acquaintances which do not necessarily intersect. A message will circulate in a particular group of acquaintances, but may never be able to make the jump to another circle. This view sees the world in terms of concentric circles of acquaintances, each within its own orbit.

☺ The Underlying Structure

Sometimes it is useful to visualize the abstract properties of a specific problem before studying it in detail; that is, we construct a model of the main features of the phenomenon as we understand them. Let us represent all the people in the United States by a number of blue points. Each point represents a person, while lines connecting two points show that the two persons are acquainted. . . . Each person has a certain number of first-hand acquaintances, which we shall represent by the letters $a, b, c, \ldots n$. Each acquaintance in turn has his own acquaintances, connected to still other points. The exact number of lines radiating from any point depends on the size of a person's circle of acquaintances. The entire structure takes on the form of a complex network of 200 million points, with complicated connections between them. . . . One way of restating the small-world problem in these terms is this: Given any two of these points chosen at random from this universe of 200 million points, through how many intermediate points would we pass before the chosen points could be connected by the shortest possible path?

☺ Research at M.I.T.

There are many ways to go about the study of the small-world problem, and I shall soon present my own approach to it. But first, let us consider the important contributions of a group of workers at The Massachusetts Institute of Technology, under the leadership of Ithiel de Sola Pool. Working closely with Manfred Kochen of IBM, Pool decided to build a theoretical model of the small-world, a model which closely parallels the idea of points and lines shown. However, unlike my own model, which is purely pictorial, Pool and Kochen translate their thinking into strict mathematical terms.

To build such a model they needed certain information. First, they had to know how many acquaintances the average man has. Surprisingly, though this is a very basic question, no reliable answers could be found in the social science literature. So the information had to be obtained, a task which Michael Gurevitch, then a graduate student at M.I.T., undertook. Gurevitch asked a variety of men and women to keep a record of all the persons they came in contact with in the course of 100 days. It turned out that on the average, these people recorded names of roughly 500 persons, so that this figure could be used as the basis of the theoretical model. Now, if every person knows 500 other people, what are the chances that any two people will know each other? Making a set of rather simple assumptions, it turns out that there is only about one chance in 200,000 that any two Americans chosen at random will know each other. However, when you ask the chances of their having a mutual acquaintance, the odds drop sharply. And quite amazingly, there is better than a 50-50 chance that any two people can be linked up with two intermediate acquaintances. Or at least, that is what the Pool-Kochen theory indicates.

Of course, the investigators were aware that even if a man has 500 acquaintances, there may be a lot of inbreeding. That is, many of the 500 friends of my friend may be actually among the people I know anyway, so that they do not really contribute to a widening net of acquaintances; the acquaintances of X simply feed back into his own circle and fail to bring any new contacts into it. . . . It is a fairly straightforward job to check up on the amount of inbreeding if one uses only one or two circles of acquaintances, but it becomes almost impossible when the acquaintance chain stretches far and wide. So many people are involved that a count just isn't practical.

So the big obstacle one runs up against is the problem of social structure. Though poor people always have acquaintances, it would probably turn out that they tend to be among other poor people, and that the rich speak mostly to the rich. It is exceedingly difficult to assess the impact of social structure on a model of this sort. If you could think of the American population as simply 200 million points, each with 500 random connections, the model would work. But the contours of social structure make this a perilous assumption, for society is not built on random connections among persons but tends to be fragmented into social classes and cliques.

⚙ *A* Harvard *A*pproach

The Pool and Kochen mathematical model was interesting from a theoretical standpoint, but I wondered whether the problem might not be solved by a more direct experimental approach. The Laboratory of Social Relations at Harvard gave me $680 to prove that it could. I set out to find an experimental method whereby it would be possible to trace a line of acquaintances linking any two persons chosen at random.

Let us assume for the moment that the actual process of establishing the linkages between two persons runs only one way: from person A to person Z. Let us call person A the *starting* person, since he will initiate the process, and person Z the *target* person, since he is the person to be reached. All that would be necessary, therefore, would be to choose a starting person at random from the 200 million people who live in the United States, and then randomly choose a target person.

This is how the study was carried out. The general idea was to obtain a sample of men and women from all walks of life. Each of these persons would be given the name and address of the same target person, a person chosen at random, who lives somewhere in the United States. Each of the participants would be asked to move a message toward the target person, using only a chain of friends and acquaintances. Each person would be asked to transmit the message to the friend or acquaintance who he thought would be most likely to know the target person. Messages could move only to persons who knew each other on a first-name basis.

As a crude beginning, we thought it best to draw our starting persons from a distant city, so we chose Wichita, Kansas for our first study and Omaha, Nebraska for our second. (From Cambridge, these cities seem vaguely "out there," on the Great Plains or somewhere.) To obtain our sample, letters of solicitation were sent to residents in these cities asking them to participate in a study of social contact in American society. The target person in our first study lived in Cambridge and was the wife of a divinity school student. In the second study, carried out in collaboration with Jeffrey Travers, the target person was a stockbroker who worked in Boston and lived in Sharon, Massachusetts. To keep matters straight, I will refer to the first study as the Kansas Study, and the second as the Nebraska Study. These terms indicate merely where the starting persons were drawn from.

Each person who volunteered to serve as a starting person was sent a folder containing a document, which served as the main tool of the investigation. Briefly, the document contains:

1. The name of the target person as well as certain information about him. This orients the participants toward a specific individual.

2. A set of rules for reaching the target person. Perhaps the most important rule is: *"If you do not know the target person on a personal basis, do not try to contact him directly. Instead, mail this folder . . . to a personal acquaintance who is more likely than you to know the target person . . . it must be someone you know on a first-name basis."* This rule sets the document into motion, moving it from one participant to the next, until it is sent to someone who knows the target person.

3. A roster on which each person in the chain writes his name. This tells the person who receives the folder exactly who sent it to him. The roster also has another practical effect; it prevents endless looping of the folder through participants who have already served as links in the chain, because each participant can see exactly what sequence of persons has led up to his own participation.

In addition to the document, the folder contains a stack of 15 business reply, or "tracer" cards. Each person receiving the folder takes out a card, fills it in, returns it to us, and sends the remaining cards along with the document to the next link.

Several other features of the procedure need to be emphasized. First, each participant is supposed to send the folder on to one other person only. Thus the efficiency with which the chain is completed depends in part on the wisdom of his choice in this matter. Second, by means of the tracer card, we have continuous feedback on the progress of each chain. The cards are coded so we know which chain it comes from and which link in the chain has been completed. The card also provides us with relevant sociological characteristics of the senders of the cards. Thus, we know the characteristics of completed, as well as incompleted, chains. Third, the procedure permits experimental variation at many points.

In short, the device possesses some of the features of a chain letter, though it does not pyramid in any way; moreover it is oriented toward a specific target, zeroes in on the target through the cooperation of a sequence of participants and contains a tracer that allows us to keep track of its progress at all times.

☺ Would It Work?

The question that plagued us most in undertaking this study was simply: Would the procedure work? Would any of the chains started in Kansas actually reach our target person in Massachusetts? Part of the excitement of experimental social psychology is that it is all so new we often have no way of knowing whether our techniques will work or simply turn out to be wispy pipe dreams.

The answer came fairly quickly. It will be recalled that our first target person was the wife of a student living in Cambridge. Four days after the folders were sent to a group of starting persons in Kansas, an instructor at the Episcopal Theological Seminary approached our target person on the street. "Alice," he said, thrusting a brown folder toward her, "this is for you." At first she thought he was simply returning a folder that had gone astray and had never gotten out of Cambridge, but when we looked at the roster, we found to our pleased surprise that the document had started with a wheat farmer in Kansas. He had passed it on to an Episcopalian minister in his home town, who sent it to the minister who taught in Cambridge, who gave it to the target person. Altogether the number of intermediate links between starting person and target person amounted to *two!*

☺ How Many Intermediaries?

As it turned out, this was one of the shortest chains we were ever to receive, for as more tracers and folders came in, we learned that chains varied from two to 10 intermediate acquaintances, with the median at five. . . . A median of five intermediate persons is, in certain ways, impressive, considering the distances traversed. Recently, when I asked an intelligent friend of mine how many steps he thought it would take, he estimated that it would require 100 intermediate persons or more to move from Nebraska to Sharon. Many people make somewhat similar estimates and are surprised to learn that only five intermediaries will—on the average—suffice. Somehow it does not accord with intuition. Later, I shall try to explain the basis of the discrepancy between intuition and fact.

On a purely theoretical basis, it is reasonable to assume that even fewer links are essential to complete the chains. First, since our participants can send the folder to only one of their 500 possible contacts, it is unlikely that even through careful selections, they will necessarily and at all times, select the contact best able to advance the chain to the target. On the whole they probably make pretty good guesses but surely, from time to time, they overlook some possibilities for short cuts. Thus, the chains obtained in our empirical study are less efficient than those generated theoretically.

Second, by working on a highly rational basis, each intermediary moves the folder toward the target person. That is, a certain amount of information about the target person—his place of employment, place of residence, schooling, and so forth—is given to the starting subject, and it is on the basis of this information alone that he selects the next recipient of the folder. Yet, in real life, we sometimes know a person because we chance to meet him on an ocean liner, or we spend a summer in camp together as teenagers, yet these haphazard bases of acquaintanceship cannot be fully exploited by the participants.

There is one factor, however, that could conceivably have worked in the opposite direction in our experiments, giving us the illusion that the chains are shorter than they really are. There is a certain decay in the number of active chains over each remove, even when they do not drop out because they reach the target person. Of 160 chains that started in Nebraska, 44 were completed and 126 dropped out. These chains die before completion because on each remove a certain proportion of participants simply do not cooperate and fail to send on the folder. Thus, the results we obtained on the distribution of chain lengths occurred within the general drift of a decay curve. It is possible that some of the incompleted chains would have been longer than those that were completed. To account for this possibility, Harrison White of Harvard has constructed a mathematical model to show what the distribution of chain lengths would look like if all chains went through to completion. In terms of this model, there is a transformation of the data, yielding slightly longer chains.

☺ Examining the Chains

Several features of the chains are worth examining, for they tell us something about the pattern of contact in American society. Consider, for example, the very pronounced tendency in our Kansas Study for females to send the folder on to females, and males to send it on to males. . . . [The] participants were three times as likely to send the folder on to someone of the same sex as to someone of the opposite sex. Exactly why this is so is not easy to determine, but it suggests that certain kinds of communication are strongly conditioned by sex roles.

Participants indicated on the reply cards whether they were sending the folder on to a friend, a relative, or an acquaintance. In the Kansas Study, 123 sent the folder to friends and acquaintances, while only 22 sent it to relatives. Cross-cultural comparison would seem useful here. It is quite likely that in societies which possess extended kinship systems, relatives will be more heavily represented in the communication network than is true in the United States. In American society, where extended kinship links are not maintained, acquaintance and friendship links provide the preponderant basis for reaching the target person. I would guess, further, that within certain ethnic groups in the United States, a higher proportion of familial lines would be found in the data. Probably, for example, if the study were limited to persons of Italian extraction, one would get a higher proportion of relatives in the chain. This illustrates, I hope, how the small-world technique may usefully illuminate varied aspects of social structure.

. . .

☺ Common Pathways

Each of us is embedded in a small-world structure. It is not true, however, that each of our acquaintances constitutes an equally important basis of contact with the larger social world. It is obvious that some of our acquaintances are more important than others in establishing contacts with broader social realms; some friends are relatively isolated, while others possess a wide circle of acquaintances, and contact with them brings us into a far-ranging network of additional persons.

Referring to our Nebraska Study, let us consider in detail the pattern of convergence crystallizing around the target person—the stockbroker living in Sharon, Massachusetts, and working in Boston. . . . A total of 64 chains reached him. (44 chains originated in Nebraska and 20 chains, from an auxiliary study, originated in the Boston area). Twenty-four of the chains reached him at his place of residence in the small town outside of Boston. Within Sharon, 16 were given to him by Mr. Jacobs, a clothing merchant in town. Thus, the clothing merchant served as the principal point of mediation between the broker and a larger world, a fact which came as a considerable surprise, and even something of a shock for the broker. At his place of work, in a Boston brokerage house, 10 of the chains passed through Mr. Jones, and five through Mr. Brown. Indeed, 48 percent of the chains to reach the broker were moved on to him by three persons: Jacobs, Jones, and Brown. Between Jacobs and Jones there is an interesting division of labor. Jacobs mediates the chains advancing to the broker by virtue of his residence. Jones performs a similar function in the occupational domain, and moves 10 chains enmeshed in the investment-brokerage network to the target person.

More detail thus fills in the picture of the small world. First, we learn that the target person is not surrounded by acquaintance points, each of which is equally likely to feed into an outside contact; rather, there appear to be highly popular channels for the transmission of the chain. Second, there is differentiation among these commonly used channels, so that certain of them provide the chief points of transmission in regard to residential contact, while others have specialized contact possibilities in the occupational domain. For each possible realm of activity in which the target person is involved, there is likely to emerge a sociometric star with specialized contact possibilities.

Geographic and Social Movement

The geographic movement of the folder from Nebraska to Massachusetts is striking. There is a progressive closing in on the target area as each new person is added to the chain. . . . In some cases, however, a chain moves all the way from Nebraska to the very neighborhood in which the target person resides, but then goes round and round, never quite making the necessary contact to complete the chain. Some chains died only a few hundred feet from the target person's house, after a successful journey of 1000 miles. Thus we see that social communication is sometimes restricted less by physical distance than by social distance.

. . .

Intuition and Fact

As we saw above, many people were surprised to learn that only five intermediaries will, on the average, suffice to link any two randomly chosen individuals, no matter where they happen to live in the United States. We ought to try to explain the discrepancy between intuition and fact.

The first point to remember is that although we deal directly with only five intermediaries, behind each of them stands a much larger group of from 500 to 2500 persons. That is, each participant has an acquaintance pool of 500 to 2500 persons from which he selects the person who, he thinks, is best able to advance the chain. Thus we are dealing only with the end product of a radical screening procedure.

The second thing to remember is that geometric progression is implicit in the search procedure, but nothing is more alien to mathematically untutored intuition than this form of thinking. As youngsters, many of us were asked the question: If you earned a penny a day and the sum were doubled each day, how much would you have earned by the end of a 30-day working period? Most frequently people give answers on the order of $1.87 or $6.45, when in fact the sum is more than $10 million for one 30-day working period, the last day alone yielding $5,268,709.12. Elements of geometric progression with an increase rate far more powerful than mere doubling underlie the small-world search procedure, and thus, with only a few removes, the search extends to an enormous number of persons.

Finally, when we state there are only five intermediate acquaintances, this connotes a closeness between the position of the starting person and the target person. But this is in large measure misleading, a confusion of two entirely different frames of reference. If two persons are five removes apart, they are far apart indeed. Almost anyone in the United States is but a few removes from the President, or from Nelson Rockefeller, but this is true only in terms of a particular mathematical viewpoint and does not, in any practical sense, integrate our lives with that of Nelson Rockefeller. Thus, when we speak of five intermediaries, we are talking about an enormous psychological distance between the starting and target points, a distance which seems small only because we customarily regard five as a small manageable quantity. We should think of the two points as being not five persons apart, but "five circles of acquaintances" apart—five "structures" apart. This helps to set it in its proper perspective.

There is a very interesting theorem based on the model of the small world. It states that if two persons from two different populations cannot make contact, then no one within the entire population in which each is embedded can make contact with any person in the other population. In other words, if a particular person, *a,* embedded in population A (which consists of his circle of acquaintances), cannot make contact with a particular person, *b,* embedded in population B, then:

1. No other person in A can make contact with *b.*

2. No other person in A can make contact with any other person in B.

3. In other words, the two sub-populations are completely isolated from each other.

Conceivably, this could happen if one of the populations were on an island never visited by the outside world. In principle, any person in the United States can be contacted by any other in relatively few steps, unless one of them is a complete and total hermit, and then he could not be contacted at all.

In sum, perhaps the most important accomplishment of the research described here is this: Although people have talked about the small-world problem, and have even theorized about it, this study achieved, as far as I know, the first empirically-created chains between persons chosen at random from a major national population.

Although the study started with a specific set of questions arising from the small-world problem, the procedure illuminates a far wider set of topics. It reveals a potential communication structure whose sociological characteristics have yet to be exposed. When we understand the structure of this potential communication net, we shall understand a good deal more about the integration of society in general. While many studies in social science show how the individual is alienated and cut off from the rest of society, this study demonstrates that, in some sense, we are all bound together in a tightly knit social fabric.

Questions

1. What is the small-world problem? Give an example.

2. Milgram's research is based on communications among white adults in Nebraska, Kansas, and Massachusetts. Based on these limitations in his work, is it fair to assume that it would take only five links for a communication to travel between members of different racial groups? What if the target people who were randomly selected lived in Grand Rapids, Michigan, and Reykjavik, Iceland? Explain your answer.

3. Design a small-world experiment that relies on the use of e-mail to move a message between two randomly selected people. What are some advantages and disadvantages of this design?

LESSONS FROM AN ARRANGED MARRIAGE

Shoba Narayan

There's an old song that goes: "Love and marriage, love and marriage. They go together like a horse and carriage . . . You can't have one without the other." Or can you? Many Americans, indeed many Westerners, would never consider marrying someone they weren't madly in love with. But in India, and in other cultures, young people marry whomever their parents choose.

This was how 25-year old Shoba Narayan was raised. But after living and working in the United States, the last thing she wanted when she returned to India was an arranged marriage. In the end, she and her parents worked out a compromise: She and her prospective husband would retain "veto power" over the match. If they didn't like each other, then they would not marry. Ultimately, Shoba agreed to marry the man her parents picked out for her, mostly because she "couldn't find a good reason to say no."

In this personal account, Narayan tells what it was like to date on her own and then to date men whom her parents picked out. She describes her first meeting with her future husband and explains how and when her love for him grew. While her experience is certainly not the rule—sadly, there are many unhappy and even abusive arranged marriages, especially among poor or uneducated women—it does give insights into what love and marriage mean in another culture and how cultures adapt traditions in response to a changing world.

I met my husband on a rainy November evening at my parents' house in India. I was 25. I had been vacationing at home after five years of art school in the States when my brother blithely suggested that I consider an arranged marriage. Before I had even digested the implications of his remark, my parents were on the lookout for "suitable boys." Six months later, I found myself face-to-face with a cheerful investment manager, the man who would later become my husband.

I was born and raised in India, and so the idea of arranged marriages wasn't foreign to me. Everyone I grew up with—my aunts, uncles, cousins, school friends—had arranged marriages that seemed to be working fine. But living and working in the States had altered my perception. I didn't want to just get married: I wanted to fall in love. I wanted to find the man of my dreams. In the end, I compromised and gave my parents a list of specifications. The man had to be an activist of some sort, I said. Perhaps someone who worked on Greenpeace ships. Either that or he could be an artist in the Himalayas. A lanky recluse like the Indian film stars I fantasized about.

Ram, the man I have been happily married to for the past six years, and the father of my daughter, Ranjini, is none of the above. He's muscular, easygoing, and business-oriented. Yet our marriage works, even though we weren't in love with each other when we got married. In fact, we both freely admit that we probably wouldn't have been attracted to each other had we met at a party.

Naturally, this seems really weird to many of my American friends. Still, living here in the United States, in a culture where most people regard sexual chemistry and falling in love as prerequisites to marriage, I've often wondered whether some of the methods my parents used to select Ram might not work for my single American friends.

True, not all arranged marriages work out well. Ram and I were free to choose each other. If we had disliked each other, our parents would have gone on looking. But sometimes a woman may not have much choice in the matter. This is especially true of poor, uneducated women who have no means of supporting themselves. Hence the ugly specter of 12-year-old girls being married off to 70-year-old men. In most Eastern countries, there is such a stigma attached to divorce that a woman might prefer to endure everything from physical abuse to infidelity just to preserve the marriage.

So I don't say that arranged marriages per se are better than your average Western marriage, where the couple meet at college, at work, at a party, or a bar. But assuming that the man and woman have veto power over the selection of their mate, I believe that some elements of the process could be

"Lessons from an Arranged Marriage," by Shoba Narayan, reprinted from *New Woman*, January, 1998, pp. 79–81, 100.

From: Shoba Narayan, reprinted from *New Woman*, January 1998, by permission of The Elizabeth Kaplan Literary Agency.

adapted for many of my single, eager-to-be-married American friends.

MATCHES AND BALANCES

The method my parents used to select my husband is a tried-and-true formula used by many Indian families: The family and economic background, religion, caste, and values of the groom must be similar, while his personality and physical traits must be different or complementary. The idea is that sameness in a relationship breeds stability and comfort; differences generate energy (including sexual energy), good health in the offspring, and spice.

A few months after my parents began their search for my husband (by spreading the word among their friends), it became apparent to me that I wouldn't get a Greenpeace activist or an artist for a mate. They were looking for someone based on a list of factors that were totally different from mine. Most Indian parents follow this same list when they look for spouses for their children, and most cultures that practice arranged marriage use some version of this list.

My parents were looking for a man from a similar family background that stressed Western education and Eastern values. It was assumed that my future husband would belong to the same religion and caste that we did. Then our horoscopes were compared to see if they matched. Only after my horoscope matched Ram's did my parents proceed with the "alliance." They met with Ram's parents first to decide if there was familiar compatibility. Both of Ram's parents had advanced degrees, they were receptive to Western ideas but valued Indian tradition, and they came from the upper middle class of society. Biological compatibility was also taken into account. My parents wanted a man whose genes balanced mine—someone muscular to balance my chronic thinness, a man with 20/20 vision to balance my shortsightedness, so that our children would get the "best of both genes," as my mother said. They were looking for a man with a logical, engineering mind to offset my artistic flights of fancy, a focused individual to rein in my impulsiveness. They were looking, in short, for my husband Ram.

LOOKS MATTER

Although nobody says it explicitly, the first meeting between the man and woman is mostly about physical chemistry. It is a chance for them to decide if they can sleep with each other, wake up to each other.

Before I met my husband, I was introduced to another man, Vikram, whom my parents considered a suitable match. After an hour of conversation, I decided that Vikram wasn't for me. Perhaps it was his drooping mustache or his gold-rimmed spectacles; perhaps it was his uninflected voice, which didn't dip in introspection or rise in excitement; perhaps it was his insistence that he would never move back to India from America. I am not sure why, but I got the impression that he was inflexible and told my parents so. They called his folks and tactfully disengaged from the relationship.

Ram, my husband, was a refreshing contrast to Vikram. I liked his unbridled laugh, his considerate manner, and the fact that he didn't mind discussing philosophy on our first meeting. Sure, he was still a corporate type and worked for an investment firm in New York; sure he seemed to be a nice, decent, likable sort. But at least he didn't rule out returning to India for good and contributing to society in some fashion. Besides, he had charmed my septuagenarian grandmother, spiritual mother, literary father, and grouchy teenage cousins, all of whom were unanimous in their approval of him.

After that first meeting, Ram went back to his job in the States. We had agreed to speak on the telephone and mutually decide where the relationship was headed, if anywhere. Either of us could call it off at any point, we agreed.

Over the next month, we spoke on the phone every day. We talked about our dreams and anxieties, argued over the spelling of the word *feisty*. Ram aid that it was spelled f-i-e-s-t-y, and I was convinced that he was wrong. So we made a bet and whoever lost had to surprise the other person. That same evening, a huge bouquet of flowers arrived at our door with a card, "Here is a feisty bunch for you. Love, R."

"What do you want out of life?" Ram asked me one day. "Why don't you come up with five words?"

His question intrigued me. "Courage, wisdom, change," I replied flippantly. "What about you?"

"Curiosity, contribution, balance, family, and fun," he said.

One month later, he proposed. I accepted, and the elders took over the wedding preparations. I don't think either of us was in love when we agreed to get married. In fact, I don't think either of us experienced when we first met the kind of physical magnetism that sparks a romantic relationship in the West. In the end, I found myself saying yes to Ram because I couldn't find a good reason to say no.

Sometimes arranged marriages can begin with physical attraction. Bhavani and her husband Srinivasan are both physicians from India who have been married for almost 20 years and now live in Long Island, New York. Their relationship began when Srinivasan saw Bhavani's photograph in a friend's wedding album and wanted to meet her. His brother duly contacted her parents, and both families waited breathlessly while the horoscopes were matched. The stars were kind to them—the astrologer reported that the two horoscopes were a good match. Bhavani agreed to marry him based on a feeling that was grounded in logic and reality. Love would come, she decided. And it did.

THE FIRST NIGHT

Sexual passion is the other big question. How can you sleep with a man you barely know? In India, my friends and I used to go into a huddle every time one of us got married. The single women in our group were curious about how the marriage was working out, and we grilled the new bride mercilessly. Was the husband as nice as he appeared? He wasn't a pervert, was he? Was he treating her well? Had they slept together? What was it like? I remember being shocked when one of my close friends announced that she had slept with her husband on the first night of their marriage. I mean, this was a guy she had met for all of two hours. How could she? "It just happened," she said, and added, a trifle defensively, "It isn't bad, you know."

Most cultures that practice arranged marriages don't encourage dating. Most couples are presumed to be virgins when they get married.

I don't know if real sexual passion happens in all arranged marriages. But then, I don't know if Western marriages are able to sustain sexual passion either. My guess is that a few lucky couples are able to ignite and sustain a good sexual relationship; the vast majority work at making their sexual experience wonderful for both parties; and a few couples are totally turned off by each other and stick to the marriage out of fear, convenience, or because they don't care about sex.

∾ WHAT'S LOVE GOT TO DO WITH IT?

Actually, love has very little to do with arranged marriages. Like most Indian girls, I was raised with the idea that friendship, commitment, support, and humor were more important to sustain a marriage than love.

When I married Ram, I wasn't sure if our marriage would work, for various reasons: America had inculcated Western values in me; Ram and I were too different; all the men I had been attracted to were outrageous and roguish musicians and artists without a regular income; Ram was muscular and I liked lanky men. But I was encouraged by the fact that all my Indian friends had had arranged marriages with the most unlikely of men and were leading happy, fulfilled lives. I had watched other couples who had arranged marriages fall in love with each other. Maybe I would too. And, unlike all my Indian friends, I thought that I could always get a divorce if all else failed. (My parents would be horrified to read this.)

The first two years of our marriage were difficult. I discovered differences between us that had not been apparent during our courtship. I loved going out dancing, trying different wines, hiking and camping, experimenting with various ethnic cuisines. Ram loved Indian food, Indian music, visiting with family. I automatically branded him old-fashioned and hide-bound, not my type.

But Ram was very Western in his thinking: He was very much a self-made, change-your-own-destiny kind of guy. When I didn't get a job I wanted, my attitude was to accept it with resignation and then feel depressed about it. Ram, on the other hand, would urge me to write another letter, go out and

∾ MATCHMAKING, AMERICAN-STYLE

In America, arranged marriages are still practiced among Turkish, Indian, Iranian, and Jewish communities. Mindy and David Schultz, for example, are religious Jews in Brooklyn whose marriage was arranged 19 years ago. They are thinking of arranging a marriage for their son, Samuel, to make sure that he marries a woman from a similar background with traditional Jewish values. Samuel and his prospective bride will be allowed to meet two or three times before deciding whether they want to get married—mainly to see if they like each other as individuals. After all, since it is assumed that both have traditional values in which the woman is in charge of the home and the man goes out to work, it is assumed that both will want the life of a religious Jew and have similar goals.

Arranged marriages also occur in most immigrant Muslim communities in the United States. Lubna Bawany, 18, of Ann Arbor, Michigan, was born and raised in the States, but her parents immigrated from Pakistan. Lubna married her husband two years ago, even though it wasn't her idea. Until recently, the couple lived apart (Lubna with her parents) while they finished school and got to know each other.

In selecting her husband, Lubna's parents were mainly concerned with his religious values, how he treated his sisters, how close he was with the rest of his family, and his education. They questioned Imran during their two meetings to find out if he would let his wife work after marriage and if he expected her to wear the purdah (veil covering he face) while living in the States, something Lubna did not want to do.

Lubna was encouraged by the fact that many other women in her community had wed when they were young and now had successful marriages. She says she did not find Imran particularly attractive when they first met. "But I thought he was a nice guy, and something inside me told me to go along with it," she says.

network. For someone so self-confessedly Western, I discovered to my chagrin that I possessed that most Eastern of values—fatalism and resignation. Where was the rabble-rousing, fighting feminist I thought I was?

It was the realization that I could learn from Ram that began my process of falling in love. Ram was detail-oriented, and, while I had once dismissed this as too "bankerish," I learned that his eye for detail could pick out flaws in my resumé, in my interviewing outfit. "Don't let your voice trail off at the end of a sentence," Ram would tell me. "It makes you appear diffident, and I know that you are a confident person. Use action words and statements instead of asking soft questions."

I learned that while I had once dismissed him for being "too nice," that niceness could have a positive effect on my career. "Why don't you pick up some souvenirs for all your business contacts," he would say when we were in India. "It is a small gesture, but they will value it." Ram routinely picked up unusual gifts for everyone in his office, including his boss, but also including the man who cleaned his office every night. In the beginning, I couldn't figure out why the man was so nice to everyone, why he went out of his way to help people. Over time, I came to realize that Ram's attitude was one of, "If I help people when I can, in the long run it will come back to me in some way, perhaps when I am stranded on a highway."

As I grew to respect his mind, his positive attitude toward life, his success, I forgot that muscular men weren't my type. Instead, I began noticing the sensual, upward curve of his lips, his generous laugh, and how hugging him felt like coming home. By our second anniversary, I could look at my marriage and honestly say that I was a happy and fulfilled woman.

Shoba Narayan is a New York City-based writer who covers relationships, finance, and the Net.

☙ Questions

1. What theory or theories of love might account for the kind of love Narayan felt for her husband when they married? What theory or theories can account for the kind of love Narayan felt for her husband on their second wedding anniversary?

2. What function does dating serve in India? Why? What function does dating serve in America? Why?

3. Do "love" and "marriage" mean the same thing to Americans as they do to people from India? Why or why not?

4. What criteria do Narayan and her family have for picking her future husband? Have you ever thought about these criteria in choosing a potential mate? Would you choose your future mate based on these criteria? Why or why not?

Chapter 7: Communication

Why Can't He Hear What You're Saying?

Your lips are moving. Sounds are coming out, and you swear you're speaking English. But he's Just. Not. Getting it. What to do? Read on for insight into why men misinterpret what women say — and how you can make yourself heard.

By Bryan Stipe

It was a novice mistake, I admit — the kind of dumb thing you do two months into a relationship, not four years. My wife and I were having dinner with friends and I was telling a story about how her brother crashed his car. Yes, maybe I hyperbolized a little bit, played it for laughs at his expense. So when Kristen shot me her death-ray look across the table — the one that means: You have committed some gaffe, said something offensive, revealed something private, etc., and should cease and desist — I ceased and desisted.

But afterward, on the car ride home, she was still mad. "I mean, at this point you shouldn't even apologize," she said. So I didn't apologize. I said I understood. I held her hand a little in the car, and when we got home I made a bowl of ice cream and watched *Big Love*. Later, Kristen came into the den, all dressed for bed, and stood silently watching Bill Paxton and wife number two in flagrante. "Well," she finally snapped, "you could have at least apologized!" When I protested that she'd told me I *shouldn't* apologize, she said, "It would have been a good place to start."

At that moment, I became a walking marriage cliché. You know the cliché I'm talking about. It goes: My wife speaks a strange alien tongue that I, no matter how hard I try, am too dumb to learn. It was one of those moments when you identify with that line from *Knocked Up*. "Marriage is an unfunny version of *Everybody Loves Raymond*."

But there's a reason the cliché exists: A lot of the time we guys *do* need help in the "What the heck are you talking about?" department. The *Everybody Loves Raymond* way of explaining this phenomenon is that we men are too thick to read between the lines. And, okay, this is kind of true. Kristen will try to tell me in every possible way about presents she'd like me to get for her. She might say, "Hey, those earrings are nice!" And nine times out of 10, I do not copy. I might think, *Wow, she really likes to talk about jewelry a lot* or *Wow, does she not realize that I'm not a woman and that I don't care about earrings? Maybe if I'm quiet for long enough she'll change the subject.*

The less *Raymond*-y way of explaining why we don't understand you is to say that we simply have different ways of talking. Men have two modes of communication: saying what we mean and repressing what we mean. We either say, "What you said the other night really pissed me off" or we say, "Hey, wanna go see *Knocked Up*?" Women, on the other hand, use a little more nuance. You *imply* things more than men do; you depend more on subtext. I remember in the beginning of our marriage, Kristen kept telling me that I looked sexy in black underwear. It took me about two months to translate that into "Your old white underpants are graying and disgusting. Please get rid of them and replace them with something that ages better."

The problem with subtext is that too often we men just don't catch it — and then we completely misinterpret you. I hate to say this, because yes, it's yet another "Men are so dumb" cliché, but it's kind of like when you pretend to throw a ball for a dog but really put the ball behind your back. The dog (man) is too stupid to keep his eye on the ball (the hidden meaning) and goes running after nothing.

This falls under my Grand Unified Theory of Male-Female Miscommunication: We misunderstand you most often when you want something but are afraid to (or don't think you should *have* to) ask for it, whether that thing is compassion or a back rub. Part of the problem is that you all are a lot nicer than we are — demure in some cases, and, it must be said, passive-aggressive in others. Kristen wanted me to "get" that she wanted those earrings without her having to ask for them. But when a man misses his cue, both parties can end up pissed. You feel like you're not being treated very well, and blurt out what it is you wanted all along (but are probably too annoyed to want anymore anyway). We feel like we've been ambushed. I'd say that's the dynamic driving fully half of the fights I have with my wife.

There is a way out. And that is: Show us some mercy. We really do want to understand you. And we are often a little intimidated in the communications department, partly because we know we have a reputation for being so bad at it. But look at us. We're trying so hard! Doesn't that count for something?

And we are not entirely untrainable: Over the course of a relationship, we'll (hopefully) pick up a few things. Recently, my friend Scott had a fight with his girlfriend about whether or not they were going to have dinner with his mother the following week. He'd been in this relationship long enough to know that what his girlfriend was really complaining about was not whether they'd see his mother, but his inability to plan anything more than five hours beforehand. So he said, "Let's plan right now for next week's dinner." That made everyone happy.

Even when your rules don't seem logical to us, we'll learn them by rote if necessary. The snafu about my wife and her brother, for example, taught me to apologize even when she tells me not to. Another rule I recently committed to memory: When the woman in your life has a crappy day, just listen and sympathize and express venomous contempt for those who have wronged her rather than trying to explain why it wasn't so bad.

Of course, that brings up a caveat. A man is not above gaming the system — that is, pretending not to understand what he doesn't really *want* to understand. "I didn't know you wanted those earrings!" he'll protest, instead of admitting, "I didn't want to spend that much money." After all, just because we're dumb doesn't mean we're stupid.

Blah, blah, blah!
For years, researchers have claimed that women talk way more than men — one oft-cited stat is that women use 20,000 words a day while men use only 7,000. But it turns out that women and men *both* use an average of 16,000 words per day, according to a recent study from the University of Texas at Austin.

Lost in translation: What he really hears when your lips are moving.

You say: "Ugh, my boss is horrible. I had the worst day."
You mean: "I really need to vent about my day."
He hears: "Tell me how to fix my relationship with my boss."

You say: "Hey, can we talk?"
You mean: "I have something important to tell you."
He hears: "You screwed up, buddy."

You say: "Oh, those shoes don't go with that belt. Why don't you wear the brown ones?"
You mean: "I just want to help you look good."

From: Bryan Stipe, reprinted from *Redbook*, Hearst Communications, Inc.

He hears: "Aw, the widdle baby can't dwess himself!"

You say: "Let's straighten up in here."
You mean: "Let's straighten up in here."
He hears: "I resent that you're a pig."

You say: "I'm so sorry you had such a rough day. You must feel terrible."
You mean: "I want you to know I empathize with you."
He hears: "I feel sorry for you, you sad sack of a man."

You say: "Do you think that woman's hot?"
You mean: "Tell me that *I'm* hot."
He hears: "DANGER! DANGER! DANGER! DO NOT ANSWER!"

Huh?!
Men's ability to process language and understand what's being said to them begins to diminish starting in their 30s. Women retain this ability until menopause.
Source: *Why Men Never Remember and Women Never Forget* by Marianne J. Legato, M.D.

Why doesn't he see what I need?
The love expert says ... he takes everything personally.

"If I call a friend and say, 'I'm having a terrible day,' she'll drop everything and ask, 'Are you okay?' A woman hears complaints as an invitation to move closer. But a man hears complaints as an indication that he's failed. He measures his very worth by his ability to provide and protect, so in his mind, if he were doing his job, she wouldn't be unhappy.

"Does this mean a woman can never complain to a man? Of course not! Men really want to please women. All you have to say is, 'Would you help me with ...' or 'I would love it if ...' Go beyond the complaint or criticism and get at the desire. High-maintenance women don't scare men. Men actually like it because it gives them a clear set of rules for how to improve, and they can tell when they're succeeding."

—Pat Love, coauthor of *How to Improve Your Marriage Without Talking About It*

Why doesn't he understand me?
The linguist says ... he assumes you're trying to be the boss of him.

"In general, men focus on hierarchy and women on connection. I always find it fascinating to go back to studies of how kids talk: Boys use talk to negotiate their status within a group, while girls use talk to negotiate closeness. This difference can cause misunderstandings with apologies, for example.

"When a man makes some small transgression, his wife might feel that if he'd just say, 'I'm sorry,' it would be over. But he won't, and then you end up arguing about why he won't apologize. For many women, an apology means, 'I care that I let you down; I care about you.' If he doesn't apologize, it's like he doesn't care. But for men, asking for an apology is a demand that he publicly humiliate himself. He thinks apologizing is a sign of weakness, and that you'll use it against him, because that's what another man would do. So when you say, 'Why won't you apologize?' he hears, 'I caught you in an error and I'm going to rub your nose in it.'"

—Deborah Tannen, Ph.D., professor of linguistics at Georgetown University and author of *You Just Don't Understand: Women and Men in Conversation*

Why doesn't he really listen?
The psychologist says ... he's too busy trying to *fix* the problem.

"There's a difference between how men and women process stress. In a woman, stress produces a reaction in the emotional center of the brain. Talking stimulates the production of serotonin to relax the brain, so she'll instinctively talk in order to feel better.

"For a man, stress triggers a reaction in the action center of the brain. So when you talk to him about a problem, he's so intent on taking action to fix it that there's no way he can actually hear your point of view. But if you tell him that the solution is just to listen, he can relax. He doesn't have to hunt for a solution, so he can listen, and maybe even empathize."

— John Gray, Ph.D., REDBOOK Love Network expert and author of the upcoming *Why Mars and Venus Collide*

Why can't he figure out what I'm really saying?
The psychiatrist says ... he's hardwired differently from you.

"In brain-imaging studies, women have more blood flow to the parts of their brains that produce and interpret language, and there are more interconnections between the emotional center and the verbal center. Men have less well-defined connections between the verbal and emotional parts of their brains. Early-childhood studies show that girls have a greater capacity for verbal communication than boys — they're more skilled at using words as a way of sharing their experience.

"The big problem between husbands and wives is that they don't realize how the other functions. A woman expects that since she is able to freely talk about her emotions, her husband is equally able to do so. Meanwhile, a man tends to view his wife's efforts to communicate as simply sharing information, not as sharing an emotional experience. So if she says, 'I'm upset that our son hasn't called to tell us he got to his friend's house,' he might say, 'I'm sure he's all right,' focusing on the 'Is he safe?' question. What she's really saying is, 'I'm anxious, I'm scared.' But he's not focusing on her emotional experience."

— Scott Haltzman, M.D., REDBOOK Love Network expert and author of the upcoming *Secrets of Happily Married Women*

"Our wires get crossed when ..."

"... the TV is on. I have to pause it and force my husband to make eye contact before I say anything. Otherwise, he will literally not hear me, much less retain any of what I said. The worst part is, there are still times when he doesn't remember what I said — and then he'll get mad at *me* when *he* doesn't remember!"

— Laura Kukucka, 30, Columbus, OH

"... something I say reminds him of something his ex-wife did or said and he thinks I'm taking him down the same path. I have to remind him that I'm not her."
— Katherine Miller, 29, Memphis

"... I criticize him, especially if I start with 'You never do ... ' or 'Why can't you ... ' I think it's because as soon as I say anything negative about him, all he hears is that negative statement. Everything after it just sounds like blah, blah, blah."
— Nature Lewis, 31, Staten Island, NY

"... there is *any* game on TV. It's like my husband's brain shifts and everything around him turns to babble. I think it's a hormonal change that happens to men during sporting events. So I'll tell him things I don't really want his opinion on — like expensive things I've bought — because he doesn't hear, and yet I haven't hidden anything!"
— Colleen Hoffman, 35, Washington Township, NJ

Told you so!
If you and he disagree about who said what when, chances are you're right (you knew it!): Studies have shown that women are better at recalling the spoken word than men.

LOOKING ASKANCE AT EYEWITNESS TESTIMONY

New Research

D. W. Miller

A typical crime takes place quickly and unexpectedly. Witnesses report that time seems to pass more slowly during the traumatic event. In addition, people often have trouble accurately recalling details from a crime that they've witnessed. Yet eyewitness testimony is so compelling that juries are more likely to vote for conviction when a trial includes such testimony.

New research on eyewitness testimony, memory, and lineup identification all suggest that our faith in eyewitness testimony is misplaced. In addition to the all-too-human errors of memory, police procedures may actually make it easy for witnesses to give a false identification in a lineup. To examine the problem of eyewitness testimony, the United States Attorney General Janet Reno convened a panel of psychological researchers, law-enforcement officials, criminal defense lawyers, and prosecutors to write a guide that police could use to better obtain effective eyewitness testimony.

This article briefly describes some of the latest psychological research on eyewitness testimony, which was incorporated in the guide published in October 1999. The guide's authors hope that the criminal justice system will apply the results of these studies to improve eyewitness identification and the entire legal process.

Ronnie Bullock was sentenced to 60 years in jail for kidnapping and raping a young Illinois girl. Edward Honaker spent a decade in a Virginia prison for sexually assaulting a woman at gunpoint. Kirk Bloodsworth was shipped off to Maryland's death row for raping and strangling a 9-year-old girl.

All three of those men were convicted in part because eyewitnesses or victims firmly placed them at the scene of the crime. But not one of them was guilty. They were among the first convicts to be exonerated by DNA tests proving that someone else was responsible.

Some psychologists believe that such mistakes happen in thousands of courtrooms every year. But most crimes leave no DNA traces to rule out the innocent. For more than two decades, psychological researchers have asked, How could so many witnesses be wrong, and what can be done about it? Only recently have they seen their findings influence the way the criminal-justice system handles eyewitness testimony.

Psychologists have conducted hundreds of studies on errors in eyewitness identification. In some cases, of course, witnesses simply lie. But research has shown that flawed police procedures and the vagaries of memory often lead witnesses to identify the wrong person, and that credulous jurors too easily credit their testimony.

To those familiar with the mountain of evidence about the way the human mind works, that comes as no surprise. "Why should people make good eyewitnesses?" asks Gary L. Wells, a psychologist at Iowa State University who is widely considered the dean of eyewitness research. In the presence of danger, he says, "we're wired for fight or flight. What helped for survival was not a quick recall of details."

The findings of Mr. Wells and his colleagues are finally gaining currency in the halls of criminal justice. In part that is due to the gradual acceptance of expert testimony on eyewitness identification.

Far more crucial, however, is the growing roster of convicts cleared by DNA evidence. In 1996, the U. S. Department of Justice released a report on the first 28 known cases of DNA exoneration. After studying those and 12 subsequent cases, Mr. Wells discovered that mistaken eyewitness testimony had played a part in about 90 percent of the convictions.

⌘ MISSING THE KEY DETAILS

Concerned about the high rate of eyewitness error in the DNA cases, U. S. Attorney General Janet Reno invited him to a meeting in early 1997. As a result of their conversation, the department's National Institute of Justice asked Mr. Wells and five fellow scholars to join a panel of law-enforcement officials, criminal-defense lawyers, and prosecutors created to write guidelines for handling eyewitness testimony.

The guide, published in October, gave scholars the opportunity to show that human memory is not a highly reliable tool for determining guilt in the courtroom. For example, contrary to popular belief, people under stress remember events no better than, and often less well than, they do under ordinary circumstances. Witnesses also perceive time as moving more slowly during traumatic events. That, in turn, leads them to overestimate how much time they had to notice details, a key factor of their credibility in court. And studies have found that witnesses to a crime are so distracted by the presence of a weapon—a phenomenon called "weapon focus"—that they remember little else with accuracy.

Researchers cannot ethically recreate the trauma of real crimes. But plenty of field research suggests that witnesses are apt to misidentify people.

For example, many studies have tested the ability of convenience-store clerks and bank tellers to recall customers they encountered in non-stressful situations. Around a third of the time, the employees wrongly identified faces from "lineups" that did not include the person they had actually met.

❧ THE DETERIORATION OF MEMORY

In addition, all sorts of factors inhibit our ability to recognize and recall facial detail. For instance, psychologists have established that most of us have more difficulty recognizing people of a different race. And memory deteriorates very quickly over time.

Elizabeth F. Loftus, a psychologist at the University of Washington and a pioneer in research on false memory, has discovered that it's remarkably easy to alter one's recollection without realizing it. Human beings are highly susceptible to incorporating "post-event information" newspaper articles, comments by police, conversations with other witnesses—into their recollections.

Witnesses also have been known to identify as criminals people they recognized from some other encounter, a process called "transference." In one bizarre example, an Australian psychologist and memory researcher named Donald Thomson was himself once identified by a rape victim as her attacker. Not only was his alibi airtight—he was being interviewed on live television at the time—but she had mistaken him for the rapist because she had seen his face on her television screen during the assault.

❧ IMPROVING POLICE PROCEDURES

Of course, policymakers can't do much to improve the flaws in our memories. So scholars like Mr. Wells, who wanted to reduce eyewitness mistakes, began to focus on things that the justice system can control—particularly police procedures.

One of the biggest problems with eyewitness identification, researchers have found, is that uncertain witnesses are often prompted to finger the person whom police have detained, even when the suspect is not the same person they spotted at the scene. Witnesses viewing a lineup tend to assume that police have caught the person they saw. So they think their job is to find the face that most resembles the description they gave to police.

The police sometimes exacerbate that tendency by designing lineups poorly. Imagine a witness to a liquor-store robbery who says the robber was white, stocky, and bearded. Based on that description, the police identify a suspect and ask the witness to look at a lineup of live individuals or at a spread of photos (known as a "six-pack").

Too often, say researchers, the "distractor" faces used by police do not match the witness's description, or the suspect's photo looks different from the others. If the suspect stands out in any way, if his is the only color photo in the six-pack, for instance, the witness is far more likely to say, "That's the guy."

Lineups are also fraught with the possibility of mistaken identity, researchers report, because of our tendency to overlook differences in facial appearance among people not of our race. Not only are white witnesses, say, more likely to mistake one black suspect for another (and vice versa), but police officers may overestimate the degree to which the distractors they choose match the suspect's description.

Recently, Mr. Wells has raised the alarm about the way a witness's confidence can be manipulated. Witnesses are easily influenced during and after the lineup—by talking with other witnesses or police interviewers—to be more certain of their choice than their recall warrants. Police investigators, for example, may praise a witness for "picking the right guy" out of the lineup.

That taint frequently makes its way to the jury box. Understandably, jurors put a lot of stock in a witness who can point to the defendant and say, "He's the one. I'll never forget his face." But scholars have learned that the degree of confidence during trial is a poor predictor of a witness's accuracy. And, they warn, jurors ought to be particularly skeptical if they learn that a witness professed more confidence on the witness stand than in the squad room. Recall, they say, doesn't improve over time.

❧ Asking the Right Questions

Until recently, the criminal-justice system made little use of those findings. Defense lawyers, of course, have embraced and exploited them at least since the 1980's. But according to Brian L. Cutler, a psychologist at Florida International University, they have rarely been able to use the research to cross-examine eyewitnesses or police.

"Defense lawyers have no special training—they don't know what questions to ask," says Mr. Cutler. "If they do ask the right questions, how well equipped are jurors to evaluate the questions?" Unfortunately, jurors cling to a belief that "the way memory works is a matter of common sense," he says. "It just isn't so."

"People expect it's like videotape, that we attend equally well to everything out there," says Roy S. Malpass, a psychologist at the University of Texas at El Paso who served on the Justice Department panel. In fact, he says, "we're highly selective."

No one knows how often eyewitness error leads to false convictions, but some scholars have taken a stab at the question. In their book *Mistaken Identification: The Eyewitness, Psychology, and the Law* (Cambridge University Press, 1995), Mr. Cutler and Steven D. Penrod, of the University of Nebraska at Lincoln, do some courtroom calculations: If just 0.5 percent of America's yearly 1.5 million convictions for serious crimes are erroneous—a rate suggested by some studies—then other research allows the authors to infer that well over half of those defendants, or around 4,500 innocent people, are convicted on false eyewitness testimony.

All that may change now that the nation's top law-enforcement officials have created new guidelines for police conduct. The Justice Department report, "Eyewitness Evidence: A Guide for Law Enforcement," reads like a primer on eyewitness research. Among other things, it instructs investigators who assemble a lineup to:

- Select "distractors" that match the witness's description, even simulating tattoos or other unusual features if necessary.

- Remind the witness that the suspect they saw may not even be in the lineup, and that the lineup is intended to clear the innocent as much as it is to identify the guilty.

- Avoid any comments that might influence the witness's selection.

- Ask for and record the witness's degree of certainty immediately.

- Photograph or film lineups to make the police more accountable to the defense.

Before they can take their new influence for granted, psychologists say, there is more to be done. For one thing, police officers and prosecutors need to be educated about the guidelines, which do not have the force of law. But Mr. Wells and others believe that both groups will embrace them once defense lawyers in the courtroom begin to hold the guidelines up as the gold standard of diligent police work.

❧ No Double-Blind Lineups

The social scientists didn't win every battle. Despite their urgings, law-enforcement officials on the Justice Department panel batted down two key suggestions for improving police lineups. Research suggests that lineups are more accurate when they are double-blind—in other words, when the investigator in charge doesn't know which person is the suspect—and sequential—when the witness sees faces one at a time.

According to participants, police representatives nixed the former idea, because logistically it would be difficult to round up investigators who didn't know who the suspect was. More important, they said, it would be a tough sell to their fellow cops, because it smacks of mistrust and requires them to cede control of an investigation to someone else.

After scholars lost the battle to include double-blind procedures, participants say, they gave up on demanding sequential line-ups. Without the first precaution, they explained, sequential lineups might be even more vulnerable to manipulation than simultaneous lineups are.

John Turtle, a panel member and psychologist at the Ryerson Polytechnic Institute, in Toronto, believes that he has a high-tech solution to all those concerns. He has developed computer software that purports to take the bias out of the photo-spread lineups, which constitute about 80 percent of those in the United States and virtually all of those in Canada.

All a police investigator would need to do is scan a photo of the suspect into a computer and sit the witness down in front of the screen. The machine would then automatically choose photos of others who match the witness's description from a large database, and offer standardized, neutral instructions that wouldn't nudge the witness toward a particular response.

Psychologists deny they are imputing bad faith to police investigators. It's human nature, they say, to want your results to match your expectations. The scholars are simply urging police officers to treat their procedures for handling witnesses with all the care of scientific experiments. "Human memory is a form of trace evidence, like blood or semen or hair, except the trace exists inside the witness's head," says Mr. Wells. "How you go about collecting that evidence and preserving it and analyzing it is absolutely vital."

ઈ Questions

1. In the article, psychologist Gary Wells asks, "Why should people make good eyewitnesses?" Are people good eyewitnesses? Why or why not? What factors, often present during a crime, make it difficult for people to be good eyewitnesses?

2. In what ways are the memories of eyewitnesses flawed?

3. In what ways do police procedures inadvertently foster misidentification by an eyewitness?

4. What has the criminal justice system done to apply the research discussed in this article in order to improve the fairness and accuracy of verdicts in criminal trials? How else could the criminal justice system use the findings discussed in this article to improve accuracy of verdicts?

ATTRIBUTIONS IN THE ADVICE COLUMNS:
ACTORS AND OBSERVERS, CAUSES AND REASONS

Thomas J. Schoeneman, *Lewis and Clark College*
Daniel E. Rubanowitz, *University of North Dakota*

If people blame their misfortunes on external causes and witnesses to bad events blame these events on the participants themselves, then what better way to test this "actor-observer effect" than by analyzing the content of letters to "Dear Abby" and "Ann Landers"? This is the basic logic behind a study by Thomas Schoeneman and Daniel Rubanowitz. However, it is one thing to find such an effect in the laboratory and quite another to document it in the real world.

This dilemma between laboratory vs. real-world and theory vs. applied research is particularly important in attribution theory. Despite all the discussion about how people think, there was very little research (at the time of this article) that actually explored whether people naturally and spontaneously think about the social world in accord with attribution theory. Schoeneman and Rubanowitz not only document the actor-observer difference, but they also demonstrate that people do think about their social world in ways theorized by attribution theory. (For clarity, only these parts of the article directly related to the actor-observer difference are presented here.)

· · ·

This study combines two approaches that stem from dissatisfaction with laboratory-based attribution theory: the use of archival sources of attributions (Bettman & Weitz, 1983; Lau & Russell, 1980; Weiner, 1985) and analyses of causes and reasons in everyday discourse (Buss, 1978; Jones, 1976; Locke & Pennington, 1928).

· · ·

In the original statement of the actor-observer divergence, Jones and Nisbett (1972) said that actors tend to attribute their own behaviors to external factors, whereas observers focus on internal dispositions as causing actors' behavior. Later, Jones (1976, p. 304) described how the cause/reason distinction refines this conception: "Under most conditions, actors do not like to think that their behavior is *caused* by either the environment or personality; at the less deterministic level of *reasons,* however, they are more likely to attribute their behavior to situational rather than to personal factors" (cf. Hinkle & Schmidt, 1984; Wolosin, Esser, & Fine, 1975). Observers do not necessarily share actors' desires to endorse rational motivation or may not have access to actors' reasons: Observers, then, should be more likely to

attribute actors' behavior to internal causes (Locke & Pennington, 1982).

METHOD

Sample

Letters and replies came from two widely syndicated advice columns: "Ann Landers" and Dear Abby." Fifteen columns from each advisor in 1980 were randomly selected; those yielded a sample of 31 letters, including replies, to "Ann Landers" and 30 to "Dear Abby."

Finding Explanatory Statements

Our coding manual described *explanatory statements* as reducible to the form of "referent because explanation," in which a *referent* is a behavior or personal attribute that is being explained in an *explanation* is the attribution being made.

Searchers worked in two-person teams. To avoid fatigue, only six letters were scrutinized at each team meeting. First, each team member individually inspected a letter, paragraph by paragraph, copied explanatory statements as they appeared in print, and translated each into "referent because explanation" form. Next, searchers compared notes and set aside items they agreed upon. Disagreements were each given one minute of discussion. At the end of this period, searchers

"Attributions in the Advise Columns: Actors and Observers, Causes and Reasons," by Thomas J. Schoeneman and Daniel E. Rubanowitz, reprinted from *Personality and Social Psychology Bulletin*, Vol. 11, No. 3, September 1985. Copyright © by the Society for Personality and Social Psychology. pp. 315–325.

From: Thomas J. Schoeneman and Daniel E. Rubanowitz, reprinted from *Personality and Social Psychology Bulletin* 11, no. 3 (September 1985), by permission of Sage Publications, Inc.

could either agree to include, agree to exclude, or reach no consensus on an item. We discarded items from the latter two categories.

Four teams looked for explanatory statements. One team, the authors, read all 61 letters. The other teams consisted of trained undergraduate psychology majors who were blind to our hypotheses. Each of these teams read 40 letters. In the end, each letter in the sample had been reviewed by three teams (the authors and two undergraduate teams).

Of the 536 explanatory statements found by single raters, 405 (75.6%) were agreed upon by at least one team. Of these, 200 were retained for analysis based on the following criteria: 126 were found by all three teams and 74 were found by the authors and one of the undergraduate teams.

Coding Explanatory Statements

After constructing a manual of coding criteria, we used a standard procedure, adopted from Lau and Russell (1980), for each of our categories. First, each of us individually coded the entire sample; then we met to compare ratings. After calculating an initial percentage agreement, we discussed disagreements until they were reconciled.

Referents and explanations were sorted into the following categories:

Referent subject. We identified the person whose behavior was being explained as *self/actor, other/observer,* or *both* (for "we/us" explanatory statements). Initial interrater agreement was 96.0%.

. . .

Locus of explanation. Attributions received labels of *internal* (inherent in or inseparable from the referent subject), *external* (implicating situations, circumstances, or other people), or *both* (for dual attributions). Rater agreement was 89.5%.

. . .

✑ Results

Sample Characteristics

Our sample contained 108 letters from "Ann Landers" and 92 from "Dear Abby." Chi-square analyses crossing column of origin with referent subject, referent mode, locus, and cause/reason turned up no significant differences.

Correspondents' letters accounted for 156 explanatory statements (78%) and columnists' replies contained the remaining 44.

. . .

Overall, the sample of explanatory statements was dominated by observers (actor = 70, observer = 115, both = 15). Attributions tended to be descriptive (161 descriptive, 39 prescriptive) and external (71 internal, 113 external, 16 both); reasons predominated over causes by a margin of 135 to 65.

Principal Analyses

The use of the "both" category was relatively infrequent for referent subject and locus (see above); in addition, these dual attributions were generally evenly distributed among the cells of the contingency tables used to assess our predictions. We therefore simplified our analyses by treating "both" ratings as missing data.

. . . Analyses using only descriptive attributions very clearly yielded the predicted trends.

Descriptive attributions. An actor-observer divergence emerged when referent subject was crossed by locus: attributions from actors were more often external . . . than internal . . . , with a slight trend toward the reverse for observers. . . . A log-linear analysis of this matrix yielded a significant interaction: $z = -2.26$, $p. < .03$ [see Table 1].[1]

. . .

✑ Discussion

Consistent with Jones and Nisbett's (1972) original prediction, actors preferred external to internal descriptive attributions and observers showed a trend toward the opposite pattern.[2] In a recent review, Watson (1982) found that although actors do produce more external attributions than observers, both types of attributor emphasize internal attributions. We believe that our findings differ from Watson's because he focused on studies of attributions that fulfill explanation and prediction functions (Forsyth, 1980) and omitted research in which motivational variables could modify the actor-observer effect. In our study, 79% of the letters involved negative outcomes; these were aired publicly in newspapers, suggesting that this set of attributions served egocentric and self-presentation functions (Forsyth, 1980). Under these conditions, a preponderance of external attributions is understandable (cf. Taylor & Koivumaki, 1976). . . .

Our investigation has . . . implications for attribution theory and research. One is that the field's focus on laboratory research has obscured the fact that naturally occurring attributions are hard to discern: Of 536 explanatory statements identified by single raters, only 200 (37%) reached the inclusion criterion of agreement by at least four raters. Our experience was that if you set yourself the task of finding explanations in everyday discourse, you will find many statements that could conceivably fit the bill.

. . .

Table 1 *Use of Causes . . . by Actors And Observers for Internal and External Descriptive Attributions*

	Internal	External
[Actor]	3	10
[Observer]	[25]	[15]

In concluding, we would like to raise two cautions. First our random selection of letters did not avoid a built-in preselection bias. Advice columnists can print only a tiny fraction of the letters they receive, and it is not clear how representative printed letters are of the total volume received.... Despite these problems, however, the predicted effects in our study were quite robust. Congruent with Lau and Russell (1980) we believe that our findings lend construct validity to our coding system and justify its use in future research.

ENDNOTES

[1] As previous investigators have noted (Bettman & Weitz, 1983; Lau & Russell, 1980), chi-square and log-linear analyses are not entirely appropriate because observations are not completely independent: In our sample, there were an average of 3.3 explanatory statements per letter. Lau and Russell (1980, p. 35) commented that "no one knows exactly how much bias any degree of dependence between observations causes."

[2] Jones and Nisbett (1972) stated that observers would cite *stable* internal factors, such as personal dispositions, as causes of actors' behavior. We coded the stability dimension of our attributions with an interrater agreement of 75.8%. In all cases of actors' and observers' internal and external descriptive attributions, stable attributions were more frequent than unstable ones. For observers' internal attributions, 27 were stable and 10 were unstable, in support of Jones and Nisbett (1972). Full details of this analysis are available from the first author.

REFERENCES

Bettman, J. R., & Weitz, B. A. (1983). Attributions in the board room: Causal reasoning in corporate annual reports. *Administrative Science Quarterly, 28,* 165–183.

Buss, A. R. (1978). Causes and reasons in attribution theory: A conceptual critique. *Journal of Personality and Social Psychology, 36,* 1311–1321.

Forsyth, D. R. (1980). The functions of attributions. *Social Psychology Quarterly, 43,* 184–189.

Hinkle, S., & Schmidt, D. F. (1984). The Buss cause/reason hypothesis: An empirical investigation. *Social Psychology Quarterly, 47,* 358–364.

Jones, E. E. (1976). How do people perceive the causes of behavior? *American Scientist, 64,* 300–305.

Jones, E. E., & Nisbett, R. E. (1972). The actor and the observer: Divergent perceptions of the causes of behavior. In E. E. Jones, D. E. Kanouse, H. H. Kelley, R. E. Nisbett, S. Valins, & B. Weiner (Eds.), *Attribution: Perceiving the causes of behavior* (pp. 79–94). Morristown, NJ: General Learning Press.

Lau, R. R., & Russell, D. (1980). Attributions in the sports pages. *Journal of Personality and Social Psychology, 39,* 29–38.

Locke, D., & Pennington, D. (1982). Reasons and other causes: Their role in attribution processes. *Journal of Personality and Social Psychology, 42,* 212–223.

Taylor, S. E., & Koivumaki, J. H. (1976). The perception of self and others: Acquaintanceship, affect, and actor-observer differences. *Journal of Personality and Social Psychology, 33,* 403–408.

Watson, D. (1982). The actor and the observer: How are their perceptions of causality different? *Psychological Bulletin, 92,* 642–700.

Weiner, B. (1985)."Spontaneous" causal thinking. *Psychological Bulletin, 97,* 74–84.

Wolosin, R. J., Esser, J., & Fine, G. A. (1975). Effect of justification and vocalization on actors' and observers' attributions of freedom. *Journal of Personality, 43,* 613–633.

ᛦ Questions

1. Schoeneman and Rubanowitz do not report any examples of the explanatory statements they found in the newspaper columns. What kinds of statements do you think people made? That is, what might people have said when they blamed the actor? What might people have said when they blamed another person? What might people have said when they blamed the situation or external factors?

2. Do you think the authors would have obtained the same results if they had analyzed letters to "Dear Heloise," an advice column about laundry and household problems? Would they have obtained the same results if they had analyzed calls to "Car Talk," a popular radio show where people call in to ask questions about their car problems? Why or why not? Is there an important difference between interpersonal problems and household or car problems that changes the attribution process?

3. Schoeneman and Rubanowitz point out a possible selection bias in their study. Since advice columnists cannot print all letters, they print a nonrandom sample of all letters received. What kinds of letters do you think they are more likely to print? How might that have affected the authors' results?

4. What other hypotheses about attribution theory can be tested via advice columns? Think about the following: success, failure, optimism, pessimism, gender differences in attributions.

ON BEING SANE IN INSANE PLACES

D. L. Rosenhan
Stanford University

D. L. Rosenhan takes the theory of fundamental attribution error (the idea that we tend to overestimate dispositional influences and underestimate situational influences in judging people's behavior) a step further. He wonders how a sane person in an insane place—a psychiatric hospital—will be judged. Will a sane person's behavior be seen for what it is—"normal"? Or will it be judged in the situational context as "insane"?

This article reports on the results of a study in which eight perfectly sane people checked into twelve mental hospitals as pseudopatients for seven to fifty-two days. Their objective was to observe the treatment and judgments of the psychiatric staff. All pseudopatients were moved by experiencing powerlessness, depersonalization, segregation, mortification (institutional adjustment), and self-labeling that patients typically experience in an institutional setting. Interestingly, their fellow patients recognized the sanity of most of the pseudopatients. Would the staff be as astute?

This classic study starkly illustrates how social situations can not only foster strange behavior, but it can also alter our perception of normal behavior.

If sanity and insanity exist, how shall we know them?

The question is neither capricious nor itself insane. However much we may be personally convinced that we can tell the normal from the abnormal, the evidence is simply not compelling. It is commonplace, for example, to read about murder trials wherein eminent psychiatrists for the defense are contradicted by equally eminent psychiatrists for the prosecution on the matter of the defendant's sanity. More generally, there are a great deal of conflicting data on the reliability, utility, and meaning of such terms as "sanity," "insanity," "mental illness," and "schizophrenia" *(1)*. Finally, as early as 1934, Benedict suggested that normality and abnormality are not universal *(2)*. What is viewed as normal in one culture may be seen as quite aberrant in another. Thus, notions of normality and abnormality may not be quite as accurate as people believe they are.

To raise questions regarding normality and abnormality is in no way to question the fact that some behaviors are deviant or odd. Murder is deviant. So, too, are hallucinations. Nor does raising such questions deny the existence of the personal anguish that is often associated with "mental illness." Anxiety and depression exist. Psychological suffering exists. But normality and abnormality, sanity and insanity, and the diagnoses that flow from them may be less substantive than many believe them to be.

At its heart, the question of whether the sane can be distinguished from the insane (and whether degrees of insanity can be distinguished from each other) is a simple matter: do the salient characteristics that lead to diagnoses reside in the patients themselves or in the environments and contexts in which observers find them? From Bleuler, through Kretchmer, through the formulators of the recently revised *Diagnostic and Statistical Manual* of the American Psychiatric Association, the belief has been strong that patients present symptoms, that those symptoms can be categorized, and, implicitly, that the sane are distinguishable from the insane. More recently, however, this belief has been questioned. Based in part on theoretical and anthropological considerations, but also on philosophical, legal, and therapeutic ones, the view has grown that psychological categorization of mental illness is useless at best and downright harmful, misleading, and pejorative at worst. Psychiatric diagnoses, in this view, are in the minds of the observers and are not valid summaries of characteristics displayed by the observed *(3–5)*.

Gains can be made in deciding which of these is more nearly accurate by getting normal people (that is, people who do not have, and have never suffered, symptoms of serious psychiatric disorders) admitted to psychiatric hospitals and then determining whether they were discovered to be sane and, if so, how. If the sanity of such pseudopatients were always detected, there would be prima facie evidence that a sane individual can be distinguished from the insane context in which he is found. Normality (and presumably abnormality) is distinct enough that it can be recognized wherever it

From: D. L. Rosenham, reprinted from *Science* 179, no. 4070 (January 19, 1973), by permission of the American Association for the Advancement of Science.

occurs, for it is carried within the person. If, on the other hand, the sanity of the pseudopatients were never discovered, serious difficulties would arise for those who support traditional modes of psychiatric diagnosis. Given that the hospital staff was not incompetent, that the pseudopatient had been behaving as sanely as he had been outside of the hospital, and that it had never been previously suggested that he belonged in a psychiatric hospital, such an unlikely outcome would support the view that psychiatric diagnosis betrays little about the patient but much about the environment in which an observer finds him.

The article describes such an experiment. Eight sane people gained secret admission to 12 different hospitals *(6)*. Their diagnostic experiences constitute the data of the first part of this article; the remainder is devoted to a description of their experiences in psychiatric institutions. Too few psychiatrists and psychologists, even those who have worked in such hospitals, know what the experience is like. They rarely talk about it with former patients, perhaps because they distrust information coming from the previously insane. Those who have worked in psychiatric hospitals are likely to have adapted so thoroughly to the settings that they are insensitive to the impact of that experience. And while there have been occasional reports of researchers who submitted themselves to psychiatric hospitalization *(7)*, these researchers have commonly remained in the hospitals for short periods of time, often with the knowledge of the hospital staff. It is difficult to know the extent to which they were treated like patients or like research colleagues. Nevertheless, their reports about the inside of the psychiatric hospital have been valuable. This article extends those efforts.

✸ PSEUDOPATIENTS AND THEIR SETTINGS

The eight pseudopatients were a varied group. One was a psychology graduate student in his 20's. The remaining seven were older and "established." Among them were three psychologists, a pediatrician, a psychiatrist, a painter, and a housewife. Three pseudopatients were women, five were men. All of them employed pseudonyms, lest their alleged diagnoses embarrass them later. Those who were in mental health professions alleged another occupation in order to avoid the special attentions that might be accorded by staff, as a matter of courtesy or caution, to ailing colleagues *(8)*. With the exception of myself (I was the first pseudopatient and my presence was known to the hospital administrator and chief psychologist and, so far as I can tell, to them alone), the presence of pseudopatients and the nature of the research program was not known to the hospital staffs *(9)*.

The settings were similarly varied. In order to generalize the findings, admission into a variety of hospitals was sought. The 12 hospitals in the sample were located in five different states on the East and West coasts. Some were old and shabby, some were quite new. Some were research-oriented, others not. Some had good staff-patient ratios, others were quite understaffed. Only one was a strictly private hospital. All of the others were supported by state or federal funds or, in one instance, by university funds.

After calling the hospital for an appointment, the pseudopatient arrived at the admissions office complaining that he had been hearing voices. Asked what the voices said, he replied that they were often unclear, but as far as he could tell they said "empty," "hollow," and "thud." The voices were unfamiliar and were of the same sex as the pseudopatient. The choices of these symptoms was occasioned by their apparent similarity to existential symptoms. Such symptoms are alleged to arise from painful concerns about the perceived meaninglessness of one's life. It is as if the hallucinating person were saying, "My life is empty and hollow." The choice of these symptoms was also determined by the *absence* of a single report of existential psychoses in the literature.

Beyond alleging the symptoms and falsifying name, vocation, and employment, no further alterations of person, history, or circumstances were made. The significant events of the pseudopatient's life history were presented as they had actually occurred. Relationships with parents and siblings, with spouse and children, with people at work and in school, consistent with the aforementioned exceptions, were described as they were or had been. Frustrations and upsets were described along with joys and satisfactions. These facts are important to remember. If anything, they strongly biased the subsequent results in favor of detecting sanity, since none of their histories or current behaviors were seriously pathological in any way.

Immediately upon admission to the psychiatric ward, the pseudopatient ceased simulating *any* symptoms of abnormality. In some cases, there was a brief period of mild nervousness and anxiety, since none of the pseudopatients really believed that they would be admitted so easily. Indeed, their shared fear was that they would be immediately exposed as frauds and greatly embarrassed. Moreover, many of them had never visited a psychiatric ward; even those who had, nevertheless had some genuine fears about what might happen to them. Their nervousness, then, was quite appropriate to the novelty of the hospital setting, and it abated rapidly.

Apart from that short-lived nervousness, the pseudopatient behaved on the ward as he "normally" behaved. The pseudopatient spoke to patients and staff as he might ordinarily. Because there is uncommonly little to do on a psychiatric ward, he attempted to engage others in conversation. When asked by staff how he was feeling, he indicated that he was fine, that he no longer experienced symptoms. He responded to instructions from attendants, to calls for medication (which was not swallowed), and to dining-hall instructions. Beyond such activities as were available to him on the admissions ward, he spent his time writing down his observations about the ward, its patients, and the staff. Initially these notes were written "secretly," but as it soon became clear that no one much cared, they were subsequently written on standard tablets of paper in such public places as the dayroom. No secret was made of these activities.

The pseudopatient, very much as a true psychiatric patient, entered a hospital with no foreknowledge of when he would be discharged. Each was told that he would have to get out by his own devices, essentially by convincing the staff that he was sane. The psychological stresses associated with hospitalization were considerable, and all but one of the pseudopatients desired to be discharged almost immediately after being admitted. They were, therefore, motivated not only to behave sanely, but to be paragons of cooperation. That their behavior was in no way disruptive is confirmed by nursing reports, which have been obtained on most of the patients. These reports uniformly indicate that the patients were "friendly," "cooperative," and "exhibited no abnormal indications."

❧ THE NORMAL ARE NOT DETECTABLY SANE

Despite their public "show" of sanity, the pseudopatients were never detected. Admitted, except in one case, with a diagnosis of schizophrenia *(10)*, each was discharged with a diagnosis of schizophrenia "in remission." The label "in remission" should in no way be dismissed as a formality, for at no time during any hospitalization had any question been raised about any pseudopatient's stimulation. Nor are there any indications in the hospital records that the pseudopatient's status was suspect. Rather, the evidence is strong that, once labeled schizophrenic, the pseudopatient was stuck with that label. If the pseudopatient was to be discharged, he must naturally be "in remission"; but he was not sane, nor, in the institution's view, had he ever been sane.

The uniform failure to recognize sanity cannot be attributed to the quality of the hospitals, for, although there were considerable variations among them, several are considered excellent. Nor can it be alleged that there was simply not enough time to observe the pseudopatients. Length of hospitalization ranged from 7 to 52 days, with an average of 19 days. The pseudopatients were not, in fact, carefully observed, but this failure clearly speaks more to traditions within psychiatric hospitals than to lack of opportunity.

Finally, it cannot be said that the failure to recognize the pseudopatients' sanity was due to the fact that they were not behaving sanely. While there was clearly some tension present in all of them, their daily visitors could detect no serious behavioral consequences—nor, indeed, could other patients. It was quite common for the patients to "detect" the pseudopatients' sanity. During the first three hospitalizations, when accurate counts were kept, 35 of a total of 118 patients on the admissions ward voiced their suspicions, some vigorously. "You're not crazy. You're a journalist, or a professor [refer-

ring to the continual note-taking]. You're checking up on the hospital." While most of the patients were reassured by the pseudopatient's insistence that he had been sick before he came in but was fine now, some continued to believe that the pseudopatient was sane throughout his hospitalization *(11)*. The fact that the patients often recognized normality when staff did not raises important questions.

Failure to detect sanity during the course of hospitalization may be due to the fact that physicians operate with a strong bias toward what statisticians call the type 2 error *(5)*. This is to say that physicians are more inclined to call a healthy person sick (a false positive, type 2) than a sick person healthy (a false negative, type 1). The reasons for this are not hard to find: it is clearly more dangerous to misdiagnose illness than health. Better to err on the side of caution, to suspect illness even among the healthy.

But what holds for medicine does not hold equally well for psychiatry. Medical illnesses, while unfortunate, are not commonly pejorative. Psychiatric diagnoses, on the contrary, carry with them personal, legal, and social stigmas *(12)*. It was therefore important to see whether the tendency toward diagnosing the sane insane could be reversed. The following experiment was arranged at a research and teaching hospital whose staff had heard these findings but doubted that such an error could occur in their hospital. The staff was informed that at some time during the following 3 months, one or more pseudopatients would attempt to be admitted into the psychiatric hospital. Each staff member was asked to rate each patient who presented himself at admissions or on the ward according to the likelihood that the patient was a pseudopatient. A 10-point scale was used, with a 1 and 2 reflecting high confidence that the patient was a pseudopatient.

Judgments were obtained on 193 patients who were admitted for psychiatric treatment. All staff who had had sustained contact with or primary responsibility for the patient—attendants, nurses, psychiatrists, physicians, and psychologists—were asked to make judgments. Forty-one patients were alleged, with high confidence, to be pseudopatients by at least one member of the staff. Twenty-three were considered suspect by at least one psychiatrist. Nineteen were suspected by one psychiatrist *and* one staff member. Actually, no genuine pseudopatient (at least from my group) presented himself during this period.

The experiment is instructive. It indicates that the tendency to designate sane people as insane can be reversed when the stakes (in this case, prestige and diagnostic acumen) are high. But what can be said of the 19 people who were suspected of being "sane" by one psychiatrist and another staff member? Were these people truly "sane," or was it rather the case that in the course of avoiding the type 2 error the staff tended to make more errors of the first sort—calling the crazy "sane"? There is no way of knowing. But one thing is certain: any diagnostic process that lends itself so readily to massive errors of this sort cannot be a very reliable one.

☙ THE STICKINESS OF PSYCHODIAGNOSTIC LABELS

Beyond the tendency to call the healthy sick—a tendency that accounts better for diagnostic behavior on admission than it does for such behavior after a lengthy period of exposure—the data speak to the massive role of labeling in psychiatric assessment. Having once been labeled schizophrenic, there is nothing the pseudopatient can do to overcome the tag. The tag profoundly colors others' perceptions of him and his behavior.

From one viewpoint, these data are hardly surprising, for it has long been known that elements are given meaning by the context in which they occur. Gestalt psychology made this point vigorously, and Asch *(13)* demonstrated that there are "central" personality traits (such as "warm" versus "cold") which are so powerful that they markedly color the meaning of other information in forming an impression of a given personality *(14)*. "Insane," "schizophrenic," "manic-depressive," and "crazy" are probably among the most powerful of such central traits. Once a person is designated abnormal, all of his other behaviors and characteristics are colored by that label. Indeed, that label is so powerful that many of the pseudopatients' normal behaviors were overlooked entirely or profoundly misinterpreted. Some examples may clarify this issue.

Earlier I indicated that there were no changes in the pseudopatients' personal history and current status beyond those of name, employment, and, where necessary, vocation. Otherwise, a veridical description of personal history and circumstances was offered. Those circumstances were not psychotic. How were they made consonant with the diagnosis of psychosis? Or were those diagnoses modified in such a way as to bring them into accord with the circumstances of the pseudopatient's life, as described by him?

As far as I can determine, diagnoses were in no way affected by the relative health of the circumstances of a pseudopatient's life. Rather, the reverse occurred: the perception of his circumstances was shaped entirely by the diagnosis. A clear example of such translation is found in the case of a pseudopatient who had had a close relationship with his mother but was rather remote from his father during his early childhood. During adolescence and beyond, however, his father became a close friend, while his relationship with his mother cooled. His present relationship with his wife was characteristically close and warm. Apart from occasional angry exchanges, friction was minimal. The children had rarely been spanked. Surely there is nothing especially pathological about such a history. Indeed, many readers may see a similar pattern in their own experiences, with no markedly deleterious consequences. Observe, however, how such a history was translated in the psychopathological context, this from the case summary prepared after the patient was discharged.

This white 39-year-old male . . . manifests a long history of considerable ambivalence in close relationships, which begins in early childhood. A warm relationship with his mother cools during his adolescence. A distant relationship to his father is described as becoming very intense. Affective stability is absent. His attempts to control emotionality with his wife and children are punctuated by angry outbursts and, in the case of the children, spankings. And while he says that he has several good friends, one senses considerable ambivalence embedded in those relationships also.

The facts of the case were unintentionally distorted by the staff to achieve consistency with a popular theory of the dynamics of a schizophrenic reaction *(15)*. Nothing of an ambivalent nature had been described in relations with parents, spouse, or friends. To the extent that ambivalence could be inferred, it was probably not greater than is found in all human relationships. It is true the pseudopatient's relationships with his parents changed over time, but in the ordinary context that would hardly be remarkable—indeed, it might very well be expected. Clearly, the meaning ascribed to his verbalizations (that is, ambivalence, affective instability) was determined by the diagnosis: schizophrenia. An entirely different meaning would have been ascribed if it were known that the man was "normal."

All pseudopatients took extensive notes publicly. Under ordinary circumstances, such behavior would have raised questions in the minds of observers, as, in fact, it did among patients. Indeed, it seemed so certain that the notes would elicit suspicion that elaborate precautions were taken to remove them from the ward each day. But the precautions proved needless. The closest any staff member came to questioning these notes occurred when one pseudopatient asked his physician what kind of medication he was receiving and began to write down the response. "You needn't write it," he was told gently. "If you have trouble remembering, just ask me again."

If no questions were asked of the pseudopatients, how was their writing interpreted? Nursing records for three patients indicate that the writing was seen as an aspect of their pathological behavior. "Patient engages in writing behavior" was the daily nursing comment on one of the pseudopatients who was never questioned about his writing. Given that the patient is in the hospital, he must be psychologically disturbed. And given that he is disturbed, continuous writing must be a behavioral manifestation of that disturbance, perhaps a subset of the compulsive behaviors that are sometimes correlated with schizophrenia.

One tacit characteristic of psychiatric diagnosis is that it locates the sources of aberration within the individual and only rarely within the complex of stimuli that surrounds him. Consequently, behaviors that are stimulated by the environment are commonly misattributed to the patient's disorder.

For example, one kindly nurse found a pseudopatient pacing the long hospital corridors. "Nervous, Mr. X?" she asked. "No, bored," he said.

The notes kept by pseudopatients are full of patient behaviors that were misinterpreted by well-intentioned staff. Often enough, a patient would go "berserk" because had had, wittingly or unwittingly, been mistreated by, say, an attendant. A nurse coming upon the scene would rarely inquire even cursorily into the environmental stimuli of the patient's behavior. Rather, she assumed that his upset derived from his pathology, not from his present interactions with other staff members. Occasionally, the staff might assume that the patient's family (especially when they had recently visited) or other patients had stimulated the outburst. But never were the staff found to assume that one of themselves or the structure of the hospital had anything to do with a patient's behavior. One psychiatrist pointed to a group of patients who were sitting outside the cafeteria entrance half an hour before lunchtime. To a group of young residents he indicated that such behavior was characteristic of the oral-acquisitive nature of the syndrome. It seemed not to occur to him that there were very few things to anticipate in a psychiatric hospital besides eating.

A psychiatric label has a life and an influence of its own. Once the impression has been formed that the patient is schizophrenic, the expectation is that he will continue to be schizophrenic. When a sufficient amount of time has passed, during which the patient has done nothing bizarre, he is considered to be in remission and available for discharge. But the label endures beyond discharge, with the unconfirmed expectation that he will behave as a schizophrenic again. Such labels, conferred by mental health professionals, are as influential on the patient as they are on his relatives and friends, and it should not surprise anyone that the diagnosis acts on all of them as a self-fulfilling prophecy. Eventually, the patient himself accepts the diagnosis, with all of its surplus meanings and expectations, and behaves accordingly (5).

The inferences to be made from these matters are quite simple. Much as Zigler and Phillips have demonstrated that there is enormous overlap in the symptoms presented by patients who have been variously diagnosed (16), so there is enormous overlap in the behaviors of the sane and the insane. The sane are not "sane" all of the time. We lose our tempers "for no good reason." We are occasionally depressed or anxious, again for no good reason. And we may find it difficult to get along with one or another person—again for no reason that we can specify. Similarly, the insane are not always insane. Indeed, it was the impression of the pseudopatients while living with them that they were sane for long periods of time—that the bizarre behaviors upon which their diagnoses were allegedly predicated constituted only a small fraction of their total behavior. If it makes no sense to label ourselves permanently depressed on the basis of an occasional depression, then it takes better evidence than is presently available to label all patients insane or schizophrenic on the basis of bizarre behaviors or cognitions. It seems more useful, as Mischel (17) has pointed out, to limit our discussion to *behaviors,* the stimuli that provoke them, and their correlates.

It is not known why powerful impressions of personality traits, such as "crazy" or "insane," arise. Conceivably, when the origins of and stimuli that give rise to a behavior are remote or unknown, or when the behavior strikes us as immutable, trait labels regarding the *behaver* arise. When, on the other hand, the origins and stimuli are known and available, discourse is limited to the behavior itself. Thus, I may hallucinate because I am sleeping, or I may hallucinate because I have ingested a peculiar drug. These are termed sleep-induced hallucinations, or dreams, and drug-induced hallucinations, respectively. But when the stimuli to my hallucinations are unknown, that is called craziness, or schizophrenia—as if that inference were somehow as illuminating as the others.

✑ THE EXPERIENCE OF PSYCHIATRIC HOSPITALIZATION

The term "mental illness" is of recent origin. It was coined by people who were humane in their inclinations and who wanted very much to raise the station of (and the public's sympathies toward) the psychologically disturbed from that of witches and "crazies" to one that was akin to the physically ill. And they were at least partially successful, for the treatment of the mentally ill *has* improved considerably over the years. But while treatment has improved, it is doubtful that people really regard the mentally ill in the same way that they view the physically ill. A broken leg is something one recovers from, but mental illness allegedly endures forever (18). A broken leg does not threaten the observer, but a crazy schizophrenic? There is by now a host of evidence that attitudes toward the mentally ill are characterized by fear, hostility, aloofness, suspicion, and dread (19). The mentally ill are society's lepers.

That such attitudes infect the general population is perhaps not surprising, only upsetting. But that they affect the professionals—attendants, nurses, physicians, psychologists, and social workers—who treat and deal with the mentally ill is more disconcerting, both because such attitudes are self-evidently pernicious and because they are unwitting. Most mental health professionals would insist that they are sympathetic toward the mentally ill, that they are neither avoidant nor hostile. But it is more likely that an exquisite ambivalence characterizes their relations with psychiatric patients, such that their avowed impulses are only part of their entire attitude. Negative attitudes are there too and can easily be detected. Such attitudes should not surprise us. They are the natural offspring of the labels patients wear and the places in which they are found.

Consider the structure of the typical psychiatric hospital. Staff and patients are strictly segregated. Staff have their own living space, including their dining facilities, bathrooms, and assembly places. The glassed quarters that contain the professional staff, which the pseudopatients came to call "the cage," sit out on every dayroom. The staff emerge primarily for caretaking purposes—to give medication, to conduct a therapy or group meeting, to instruct or reprimand a patient. Otherwise, staff keep to themselves, almost as if the disorder that afflicts their charges is somehow catching.

So much is patient-staff segregation the rule that, for four public hospitals in which an attempt was made to measure the degree to which staff and patients mingle, it was necessary to use "time out of the staff cage" as the operational measure. While it was not the case that all time spent out of the cage was spent mingling with patients (attendants, for example, would occasionally emerge to watch television in the dayroom), it was the only way in which one could gather reliable data on time for measuring.

The average amount of time spent by attendants outside of the cage was 11.3 percent (range, 3 to 52 percent). This figure does not represent only time spent mingling with patients, but also includes time spent on such chores as folding laundry, supervising patients while they shave, directing ward cleanup, and sending patients to off-ward activities. It was the relatively rare attendant who spent time talking with patients or playing games with them. It proved impossible to obtain a "percent mingling time" for nurses, since the amount of time they spent out of the cage was too brief. Rather, we counted instances of emergence from the cage. On the average, daytime nurses emerged from the cage 11.5 times per shift, including instances when they left the ward entirely (range, 4 to 39 times). Late afternoon and night nurses were even less available, emerging on the average 9.4 times per shift (range, 4 to 41 times). Data on early morning nurses, who arrived usually after midnight and departed at 8 a.m., are not available because patients were asleep during most of this period.

Physicians, especially psychiatrists, were even less available. They were rarely seen on the wards. Quite commonly, they would be seen only when they arrived and departed, with the remaining time being spent in their offices or in the cage. On the average, physicians emerged on the ward 6.7 times per day (range, 1 to 17 times). It proved difficult to make an accurate estimate in this regard, since physicians often maintained hours that allowed them to come and go at different times.

The hierarchical organization of the psychiatric hospital has been commented on before (20), but the latent meaning of that kind of organization is worth noting again. Those with the most power have least to do with patients, and those with the least power are most involved with them. Recall, however, that the acquisition of role-appropriate behaviors occurs mainly through the observation of others, with the most powerful having the most influence. Consequently, it is understandable that attendants not only spend more time with patients than do any other members of the staff—that is required by their station in the hierarchy—but also, insofar as they learn from their superiors' behavior, spend as little time with patients as they can. Attendants are seen mainly in the cage, which is where the models, the action, and the power are.

I turn now to a different set of studies, these dealing with staff response to patient-initiated contact. It has long been known that the amount of time a person spends with you can be an index of your significance to him. If he initiates and maintains eye contact, there is reason to believe that he is considering your requests and needs. If he pauses to chat or actually stops and talks, there is added reason to infer that he is individuating you. In four hospitals, the pseudopatient approached the staff member with a request which took the following form: "Pardon me, Mr. [or Dr. or Mrs.] X, could you tell me when I will be eligible for grounds privileges?" (or ". . . when I will be presented at the staff meeting?" or ". . . when I am likely to be discharged?"). While the content of the question varied according to the appropriateness of the target and the pseudopatient's (apparent) current needs the form was always a courteous and relevant request for information. Care was taken never to approach a particular member of the staff more than once a day, lest the staff member become suspicious or irritated. In examining these data, remember that the behavior of the pseudopatients was neither bizarre nor disruptive. One could indeed engage in good conversation with them.

The data for these experiments are shown in Table 1, separately for physicians (column 1) and for nurses and attendants (column 2). Minor differences between these four institutions were overwhelmed by the degree to which staff avoided continuing contacts that patients had initiated. By far, their most common response consisted of either a brief response to the question, offered while they were "on the move" and with head averted, or no response at all.

The encounter frequently took the following bizarre form: (pseudopatient) "Pardon me, Dr. X. Could you tell me when I am eligible for grounds privileges?" (physicians) "Good morning, Dave. How are you today?" (Moves off without waiting for a response.)

It is instructive to compare these data with data recently obtained at Stanford University. It has been alleged that large and eminent universities are characterized by faculty who are so busy that they have no time for students. For this comparison, a young lady approached individual faculty members who seemed to be walking purposefully to some meeting or teaching engagement and asked them the following six questions.

1. "Pardon me, could you direct me to Encina Hall?" (at the medical school: ". . . to the Clinical Research Center?").
2. "Do you know where Fish Annex is?" (there is no Fish Annex at Stanford).
3. "Do you teach here?"
4. "How does one apply for admission to the college?" (at the medical school: ". . . to the medical school?").
5. "Is it difficult to get in?"
6. "Is there financial aid?"

Table 1 *Self-initiated contact by pseudopatients with psychiatrists and nurses and attendants, compared to contact with other groups.*

Contact	Psychiatric hospitals		University campus (nonmedical)	University medical center		
				Physicians		
	(1) Psychiatrists	(2) Nurses and attendants	(3) Faculty	(4) "Looking for a psychiatrist"	(5) "Looking for an internist"	(6) No additional comment
Responses						
Moves on, head averted (%)	71	88	0	0	0	0
Makes eye contact (%)	23	10	0	11	0	0
Pauses and chats (%)	2	2	0	11	0	10
Stops and talks (%)	4	0.5	100	78	100	90
Mean number of questions answered (out of 6)	*	*	6	3.8	4.8	4.5
Respondents (No.)	13	47	14	18	15	10
Attempts (No.)	185	1283	14	18	15	10

*Not applicable.

Without exception, as can be seen in Table 1 (column 3), all of the questions were answered. No matter how rushed they were, all respondents not only maintained eye contact, but stopped to talk. Indeed, many of the respondents went out of their way to direct or take the questioner to the office she was seeking, to try to locate "Fish Annex," or to discuss with her the possibilities of being admitted to the university.

Similar data, also shown in Table 1 (columns 4, 5, and 6), were obtained in the hospital. Here too, the young lady came prepared with six questions. After the first question, however, she remarked to 18 of her respondents (column 4), "I'm looking for a psychiatrist," and to 15 others (column 5), "I'm looking for an internist." Ten other respondents received no inserted comment (column 6). The general degree of cooperative responses in considerably higher for these university groups than it was for pseudopatients in psychiatric hospitals. Even so, differences are apparent within the medical school setting. Once having indicated that she was looking for a psychiatrist, the degree of cooperation elicited was less than when she sought an internist.

☙ POWERLESSNESS AND DEPERSONALIZATION

Eye contact and verbal contact reflect concern and individuation; their absence, avoidance and depersonalization. The date I have presented do not do justice to the rich daily encounters that grew up around matters of depersonalization and avoidance. I have records of patients who were beaten by staff for the sin of having initiated verbal contact. During my own experience, for example, one patient was beaten in the presence of other patients for having approached an attendant and told him, "I like you." Occasionally, punishment meted out to patients for misdemeanors seemed so excessive that it could not be justified by the most radical interpretations of psychiatric canon. Nevertheless, they appeared to go unquestioned. Tempers were often short. A patient who had not heard a call for medication would be roundly excoriated, and the morning attendants would often wake patients with, "Come on, you m——f——s, out of bed!"

Neither anecdotal nor "hard" data can convey the overwhelming sense of powerlessness which invades the individual as he is continually exposed to the depersonalization of the psychiatric hospital. It hardly matters *which* psychiatric hospital—the excellent public ones and the very plush private hospital were better than the rural and shabby ones in this regard, but, again, the features that psychiatric hospitals had in common overwhelmed by far their apparent differences.

Powerlessness was evident everywhere. The patient is deprived of many of his legal rights by dint of his psychiatric commitment *(21)*. He is shorn of credibility by virtue of his psychiatric label. His freedom of movement is restricted. He cannot initiate contact with the staff, but may only respond to such overtures as they make. Personal privacy is minimal. Patient quarters and possessions can be entered and examined by any staff member, for whatever reason. His personal history and anguish is available to any staff member (often including the "grey lady" and "candy striper" volunteer) who chooses to read his folder, regardless of their therapeutic relationship to him. His personal hygiene and waste evacuation are often monitored. The water closets [toilets] may have no doors.

At times, depersonalization reached such proportions that pseudopatients had the sense that they were invisible, or at least unworthy of account. Upon being admitted, I and other pseudopatients took the initial physical examinations in a semipublic room, where staff, members went about their own business as if we were not there.

On the ward, attendants delivered verbal and occasionally serious physical abuse to patients in the presence of other observing patients, some of whom (the pseudopatients) were writing it all down. Abusive behavior, on the other hand, terminated quite abruptly when other staff members were known to be coming. Staff are credible witnesses. Patients are not.

A nurse unbuttoned her uniform to adjust her brassiere in the presence of an entire ward of viewing men. One did not have the sense that she was being seductive. Rather, she didn't notice us. A group of staff persons might point to a patient in the dayroom and discuss him animatedly, as if he were not there.

One illuminating instance of depersonalization and invisibility occurred with regard to medications. All told, the pseudopatients were administered nearly 2100 pills, including Elavil, Stelazine, Compazine, and Thorazine, to name but a few. (That such a variety of medication should have been administered to patients presenting identical symptoms is itself worthy of note.) Only two were swallowed. The rest were either pocketed or deposited in the toilet. The pseudopatients were not alone in this. Although I have no precise records on how many patients rejected their medications, the pseudopatients frequently found the medications of other patients in the toilet before they deposited their own. As long as they were cooperative, their behavior and the pseudopatients' own in this matter, as in other important matters, went unnoticed throughout.

Reactions to such depersonalization among pseudopatients were intense. Although they had come to the hospital as participant observers and were fully aware that they did not "belong," they nevertheless found themselves caught up in and fighting the process of depersonalization. Some examples: a graduate student in psychology asked his wife to bring his textbooks to the hospital so he could "catch up on his homework"—this despite the elaborate precautions taken to conceal his professional association. The same student, who had trained for quite some time to get into the hospital, and who had looked forward to the experience, "remembered" some drag races that he had wanted to see on the weekend and insisted that he be discharged by that time. Another pseudopatient attempted a romance with a nurse. Subsequently, he informed the staff that he was applying for admission to graduate school in psychology and was very likely to be admitted, since a graduate professor was one of his regular hospital visitors. The same person began to engage in psychotherapy with other patients—all of this as a way of becoming a person in an impersonal environment.

ᕱ THE SOURCE OF DEPERSONALIZATION

What are the origins of depersonalization? I have already mentioned two. First are attitudes held by all of us toward the mentally ill—including those who treat them—attitudes characterized by fear, distrust, and horrible expectations on the one hand, and benevolent intentions on the other. Our ambivalence leads, in this instance as in others, to avoidance.

Second, and not entirely separate, the hierarchical structure of the psychiatric hospital facilitates depersonalization. Those who are at the top have least to do with patients, and their behavior inspires the rest of the staff. Average daily contact with psychiatrists, psychologists, residents, and physicians combined ranged from 3.9 to 25.1 minutes, with an overall mean of 6.8 (six pseudopatients over a total of 129 days of hospitalization). Included in this average is time spent in the admissions interview, ward meetings in the presence of a senior staff member, group and individual psychotherapy contacts, case presentation conferences, and discharge meetings. Clearly, patients do not spend much time in interpersonal contact with doctoral staff. And doctoral staff serve as models for nurses and attendants.

There are probably other sources. Psychiatric installations are presently in serious financial straits. Staff shortages are pervasive, staff time at a premium. Something has to give, and that something is patient contact. Yet, while financial stresses are realities, too much can be made of them. I have the impression that the psychological forces that result in depersonalization are much stronger than the fiscal ones and that the addition of more staff would not correspondingly improve patient care in this regard. The incidence of staff meetings and the enormous amount of record-keeping on patients, for example, have not been as substantially reduced as has patient contact. Priorities exist, even during hard times. Patient contact is not a significant priority in the traditional psychiatric hospital, and fiscal pressures do not account for this. Avoidance and depersonalization may.

Heavy reliance upon psychotropic medication tacitly contributes to depersonalization by convincing staff that treatment is indeed being conducted and that further patient contact may not be necessary. Even here, however, caution needs to be exercised in understanding the role of psychotropic drugs. If patients were powerful rather than powerless, if they were viewed as interesting individuals rather than diagnostic entities, if they were socially significant rather than social lepers, if their anguish truly and wholly compelled our sympathies and concerns, would we not *seek* contact with them, despite the availability of medications? Perhaps for the pleasure of it all?

☙ THE CONSEQUENCES OF LABELING AND DEPERSONALIZATION

Whenever the ratio of what is known to what needs to be known approaches zero, we tend to invent "knowledge" and assume that we understand more than we actually do. We seem unable to acknowledge that we simply don't know. The needs for diagnosis and remediation of behavioral and emotional problems are enormous. But rather than acknowledge that we are just embarking on understanding, we continue to label patients "schizophrenic," "manic-depressive," and "insane," as if in those words we had captured the essence of understanding. The facts of the matter are that we have known for a long time that diagnoses are often not useful or reliable, but we have nevertheless continued to use them. We now know that we cannot distinguish insanity from sanity. It is depressing to consider how that information will be used.

Not merely depressing, but frightening. How many people, one wonders, are sane but not recognized as such in our psychiatric institutions? How many have been needlessly stripped of their privileges of citizenship, from the right to vote and drive to that of handling their own accounts? How many have feigned insanity in order to avoid the criminal consequences of their behavior, and, conversely, how many would rather stand trial than live interminably in a psychiatric hospital—but are wrongly thought to be mentally ill? How many have been stigmatized by well-intentioned, but nevertheless erroneous, diagnoses? On the last point, recall again that a "type 2 error" in psychiatric diagnosis does not have the same consequences it does in medical diagnosis. A diagnosis of cancer that has been found to be in error is cause for celebration. But psychiatric diagnoses are rarely found to be in error. The label sticks, a mark of inadequacy forever.

Finally, how many patients might be "sane" outside the psychiatric hospital but seem insane in it—not because craziness resides in them, as it were, but because they are respond-

ing to a bizarre setting, one that may be unique to institutions which harbor nether people? Goffman *(4)* calls the process of socialization to such institutions "mortification"—an apt metaphor that includes the processes of depersonalization that have been described here. And while it is impossible to know whether the pseudopatients' responses to these processes are characteristic of all inmates—they were, after all, not real patients—it is difficult to believe that these processes of socialization to a psychiatric hospital provide useful attitudes or habits of response for living in the "real world."

☙ SUMMARY AND CONCLUSIONS

It is clear that we cannot distinguish the sane from the insane in psychiatric hospitals. The hospital itself imposes a special environment in which the meanings of behavior can easily be misunderstood. The consequences to patients hospitalized in such an environment—the powerlessness, depersonalization, segregation, mortification, and self-labeling—seem undoubtedly countertherapeutic.

I do not, even now, understand this problem well enough to perceive solutions. But two matters seem to have some promise. The first concerns the proliferation of community mental health facilities, of crisis intervention centers, of the human potential movement, and of behavior therapies that, for all of their own problems, tend to avoid psychiatric labels, to focus on specific problems and behaviors, and to retain the individual in a relatively nonpejorative environment. Clearly, to the extent that we refrain from sending the distressed to insane places, our impressions of them are less likely to be distorted. (The risk of distorted perceptions, it seems to me, is always present, since we are much more sensitive to an individual's behaviors and verbalizations than we are to the subtle contextual stimuli that often promote them. At issue here is a matter of magnitude. And, as I have show, the magnitude of distortion is exceedingly high in the extreme context that is a psychiatric hospital.)

The second matter that might prove promising speaks to the need to increase the sensitivity of mental health workers and researchers to the *Catch 22* position of psychiatric patients. Simply reading materials in this area will be of help to some such workers and researchers. For others, directly experiencing the impact of psychiatric hospitalization will be of enormous use. Clearly, further research into the social psychology of such total institutions will both facilitate treatment and deepen understanding.

I and the other pseudopatients in the psychiatric setting had distinctly negative reactions. We do not pretend to describe the subjective experiences of true patients. Theirs may be different from ours, particularly with the passage of time and the necessary process of adaptation to one's environment. But we can and do speak to the relatively more objective indices of treatment within the hospital. It could be a mistake, and a very unfortunate one, to consider that what happened to us derived from malice or stupidity on the part of the staff. Quite the contrary, our overwhelming impression of them was of people who really cared, who were committed and who were uncommonly intelligent. Where they failed, as they sometimes did painfully, it would be more accurate to attribute those failures to the environment in which they, too, found themselves than to personal callousness. Their perceptions and behavior were controlled by the situation, rather than being motivated by a malicious disposition. In a more benign environment, one that was less attached to global diagnosis, their behaviors and judgments might have been more benign and effective.

References and Notes

[1] P. Ash, *J. Abnor. Soc. Psychol.* 44, 272 (1949); A. T. Beck, *Amer. J. Psychiat.* 119, 210 (1962); A. T. Boisen, *Psychiatry* 2, 233 (1938); N. Kreitman, *J. Ment. Sci.* 107, 876 (1961); N. Kreitman, P. Sainsbury, J. Morrisey, J. Towers, J. Scrivener, *ibid.*, p. 887; H. O. Schmitt and C. P Fonda, *J. Abnorm. Soc. Psychol*, 52, 262 (1956); W. Seeman, *J. Nerv. Ment. Dis.* 118, 541 (1953). For an analysis of these artifacts and summaries of the disputes, see J. Zubin, *Annu. Rev. Psychol.* 13, 373 (1967); L. Phillips and J. G. Draguns, *ibid.* 22, 447 (1971).

[2] R. Benedict, J. *Gen. Psychol.* 10, 59 (1934).

[3] See in this regard H. Becker, *Outsiders: Studies in the Sociology of Deviance* (Free Press, New York, 1963): B. M. Braginsky, D. D. Braginsky, K. Ring, *Methods of Madness: The Mental Hospital as a Last Resort* (Holt, Rinehart & Winston, New York, 1969); G. M. Crocetti and P. V. Lemkau, *Amer. Sociol. Rev.* 30, 577 (1965); E. Goffman, *Behavior in Public Places* (Free Press, New York, 1964); R. D. Laing, *The Divided Self: A Study of Sanity and Madness* (Quadrangle, Chicago, 1960); D. L. Phillips, *Amer. Sociol. Rev.* 28, 963 (1963); T. R. Sarbin, *Psychol. Today* 6, 18 (1972); E. Schur, *Amer. J. Sociol.* 75, 309 (1969); T. Szasz, *Law, Liberty, and Psychiatry* (Macmillan, New York, 1963); *The Myth of Mental Illness: Foundations of a Theory of Mental Illness* (Hoeber-Harper, New York, 1963). For a critique of some of these views, see W. R. Gove. *Amer. Sociol. Rev.* 35, 873 (1970).

[4] E. Goffman, *Asylums* (Doubleday, Garden City, N.Y., 1961).

[5] T. J. Scheff, *Being Mentally Ill: A Sociological Theory* (Aldine, Chicago, 1966).

[6] Data from a ninth pseudopatient are not incorporated in this report because, although his sanity went undetected, he falsified aspects of his personal history, including his marital status and parental relationships. His experimental behaviors therefore were not identical to those of the other pseudopatients.

[7] A. Barry, *Bellevue Is A State of Mind* (Harcourt Brace Jovanovich, New York, 1971); I. Belknap, *Human Problems of a State Mental Hospital* (McGraw-Hill, New York, 1956); W. Caudill, F. C. Redlich, H. R. Gilmore, E. B. Brody, *Amer. J. Orthopsychiat.* 22, 314 (1952); A. R. Goldman, R. H. Bohr, T. A. Steinberg, *Prof. Psychol.* 1, 427 (1970); unauthored, *Roche Report* 1 (No. 13), 8 (1971).

[8] Beyond the personal difficultues that the pseudopatient is likely to experience in the hospital, there are legal and social ones that, combined, require considerable attention before entry. For example, once admitted to a psychiatric institution, it is difficult, if not impossible, to be discharged on short notice, state law to the contrary notwithstanding. I was not sensitive to these difficulties at the outset of the project, nor to the personal and situational emergencies that can arise, but later a writ of habeas corpus was prepared for each of the entering pseudopatients and an attorney was kept "on call" during every hospitalization. I am grateful to John Kaplan and Robert Bartels for legal advice and assistance in these matters.

[9] However distasteful such concealment is, it was a necessary first step to examining these questions. Without concealment, there would have been no way to know how valid these experiences were; nor was there any way of knowing whether whatever detections occurred were a tribute to the diagnostic acumen of the staff or to the hospital's rumor network. Obviously, since my concerns are general ones that cut across individual hospitals and staffs, I have respected their anonymity and have eliminated clues that might lead to their identification.

[10] Interestingly, of the 12 admissions, 11 were diagnosed as schizophrenic and one, with the identical symptomatology, as manic-depressive psychosis. This diagnosis has a more favorable prognosis, and it was given by the only private hospital in our sample. On the relations between social class and psychiatric diagnosis, see A. deB. Hollingshead and F. C. Redlich, *Social Class and Mental Illness: A Community Study* (Wiley, New York, 1958).

[11] It is possible, of course, this patients have quite broad latitudes in diagnosis and therefore are inclined to call many people sane, even those whose behavior is patently aberrant. However, although we have no hard data on this matter, it was our distinct impression that this was not the case. In many instances, patients not only singled us out for attention, but came to imitate our behaviors and styles.

[12] J. Cumming and E. Cumming, *Community Ment. Health* 1, 135 (1965); A Farina and K. Ring. *J. Abnorm. Psychol.* 70, 47 (1965); H. E. Freeman and O. G. Simmons, *The Mental Patient Comes Home* (Wiley, New York, 1963); W. J. Johannsen, *Ment. Hygiene* 53, 218 (1969); A. S. Linsky, *Soc. Psychiat.* 5, 166 (1970).

[13] S. E. Asch, *J. Abnorm. Soc. Psychol.* 41, 258 (1946); *Social Psychology* (Prentice-Hall, New York, 1952).

[14] See also I. N. Mensh and J. Wishner, *J. Personality 16*, 188 (1947); J. Wishner, *Psychol. Rev.* 67, 96 (1960); J. S. Bruner and R. Tagiuri, in *Handbook of Social Psychology*. G. Lindzey, Ed. (Addison-Wesley, Cambridge, Mass., 1954), vol. 2, pp. 634–654; J. S. Bruner, D. Shapiro, R. Tagiuri, in *Person Perception and Interpersonal Behavior*, R. Tagiuri and L. Petrullo, Eds. (Stanford Univ. Press, Stanford, Calif., 1958), pp. 277–288.

[15] For an example of a similar self-fulfilling prophecy, in this instance dealing with the "central" trait of intelligence, see R. Rosenthal and L. Jacobson, *Pygmalion in the Classroom* (Holt, Rinehart & Winston, New York, 1968).

[16] E. Zigler and L. Phillips, *J. Abnorm. Soc. Psychol.* 63, 69 (1961). See also R. K. Freudenberg and J. P. Robertson, *A.M.A. Arch. Neurol. Psychiatr.* 76, 14 (1956).

[17] W. Mischel, *Personality and Assessment* (Wiley, New York, 1968).

[18] The most recent and unfortunate instance of this tenet is that of Senator Thomas Eagleton.

[19]T. R. Sarbin and J. C. Mancuso, *J. Clin. Consult, Psychol.* 35, 159 (1970); T. R. Sarbin, *ibid.* 31, 447 (1967); J. C. Nunnally, Jr., *Popular Conceptions of Mental Health* (Holt, Rinehart & Winston, New York, 1961).

[20]A. H. Stanton and M. S. Schwartz, *The Mental Hospital: A Study of Institutional Participation in Psychiatric Illness and Treatment* (Basic, New York, 1954).

[21]D. B. Wexler and S. E. Scoville, *Ariz. Law Rev.* 13, 1 (1971).

[22]I thank W. Mischel, E. Orne, and M. S. Rosenhan for comment on an earlier draft of this manuscript.

ತಿ Questions

1. Rosenhan starts with the provocative question, "If sanity and insanity exist, how shall we know them?" Can we tell the normal from the abnormal? When might it be difficult to do so?

2. Do you think doctors, lawyers, police officers, psychologists, psychiatrists, teachers, and other professionals would benefit from experiencing firsthand the environments they work in, as one of their own clients? Why?

3. Is mental illness a manifestation of the person or the situation they're in? To answer this question, consider the environment of both the evaluator and the target. What are the implications of saying it's one or the other?

4. How does this article illustrate the power of labels? How do labels function? Consider the personal, legal, and social stigmas associated with labels and the impact of labels on both the person and the evaluator.

Chapter 9
Attitudes

My dad was always very clear when we were young. All people of all races and religions are to be treated with respect and are considered equal. I really thought that was an important part of the way he was raising us. Then my little sister started dating someone of a different race. He did not exactly freak out, nor did he forbid the relationship, but you just knew that all of his negative comments were because this kid was black. My dad couldn't stand it and seemed very stressed out for seven months until they broke up.

—Melinda, senior Physical Education major

An **attitude** is a positive or negative evaluation of an object, a person or group, or an idea. Although political scientists, psychologists, and sociologists study attitudes, they approach the field in different ways. Political scientists study attitudes in the form of polls measuring people's evaluations of government policies or politicians. Psychologists tend to focus on the nature and formation of attitudes. Sociologists examine how our positions in society affect attitude formation, often emphasizing the roles of social class, race, gender, and/or generation in how we develop and maintain attitudes about the world around us (Schuman 1995).

The social psychological study of attitudes seeks to explain how social forces affect individuals' attitudes and how these attitudes in turn relate to behavior. One of the interesting things you will learn in this chapter is that our attitudes are not necessarily linked with parallel behaviors. Melinda's experience with her father shows just that. Positive attitudes toward some object don't necessarily lead to positive behaviors toward that object. Although attitudes are sometimes correlated with behaviors, the relationship is complex. First, the relationship between our attitudes and behavior is often quite weak. Second, general attitudes do not necessarily lead to specific behaviors—you may have a positive attitude about the importance of exercise but find that you never set aside time to work out. Finally, people can change certain attitudes somewhat readily, thus making the relationship between attitudes and behavior difficult to study.

From: *Social Psychology: Sociological Perspectives*, Second Edition by David E. Rohall, Melissa A. Milkie, and Jeffrey W. Lucas.

The Construction of Attitudes

I never really thought much about marijuana until I joined the fraternity. I had seen all of the advertisements about how bad drugs are, but then my friends kept telling me it was OK. Of course, they were all doing it. I gave it a shot. It wasn't so bad. I guess I would be for legalizing it. . . .

—Darrell, junior Economics major

The interactionist perspective views attitudes like any other aspect of social life: They are continually being constructed based on our interactions with other people. Direct experience with specific people or objects may have as strong or stronger an effect on attitude development than preexisting values and beliefs (Maio et al. 2003). These findings probably reflect the fact that values and beliefs are largely derived from indirect experience, whereas direct exposure to a person or an object provides tangible information from which to form attitudes.

Darrell's experience with marijuana reflects these research findings: Despite all the advertising against the use of drugs, he tries it and decides that it is not so bad after all. Of course, his friends have a lot to do with his attitude change, providing additional arguments in support of the drug. The positive experience he derives from using the drug probably influences his opinion on the matter too. The goal of this section is to review the basic components of attitudes, the major interactionist perspectives on attitude construction, and the relationship between attitudes and behavior.

Dimensions of Attitudes

We have defined attitudes as positive or negative evaluations of an object, person, or group. Attitudes can be malleable in nature, changing quite readily. However, people have more enduring thoughts and feelings about objects as well. We also ponder what other people think about the topics that concern us. The role of larger norms and values come into play in complex ways. **Values and beliefs** refer to strongly held, relatively stable sets of attitudes. Values may be learned through socialization in families and school, as well as in society at large.

Attitudes are composed of several dimensions. First, there are "thinking" and "feeling" components of our attitudes toward any object. The cognitive or "thinking" aspect of an attitude is formally called an **opinion**. This distinction is important because people can think about a person or object in one way but then *feel* very different about that same object. You may cognitively think that homosexuality is okay but still feel uneasy among a group of gay men. Therefore, if you simply ask someone for an opinion, you may not get a true sense of that person's attitude because you will only capture one aspect of it. Nevertheless, most public opinion polls focus on our cognitions about a particular topic.

In addition to dividing attitudes into thinking and feeling components, attitudes can be measured in terms of direction and strength:

- Direction—whether attitudes toward an object are negative or positive.
- Strength—the level of positive or negative response to that object.

Modern perspectives on attitudes incorporate the idea that there are situations in which attitudes do not exist or in which someone has mixed feelings about an object. So, it is possible to have a **nonattitude** toward an object when you do not care either way about it. For instance, you may have no opinion about a political candidate because you do not have enough information to form a view. Some research also shows that people will give you an attitude or opinion of a person or issue even when they have limited or no information about the topic (Converse and Presser 1986; Fletcher and Chalmers 1991; Schuman and Presser 1980). Alternatively, people may have both negative and positive attitudes toward the person; you may dislike her personality but appreciate her beliefs on a topic. Such complexities make it difficult to use public opinion to predict people's behavior or to precisely define what a person thinks about a person, an object, or an issue.

Linking Attitudes and Behavior

One of the reasons people study attitudes is to predict their behaviors. How is knowing something about someone's attitude useful in predicting her behavior? One of the earliest uses of polling was to predict election results, using public opinion surveys to predict how people would actually vote. Polls successfully predicted that Theodore Roosevelt would beat Alfred Landon in the 1936 presidential race (Sudman, Bradburn, and Schwarz 1996). Polls became increasingly used for predicting election results. However, pollsters failed to predict Harry Truman's victory over Thomas Dewey in 1948, causing many to question the ability to use polling to predict how people will act in the voting booths.

The relationship between our attitudes and behavior is typically small, with an average correlation of about 0.38 (Kraus 1995). A correlation of 0 means that attitudes and behavior are completely unrelated, whereas a correlation of 1 means that attitudes and behavior are perfectly correlated (they vary together perfectly). Thus, if our attitudes toward keeping the workplace "green" through reducing, reusing, and recycling paper and plastic were completely unrelated to our recycling behavior, the correlation would be 0. If very positive attitudes were perfectly correlated to very frequent green behaviors, the correlation would be 1. The fact that attitudes are typically correlated at 0.38 with corresponding behaviors means that we cannot assume a whole lot about their interrelations. And even if we found that a particular type of attitude is highly correlated with its corresponding behavior, we cannot assume the attitude causes the behavior. It could be that behaving in particular ways is what shapes people's attitudes. In the recycling example, if people are forced to recycle due to new rules, laws, or shortages, it is very possible that their attitudes about recycling will become more favorable.

Ajzen's Theory of Planned Behavior

One prominent theory linking attitudes and behavior comes from two psychologists, Icek Ajzen and Martin Fishbein. Ajzen and Fishbein tried to understand how our attitudes interact with our larger sets of beliefs and social norms in our decision-making processes. They argued that one of the reasons we do not find large correlations between attitudes and behavior is that we must incorporate social norms into our predictive models. In addition, our attitudes only predict our intention to act toward an object rather than the actual behavior. For instance, you may dislike someone (attitude) and plan to cause them harm (intention), but that does not necessarily mean that you will actually harm them (behavior).

The following model is one of the most recent versions of the model. It includes individuals' attitudes toward a behavior but also includes the idea that people consider the likelihood of their actions having the intended effect (perceived behavioral control) before acting. Using the previous example, the intention to hurt someone may be curbed if you believe that you are not capable of producing harm to the other person.

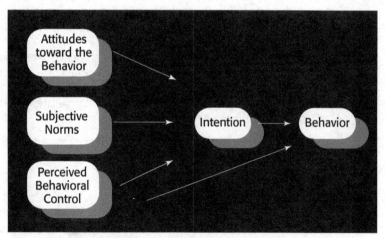

Source: Based on Icek Ajzen's Web site accessed at http://www.people.umass.edu/~aizen/.
See also Ajzen (1991).

The Theory of Planned Behavior (also known as the Theory of Reasoned Action) also incorporates our beliefs about what other people would think about the behavior under the heading "subjective norms." If we believe that other people will support the behavior, we are much more likely to act on an attitude than we would if they do not support it. Hence, this model recognizes the importance of social relationships in deciding whether to act on an attitude, helping to explain why some attitudes lead people to act in some cases and not others.

The Weighted Average Model in Psychology

The weighted average model assumes that we process information such as attitudes in the same way as adding new numbers to a pool of existing numbers, with new numbers getting averaged into the existing set of numbers. Hence, if you have a negative opinion about someone and learn that she did something nice, you will not immediately develop a favorable opinion of her. Instead, you will average the new positive information with the existing data that says that she is not a good person. Your new image of the person may be less negative but still negative overall.

The model does not assume that all information is equally assessed. Some information will have more power over your assessment than other information. We bias information about a person or an object based on the person who is giving us the new information as well as the nature of the information. For instance, you will probably weight information from trustworthy resources, such as family and friends, more than information from strangers or acquaintances. Further, we tend to weight early information (e.g., first impressions) more than subsequent information. This dynamic is called the primacy effect. However some research shows that a recency effect can also occur, when the most recent information is weighted more than other information. The recency effect is particularly likely when much time has passed since the first impression.

The weighted average model incorporates interactionist conceptions of the relationship between agency and interaction—that people take information about the world and process it before making any conclusions. That is, people are not simply empty vessels being manipulated by outside forces but active participants in attitudinal processes.

The small relationship between attitudes and behavior—and between attitudes and other attitudes—may simply reflect poor measurement of attitudes and/or behaviors (Raden 1985; Schuman 1995). Several conditions increase the likelihood that researchers will find relationships between attitudes and behaviors or between attitudes and other attitudes. First, researchers need to be very specific about the attitudes and behaviors in question. Asking respondents their attitude about abortion generally, for example, will sometimes elicit different responses than when asking about abortion in which the life of the mother is at risk. In addition, general attitudes are often called on when people are unaware of the specificities associated with a particular issue. For instance, if you want to ask people their opinions toward building a nuclear power plant in their town, they may have very little knowledge of the costs and benefits of nuclear power for their town, leaving them to rely on more general attitudes toward nuclear power to make their decisions. Hence, most people will provide an opinion on a topic when asked, but some people are more informed about the topic than others, making their responses more reliable and consistent over time than people with less knowledge.

The Effects of Social Status on Attitudes and Behavior

Gendered Attitudes and Behaviors

Few pollsters would conduct a survey or poll without including a series of questions about socioeconomic characteristics such as race, income, and gender. Social structure and personality researchers are also interested in whether social statuses affect attitudes. And they do. For instance, about 40% of Americans identify themselves as "very conservative" or "conservative," 21% say they are "liberal" or "very liberal," and 36% say they are "moderate" on social issues (Saad 2010). Therefore, on average, Americans' political attitudes can be defined as moderate to conservative. However, these values vary by region and social location. For instance, in the United States, people living on the west coast or in the northeastern states lean toward the Democratic Party (Jones 2009). Married people tend to be more conservative than singles and young adults tend to be more liberal than older adults (Jones 2003; Saad 2009).

The relationship between gender and attitudes depends on the topic. Women, for instance, were less supportive of invading Iraq with U.S. ground troops than men (Moore 2002). The biggest support gap occurred in November 2001, when 80% of men but only 68% of women supported the invasion of Iraq. Similarly, Smith (1984) found women to be less supportive of the use of force or violence in an array of law enforcement situations. However, there are not a lot of differences in men's and women's attitudes toward some topics such as race attitudes (Hughes and Tuch 2003). Therefore, gender may be more relevant for understanding some attitudes than others.

Race/Ethnicity and Attitudes

Our racial or ethnic groups also influence our attitudes. Polls and studies regularly show that African Americans and whites often disagree on average on a number of social issues. Specifically, African Americans tend to be more supportive of public policies related to civil rights (Wolf 1998), including gay civil liberties (Lewis 2003; Wolf 1998) and affirmative action (Bobo 1998). They are also less likely to support the death penalty than whites (Unnever and Cullen 2007). Matthew Hunt (2007) studied data from the General Social Survey collected between 1977 and 2004. Overall, he found a decline in the support of the purely racist belief that the disadvantaged social positions of African Americans' are due to innate inferiority. He also found that whites were most likely to attribute inequality between groups to a lack of motivation or will power (50%) and lack of chance for education (43%). Among African Americans, 61% attributed it to discrimination, with only 41% of Latinos and 31% of whites agreeing. Finally, Hunt concludes that there has been a growing similarity in beliefs about discrimination among all racial groups as African Americans and Latinos today are less likely to endorse a discrimination-based explanation than in the past.

These differences in values and beliefs among racial groups may reflect structural positions of African Americans in U.S. society who share a history of discrimination and lack of entitlements (Wolf 1998) or may reflect different cultural identities and beliefs, an issue that will be addressed in more detail under the rubric of social identity theory later in this chapter. In any case, race and ethnic status continue to predict differences in many social values.

The Social Context of Attitudes

Because individuals have multiple statuses, understanding attitudes requires examining people's multiple characteristics and social contexts. For instance, both men and whites in the United States have generally supported the use of the death penalty more than women and African Americans. The greatest differences are between African Americans and whites, with 71% of whites but only 44% of African Americans favoring the death penalty (Carroll 2004).

Do some of our group memberships have more power over our attitude formation than others? One way to study these relationships is to examine multiple affiliations at the same time. In a study of support for the Iraq War, for instance, David Rohall and his colleagues (2006) found that military academy and Reserve Officers Training Corps students were significantly more supportive of the war than civilian students. Traditionally, these differences have been explained by arguing that military personnel are socialized to be more accepting

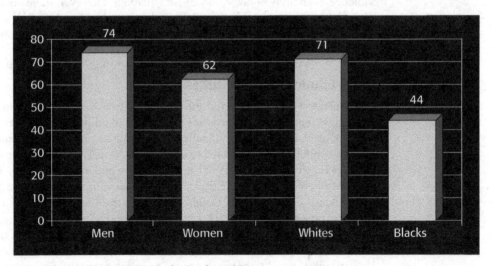

Percent Favoring the Death Penalty by Gender and Race

Based on the question: "Are you in favor of the death penalty for a person convicted of murder?"

Source: Adapted from Carroll (2004).

of war than their civilian counterparts, creating a culture of war. However, almost half of the effects of military affiliation on attitudes toward war were explained by the disproportionate number of males who were in the military—men (both military and civilian) are generally more supportive of this war than women. In this case, gender had a greater effect on attitudes toward war than military affiliation.

The relationship between group affiliations and attitudes becomes even more complex when we consider the context of community. Does our neighborhood affect the way we think about the world? In one study, Scott Schieman and Leonard Pearlin (2006) studied the impact of community-level disadvantage, measured using census indicators such as the number of households below the poverty line and individuals receiving public assistance, as well as subjective perceptions of neighborhood problems, and the degree to which respondents believed their neighborhoods to be noisy and run down. People living in poor neighborhoods (measured by census conditions) believed their neighborhoods were more disordered. But Schieman and Pearlin also found that this relationship was strongest among people who feel relatively advantaged, people who themselves believed that they were better off financially than their neighbors. Here, we see how personal biography intersects with neighborhood conditions to impact our perceptions of the world around us.

In another study, researchers found perceptions of discrimination went down as the percentage of African Americans went up in a neighborhood (Hunt et al. 2007). The researchers used data from a large-scale survey of over 40,000 African American women, measuring the frequency of both lifetime experiences with racism (e.g., being treated unfairly because of race) as well as everyday racism (e.g., receiving poor service in a restaurant). The researchers found that respondents' perceptions of discriminatory behavior went down in relatively mixed neighborhoods and neighborhoods primarily composed of African Americans relative to those neighborhoods in which African Americans were a minority.

Attitudes across the Life Course

Symbolic interactionists show that our attitudes can change over time as we interact with different people and that the expression of behaviors related to our attitudes is tied to our current social contexts. We also know that whole groups of people change over time as they are exposed to similar life events. Large-scale events such as wars, social movements, and assassinations provide similar identity-forming contexts among people who experience them at the same time. The Great Depression had long-term effects on some of the children growing up at that time. The amalgamation of such events for a particular group who are exposed to them creates a unique cohort of people. Generational changes due to exposure to unique life events may also account for change in societal values and beliefs over time. If newer cohorts are more liberal, for instance, they make the average American (or Canadian or whatever group is being examined) more liberal when they replace the earlier, more conservative cohorts. Social structure and personality researchers study cohort replacement by comparing attitudes toward social issues based on the birth cohort, or generation, to which people belong.

Attitude Stability and Change

Americans' attitudes toward social issues have changed in a number of ways over the years. Duane Alwin (Alwin 2002, p. 43) cited several examples, including the following:

- In 1977, 66% of Americans said that it is better if the man works and the woman stays home; in 2000, only 35% did.
- In 1972, 48% said that sex before marriage is wrong; in 2000, 36% did.
- In 1972, 39% said that there should be a law against interracial marriage; in 2000, 12% did.
- In 1958, 78% said that one could trust the government in Washington to do right; in 2000, only 44% did.

Historical experiences such as the Great Depression can affect some groups of people, whereas other groups are left relatively unaffected as discussed in Chapter 6. Thus, many of the social changes that have occurred in the United States occurred unevenly across groups.

Understanding attitude change is complicated by the fact that support for an issue can change across time while the overall level of support for that issue remains limited. For instance, attitudes toward penalties for the possession of marijuana have changed since the 1970s, but the majority of Americans still do not support its legalization (Rohall 2003). Only 12% of Americans believed that marijuana should be legalized in 1970; that percentage had increased to 34% by 2002. Despite increased support for the legalization of marijuana over the last 30 years, it is clear that Americans are not ready to make the drug legal. In one sense, opinions about illegal drugs have changed dramatically over the last 30 years. On the other hand, Americans as a whole continue to think that it should remain illegal. In essence, we should care about both the trends in and the overall levels of support for various issues.

Chapter 10

Stereotypes, Prejudice, and Discrimination

Learning Racism

The subtle nature of children's play can help us understand the roots of the replication of racist attitudes and behaviors. Children find creative ways to develop independence from adults as well as ways of excluding others from their play (Corsaro 2005). Race and ethnicity can be one of the ways children distinguish themselves or their group from others (Ausdale and Feagin 2002). Thus, race can serve as one of many markers among groups of people, especially if racial differences are readily apparent (e.g., skin color). However, children are capable of finding ways to differentiate among groups based on things other than the color of skin. If language is the building block of symbolic interaction, then language differences can be one of the first methods of differentiation. Language can serve as a way to exclude children from play. For example, children may interact such that only Spanish or English is allowed, excluding those who do not speak a particular language.

Debra Van Ausdale and Joe Feagin's (2002) research shows that racist ideas can be brought into children's interaction at a very young age, even before they have the ability to fully understand their ramifications. Some racist epithets may simply be heard and repeated among peers as young as three years old. Racist language may start with simple imitation, but children can use those to create more extensive conceptualizations of race and ethnicity. From an interactionist perspective, children can actively develop and manipulate simple statements about skin color into complex sets of meaning about categories of people. The process involves intellectual and social components, some related to race and some not. For instance, a child may hear a racial epithet but do nothing with the thought until social conditions require some means of differentiation among peers. The child may then use and elaborate on a simple epithet as a means of defining oneself and others in an interaction. Therefore, some of the same basic interactionist principles of socialization are used to negotiate racist and ethnocentric attitudes and behaviors.

From: *Social Psychology: Sociological Perspectives*, Second Edition by David E. Rohall, Melissa A. Milkie, and Jeffrey W. Lucas.

Prejudicial Attitudes and Behavior

One major application of symbolic interactionism to the study of attitudes and behaviors is the understanding of **prejudice**, an attitude of dislike or active hostility toward a particular group in society. One of the earliest writers on American racial prejudice was W. E. B. Du Bois. Du Bois made very frank observations of the poor relationships between African Americans and whites in both the United States and Europe. In a work originally published in 1920, he wrote,

> The discovery of whiteness among the world's peoples is a very modern thing—nineteenth and twentieth century matter, indeed. The ancient world would have laughed at such distinction. . . . Today we have changed all that, and the world in a sudden, emotional conversion has discovered that it is white and by that token, wonderful! This assumption that of all hues of God whiteness alone is inherently and obviously better than brownness or tan leads to curious acts. . . . (Du Bois 2003, originally 1920, p. 44)

Du Bois considered the subtle and not-so-subtle ways that prejudice manifests itself in society, through both words and deeds. In the same article about white people he wrote:

> (W)hite faces . . . I see again and again, often and still more often, a writing of human hatred, a deep and passionate hatred, vast by the vagueness of its expression . . . I have seen a man—an educated gentleman—grow livid with anger because a little, silent, black woman is sitting by herself in a Pullman car. I have seen a great grown man curse a little child, who had wandered into the wrong waiting room. (Du Bois 2003, originally 1920, pp. 46–47)

Although many Western cultures have changed since Du Bois's observations, prejudice is still common, and researchers continue to study prejudicial attitudes, examining how and why they develop and how they relate to specific behaviors.

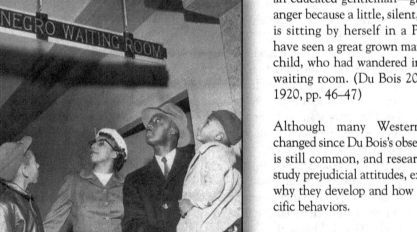

Prejudicial attitudes are reflected in many ways in society, some more clearly than others. These attitudes help to maintain group boundaries.

Conscious and Unconscious Racism

Earlier in this chapter we distinguished between cognitive and emotional dimensions of attitudes. Conscious racism can be measured by asking people if they dislike a particular group or if they believe themselves to be superior to one group or another. Many researchers today are finding unique ways to assess **unconscious racism**, ways in which we may be biased against a group without being aware of it. Public opinion polls show that most Americans and Europeans are not consciously racist, for instance, when asked whether any form of racial inequality is acceptable. Yet we know that there are still inequalities in society based on race. Some critics cite the devastating effects of Hurricane Katrina on New Orleans's population, questioning whether the poor treatment of the hurricane victims would have occurred if the victims were predominately white and middle class (Brunsma, Overfelt, and Picou 2007). National leaders publicly denied any conscious decisions based on the race and class of the victims, who were predominately African Americans of limited means. Could some sort of unconscious racism have contributed to the slow response to help these victims?

Is there any real evidence of unconscious racism? The short answer is yes. First, we will review two classic studies of prejudice that reveal the complex relationship between conscious and unconscious racism. We will then examine modern attempts to study unconscious prejudice.

One way to assess prejudicial attitudes is by examining social distance. **Social distance** refers to how close we feel to other people. The strength of attitudes toward people in other groups may reflect our prejudices toward people in those groups. Emory Borgardus (1882–1973) developed an instrument in 1958 called the social distance scale to assess individuals' senses of social distance to people of other ethnic and racial groups. The original social distance scale asked respondents the most that they were willing to do with a person from each of the racial or ethnic groups listed in the survey. The statements included the following activities:

1. Would marry
2. Would have as close friends
3. Would have as neighbor
4. Would have as co-worker
5. Would have as speaking acquaintances only
6. Would have as visitors only to my nation
7. Would bar from my country

The most positive score for attitudes toward people from a particular group would be a 1 (would marry), and the most negative score would be a 7 (would bar from my country). The average score for each group represents the average social distance people feel toward those groups.

Findings from 40 years' worth of research in the United States through the middle of the twentieth century using this scale shows that among college and university students, respondents felt "closest" to "Canadians," "Americans," and "English" (Owen, Eisner, and McFaul 1981). Groups with the worst scores included Asians and blacks. The worst scores rarely exceeded 4 (remember, higher scores reflect greater social distance), suggesting that respondents' prejudicial

Research Using the Bogardus Social Distance Scale

Rank	1926 Group	Score	1946 Group	Score	1956 Group	Score	1966 Group	Score
1	English	1.06	Americans	1.04	Americans	1.08	Americans	1.07
2	Americans	1.10	Canadians	1.11	Canadians	1.16	English	1.14
3	Canadians	1.13	English	1.13	English	1.23	Canadians	1.15
4	Scots	1.13	Irish	1.24	French	1.47	French	1.36
5	Irish	1.30	Scots	1.26	Irish	1.56	Irish	1.40
26	Negroes	3.28	Japanese Am	2.90	Japanese	2.70	Turks	2.48
27	Turks	3.30	Koreans	3.05	Negroes	2.74	Koreans	2.51
28	Chinese	3.36	Indians, Asia	3.43	Mexicans	2.79	Mexicans	2.56
29	Koreans	3.60	Negroes	3.60	Indians, Asia	2.80	Negroes	2.56
30	Indians, Asia	3.91	Japanese	3.61	Koreans	2.83	Indians, Asia	2.62

Source: Adapted from Owen and colleagues (1981).

attitudes were usually centered around neighbors, intimate friendships and family relationships.

More recent attempts to study social distance attitudes have shown the scale to be reliable. Parrillo and Donoghue (2005) found some similarities and difference regarding levels of social distance in a national study of college students conducted in 2001 with an overall score of 1.45 among 30 groups. As with the earlier studies, European Americans received the most positive scores. However, in this sample, the most negative scores included Arabs (1.94), Muslims (1.88), and Vietnamese (1.69). Consistent with earlier findings, women appear to be more tolerant than men. The authors also pointed out that overall distance scores and the spread between social groups have both decreased over the years, suggesting that attitudes have generally become more tolerant toward people of different racial and ethnic backgrounds. The social distance scale has been adapted to study racial and ethnic attitudes in places such as Canada (Weinfurt and Moghaddam 2001), the Czech Republic (Rysavy 2003), and the Ukraine (Panina 2004).

LaPiere's Study of Prejudice

Another classic study of prejudicial attitudes was conducted by Richard T. LaPiere over 50 years ago in the United States. His research is important because it showed that prejudicial attitudes and social distance do not necessarily lead to aggressive or hostile behavior among groups. That is, just because you feel prejudice toward an individual—or people from a particular race, class, or gender—does not mean that you will necessarily act on those attitudes. LaPiere (1934) spent two years traveling extensively with a Chinese couple in the United States, staying at various hotels and eating at local restaurants. His work was being conducted during a time in the United States when racial segregation was still considered acceptable by many people. He wanted to know if people's attitudes toward different races coincided with the treatment of people of those races. To study this relationship, he conducted a survey of racial attitudes from the owners of the establishments he had visited during his travels with the couple as well as some restaurants and hotels he did not visit over that period of time.

LaPiere's (1934) primary survey question was, "Will you accept members of the Chinese race as guests in your establishment?" He then compared their verbal responses to their actual experiences at those establishments. One hundred and twenty-eight hotels and restaurants that had been visited responded to the survey. Of those that responded, 92% indicated that they would *not* give service to Chinese people. Only one of the respondents said that they would provide service to this group. The rest were undecided. However, their actual experiences differed markedly from the attitudes expressed in the survey. Of the 251 hotel and restaurant visits (both accompanied and unaccompanied by the author), the Chinese couple was refused service at only one hotel. In fact, almost 40% of the visits were coded as being "very much better than [the] investigator would expect to have received (himself) . . ." (p. 235). A summary of his findings can be found in Table 9.3.

LaPiere's (1934) study was one of the first to show that attitudinal research is limited in its ability to predict individuals' behaviors. According to LaPiere, attitudes exist as symbolic representations in the minds of individuals. What individuals do with those symbolic representations is highly dependent on the social conditions surrounding those individuals, especially when confronted with real people and tangible physical conditions.

Summary of LaPiere's Attitude-Behavior Experiment

	Responses to Survey about Service to Chinese People*	Actual Experience with Service at the Same Hotels and Restaurants
Would not provide service to Chinese patrons or Undecided	127	1
Would provide service to Chinese patrons	1	250

*Based on responses to the question: "Will you accept members of the Chinese race as guests in your establishment?" Only 128 hotels and restaurants visited responded to the survey.

Source: Adapted from LaPiere (1934).

Since Lapiere's time, conscious racism seems to have dissipated somewhat. At a minimum, it is less acceptable to openly share those thoughts. Polls showing outward tolerance may either be misleading because people are being dishonest in their answers or might reveal that racism has become (or remained) unconscious. Some modern researchers employ measures of unconscious racism such as the Implicit Association Test (IAT) (Tetlock and Mitchell 2008) to study racism today. Subjects taking the IAT are asked to categorize a series of items that appear on a computer screen. Studies generally show that people pair concepts, such as, for example, white with good and black with bad. People do not have time to ponder these associations, leading researchers to believe that they are learned associations. We also know that IAT scores are positively associated with conscious racial beliefs (Dambrun, Villate, and Richetin 2008).

Other studies rely on indirect evidence of racial bias. Tanya Stivers and Asifa Majid (2007) revealed unconscious racism by examining pediatric physicians' interactions with children and their parents. They found that African American and Latino children were less likely to be selected to answer physicians' questions than their white peers. It appears that the physicians trusted white children to be more competent in responding to their questions than minorities. In another study, Devah Pager and Lincoln Quillian (2005) compared employers' self-reports about their willingness to hire black and white ex-offenders and their actual hiring behavior in a creative field experiment. Although there were no differences in employers' statements about hiring ex-offenders of either race, the study showed that (pseudo) white ex-offender candidates were more likely to get callbacks from employers than (pseudo) black ex-offenders who presented the exact same resumes. The results suggest that employers consciously or unconsciously acted against their stated attitudes.

The role of prejudice encompasses much more than interactions between individuals. Norman Denzin (2007) argued that racism is entrenched in our cultural heritage, in our interpretations of history, among other things. In his historical analysis of the Lewis and Clark expedition (1804–1806) to the West at the request of Thomas Jefferson, he finds the story laden with racism and ethnocentrism. Modern historical interpretations of the story focus on the struggles Lewis and Clark overcame, their positive interactions with Native Americans, and their great discoveries. Denzin points out that slavery and racism were alive and well at the time of the journey, and these men were not immune to these biases as they interacted with Native Americans. A number of examples of racial prejudice and discrimination toward the Native Americans abound. However, he says, we have reconstructed the memory of the journey to fit the norms and standards of our times. From an interactionist perspective, personal and collective memories of interactions or events are reinterpreted to help maintain a positive self-attitude or to match the standards of our society.

The connection between unconscious racism and conscious choices is not well established. From a symbolic interaction perspective, there are dozens of situational conditions that may intervene between our unconscious mind and social reality—much like LaPiere showed that conscious racism does not always lead to discrimination. In addition to laws limiting discrimination in the workplace, people must manage cultural norms against discrimination in their day-to-day lives. Mica Pollock (2004) conducted an ethnographic study of race interactions in a California high school. She found that people publicly discussed race freely under some conditions and not others. When it was a sensitive issue, race talk occurred only behind the scenes. Kristin Myers (2005) conducted a systematic observation of how people talk about race in their day-to-day lives. Not only did she find that talk of race was commonly used in everyday life but that people relied heavily on racial stereotypes in their interactions. Monica McDermott's (2006) study showed that race relations vary by context: Working-class whites, she found, were much more likely to express prejudice against African Americans when African Americans were not present. It is clear from these studies that the norms governing racial attitudes and behaviors are highly structured to include our own conscious and unconscious biases, situational dynamics, information from the larger culture (e.g., stereotypes), and sets of norms governing the appropriate contexts to share thoughts regarding race.

Subtle Sexism

Conscious and unconscious prejudices toward someone's race, class, and gender can exist for any group of people. As with race, prejudice against women can be conscious or unconscious. Very few people admit to being consciously sexist or prejudiced against women. However, researchers have observed cases of **subtle sexism**, unequal treatment of women that go unnoticed (Swim and Cohen 1997). Manifestations of subtle sexism abound. Martha Foschi and her colleagues (1994) conducted an experiment in which 85 college students in Canada were asked to review job applications of men and women applying for an engineering position. When men had better records, they were chosen more often for the job and given higher competency ratings than when women's records were better. These differences only held true for the male subjects; sex of the applicant did not affect female subjects' assessments.

There are other ways to assess subtle sexism in everyday life. Irene Padavic (1991) conducted a participant observation of gender relations on a shop floor. She found that men would define women on the floor as feminine or unfeminine and treat them differently as a result. She concluded that stereotypes caused many women to feel isolated from the larger work culture. Sexist cultural beliefs can also affect men's and women's career aspirations. In one study, Shelley Correll (2004) informed undergraduate students that men were better at a particular task and then asked them to complete that task. She found that the men in the experiment assessed their abilities higher than the women even though their scores were the same. What is more, men also reported higher aspirations to do jobs related to that task. How might this study apply to the "real world"? Perhaps men and women come to believe that they are better or worse at a particular profession because of subtle gender beliefs in the culture that disadvantage women. And women more than men self-select out of good jobs when they have the same skills. In this case, they truly believe that they are less competent but maybe using "flawed" data in their assessments.

Theory of Group Position

If prejudice exists, how does it form? This question is especially important to answer considering most people do not consider themselves to be racist. Herbert Blumer was one of the most influential interactionists in the study of racial prejudice (Williams and Correa 2003). Blumer (1958) argued that prejudice is largely a group phenomenon rather than an individual attribute because it defines a group characteristic: one's race. According to the **theory of group position**, prejudicial attitudes reflect a group's relative position in society. Negative attitudes are defined to maintain a group's relative position in society. Specifically, among the dominant group, themes of group superiority (toward one's own group) and inferiority (toward the minority group) help to sustain one's higher status in society. These two factors influence the development of the feeling of entitlement among the dominant group, believing they deserve their position, and fear of the lower-status group. Ultimately, it establishes antipathy among the groups.

Although Blumer's work was focused on African American/white relationships in America, it can also be applied to other ethnic groups (Williams and Correa 2003). Race serves as a source of identity relevant to other groups in society who compete for limited resources. Greater competition among groups increases hostility among them as they each vie for relative position (Bobo and Hutchings 1996). Prejudicial attitudes are linked to groups that are seen as a threat to economic and cultural interests of another group, leading to the development of negative attitudes toward those groups (Perry 2007).

Changing Prejudicial Attitudes

Regardless of how we become prejudiced, how do you fix the problem? One of the most cited theories about improving relationships between groups is the social contact hypothesis. The social contact hypothesis is attributed to psychologist Gordon Allport (1897–1967). Allport proposed that groups can be taught to have better attitudes toward each other but only under very specific conditions. Simply putting them together in a room will not do it. First, the members of each group must have equal status. Second, they must have some kind of shared goal to complete together, something that they can accomplish as a team. Third, there must be interaction among group members. Finally, there must be some authority supporting and guiding the process.

Sociological research generally supports the contact hypothesis if most or all of these factors are taken into account (e.g., Caspi 1984; Lee, Farrell, and Link 2004; Sigelman and Welch 1993). But this method of changing attitudes works from the ground up: you have to change society by changing individuals' everyday lives. National-level policies such as desegregation may aid in such endeavors, but it does not guarantee people will choose to interact with people outside of their own groups, supporting the concept of agency. It also does not provide for the other factors in the social contact model such as having a superordinate goal to be followed.

REDUCING PREJUDICE:
COMBATING INTERGROUP BIASES

John F. Dovidio, Colgate University
Samuel L. Gaertner, University of Delaware

Here's something to think about: How is it that major league baseball players can play fiercely all season against each other and then suddenly become cooperative teammates during the all-star game? It's all in the categorization, you might say.

This simple example illustrates the power behind the work of John Dovidio and Samuel Gaertner. In this review article, they summarize the traditional approach to prejudice: using persuasion, education, and socialization to change the false beliefs that perpetuate prejudice. They note that today there are fewer overt expressions of prejudice. Instead, we see what's called "modern" racism, which involves nonconscious or unintentional forms of prejudice. To combat these forms, Dovidio and Gaertner suggest that psychologists get people to change their cognitive categories through changing conditions of contact. Much as the baseball player has to stop thinking of his new teammates and his former enemies as them *and instead think of* them *as* us *in order to play in the all-star game, prejudice could lessen if people de*categorized *or re*categorized *others by emphasizing similarity or solidarity rather than differences.*

What Dovidio and Gaertner suggest challenges people's innermost identities and group loyalties. However, their work is rich and exciting and provides a new way of understanding why techniques like the "jigsaw classroom" and superordinate goals help reduce prejudice. When it comes to reducing prejudice, you might say that everybody wins through these researchers' work.

Prejudice is commonly defined as an unfair negative attitude toward a social group or a member of that group. Stereotypes, which are overgeneralizations about a group or its members that are factually incorrect and inordinately rigid, are a set of beliefs that can accompany the negative feelings associated with prejudice. Traditional approaches consider prejudice, like other attitudes, to be acquired through socialization and supported by the beliefs, attitudes, and values of friends and peer groups (see Jones, 1977). We consider the nature of traditional and contemporary forms of prejudice, particularly racial prejudice, and review a range of techniques that have been demonstrated empirically to reduce prejudice and other forms of intergroup bias. Bias can occur in many forms, and thus it has been assessed by a range of measures. These measures include standardized tests of prejudice toward another social group, stereotypes, evaluations of and feelings about specific group members and about the group in general, support for policies and individual actions benefiting the other group, and interaction and friendship patterns.

In part because of changing norms and the Civil Rights Act and other legislative interventions that made discrimination not simply immoral but also illegal, overt expressions of prejudice have declined significantly over the past 35 years. Contemporary forms of prejudice, however, continue to exist and affect the lives of people in subtle but significant ways (Dovidio & Gaertner, 1998; Gaertner & Dovidio, 1986). The negative feelings and beliefs that underlie contemporary forms of prejudice may be rooted in either individual processes (such as cognitive and motivational biases and socialization) or intergroup processes (such as realistic group conflict or biases associated with the mere categorization of people into in-groups and out-groups). These negative biases may occur spontaneously, automatically, and without full awareness.

Many contemporary approaches to prejudice based on race, ethnicity, or sex acknowledge the persistence of overt, intentional forms of prejudice but also consider the role of these automatic or unconscious processes and the consequent indirect expressions of bias. With respect to the racial preju-

From: John F. Dovidio and Samuel L. Gaertner, reprinted from *Current Directions in Psychological Science* 8, no. 4 (August 1999), by permission of Sage Publications, Inc.

dice of white Americans toward blacks, for example, in contrast to "old-fashioned" racism, which is blatant, aversive racism represents a subtle, often unintentional, form of bias that characterizes many white Americans who possess strong egalitarian values and who believe that they are nonprejudiced. Aversive racists also possess negative racial feelings and beliefs (which develop through normal socialization or reflect social-categorization biases) that they are unaware of or that they try to dissociate from their nonprejudiced self-images. Because aversive racists consciously endorse egalitarian values, they will not discriminate directly and openly in ways that can be attributed to racism; however, because of their negative feelings, they will discriminate, often unintentionally, when their behavior can be justified on the basis of some factor other than race (e.g., questionable qualifications for a position). Thus aversive racists may regularly engage in discrimination while they maintain self-images of being nonprejudiced. According to symbolic racism theory, a related perspective that has emphasized the role of politically conservative rather than liberal ideology (Sears, 1988), negative feelings toward blacks that whites acquire early in life persist into adulthood but are expressed indirectly and symbolically, in terms of opposition to busing or resistance to preferential treatment, rather than directly or overtly, as in support for segregation.

Contemporary expressions of bias may also reflect a dissociation between cultural stereotypes, which develop through common socialization experiences and because of repeated exposure generally become automatically activated, and individual differences in prejudicial motivations. Although whites both high and low in prejudice may be equally aware of cultural stereotypes and show similar levels of automatic activation, only those low in prejudice make a conscious attempt to prevent those negative stereotypes from influencing their behavior (Devine & Monteith, 1993).

INDIVIDUAL PROCESSES AND PREJUDICE REDUCTION

Attempts to reduce the direct, traditional form of racial prejudice typically involve educational strategies to enhance knowledge and appreciation of other groups (e.g., multicultural education programs), emphasize norms that prejudice is wrong, and involve direct persuasive strategies (e.g., mass media appeals) or indirect attitude-change techniques that make people aware of inconsistencies in their attitudes and behaviors (Stephan & Stephan, 1984). Other techniques are aimed at changing or diluting stereotypes by presenting counter-stereotypic or nonstereotypic information about group members. Providing stereotype-disconfirming information is more effective when the information concerns a broad range of group members who are otherwise typical of their group rather than when the information concerns a sin-

gle person who is not a prototypical representative of the group. In the latter case, people are likely to maintain their overall stereotype of the group while subtyping, with another stereotype, group members who disconfirm the general group stereotype (e.g., black athletes; Hewstone, 1996). The effectiveness of multicultural education programs is supported by the results of controlled intervention programs in the real world; evidence of the effectiveness of attitude- and stereotype-change approaches, and the hypothesized underlying processes, comes largely (but not exclusively) from experimental laboratory research.

Approaches for dealing with the traditional form of prejudice are generally less effective for combating the contemporary forms. With respect to contemporary racism, for example, whites already consciously endorse egalitarian, nonprejudiced views and disavow traditional stereotypes. Instead, indirect strategies that benefit from people's genuine motivation to be nonprejudiced may be more effective for reducing contemporary forms of prejudice. For example, techniques that lead people who possess contemporary prejudices to discover inconsistencies among their self-images, values, and behaviors may arouse feelings of guilt, tension about the inconsistencies, or other negative emotional states that can motivate the development of more favorable racial attitudes and produce more favorable intergroup behaviors (even nonverbal behaviors) several months later. Also, people who consciously endorse nonprejudiced attitudes, but whose behaviors may reflect racial bias, commonly experience feelings of guilt and compunction when they become aware of discrepancies between their potential behavior toward minorities (i.e., what they *would* do) and their personal standards (i.e, what they *should* do) during laboratory interventions. These emotional reactions, in turn, can motivate people to control subsequent spontaneous stereotypical responses and behave more favorably in the future (Devine & Monteith, 1993). People's conscious efforts to suppress stereotypically biased reactions can inhibit even the immediate activation of normally automatic associations, and with sufficient practice, these efforts can eliminate automatic stereotype activation over the long term.

Approaches oriented toward the individual, however, are not the only way to combat contemporary forms of prejudice. Strategies that emphasize intergroup processes, such as intergroup contact and social categorization and identity, are alternative, complementary approaches.

INTERGROUP CONTACT

Real-world interventions, laboratory studies, and survey studies have demonstrated that intergroup contact under specified conditions (including equal status between the groups, cooperative intergroup interactions, opportunities for personal acquaintance, and supportive egalitarian norms) is a powerful technique for reducing intergroup bias and conflict (Pettigrew, 1998). Drawing on these principles cooperative learning and "jigsaw" classroom interventions (Aronson & Patnoe, 1997) are designed to increase interdependence between members of different groups working on a designated problem-solving task and to enhance appreciation for the resources they bring to the task. Cooperation is effective for reducing subsequent intergroup bias when the task is completed successfully, group contributions to solving the problem are seen as different or complementary, and the interaction among participants during the task is friendly, personal, and supportive.

Recent research has attempted to elucidate how the different factors of intergroup contact (e.g., cooperation, personal interaction) operate to reduce bias. Engaging in activities to achieve common, superordinate goals for instance, changes the functional relations between groups from actual or symbolic competition to cooperation. Through psychological processes to restore cognitive balance or reduce inconsistency between actions and attitudes, attitudes toward members of the other group and toward the group as a whole may improve to be consistent with the positive nature of the interaction. Also, the rewarding properties of achieving success may become associated with members of other groups, thereby increasing attraction.

✎ SOCIAL CATEGORIZATION AND IDENTITY

Factors of intergroup contact, such as cooperation, may also reduce bias through reducing the salience of the intergroup boundaries, that is, through *decategorization*. According to this perspective, interaction during intergroup contact can individuate members of the out-group by revealing variability in their opinions (Wilder, 1986) or can produce interactions in which people are seen as unique individuals (personalization), with the exchange of intimate information (Brewer & Miller, 1984). Alternatively, intergroup contact may be structured to maintain but alter the nature of group boundaries, that is, to produce *recategorization*. One recategorization approach involves either creating or increasing the salience of crosscutting group memberships. Making interactants aware that members of another group are also members of one's own group when groups are defined by a different dimension can improve intergroup attitudes (Urban & Miller, 1998). Another recategorization strategy, represented by our own work on the Common In-Group Identity Model, involves interventions to change people's conceptions of groups, so that they think of membership not in terms of several different groups, but in terms of one, more inclusive group (Gaertner, Dovidio, Anastasio, Bachman, & Rust, 1993).

The Common In-Group Identity Model recognizes the central role of social categorization in reducing as well as in creating intergroup bias (Tajfel & Turner, 1979). Specifically, if members of different groups are induced to conceive of themselves more as members of a single, super-

ordinate group rather than as members of two separate groups, attitudes toward former out-group members will become more positive through processes involving pro-in-group bias. Thus, changing the basis of categorization from race to an alternative dimension can alter who is a "we" and who is a "they," undermining a contributing force to contemporary forms of racism, such as aversive racism. The development of a superordinate identity does not always require people to abandon their previous group identities; they may possess dual identities, conceiving of themselves as belonging both to the superordinate group and to one of the original two groups included within the new, larger group. The model also recognizes that decategorization (seeing people as separate individuals) can also reduce bias. In contrast, perceptions of the groups as different entities (we/they) maintains and reinforces bias. The Common In-Group Identity Model is presented schematically in Figure 1.

In experiments in the laboratory and in the field, and in surveys in natural settings (a multi-ethnic high school, banking mergers, and blended families), we have found evidence consistent with the Common In-Group Identity Model and hypothesis that intergroup contact can reduce prejudice. Specifically, we have found that key aspects of intergroup contact, such as cooperation, decrease intergroup bias in part through changing cognitive representations of the groups. The development of a common in-group identity also facilitates helping behaviors and self-disclosing interactions that can produce reciprocally positive responses and that can further reduce intergroup prejudices through other mechanisms such as personalization.

Moreover, the development of a common in-group identity does not necessarily require groups to forsake their original identities. Threats to important personal identities or the "positive distinctiveness" of one's group can, in fact, exacerbate intergroup prejudices. The development of a dual identity (two subgroups in one group; see Fig. 1), in which original and superordinate group memberships are simultaneously salient, is explicitly considered in the model. Even when racial or ethnic identity is strong, perceptions of a superordinate connection enhance interracial trust and acceptance. Indeed, the development of a dual identity, in terms of a bicultural or multicultural identity, not only is possible but can contribute to the social adjustment, psychological adaptation, and overall well-being of minority-group members (LaFromboise, Coleman, & Gerton, 1993). Recognizing both different and common group membership, a more complex form of a common in-group identity, may also increase the generalizability of the benefits of intergroup contact for prejudice reduction. The development of a common in-group identity contributes to more positive attitudes toward members of other groups present in the contact situation, whereas recognition of the separate group memberships provides the associative link by which these more positive attitudes may generalize to other members of the groups not directly involved in the contact situation.

Figure 1. *The Common I-Group Identity Model. In this model, elements of an intergroup contact situation (e.g., intergroup independence) influence cognitive representations of the groups as one superordinate group (recategorization), as two subgroups in one group (recategorization involving a dual identity), as two groups (categorization), or as separate individuals (decategorization). Recategorization and decategorization, in turn, can both reduce cognitive, effective, and behavioral biases, but in different ways. Recategorization reduces bias by extending the benefits of in-group favoritism to former out-group members. Attitudes and behavior toward these former out-group members thus become more favorable, approaching attitudes and behaviors toward in-group members. Decategorization, in contrast, reduces favoritism toward original in-group members as they become perceived as separate individuals rather than members of one's own group.*

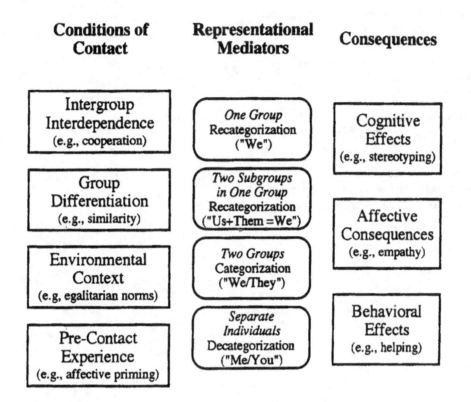

☜ CONCLUSION

Prejudice can occur in its blatant, traditional form, or it may be rooted in unconscious and automatic negative feelings and beliefs that characterize contemporary forms. Whereas the traditional form of prejudice may be combated by using direct techniques involving attitude change and education, addressing contemporary forms requires alternative strategies. Individual-level strategies engage in genuine motivations of people to be nonprejudiced. Intergroup approaches focus on realistic group conflict or the psychological effects of categorizing people into in-groups and out-groups. The benefits of intergroup contact can occur through many routes, such as producing more individuated perceptions of out-group members and more personalized relationships. Intergroup contact can also produce more inclusive, superordinate representations of the groups, which can harness the psychological forces that contribute to intergroup bias and redirect them to improve attitudes toward people who would otherwise be recognized only as out-group members. Understanding the processes involved in the nature and development of prejudice can thus guide, both theoretically and pragmatically, interventions that can effectively reduce both traditional and contemporary forms of prejudice.

RECOMMENDED READING

Brewer, M. B., & Miller, N. (1996). *Intergroup relations.* Pacific Grove, CA: Brooks/Cole.

Brown, R. J. (1995). *Prejudice.* Cambridge, MA: Blackwell.

Hawley, W. D., & Jackson, A. W. (Eds.). (1995). *Toward a common destiny: Improving race and ethnic relations in America.* San Francisco: Jossey-Bass.

Landis, D., & Bhagat, R. S. (Eds.). (1996). *Handbook of intercultural training.* Thousand Oaks, CA: Sage.

Stephan, W. G., & Stephan, C. W. (1996). *Intergroup relations.* Boulder, CO: Westview Press.

❦ Questions

1. Dovidio and Gaertner discuss individual and intergroup processes behind stereotyping and prejudice. Which set of processes should be targeted in order to reduce traditional forms of racism? Why? Which set of processes should be targeted in order to reduce current forms of racism? Why?

2. Thing about groups to which you belong (race, sex, nationality, sexual orientation, sports teams, clubs, fraternities, sororities, etc.). Using these groups, give examples of categorization, decategorization, and recategorization. Which of these three would be most effective at reducing group tensions among these various groups?

3. Dovidio and Gaertner claim that recategorization can change cognitive beliefs, affective consequences, and behavioral effects. If this is true, which one should we reduce to have the greatest impact on lessening prejudice?

4. In a diverse world both within the United States and globally, which technique, individual processes or intergroup process, is more likely to help increase peace? Why?

TALKING OPENLY ABOUT RACE
THWARTS RACISM IN CHILDREN

Erin Burnette

Nobody is born a racist. If we knew when and how we develop prejudices, then we could design programs to counteract racism. This is the idea behind the three research programs described in this article. First, we know that infants are able to classify their world. But can they recognize different skin tones of faces? If so, then this may be the foundation for why stereotypes are so readily learned. Second, do children get their racial attitudes from their parents and peers? If not, then where do prejudicial attitudes come from? Finally, is it possible to prevent racism? If so, what kinds of programs are most effective at reducing and preventing racism in children and teens? All three of these research programs have something in common: They found that if nothing is done to actively counteract children's beliefs, then racism will persist.

Many parents believe that their own children are oblivious to racial differences, and believe racist behavior in youngsters is created when bigoted parents pass intolerant views to their children.

But research suggests otherwise. Racism among children, say psychologists, can be caused by another parental behavior: *not* talking about race. A lack of discussion makes racial differences a taboo subject and contributes to children's negative ideas.

A key factor in preventing racism, say many psychologists, is to get children to talk about it.

WHEN STEREOTYPES START

Young children have a tendency to categorize the world along simple and rigid lines, said Rebecca Bigler, Ph.D., a researcher and psychology professor at the University of Texas at Austin, who studies stereotyping and cognitive skills such as classification.

"Studies demonstrate that children are classifiers—they set up their world in categories such as male and female, black and white, and good and bad—in order to make sense of their environment," Bigler said.

To measure children's racial awareness, investigators at the Institute for Research on Social Problems in Boulder, Colorado, conducted habituation tests—repeatedly showing an object to study participants until they lost interest in it.

They conducted the tests on a sample of 100 African-American and 100 white 6-month-old children. The investigators showed the infants pictures of either four different white faces or four different African-American faces until they were habituated to the race in the pictures. The team then showed the children a picture of someone from a different ethnicity.

The researchers found that when the infants saw a picture of a face from a different race, they spent a significantly longer period of time looking at it, demonstrating that they noticed the difference.

The infants are treating the pictures as if they have a preverbal concept of race," said Phyllis A. Katz, Ph.D., who led the study. "The results show that children are sensitive to race cues even before they develop language skills."

ENVIRONMENTAL FACTORS

A widespread societal belief holds that parental and peer attitudes are the primary factors that shape a child's attitudes about race. But studies conducted by Frances Aboud, Ph.D., and her colleagues at McGill University found otherwise.

In one study, Aboud and her colleagues gave 39 white, middle-class parents and their 8- to 10-year-old children the Preschool Racial Attitude Measure and the Multi-response Racial Attitude Measure to determine whether the children's beliefs about race mirrored those of their parents. The researchers also asked the children to predict their parents' answers to the measure.

The investigators found that the children's attitudes toward race are not the same as their parents' or their friends'.

"Talking Openly About Race Thwarts Racism in Children," by Erin Burnette, reprinted from *APA Monitor*, June, 1997, p. 33.

From: Erin Burnette, reprinted from *APA Monitor* (June 1997), American Psychological Association.

But while parents' and peers' attitudes toward race may not influence a child's own racial outlook, psychologists contend that the lack of dialogue about race in school and at home fosters children's development of negative stereotypes.

"Some parents don't talk about racial differences because they don't want to make it a big deal," Bigler said. "In not talking about it, however, children tend to guess what their parents' beliefs are and they are usually wrong."

People who don't see themselves as prejudiced often don't talk about race issues, said Vonnie McLoyd, Ph.D., a professor at Duke University.

"But the societal circumstances that African-Americans confront are much different than those that white people experience," she said. "We need to explore those differences and teach our children that differences don't translate into deficits."

Parents give their children subtle messages without realizing it, says Beverly Tatum, Ph.D., a psychology professor at Mt. Holyoke College who studies racial identity in children.

"A young child, for example, asks his mother why the man in the grocery store is so dark. Instead of answering, his mother tells him to be quiet, which tells the child it's not okay to discuss differences."

ഐ THWARTING RACISM

Several psychologists are developing programs to prevent racism in children. Tatum and her colleague Phyllis Brown, a doctoral education student at the University of Massachusetts, have designed a three-pronged program that increases diversity awareness in teachers and students from the North Hampton public school district in western Massachusetts. The two-year pilot project started in September and involves three components:

- **Staff development,** which offers teachers a four-month course that defines racism, explores how educators and children manifest it, and provides tips on handling it in school.

- **Youth groups,** whereby students meet after school once a week for seven weeks with members of their own culture to discuss what it means to be part of that culture. There's a group for Asian-Americans, African-Americans, Jewish-Americans, Latinos, whites and bi-racial students. The group facilitators then mix the groups so that they include a member of each culture. They meet for seven more weeks to discuss their differences and how they can get along.

- **Parent groups,** which meet once a month to educate parent about racism and help them more comfortably discuss race issues with their children.

Tatum says teachers who have taken a similar course in the greater Boston area are implementing the youth groups in their own schools.

The key to combating racism, says McLoyd is being honest with children.

"Racism is so deeply rooted. It's going to take hard work by open, honest, fair-minded people who are not easily discouraged," she says.

ഐ Questions

1. Do infants recognize race? Explain your reasoning.

2. If children's racial attitudes are not like the racial attitudes of their parents or friends, where do children get these attitudes?

3. If children are natural classifiers of the world, is racism inevitable?

4. If we ignore racial differences, will prejudice go away? Why or why not? What might combat stereotyping and prejudice? Why?

Chapter 11
Group Dynamics

Group Structures

The effect of a group on its members depends, in part, on how the group is configured. Groups can be configured in a number of ways—by size, function (e.g., work or pleasure), or goals, among other things. Each of these configurations can produce different expectations about how to behave in the group.

Group Size

Small groups are defined as groups of two or more individuals—typically between 2 and 20 people—whose members are able to engage in direct, face-to-face interactions. Although there is no official group size at which face-to-face interaction becomes impossible, it is difficult for personal relationships to develop in groups of more than 20. In a five-person group, for example, each person can interact with every other group member. But in a group of 50 people, a leader might direct the entire group (for example, by presenting a lecture) or instead might break the 50-person group into smaller, more intimate groups. An interaction among all 50 group members, however, is unlikely.

Anyone who has been part of a class of 90 students meeting in a large auditorium and has also participated in small classes of about 15 students can understand the impact of group size on interactions. You may enjoy smaller classes more than larger ones. Why? Probably because smaller classes allow for more intimate interactions between students, opening up discussions and giving class members an opportunity to get to know one another. In short, by allowing for more intimacy among their members, smaller classes provide better learning environments.

Dyads and Triads

One of the earliest sociologists to study the effects of group dynamics on individuals was Georg Simmel. Simmel (1950) argued that the size of a group restricts the level of intimacy possible within the group. A two-person group, or **dyad**, is limited to a single relationship. But adding just one more person to that group, to form a **triad**, creates two additional relationships. Thus, simply adding a person

From: *Social Psychology: Sociological Perspectives*, Second Edition by David E. Rohall, Melissa A. Milkie, and Jeffrey W. Lucas.

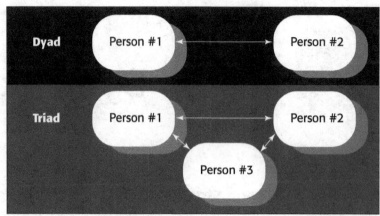

Relationships in Dyads and Triads

to a group increases the number of relationships in the group exponentially while simultaneously decreasing intimacy levels. The effects of group size on group members' thoughts, feelings, and behaviors occur above and beyond the specific individuals involved in the group.

The change from a dyad to a triad is an example of a process that occurs in small groups. The process can be illustrated through considering personal relationships. Suppose you go to a party and meet someone to whom you are attracted. As you start to talk, you become more interested in the other person, exchanging ideas about topics you both enjoy. A little later, a friend of yours enters the room and approaches your dyad, transforming it into a triad.

What happens now? Your discussion will very likely change, not only because a new group member brings a different point of view, but also because the group now has two new relationships to balance. As a result, someone will likely talk less, and there will be less opportunity to develop intimacy. Adding still more people to the triad will again create an exponential increase in the number of relationships—for example, a four-person group involves six different relationships—and a corresponding decrease in intimacy.

At the small-group level, group-processes theories in sociology focus on the exchanges—of resources, of information, of emotion—that take place between people and on how our positions in groups affect these exchanges. According to many scholars who study small groups, a primary source of motivation for individuals in groups is to obtain the things they need in life. Those "things" can include physical as well as social objects.

Types of Groups

Social psychologists distinguish between three broad types of groups, which are configured in different ways and serve different purposes:

- **Primary groups:** family members and close friends—the people we are close to and interact with regularly (Cooley 1909).

- **Secondary groups:** people we affiliate with to achieve similar goals or needs—for example, co-workers or teammates.
- **Reference groups:** people we do not necessarily know personally but look to as a source of standards and identity.

Each type of group holds different expectations of its members. Primary groups serve more emotional needs, whereas secondary groups usually serve instrumental needs. Reference groups, however, can vary considerably. Your membership in the Democratic or Republican Party may serve instrumental needs (e.g., a push for public policy) as well as reference needs (to find support for your ideals). Unlike your relationship to most primary and secondary groups, you may not actually interact with members of your reference groups. Even if you identify with your party's goals and use its ideals as a standard of behavior, for example, you may never actually go to party meetings.

Relationships among Groups

In our previous review of group processes, we looked at behavior within groups, or "intra-group" dynamics. But social psychologists are also interested in intergroup dynamics, that is, relationships between two or more groups. Thus, groups themselves—beyond their individual members—can serve as a unit of analysis. Going along with this, groups can develop identities that later have effects on the members of the group.

Intergroup relationships can occur on several levels, ranging from a small group of friends to larger, more formal groups. An important social psychological theory of intergroup relationships, social identity theory, is reviewed in detail later in this book. One area of interest to social psychologists who study intergroup relationships is the causes and consequences of prejudice and discrimination. Sociologists also study the behavior of larger groups through research on such acts as protests and riots.

Both inter- and intra-group behavior can be studied as aspects of **collective behavior**—the action or behavior of people in groups or crowds (Lofland 1992; Miller 2000). Collective behavior has traditionally been associated with riots, protests, and revolutions. But the field can also include the study of popular trends and fads. Theories of collective behavior can vary considerably, with some, such as mass hysteria theory, emphasizing its emotional aspects, whereas others, such as emergent norm theory, focus instead on the rational nature of human behavior in larger groups (Miller 2000).

As you can see from this discussion, the broad heading of "group processes" includes a variety of work. Because the emphasis in this book is on sociological social psychology, we will focus on the aspect of group processes that is of greatest interest to sociological social psychologists; that is, on the processes that occur in groups rather than on features of the groups themselves. In the chapters that follow, our discussions of group processes will generally (but not exclusively) look at social processes such as status, power, justice, and legitimacy.

Section Summary

This section of the chapter answered the questions: What is the group processes perspective? What are some basic social processes that play out in group contexts? What are the elements of group structure? Group process researchers emphasize the role of status and power in groups. They also study how notions of justice and legitimacy play out in group contexts. Group structures vary by size as well as complexities associated with size. They can also include group types such as primary, secondary, and reference groups. Group size and type can have large impacts on the interaction of members within a group.

Networks and Social Capital

Friends, family, and organizations of which we are a part provide access to a wide variety of social networks. Our friends link us to their friends and to organizations and groups with which they associate. Social networks act as conduits between different people, providing resources and information that may not be readily available from the people with whom we have direct contact. Organizations provide a bridge between strangers, a way of giving someone a sense that the other can be trusted in some way.

We often think of collateral in economic terms. However, collateral can exist in relationships. We trust people because we know them well enough to share important things with them, perhaps even money. Social networks serve as the basis for the exchange of both fiscal and **social capital**, the trust and social support found in relationships with other people (Coleman 1988; Putnam 2000). The number and types of people we have access to determine the availability of social capital. Not only do we turn to people for emotional support, but we also turn to others for advice and help in pursuing our goals. Our networks determine the amount and types of social capital available to us.

The effects of networking between individuals from different groups create a variety of outcomes for individuals, depending on the status of the individuals in a group as well as the status of the group itself. A group of neighbors at a local pub is likely have less clout in the larger world than a group of senior business executives. Hence, having access to the relationships in the latter group will likely provide different resources, including things such as money, useful knowledge about how to find good jobs, investments, and access to better medical and mental health services.

The Strength of Weak Ties

A typical way that relationships are important to us is found in research assessing how people find work. A Harvard accounting student probably has access to people with more powerful positions than a student at a community college. The job outcomes of these students are going to be related to the information available within their respective networks. The Harvard network is likely to provide information about and access to higher-level accounting jobs than the community-college network. In this way, our social class position is intimately tied to social networks, affecting our ability to succeed in society.

Two ways by which we are connected to other people are strong and weak ties. **Strong ties** refer to people with whom we are close, such as friends and family. **Weak ties** refer to people we do not know as well, such as acquaintances or more distant friends. We can further contrast both of these types of ties with more formal relationships in which people are connected via structured positions in organizations. Mark Granovetter (1973), in the original theoretical discussion of weak ties, said that "those to whom we are weakly tied are more likely to move in circles different from our own and will thus have access to information different from that which we receive" (p. 1371). For job seekers, the quantity of ties is typically more important to finding work than the quality of those ties. Granovetter's research supported the contention that weak ties are more important than strong ties for finding work. He reports that of people who find work through contacts, 84% reported seeing those contacts only rarely or occasionally.

Granovetter's (1995) more recent work combines ideas about both strong and weak ties in assessing job-searching strategies. He found that 56% of the professional, technical, and managerial workers experiencing job transitions in New England reported finding work via **personal ties** (both strong and weak), followed by another 19% who found jobs through formal means (e.g., ads or employment agencies), 19% through direct applications, and the rest via miscellaneous other methods. Personal ties not only produce jobs but are also associated with finding better jobs: workers who found jobs via networks (personal ties) were more satisfied with their work and reported higher incomes than those who found work through other means.

Levels and types of social capital vary. Immigrants and other groups with high levels of mobility may have limited access to social capital because they are not in one place long enough to establish social networks (Ream 2005). Poor people may have strong social ties that help them through their economic circumstances, but the ties may also limit their upward mobility because the networks are horizontal in nature, connecting people to jobs within their social class. Government programs can help build social capital among these people by providing venues to bridge them with people outside of their own social classes, such as mentoring or job tutoring (Strathdee 2005).

Collective Behavior

I knew almost nothing about basketball. I joked that I was not even sure how many players were on a basketball team. Nonetheless, when my daughters were playing high school basketball in rural Illinois "basketball country," I shouted, cheered, and booed along with hundreds of other fans in steamy gyms on many cold winter nights in spite of the fact that I know so little about the game! I felt strong allegiance with the parents of our players, and I also began to feel animosity toward the opposing fans. I often left the gym with sore hands from clapping loudly with others to try to urge our team on to victory.

—Steve, nontraditional student

Most of the earlier chapters focus on the influence of social forces on individuals. In this chapter, we will review social psychological theories and research that try to explain the behavior of large groups. Steve reflects on how engrossed he became while watching his daughters' basketball games. Steve was not a basketball fan outside the stadium. However, when he was at the game, he could not resist succumbing to the exaggerated emotions of the crowd. What drove this change in his thoughts and feelings? Of course he was motivated to support his daughters. But what other social processes were going on that could account for his "basketball fever"?

Sociologists have studied sports crowds and many other types of collective events, including celebrations, ceremonies, riots, fads, disasters, demonstrations, and social movements. This chapter will provide you with a brief overview of social psychological theory and research on collective behavior. Earlier we defined collective behavior as action or behavior of people in groups or crowds, usually as a reaction to an event or to express a common sentiment (Rohlinger and Snow 2003). This behavior typically includes situations in which individuals act differently in group contexts than they would in ordinary environments. Collective behavior can take the form of protests, riots, or panics. It may also include fads and trends in which large numbers of people become obsessed with an object or idea for a period of time.

The term collective behavior came into use in the 1920s when Samuel Henry Prince (1920) discussed "collective behavior" in his study of the great Halifax, Nova Scotia, explosion of 1917. The first introductory sociology text ever published, Robert Park and Ernest Burgess's *Introduction to the Science of Sociology* (1921) also included a chapter on collective behavior. Although crowds are viewed by sociologists as a form of collective behavior, one of the earliest books written about crowds, Charles Mackay's (1852) *Memoirs of Extraordinary Popular Delusions and the Madness of Crowds*, never used the term collective behavior. Likewise, Gustave LeBon (1960, originally 1895), who is often credited as the "father of collective behavior," never used the term when he wrote his book *The Crowd*. The early work of Mackay and LeBon focused on crowd excitement and included many discussions of the fickleness, sentimentality, mania, and amorality of crowds. This treatment of crowds as irrational entities came to dominate most of the first century of sociological writing about the crowd and collective behavior.

In 1968, Carl Couch challenged these views when he suggested crowds are no more or no less bizarre than other social systems (Couch 1968). Evidence to support his view was soon forthcoming. Researchers working through the newly established Disaster Research Center at Ohio State University began to regularly find that survivors of disasters were capable of caring for themselves and others and restoring order to their communities rather quickly; they did not stampede from danger or become helpless because of emotional shock, as earlier stereotypes suggested.

In the 1970s Clark McPhail led teams of observers to demonstrations, civil disorders, sporting events, and shopping malls to systematically observe crowds. McPhail's teams utilized multimedia data-collection techniques. They first used notepads and check sheets for recording data manually and later augmented these with film and video cameras. Simultaneous observations were made at several locations in or near crowds. After studying and comparing data from hundreds of events, McPhail concluded that much of what had been previously written about crowds and collective behavior was not accurate (Miller 2000). To distinguish his work from earlier treatments, he began to refer to crowds as gatherings and to write about collective action within gatherings. By the 1980s, sociologists generally began to use the term **collective action** to reflect the seemingly purposive nature of people's behavior when they collectively celebrate, mourn, worship, protest, compete in athletics, or confront disasters.

Another concept related to collective behavior and action is social movements. Herbert Blumer (1972) defined **social movements** as collective action designed to produce new social orders. Hence, collective action may turn into a social movement, but social movements incorporate large-scale goals and plans that often exceed the temporary nature of most other forms of collective behavior or action.

Constructing Collective Behavior

It will be remarked that among the special characteristics of crowds there are several—such as impulsiveness, irritability, incapacity to reason, the absence of judgment, and of the critical spirit, the exaggeration of the sentiments, and others besides are almost always observed in beings belonging to inferior forms of evolution—in women, savages, and children, for instance.

—Gustave LeBon (1960, originally 1895, p. 36)

The French Revolution (1789–1794) is associated with some of the most ghastly behavior by groups in the history of humankind. Mobs of French citizens would go through the streets of Paris, collecting people to be killed in the name of the Revolution. A state of paranoia existed in France at the time. Although LeBon lived after the French Revolution, he sought to understand why such "cultured" people could become like dogs killing their victims in packs. The French went from being among the most "developed" and "civilized" peoples of the world to individuals willing to commit the most barbaric acts.

Since LeBon's writings, social scientists have tried to understand the social conditions that produce such changes in individuals. Some contemporary perspectives stem from LeBon's early work, emphasizing the emotional changes in people as a result of being in a crowd. Other people emphasize the rational

Media images of collective behavior emphasize emotional outbursts and reactions.

aspects of crowd behavior. The first part of this chapter will examine ways in which crowds have been shown to transform individuals' thoughts, feelings, and behavior. Later sections will review current research on crowd behavior.

Mass Hysteria Theory

Everyday life is composed of a wide variety of collective events, such as high school basketball games, that are characterized by the joined expression of intense feeling. Early writers such as Mackay (1852) found such "crowd madness" a worthy subject for pioneering work. LeBon was struck by the even more spectacular, emotion-laden events that were part of revolutions that overthrew the monarchies of Europe. The concern for collectively experienced and expressed emotion is the basis of the earliest general theory in the field of collective behavior.

LeBon probed the workings of crowds, representative forms of government, and social movements throughout his writing career. In bold terms, LeBon frequently wrote that all crowds exert an inherently negative influence on people. This thinking is the basis of **mass hysteria theory** (also called **contagion theory**), in which individuals in crowds lose their ability to think and act rationally.

The Case of the Stairway of the Stars Concert

A dozen police cars, fire trucks, and ambulances were parked on the lawn of the Santa Monica Civic Auditorium late on Thursday evening, April 13, 1989. Their flashing lights illuminated the faces of hundreds of people moving about the vehicles. Many of the faces were young, some showed fear, some were crying. Police, firefighters, and paramedics moved among the people on the lawn. Near a medical tent, there were rows of stretchers, and many of them were occupied. It was not an earthquake or a terrorist bomb that had forced one of the largest evacuations in Santa Monica history. The Civic Auditorium had been emptied by what was to be later identified as "mass hysteria."

Nearly a thousand young musicians and singers of the Santa Monica-Malibu Unified School District had rehearsed since ten o'clock that morning for the 40th Annual Stairway of the Stars concert. This was the big concert of the year for band, orchestra, and chorus students in grades four through high school. None of the musicians, or their teachers and parents, had expected this gala event to end in this fashion.

During the afternoon rehearsals, however, students and teachers had complained that the auditorium was hot, stuffy, and "smelled funny." Many students said they had to sit and rest during the day because they had headaches and felt dizzy. At least two students fainted during the day, and several students had been unable to complete rehearsal because of nausea and fever. Even though rehearsals had been difficult and uncomfortable, the classical music concert started on time.

During the concert, students continued to experience many flulike symptoms, including headaches, dizziness, weakness, abdominal pains, nausea, and shortness of breath. Spectators also reported experiencing similar discomforts. Toward the end of the Stairway of the Stars program, some performers had collapsed or fainted, and many others were too ill to continue. School officials called an early end to the concert and ordered the evacuation of the auditorium.

Did the students experience a major viral illness or simply some sort of mass hysteria? This incident led many to believe that a mild form of hysteria occurred in which students transferred some physiological symptoms to other people. In other words, people began to believe that they were sick, even when they had no real ailments. Just like viruses, behavior can be contagious!

LeBon describes groups' influence on their members as a rapidly transmitted, **contagious mental unity**, a sense of a shared emotional bond that emerges whenever people interact in a group—be it a revolutionary street crowd or a parliament—making individuals act more on animalist emotions than reason. For LeBon, contagious mental unity, or when people are overcome with a shared emotion in a crowd, was the root cause of the horrors he witnessed during the Paris riots of 1871.

Value-Added Theory

Another major theoretical perspective in the study of collective behavior is **value-added theory**, associated with Neil Smelser (Miller 2000). From this perspective, there are different types of collective behavior and several social-structural determinants of collective behavior. Hence, to fully understand the causes of a particular event or events, according to the value-added theory, we need to distinguish the type of collective behavior in question and the social conditions surrounding it.

Types of Collective Behavior

According to value-added theory, there are five types of collective behavior: the panic, the craze, the hostile outburst, the norm-oriented social movement, and the value-oriented social movement. One of the reasons it is difficult to predict behaviors in a crowd setting is that the people may be gathered for very different reasons, producing different kinds of outcomes. People in these different types of groupings have different goals and expectations.

Value-added theory defines the five different types of crowd settings as follows:

1. **Panic**—when large numbers of people are overwhelmed with a common fear.
2. **Craze**—when large numbers of people become obsessed with a product, behavior, or idea.
3. **Hostile outbursts**—any type of mass violence or killings.
4. **Norm-oriented social movements**—movements to change the way things are regulated in society.
5. **Value-oriented social movements**—attempts to change the social order of society.

A panic refers to a situation in which large numbers of people are overwhelmed with a common fear. The 1929 stock market crash is often used as an example of a wide-scale panic. A craze simply refers to when large numbers of people become obsessed with something, such as the purchase of a product (e.g., hula hoops) or an activity (e.g., disco dancing). Hostile outbursts include any type of mass violence or killings, such as the Rwandan genocide in the 1990s. Norm-oriented social movements include movements to change the way things are regulated in society, such as the Temperance Movement in the United States during the 1920s. Finally, value-oriented social movements include attempts to change the social order of society—replacing a religious government with a secular democracy, for instance.

From the value-added approach, the role of emotion in collective behavior depends, in part, on the type of group behavior being considered. We would expect the most rational behavior to occur in social movements (both norm- and value-oriented) because they require some level of coordination and communication to succeed. Alternatively, panics, by definition, are based on emotion.

Therefore, we would predict more emotional behavior in those cases than during social movements.

Determinants of Collective Behavior

According to value-added theory, there are five determinants of collective behavior.

1. There must be **structural conduciveness**—a society must be in a condition amenable to the formation of movements.
2. There must be some level of **structural strain** in society over some issue or problem, the driving force of a collective behavior that provides a motivation to reduce strain.
3. There must be a **generalized belief**, a shared view of the problem and how to resolve the tension.
4. There must be some sort of **mobilization for action**, individuals' reaction to an immediate threat.
5. There must be **action of social control** in terms of how authorities react to the behavior, which determines how an event will be manifested in society.

Specifically, the social control agents in society—such as the government and police—can relieve or instigate fears and anxieties by modifying any of the previous components. For instance, the government may issue a statement to tell citizens not to panic during a crisis event.

According to value-added theory, each determinant of collective behavior must be present for collective action to take place. For instance, the stock market crash of 1929 could not occur in a small hunting-and-gathering society without an advanced economy (structural conduciveness). Nor could it occur in a society that had not inflated the stock market in a way that required a large-scale shift to correct itself (structural strain). Investors shared the same idea about how to fix the problem: Get out of the market before losing all of their investments (generalized belief). In the case of the stock market crash, investors reacted to the lack of information available to make investment decisions (mobilization for action), causing them to fear for their financial lives. Finally, the inaction of financial and government leaders to the crisis left people to act on their worst fears (action of social control). The compilation of these determinants led to wide-scale panic, producing a massive financial downturn.

Perception Control Theory

Another rational choice approach to collective behavior is perception control theory. **Perception control theory** is based on the premise that people must be able to monitor and interpret one another's behavior in order for collective action to occur. In short, people adjust their actions to make them congruent with what is expected of them. According to McPhail (1994), there are three sources of perception control input:

1. **Independent instructions**—individual decisions.
2. **Interdependent instruction**—assumes that individuals work together to make decisions.
3. **Organizational instruction**—information provided by a movement's leadership or some other outside force.

Each form of instruction occurs naturally in different types and stages of collective behavior. The latter form of instruction is probably most necessary in larger demonstrations where coordination is more difficult to maintain than in smaller groups. Interdependent instruction is important amid the crowd members themselves, as they turn to each other for assistance and cooperation during an event. This perspective is supported by the finding that most violence and looting in riots occur sporadically and in small groups rather than en masse (the larger group) (McPhail 1994). Perception control theory extends rational views of collective behavior by narrowing the range of interaction among people, helping to examine the ways people try to maintain order in groups. As in Blumer's theory of circular reaction, however, these communication lines, regardless of their form, often break down, leading to confusion, perhaps explaining both rational (when communication lines are intact) and irrational (when they break down) behaviors.

EXPERIMENTS IN GROUP CONFLICT

Muzafer Sherif
University of Oklahoma

In the notes accompanying the original reprint of this reading, Muzafer Sherif was described as having experienced "war and revolution in Turkey, mass hysteria in 1932 Germany and social decay in prewar France." It was therefore no wonder that when he came to the United States, he energetically sought solutions to important social problems. In the process, he became one of the founders of social psychology.

 The experiment described below, often referred to as the Robber's Cave Experiment because of the location of the last study, represents an ideal social psychological research project. Sherif meticulously devised a controlled field experiment that created group loyalty, incited group animosity, and resolved group conflict. The fact that the young experimental participants and their parents thought of the experience as just a fun summer-camp adventure attests to the realism that his design achieved. The fact that Sherif's findings have been replicated and applied to solve real problems in prejudice and conflict resolution reveals the power of his findings.

 In this article, Sherif discusses the conditions and results of three different summer-camp experiments. The results of this series of experiments have helped social psychologists understand the kinds of circumstances that can lead to conflict between groups and—more importantly—the keys to reducing conflict.

Conflict between groups–whether between boys' gangs, social classes, "races" or nations–has no simple cause, nor is mankind yet in sight of a cure. It is often rooted deep in personal, social, economic, religious and historical forces. Nevertheless it is possible to identify certain general factors which have a crucial influence on the attitude of any group toward others. Social scientists have long sought to bring these factors to light by studying what might be called the "natural history" of groups and group relations. Intergroup conflict and harmony is not a subject that lends itself easily to laboratory experiments. But in recent years there has been a beginning of attempts to investigate the problem under controlled yet lifelike conditions, and I shall report here the results of a program of experimental studies of groups which I started in 1948. Among the persons working with me were Marvin B. Sussman, Robert Huntington, O. J. Harvey, B. Jack White, William R. Hood and Carolyn W. Sherif. The experiments were conducted in 1949, 1953 and 1954; this article gives a composite of the findings.

 We wanted to conduct our study with groups of the informal type, where group organization and attitudes would evolve naturally and spontaneously, without formal direction or external pressures. For this purpose we conceived that an isolated summer camp would make a good experimental setting, and that decision led us to choose as subjects boys about 11 or 12 years old, who would find camping natural and fascinating. Since our aim was to study the development of group relations among these boys under carefully controlled conditions, with as little interference as possible from personal neuroses, background influences or prior experiences, we selected normal boys of homogeneous background who did not know one another before they came to the camp.

 They were picked by a long and thorough procedure. We interviewed each boy's family, teachers and school officials, studied his school and medical records, obtained his scores on personality tests and observed him in his classes and at play with his schoolmates. With all this information we were able to assure ourselves that the boys chosen were of like kind and background: all were healthy, socially well-adjusted, somewhat above average in intelligence and from stable, white, Protestant, middle-class homes.

 None of the boys was aware that he was part of an experiment on group relations. The investigators appeared as a regular camp staff–camp directors, counselors and so on. The boys met one another for the first time in buses that took them to the camp, and so far as they knew it was a normal summer of camping. To keep the situation as lifelike as possible, we

"Experiments in Group Conflict," by Muzafer Sherif, reprinted from *Scientific American*, November 1956. Pp. 54–56.

From: Muzafer Sherif, reprinted by permission from *Scientific American*, November 1956.

conducted all our experiments within the framework of regular camp activities and games. We set up projects which were so interesting and attractive that the boys plunged into them enthusiastically without suspecting that they might be test situations. Unobtrusively we made records of their behavior, even using "candid" cameras and microphones when feasible.

We began by observing how the boys became a coherent group. The first of our camps was conducted in the hills of northern Connecticut in the summer of 1949. When the boys arrived, they were all housed at first in one large bunkhouse. As was to be expected, they quickly formed particular friendships and chose buddies. We had deliberately put all the boys together in this expectation, because we wanted to see what would happen later after the boys were separated into different groups. Our object was to reduce the factor of personal attraction in the formation of groups. In a few days we divided the boys into two groups and put them in different cabins. Before doing so, we asked each boy informally who his best friends were, and then took pains to place the "best friends" in different groups so far as possible. (The pain of separation was assuaged by allowing each group to go at once on a hike and camp-out.)

As everyone knows, a group of strangers brought together in some common activity soon acquires an informal and spontaneous kinds of organization. It comes to look upon some members as leaders, divides up duties, adopts unwritten norms of behavior, develops an *esprit de corps*. Our boys followed this pattern as they shared a series of experiences. In each group the boys pooled their efforts, organized duties and divided up tasks in work and play. Different individuals assumed different responsibilities. One boy excelled in cooking. Another led in athletics. Others, though not outstanding in any one skill, could be counted on to pitch in and do their level best in anything the group attempted. One or two seemed to disrupt activities, to start teasing at the wrong moment or offer useless suggestions. A few boys consistently had good suggestions and showed ability to coordinate the efforts of others in carrying them through. Within a few days one person had proved himself more resourceful and skillful than the rest. Thus, rather quickly, a leader and lieutenants emerged. Some boys sifted toward the bottom of the heap, while others jockeyed for higher positions.

We watched these developments closely and rated the boys' relative positions in the group, not only on the basis of our own observations but also by informal sounding of the

Friendship choices of campers for others in their own cabin are shown for Red Devils (white) and Bulldogs (black). At first a low percentage of friendships were in the cabin group (left). After five days, most friendship choices were within the group (right).

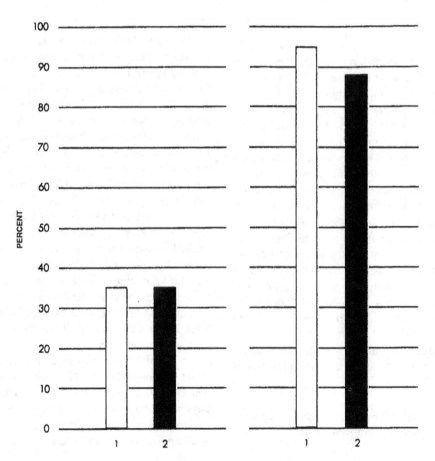

During conflict between the two groups in the Robber's Cave experiment there were few friendships between cabins (left). After cooperation toward common goals had restored good feelings, the number of friendships between groups rose significantly (right).

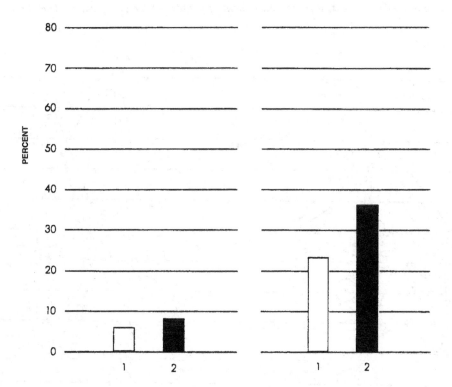

boys' opinions as to who got things started, who got things done, who could be counted on to support group activities.

As the group became an organization, the boys coined nicknames. The big, blond, hardy leader of one group was dubbed "Baby Face" by his admiring followers. A boy with a rather long head became "Lemon Head." Each group developed its own jargon, special jokes, secrets and special ways of performing tasks. One group, after killing a snake near a place where it had gone to swim, named the place "Moccasin Creek" and thereafter preferred this swimming hole to any other, though there were better ones nearby.

Wayward members who failed to do things "right" or who did not contribute their bit to the common effort found themselves receiving the "silent treatment," ridicule or even threats. Each group selected symbols and a name, and they had these put on their caps and T-shirts. The 1954 camp was conducted in Oklahoma, near a famous hideaway of Jesse James called Robber's Cave. The two groups of boys at this camp named themselves the Rattlers and the Eagles.

Our conclusions on every phase of the study were based on a variety of observations, rather than on any single method. For example, we devised a game to test the boys' evaluations of one another. Before an important baseball game, we set up a target board for the boys to throw at, on the pretense of making practice for the game more interesting. There are no marks on the front of the board for the boys to judge objectively how close the ball came to a bull's-eye, but, unknown to them, the

board was wired to flashing lights behind so that an observer could see exactly where the ball hit. We found that the boys consistently overestimated the performances by the most highly regarded members of their group and underestimated the scores of those of low social standing.

The attitudes of group member were even more dramatically illustrated during a cook-out in the woods. The staff supplied the boys with unprepared food and let them cook it themselves. One boy promptly started to build a fire, asking for help in getting wood. Another attacked the raw hamburger to make patties. Others prepared a place to put buns, relishes and the like. Two mixed soft drinks from flavoring and sugar. One boy who stood around without helping was told by the others to "get to it." Shortly the fire was blazing and the cook had hamburgers sizzling. Two boys distributed them as rapidly as they became edible. Soon it was time for the watermelon. A low-ranking member of the group took a knife and started toward the melon. Some of the boys protested. The most highly regarded boy in the group took over the knife, saying, "You guys who yell the loudest get yours last."

When the two groups in the camp had developed group organization and spirit, we proceeded to the experimental studies of intergroup relations. The groups had had no previous encounters; indeed, in the 1954 camp at Robber's Cave the two groups came in separate buses and were kept apart while each acquired a group feeling.

Sociograms represent patterns of friendship choices within the fully developed groups. One-way friendships are indicated by the broken arrows; reciprocated friendships, by solid lines. Leaders were among those highest in the popularity scale. Bulldogs (left) had a close-knit organization with good group spirit. Low-ranking members participated less in the life of the group but were not rejected. Red Devils (right) lost the tournament of games between the groups. They had less group unity and were sharply stratified.

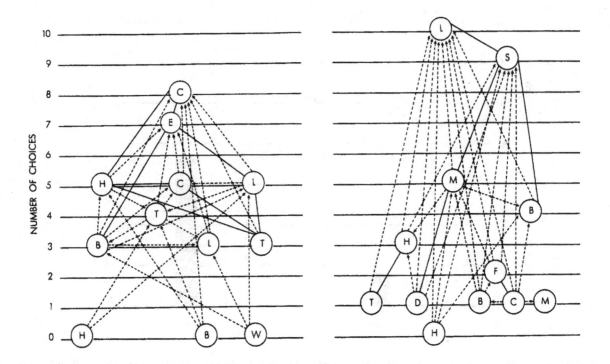

Our working hypothesis was that when two groups have conflicting aims—*i.e.,* when one can achieve its ends only at the expense of the other—their members will become hostile to each other even though the groups are composed of normal well-adjusted individuals. There is a corollary to this assumption which we shall consider later. To produce friction between the groups of boys we arranged a tournament of games: baseball, touch football, a tug-of-war, a treasure hunt and so on. The tournament started in a spirit of good sportsmanship. But as it progressed good feeling soon evaporated. The members of each group began to call their rivals "stinkers," "sneaks" and "cheaters." They refused to have anything more to do with individuals in the opposing group. The boys in the 1949 camp turned against buddies whom they had chosen as "best friends" when they first arrived at the camp. A large proportion other boys in each group gave negative ratings to all the boys in the other. The rival groups made threatening posters and planned raids, collecting secret hoards of green apples for ammunition. In the Robber's Cave camp the Eagles, after a defeat in a tournament game, burned a banner left behind by the Rattlers; the next morning the Rattlers seized the Eagles' flag when they arrived on the athletic field. From that time on name-calling, scuffles and raids were the rule of the day.

Within each group, of course, solidarity increased. There were changes: one group deposed its leader because he could not "take it" in the contests with the adversary; another group overnight made something of a hero of a big boy who had previously been regarded as a bully. But morale and cooperativeness within the group became stronger. It is noteworthy that this heightening of cooperativeness and generally democratic behavior did not carry over to the group's relations with other groups.

We now turned to the other side of the problem: How can two groups in conflict be brought into harmony? We first undertook to test the theory that pleasant social contacts between members of conflicting groups will reduce friction between them. In the 1954 camp we brought the hostile Rattlers and Eagles together for social events: going to the movies, eating in the same dining room and so on. But far from reducing conflict, these situations only served as opportunities for the rival groups to berate and attack each other. In the dining-hall line they shoved each other aside, and the group that lost the contest for the head of the line shouted "Ladies first!" at the winner. They threw paper, food and vile name at each other at the tables. An Eagle bumped by a Rattler was admonished by his fellow Eagles to brush "the dirt" off his clothes.

We then returned to the corollary of our assumption about the creation of conflict. Just as competition generates friction, working in a common endeavor should promote harmony. It seemed to us, considering group relations in the everyday world, that where harmony between groups is established, the most decisive factor is the existence of "superordinate" goals which have a compelling appeal for both but which neither could achieved without the other. To test this hypothesis experimentally, we created a series of urgent, and natural, situations which challenged our boys.

One was a breakdown in the water supply. Water came to our camp in pipes from a tank about a mile away. We arranged to interrupt it and then called the boys together to inform them of the crisis. Both groups promptly volunteered to search the water line for the trouble. They worked together harmoniously, and before the end of the afternoon they had located and corrected the difficulty.

A similar opportunity offered itself when the boys requested a movie. We told them that the camp could not afford to rent one. The two groups then got together, figured out how much each group would have to contribute, chose the film by a vote and enjoyed the showing together.

One day the two groups went on an outing at a lake some distance away. A large truck was to go to town for food. But when everyone was hungry and ready to eat, it developed that the truck would not start (we had taken care of that). The boys got a rope–the same rope they had used in their acrimonious tug-of-war–and all pulled together to start the truck.

These joint efforts did not immediately dispel hostility. At first the groups returned to the old bickering and name-calling as soon as the job in hand was finished. But gradually the series of cooperative acts reduced friction and conflict. The members of the two groups began to feel more friendly to each other. For example, a Rattler whom the Eagles disliked for his sharp tongue and skill in defeating them became a "good egg." The boys stopped shoving in the meal line. They no longer called each other names, and sat together at the table. New friendships developed between individuals in the two groups.

In the end the groups were actively seeking opportunities to mingle, to entertain and "treat" each other. They decided to hold a joint campfire. They took turns presenting skits and songs. Members of both groups requested that they go home together on the same bus, rather than on the separate buses in which they had come. On the way the bus stopped for refresh-

Negative ratings of each group by the other were common during the period of conflict (left) but decreased when harmony was restored (right). The graphs show percent who thought that all *(rather than* some *or* none*) of the other group were cheaters, sneaks, etc.*

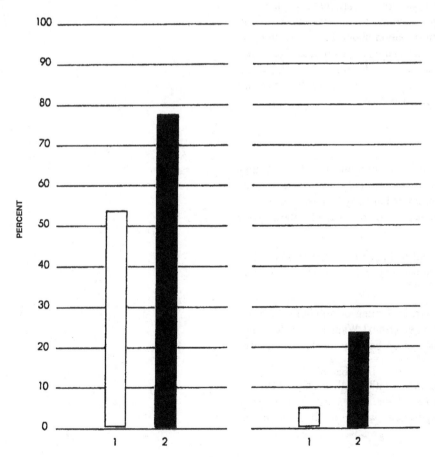

ments. One group still had five dollars which they had won as a prize in a contest. They decided to spend this sum on refreshments. On their own initiative they invited their former rivals to be their guests for malted milks.

Our interviews with the boys confirmed this change. From choosing their "best friends" almost exclusively in their own group, many of them shifted to listing boys in the other group as best friends. They were glad to have a second chance to rate boys in the other group, some of them remarking that they had changed their minds since the first rating made after the tournament. Indeed they had. The new ratings were largely favorable *[see chart]*.

Efforts to reduce friction and prejudice between groups in our society have usually followed rather different methods. Much attention has been given to bringing members of hostile groups together socially, to communicating accurate and favorable information about one group to the other, and to bringing the leaders of groups together to enlist their influence. But as everyone knows, such measures sometimes reduce intergroup tensions and sometimes do not. Social contacts, as our experiments demonstrated, may only serve as occasions for intensifying conflict. Favorable information about a disliked group may be ignored or reinterpreted to fit stereotyped notions about the group. Leaders cannot act with regard for the prevailing temper in their own groups.

What our limited experiments have shown is that the possibilities for achieving harmony are greatly enhanced when groups are brought together to work toward common ends. Then favorable information about a disliked group is seen in a new light, and leaders are in a position to take bolder steps toward cooperation. In short, hostility gives way when groups pull together to achieve overriding goals which are real and compelling to all concerned.

๙ Questions

1. Does competition always promote conflict? Under what conditions is it most likely to do so? Does cooperation always promote harmony? Under what conditions is it most likely to do so? Explain your reasoning.

2. Will social contact tend to increase or decrease conflict? Why? In what circumstances will it increase conflict? Decrease conflict?

3. What impact does ingroup feeling or solidarity have on animosity toward another group? What impact does animosity toward another group have on ingroup solidarity? Why?

From: TK (Charon)

4. Think of groups who today don't get along in your school, city, or town, or in the United States. According to the results of Sherif's experiment, what could be done to promote harmony between these groups?

GROUP DECISION FIASCOES CONTINUE: SPACE SHUTTLE CHALLENGER AND A REVISED GROUPTHINK FRAMEWORK

Gregory Moorhead, Richard Ference, and Chris P. Neck

Arizona State University

In January 1986, the Challenger space shuttle mission ended in disaster. The shuttle exploded moments after being launched, killing all on board instantly.

What went wrong? If you said that the O-ring seals on the rocket failed, then you are partially right. For most social psychologists, however, what really failed was the decision-making process that led to the launch.

It might be tempting to think that groups are superior than individuals when it comes to making complicated decisions. But this is not necessarily so. The soundness of any decision depends on how well the group functions. One all too frequent way that a group can misfunction is when the individuals in the group get such a strong feeling of cohesiveness that preserving this feeling and fostering a sense of moral rightness about what they are doing becomes more important than making a smart decision. When this phenomenon kicks in, members may hesitate to speak up, may follow the leader unquestioningly, or may protect the group from dissenting information. In short, they become victims of what sociol psychologist Irving Janis calls groupthink. And the immediate result of groupthink is poor decision-making.

Janis has analyzed the background and decision-making process behind many famous historical events. Based on this research, he formulated a theory about what conditions may inadvertently foster groupthink. He has also explored the typical symptoms of groupthink and the decision-making problems that it can cause. For example, Janis believes that the Bay of Pigs Invasion, the United States' lack of preparedness for the bombing of Pearl Harbor, America's entry into the Vietnam conflict, and the Watergate cover-up are all examples of instances when groupthink led to poor decision-making. On the other hand, Janis believes that the Cuban Missile Crisis and the formulation of the Marshall Plan to rebuild Europe after World War II examplify times when participants prevented groupthink from harming the decision-making process.

Following Janis's lead, Gregory Moorhead, Richard Ference, and Chris Neck conducted a similar historical analysis of the Challenger tragedy. In the article below, they conclude that groupthink ran rampant among the executives who made the final decision to launch on that fateful day. In addition, the authors suggest two modifications to Janis's original theory.

As the American philosopher and poet George Santayana once said, "Those who cannot remember the past are condemned to repeat it." If we truly hope to avoid making the kinds of errors in our decision-making that can lead to disasters like the Challenger explosion, studying the nature of groupthink is a powerful first step.

INTRODUCTION

In 1972, a new dimension was added to our understanding of group decision making with the proposal of the groupthink hypothesis by Janis (1972). Janis coined the term "groupthink" to refer to "a mode of thinking that people engage in when they are deeply involved in a cohesive in-group, when the members' striving for unanimity override their motivation to realistically appraise alternative courses of action" (Janis, 1972, p. 8). The hypothesis was supported by his hindsight analysis of several political-military fiascoes and successes that are differentiated by the occurrence or non-occurrence of antecedent conditions, groupthink symptoms, and decision making defects.

From: Gregory Moorhead, Richard Ference, and Chris P. Neck, reprinted from *Human Relations* 44, no. 6 (June 1991), by permission of Sage Publications, Inc.

In a subsequent volume, Janis further explicates the theory and adds an analysis of the Watergate transcripts and various published memoirs and accounts of principals involved, concluding that the Watergate cover-up decision also was a result of groupthink (Janis, 1983). Both volumes propose prescriptions for preventing the occurrence of groupthink, many of which have appeared in popular press, in books on executive decision making, and in management textbooks. Multiple advocacy decision-making procedures have been adopted at the executive levels in many organizations, including the executive branch of the government. One would think that by 1986, 13 years after the publication of a popular book, that its prescriptions might be well ingrained in our management and decision-making styles. Unfortunately, it has not happened.

On January 28, 1986, the space shuttle Challenger was launched from Kennedy Space Center. The temperature that morning was in the mid-20's, well below the previous low temperatures at which the shuttle engine had been tested. Seventy-three seconds after launch, the Challenger exploded, killing all seven astronauts aboard, and becoming the worst disaster in space flight history. The catastrophe shocked the nation, crippled the American space program, and is destined to be remembered as the most tragic national event since the assassination of John F. Kennedy in 1963.

The Presidential Commission that investigated the accident pointed to a flawed decision-making process as a primary contributory cause. The decision was made the night before the launch in the Level I Flight Readiness Review meeting. Due to the work of the Presidential Commission, information concerning that meeting is available for analysis as a group decision possibly susceptible to groupthink.

In this paper, we report the results of our analysis of the Level I Flight Readiness Review meeting as a decision-making situation that displays evidence of groupthink. We review the antecedent conditions, the groupthink symptoms, and the possible decision-making defects, as suggested by Janis (1983). In addition, we take the next and more important step of going beyond the development of another example of groupthink to make recommendations for renewed inquiry into group decision-making processes.

✑ THEORY AND EVIDENCE

The groupthink hypothesis has been presented in detail in numerous publications other than Janis' books (Flowers, 1977; Courtright, 1978; Leana, 1985; Moorhead, 1982; Moorhead & Montanari, 1986) and will not be repeated here. The major categories will be used as a framework for organizing the evidence from the meeting. Within each category the key elements will be presented along with meeting details that pertain to each.

The meeting(s) took place throughout the day and evening from 12.36 pm (EST), January 27, 1986 following the decision to not launch the Challenger due to high crosswinds at the launch site. Discussions continued through about

12:00 midnight (EST) via teleconferencing and Telefax systems connecting the Kennedy Space Center in Florida, Morton Thiokol (MTI) in Utah, Johnson Space Center in Houston, and the Marshall Space Flight Center. The Level I Flight Readiness Review is the highest level of review prior to launch. It comprises the highest level of management at the three space centers and at MTI, the private supplier of the solid rocket booster engines.

To briefly state the situation, the MTI engineers recommended not to launch if temperatures of the O-ring seals on the rocket were below 53 degrees Fahrenheit, which was the lowest temperature of any previous flight. Laurence B. Mulloy, manager of the Solid Rocket Booster Project at Marshall Space Flight Center, states:

> . . . The bottom line of that, though, initially was that Thiokol engineering, Bob Lund, who is the Vice President and Director of Engineering, who is here today, recommended that 51-L [the Challenger] not be launched if the O-ring temperatures predicted at launch time would be lower than any previous launch, and that was 53 degrees . . . (*Report of the Presidential Commission on the Space Shuttle Accident*, 1986, p. 91–92).

This recommendation was made at 8:45 pm, January 27, 1986 (*Report of the Presidential Commission on the Space Shuttle Accident*, 1986). Through the ensuing discussions the decision to launch was made.

Antecedent Conditions

The three primary antecedent conditions for the development of groupthink are: a highly cohesive group, leader preference for a certain decision, and insulation of the group from qualified outside opinions. These conditions existed in this situation.

Cohesive Group. The people who made the decision to launch had worked together for many years. They were familiar with each other and had grown through the ranks of the space program. A high degree of *esprit de corps* existed between the members.

Leader Preference. Two top level manager actively promoted their pro-launch opinions in the face of opposition. The commission report states that several managers at space centers and MTI pushed for launch, regardless of the low temperatures.

Insulation from Experts. MTI engineers made their recommendations relatively early in the evening. The top level decision-making group knew of their objections but did not meet with them directly to review their data and concerns. As Roger Boisjoly, a Thiokol engineer, states in his remarks to the Presidential Commission:

... and the bottom line was that the engineering people would not recommend a launch below 53 degrees Fahrenheit ... From this point on, management formulated the points to base their decision on. There was never one comment in favor, as I have said, of launching by any engineer or other nonmanagement person. ... I was not even asked to participate in giving any input to the final decision charts (*Report of the Presidential Commission on the Space Shuttle Accident,* 1986, p. 91–92).

This testimonial indicates that the top decision-making team was insulated from the engineers who possessed the expertise regarding the functioning of the equipment.

Groupthink Symptoms

Janis identified eight symptoms of groupthink. They are presented here along with evidence from the *Report of the Presidential Commission on the Space Shuttle Accident* (1986).

Invulnerability. When groupthink occurs, most or all of the members of the decision-making group have an illusion of invulnerability that reassures them in the face of obvious dangers. This illusion leads the group to become overly optimistic and willing to take extraordinary risks. It may also cause them to ignore clear warnings of danger.

The solid rocket joint problem that destroyed Challenger was discussed often at flight readiness review meetings prior to flight. However, Commission member Richard Feynman concluded from the testimony that a mentality of overconfidence existed due to the extraordinary record of success of space flights. "Every time we send one up it is successful. Involved members may seem to think that on the next one we can lower our standards or take more risks because it always works" (*Time,* 1986).

The invulnerability illusion may have built up over time as a result of NASA's own spectacular history. NASA had not lost an astronaut since 1967 when a flash fire in the capsule of Apollo 1 killed three. Since that time NASA had a string of 55 successful missions. They had put a man on the moon, built and launched Skylab and the shuttle, and retrieved defective satellites from orbit. In the minds of most Americans and apparently their own, they could do no wrong.

Rationalization. Victims of groupthink collectively construct rationalizations that discount warnings and other forms of negative feedback. If these signals were taken seriously when presented, the group members would be forced to reconsider their assumptions each time they re-commit themselves to their past decisions.

In the Level I flight readiness meeting when the Challenger was given final launch approval, MTI engineers presented evidence that the joint would fail. Their argument was based on the fact that in the coldest previous launch (air temperature 30 degrees) the joint in question experienced serious erosion and that no data existed as to how the joint would perform at colder temperatures. Flight center officials put forth numerous technical rationalizations faulting MTI's analysis. One of these rationalizations was that the engineer's data were inconclusive. As Mr. Boisjoly emphasized to the Commission:

... I was asked, yes, at that point in time I was asked to quantify my concerns, and I said I couldn't. I couldn't quantify it. I had no data to quantify it, but I did say I knew that it was away from goodness in the current data base. Someone on the net commented that we had soot blow-by on SRM–22 [Flight 61-A, October, 1985] which was launched at 75 degrees. I don't remember who made the comment, but that is where the first comment came in about the disparity between my conclusion and the observed data because SRM-22 [Flight 61-A, October 1985] had blow-by at essentially a room temperature launch. I then said that SRM-15 [Flight 51–C, January, 1985] had much more blow-by indication and that it was indeed telling us that lower temperature was a factor. I was asked again for data to support my claim, and I said I had none other than what is being presented (*Report of the Presidential Commission on the Space Shuttle Accident,* 1986, p. 89).

Discussions became twisted (compared to previous meetings) and no one detected it. Under normal conditions, MTI would have to prove the shuttle boosters readiness for launch, instead they found themselves being forced to prove that the boosters were unsafe. Boisjoly's testimony supports this description of the discussion:

... This was a meeting where the determination was to launch, and it was up to us to prove beyond a shadow of a doubt that it was not safe to do so. This is in total reverse to what the position usually is in a preflight conversation or a flight readiness review. It is usually exactly opposite of that ... (*Report of the Presidential Commission on the Space Shuttle Accident,* 1986, p. 93).

Morality. Group members often believe, without quesiton, in the inherent morality of their position. They tend to ignore the ethical or moral consequences of their decision.

In the Challenger case, this point was raised by a very high level MTI manager, Allan J. McDonald, who tried to stop the launch and said that he would not want to have to defend the decision to launch. He stated to the Commission:

... I made the statement that if we're wrong and something goes wrong on this flight, I wouldn't want to have to be the person to stand up in front of board in inquiry and say that I went ahead and told them to go ahead and fly this thing outside what the motor was qualified to . . . (*Report of the Presidential Commission on the Space Shuttle Accident,* 1986, p. 95).

Some members did not hear this statement because it occurred during a break. Three top officials who did hear it ignored it.

Stereotyped Views of Others. Victims of groupthink often have a stereotyped view of the opposition of anyone with a competing opinion. They feel that the opposition is too stupid or too weak to understand or deal effectively with the problem.

Two of the top three NASA officials responsible for the launch displayed this attitude. They felt that they completely understood the nature of the joint problem and never seriously considered the objections raised by the MTI engineers. In fact they denigrated and badgered the opposition and their information and opinions.

Pressure on Dissent. Group members often apply direct pressure to anyone who questions the validity of the arguments supporting a decision or position favored by the majority. These same two officials pressured MTI to change its position after MTI originally recommended that the launch not take place. These two officials pressured MTI personnel to prove that it was not safe to launch, rather than to prove the opposite. As mentioned earlier, this was a total reversal of normal preflight procedures. It was this pressure that top MTI management was responding to when they overruled their engineering staff and recommended launch. As the Commission report states:

> . . . At approximately 11 p.m. Eastern Standard Time, the Thiokol/NASA teleconference resumed, the Thiokol management stating that they had reassessed the problem, that the temperature effects were a concern, but that the data was admittedly inconclusive . . . (p. 96).

This seems to indicate that NASA's pressure on these Thiokol officials forced them to change their recommendation from delay to execution of the launch.

Self-Censorship. Group members tend to censor themselves when they have opinions or ideas that deviate from the apparent group consensus. Janis feels that this reflects each member's inclination to minimize to himself or herself the importance of his or her own doubts and counter–arguments.

The most obvious evidence of self-censorship occurred when a vice president of MTI, who had previously presented information against launch, bowed to pressure from NASA and accepted their rationalizations for launch. He then wrote these up and presented them to NASA as the reasons that MTI had changed its recommendation to launch.

Illusion of Unanimity. Group members falling victim to groupthink share an illusion of unanimity concerning judgments made by members speaking in favor of the majority view. This symptom is caused in part by the preceding one and is aided by the false assumption that any participant who remains silent is in agreement with the majority opinion. The group leader and other members support each other by playing up points of convergence in their thinking at the expense of fully exploring points of divergence that might reveal unsettling problems.

No participant from NASA ever openly agreed with or even took sides with MTI in the discussion. The silence from NASA was probably amplified by the fact that the meeting was a teleconference linking the participants at three different locations. Obviously, body language which might have been evidenced by dissenters was not visible to others who might also have held a dissenting opinion. Thus, silence meant agreement.

Mindguarding. Certain group members assume the role of guarding the minds of others in the group. They attempt to shield the group from adverse information that might destroy the majority view of the facts regarding the appropriateness of the decision.

The top management at Marshall knew that the rocket casings had been ordered redesigned to correct a flaw five months previous to this launch. This information and other technical details concerning the history of the joint problem was withheld at the meeting.

Decision-Making Defects

The result of the antecedent conditions and the symptoms of groupthink is a defective decision-making process. Janis discusses several defects in decision making that can result.

Few Alternatives. The group considers only a few alternatives, often only two. No initial survey of all possible alternatives occurs. The Flight Readiness Review team had a launch/no-launch decision to make. These were the only two alternatives considered. Other possible alternatives might have been to delay the launch for further testing, or to delay until the temperatures reached an appropriate level.

No Re-Examination of Alternatives. The group fails to re-examine alternatives that may have been initially discarded based on early unfavorable information. Top NASA officials spent time and effort defending and strengthening their position, rather than examining the MTI position.

Rejecting Expert Opinions. Members make little or no attempt to seek outside experts' opinions. NASA did not seek out other experts who might have some expertise in this area. They assumed that they had all the information.

Rejecting Negative Information. Members tend to focus on supportive information and ignore any data or information that might cast a negative light on their preferred alternative. MTI representatives repeatedly tried to point out errors in the rationale the NASA officials were using to justify the launch. Even after the decision was made, the argument continued until a NASA official told the MTI representative that it was no longer his concern.

No Contingency Plans. Members spend little time discussing the possible consequences of the decision and, therefore, fail to develop contingency plans. There is no documented evidence in the Rogers Commission Report of any discussion of the possible consequences of an incorrect decision.

Summary of the Evidence

The major categories and key elements of the groupthink hypothesis have been presented (albeit somewhat briefly) along with evidence from the discussions prior to the launching of the Challenger, as reported in the President's Commission to investigate the accident. The antecedent conditions were present in the decision-making group, even though the group was in several physical locations. The leaders had a preferred solution and engaged in behaviors designed to promote it rather than critically appraise alternatives. These behaviors were evidence of most of the symptoms leading to a defective decision-making process.

ᓂ DISCUSSION

This situation provides another example of decision making in which the group fell victim to the groupthink syndrome, as have so many previous groups. It illustrates the situation characteristics, the symptoms of groupthink, and decision-making defects as described by Janis. This situation, however, also illustrates several other aspects of situations that are critical to the development of groupthink that need to be included in a revised formulation of the groupthink model. First, the element of time in influencing the development of groupthink has not received adequate attention. In the decision to launch the space shuttle Challenger, time was a crucial part of the decision-making process. The launch had been delayed once, and the window for another launch was fast closing. The leaders of the decision team were concerned about public and congressional perceptions of the entire space shuttle program and its continued funding and may have felt that further delays of the launch could seriously impact future funding. With the space window fast closing, the decision team was faced with a launch now or seriously damage the program decision. On top level manager's response to Thiokol's initial recommendation to postpone the launch indicates the presence of time pressure:

With this LLC (Launch Commit Criteria), i.e., do not launch with a temperature greater [sic] than 53 degrees, we may not be able to launch until next April. We need to consider this carefully before we jump to any conclusions . . . (*Report of the Presidential Commission on the Space Shuttle Accident,* 1986, p. 96).

Time pressure could have played a role in the group choosing to agree and to self-censor their comments. Therefore, time is a critical variable that needs to be highlighted in a revised groupthink framework. We propose that time is an important moderator between group characteristics and the development of the groupthink symptoms. That is, in certain situations when there is pressure to make a decision quickly, the elements may combine to foster the development of groupthink.

The second revision needs to be in the role of the leadership of the decision-making group. In the space shuttle Challenger incident, the leadership of the group varied from a shared type of leadership to a very clear leader in the situation. This may indicate that the leadership role needs to be clearly defined and a style that demands open disclosure of information, points of opposition, complaints, and dissension. Inclusion of leadership in a more powerful role of the groupthink framework needs to be more explicit than in the Janis formulation in which leadership is one of several group characteristics that can lead to the development of the groupthink symptoms. We propose the leadership style is a critical variable that moderates the relationship between the group characteristics and the development of the symptoms. Janis (1983) is a primary form of evidence to support the inclusion of leadership style in the enhanced model. His account of why the *same* group succumbed to groupthink in one decision (Bay of Pigs) and not in another (Cuban Missile Crisis) supports the depiction of the leadership style as a moderator variable. In these decisions, the only condition that changed was the leadership style of the President. In other words, the element that seemed to distinguish why groupthink occurred in the Bay of Pigs decision and not in the Cuban Missile Crisis situation is the president's change in his behavior.

These two variables, time and leadership style, are proposed as moderators of the impact of the group characteristics on groupthink symptoms. This relationship is portrayed graphically in Fig. 1. In effect, we propose that the groupthink symptoms result from the group characteristics, as proposed by Janis, but only in the presence of the moderator variables of time and certain leadership styles.

Time, as an important element in the model, is relatively straightforward. When a decision must be made within a very short time frame, pressure on members to agree, to avoid time-consuming arguments and reports from outside experts, and to self-censor themselves may increase. These pressures inevitably cause group members to seek agreement. In Janis's original model, time was included indirectly as a function of the antecedent condition, group cohesion. Janis (1983)

Figure 1 *Revised Groupthink Framework*

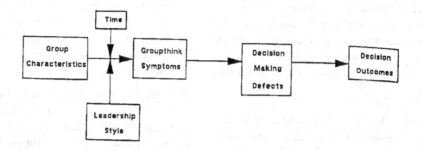

argued that time pressures can adversely affect decision quality in two ways. First, it affects the decision makers' mental efficiency and judgment, interfering with their ability to concentrate on complicated discussions, to absorb new information, and to use imagination to anticipate the future consequences of alternative courses of action. Second, time pressure is a source of stress that will have the effect of inducing a policy-making group to become more cohesive and more likely to engage in groupthink.

Leadership style is shown to be a moderator because of the importance it plays in either promoting or avoiding the development of the symptoms of the groupthink. The leader, even though she or he may not promote a preferred solution, may allow or even assist the group seeking agreement by not forcing the group to critically appraise all alternative courses of action. The focus of this leadership variable is on the degree to which the leader allows or promotes discussion and evaluation of alternatives. It is not a matter of simply not making known a preferred solution; the issue is one of stimulation of critical thinking among the group.

Impact on Prescriptions for Prevention

The revised model suggests that more specific prescriptions for prevention of groupthink can be made. First, group members need to be aware of the impact that a short decision time frame has on decision processes. When a decision must be made quickly, there will be more pressure to agree, i.e., discouragement of dissent, self-censorship, avoidance of expert opinion, and assumptions about unanimity. The type of leadership suggested here is not one that sits back and simply does not make known her or his preferred solution. This type of leader must be one that requires all members to speak up with concerns, questions, and new information. The leader must know what some of these concerns are and which members are likely to have serious doubts so that the people with concerns can be called upon to voice them. This type of group leadership does not simply assign the role of devil's advocate and step out of the way. This leader actually plays the role or makes sure that others do. A leader with the required style to avoid groupthink is not a laissez faire leader or noninvolved

participative leader. This leader is active in directing the activities of the group but does not make known a preferred solution. The group still must develop and evaluate alternative courses of action, but under the direct influence of a strong, demanding leader who forces critical appraisal of all alternatives.

Finally, a combination of the two variables suggests that the leader needs to help members to avoid the problems created by the time element. For example, the leader may be able to alter an externally imposed time frame for the decision by negotiating an extension or even paying late fees, if necessary. If an extension is not possible, the leader may need to help the group eliminate the effects of time on the decision processes. This can be done by forcing attention to issues rather than time, encouraging dissension and confrontation, and scheduling special sessions to hear reports from outside experts that challenge prevailing views within the group.

Janis presents, in both editions of his book, several recommendations for preventing the occurrence of groupthink. These recommendations focus on the inclusion of outside experts in the decision-making process, all members taking the role of devil's advocate and critically appraising all alternative courses of action, and the leader not expressing a preferred solution. The revised groupthink framework suggests several new prescriptions that may be helpful in preventing further decision fiascoes similar to the decision to launch the space shuttle Challenger.

Much additional research is necessary to test the revised framework. First, laboratory research is needed to refine details of how time affects the development of groupthink. Second, the impact of various types of leadership style that may be appropriate for group decision-making situations needs to be investigated. Finally, research which tests the revised framework with real decision-making groups will be needed to refine new prescriptions or preventing groupthink.

✄ CONCLUSION

This paper has reviewed the basic tenets of groupthink and examined the decision to launch the space shuttle Challenger in January 1986. The report of the Presidential Commission provided enough evidence of the antecedent conditions, the symptoms, and the decision-making defects to support a conclusion that the decision to launch can be classified as a groupthink situation. We have proposed, in addition, that other conditions may play important roles in the development of groupthink. These two variables, time and leadership style, are proposed as moderators of the relationship between group characteristics and groupthink symptoms. These two moderators lead to new prescriptions for the prevention of groupthink. Much additional research is needed to test the degree to which the revised framework can be used to guide prescriptions for prevention.

REFERENCES

Courtright, J. A. (1978). A laboratory investigation of groupthink. *Communications Monographs, 45,* 229–246.

Fixing NASA. (1986, June 9). *Time.*

Flowers, M. L. (1977). A laboratory test of some implications of Janis's groupthink hypothesis. *Journal of Personality and Social Psychology, 35,* 888–896.

Janis, I. L. (1972). *Victims of groupthink.* Boston: Houghton Mifflin.

Janis, I. L. (1983). *Groupthink* (2nd ed.). Boston: Houghton Mifflin.

Leana, C. R. (1985). A partial test of Janis's groupthink model: Effects of group cohesiveness and leader behavior on defective decision making. *Journal of Management, 11,* 5–17.

Moorhead, G. (1982). Groupthink: Hypothesis in need of testing. *Group and Organization Studies, 7,* 429–444.

Moorhead, G., & Montanari, J. R. (1986). Empirical analysis of the groupthink phenomenon. *Human Relations, 39,* 399–410.

Report of the Presidential Commission on the Space Shuttle Accident. (1986, July). Washington, DC.

❧ Questions

1. What two modifications do Moorhead et al. make to Janis's original theory of groupthink? What is the reasoning behind these modifications?

2. How could groupthink have been prevented from causing the Challenger disaster? Hint: Consider the symptoms of groupthink and the conditions surrounding the decision to launch the shuttle. Specifically, what should participants have done differently at various points in the process in order to avoid the damaging effects of groupthink?

3. How does groupthink affect participants' perception of facts? Did knowledge of launch-pad conditions prevent groupthink from occurring in the Challenger launch? Why or why not?

4. If, as Moorhead et al. suggest, a group leader plays an role in whether groupthink will occur, what kinds of leaders are more likely to foster groupthink? Why? What kinds of groups are most vulnerable to groupthink? Why? Discuss by applying principles of conformity and obedience.

SOME CONDITIONS OF OBEDIENCE AND DISOBEDIENCE TO AUTHORITY

▓ *Historical Milestone* ▓

Stanley Milgram[1]

Do you agree with the author C. P. Snow that "more hideous crimes have been committed in the name of obedience than in the name of rebellion"? Social psychologist Stanley Milgram investigated this very question. Would ordinary people—much like the war criminals who were tried during the Nuremberg trials of 1945-1956, which inspired Milgram's study—hurt another human being with the claim "I was just following orders"?

To test just how far people would go in order to obey an authority, Milgram designed his now-famous obedience to authority studies. As part of what they thought was an experiment on the effect of punishment on learning, participants administered what they thought were electric shocks to another person. (This other person was really a confederate of the experimenter and received no actual shocks.) The design of the experiment required subjects to administer greater and greater "shocks"—supposedly up to 300 volts—each time the confederate gave a wrong answer. How far would subjects go in administering shocks at the command of the experimenter?

In this article, Milgram presents the results of the basic design and a number of variations on the study. He also discusses the dilemma that the participants faced and the psychological pressures that made it difficult for them to disobey. Milgram's results show that obedience—and the entire context of the experimental setup—was so powerful that the majority of subjects administered the highest level of shock.

Despite the extraordinary findings and implications of this research, many critics believe that it was unethical for Milgram to have conducted these studies because they subjected participants to extreme duress. The experiment sparked intense debate among social psychologists, which culminated in the establishment of ethical guidelines for research and ethical review boards to protect participants' rights.

The situation in which one agent commands another to hurt a third turns up time and again as a significant theme in human relations. It is powerfully expressed in the story of Abraham, who is commanded by God to kill his son. It is no accident that Kierkegaard, seeking to orient his thought to the central themes of human experience, chose Abraham's conflict as the springboard to his philosophy.

War too moves forward on the triad of an authority which commands a person to destroy the enemy, and perhaps all organized hostility may be viewed as a theme and variation on the three elements of authority, executant, and victim.[2] We describe an experimental program, recently concluded at Yale University, in which a particular expression of this conflict is studied by experimental means.

In its most general form the problem may be defined thus: if *X* tells *Y* to hurt *Z*, under what conditions will *Y* carry out the command of *X* and under what conditions will he refuse. In the more limited form possible in laboratory research, the question becomes: if an experimenter tells a subject to hurt another person, under what conditions will the subject go along with this instruction, and under what conditions will he refuse to obey. The laboratory problem is not so much a dilution of the general statement as one concrete expression of the many particular forms this question may assume.

One aim of the research was to study behavior in a strong situation of deep consequence to the participants, for the psychological forces operative in powerful and lifelike forms of the conflict may not be brought into play under diluted conditions.

This approach meant, first, that we had a special obligation to protect the welfare and dignity of the persons who took part in the study; subjects were, of necessity, placed in a difficult predicament, and steps had to be taken to ensure

"Some Conditions of Obedience and Disobedience to Authority," by Stanley Milgram, reprinted from *Human Relations*, vol. 18, no. 1, 1965, pp. 57–75.

From: Stanley Milgram, reprinted from *Human Relations* 18, no. 1 (February 1965), by permission of Sage Publications, Inc.

their wellbeing before they were discharged from the laboratory. Toward this end, a careful, post-experimental treatment was devised and has been carried through for subjects in all conditions.[3]

TERMINOLOGY

If *Y* follows the command of *X* we shall say that he has obeyed *X;* if he fails to carry out the command *of X,* we shall say that he has disobeyed *X*. The terms *to obey* and to *disobey,* as used here, refer to the subject's overt action only, and carry no implication for the motive or experiential states accompanying the action.[4]

To be sure, the everyday use of the word *obedience* is not entirely free from complexities. It refers to action within widely varying situations, and connotes diverse motives within those situations: a child's obedience differs from a soldier's obedience, or the love, honor, and *obey* of the marriage vow. However, a consistent behavioral relationship is indicated in most uses of the term: in the act of obeying, a person does what another person tells him to do. *Y* obeys *X* if he carries out the prescription for action which *X* has addressed to him; the term suggests, moreover, that some form of dominance-subordination, or hierarchical element, is part of the situation in which the transaction between *X* and *Y* occurs.

A subject who complies with the entire series of experimental commands will be termed an *obedient* subject; one who at any point in the command series defies the experimenter will be called a *disobedient* or *defiant* subject. As used in this report, the terms refer only to the subject's performance in the experiment, and do not necessarily imply a general personality disposition to submit to or reject authority.

SUBJECT POPULATION

The subjects used in all experimental conditions were male adults, residing in the greater New Haven and Bridgeport areas, aged 20 to 50 years, and engaged in a wide variety of occupations. Each experimental condition described in this report employed 40 fresh subjects and was carefully balanced for age and occupational types. The occupational composition for each experiment was: workers, skilled and unskilled: 40%; white collar, sales, business: 40%; professionals: 20%. The occupations were intersected with three age categories (subjects in 20s, 30s, and 40s, assigned to each condition in the proportions of 20, 40, and 40% respectively).

THE GENERAL LABORATORY PROCEDURE[5]

The focus of the study concerns the amount of electric shock a subject is willing to administer to another person when ordered by an experimenter to give the "victim" increasingly more severe punishment. The act of administering shock is set in the context of a learning experiment, ostensibly designed to study the effect of punishment on memory. Aside from the experimenter, one naive subject and one accomplice perform in each session. On arrival each subject is paid $4.50. After a general talk by the experimenter, telling how little scientists know about the effect of punishment on memory, subjects are informed that one member of the pair will serve as teacher and one as learner. A rigged drawing is held so that the naive subject is always the teacher, and the accomplice becomes the learner. The learner is taken to an adjacent room and strapped into an "electric chair."

The naïve subject is told that it is his task to teach the learner a list of paired associates, to test him on the list, and to administer punishment whenever the learner errs in the test. Punishment takes the form of electric shock, delivered to the learner by means of a shock generator controlled by the naive subject. The teacher is instructed to increase the intensity of electric shock one step on the generator on each error. The learner, according to plan, provides many wrong answers, so that before long the naïve subject must give him the strongest shock on the generator. Increases in shock level are met by increasingly insistent demands from the learner that the experiment be stopped because of the growing discomfort to him. However, in clear terms the experimenter orders the teacher to continue with the procedure in disregard of the learner's protests. *Thus, the naive subject must resolve a conflict between two mutually incompatible demands from the social field. He may continue to follow the orders of the experimenter and shock the learner with increasing severity, or he may refuse to follow the orders of the experimenter and heed the learner's pleas. The experimenter's authority operates not in a free field, but against ever-mounting countervailing pressures from the person being punished.*

A few technical points need to be considered before the findings of the study are described. For the purpose of delivering shock, a simulated shock generator is used, with 30 clearly marked voltage levels that range from 15 to 450 volts (and each activated by one of 30 individual lever switches set in a horizontal line). The naïve subject is given a sample shock of 45 volts to convince him of the authenticity of the instrument. The generator bears verbal designations that range from "Slight Shock" to "Danger: Severe Shock."

The responses of the victim are standardized on tape, and each protest is coordinated to a particular voltage level on the shock generator. Starting with 75 volts the learner begins to grunt and moan. At 150 volts he demands to be let out of the experiment. At 180 volts he cries out that he can no longer stand the pain. At 300 volts he refuses to provide any more answers to the memory test, insisting that he is no longer a participant in the experiment and must be freed. In response to this last tactic, the experimenter instructs the naïve subject to treat the absence of an answer as equivalent to a wrong answer, and to follow the usual shock procedure. The experimenter reinforces his demand with the statement: "You have no other choice, you must go on!" (This imperative is used whenever the naïve subject tries to break off the experiment.) If the subject refuses to give the next higher level of shock, the experiment is considered at an end. A quantitative value is assigned to the subject's performance based on the maximum intensity shock he administered before breaking off. Thus any subject's score may range from zero (for a subject unwilling to administer the first shock level) to 30 (for a subject who proceeds to the highest voltage level on the board). For any particular subject and for any particular experimental condition the degree to which participants have followed the experimenter's orders may be specified with a numerical value, corresponding to the metric on the shock generator.

This laboratory situation gives us a framework in which to study the subject's reactions to the principal conflict of the experiment. Again, this conflict is between the experimenter's demands that he continue to administer the electric shock, and the learner's demands, which become increasingly more insistent, that the experiment be stopped. The crux of the study is to vary systematically the factors believed to alter the degree of obedience to the experimental commands, to learn under what conditions submission to authority is most probable, and under what conditions defiance is brought to the fore.

ℰ Pilot Studies

Pilot studies for the present research were completed in the winter of 1960; they differed from the regular experiments in a few details: for one, the victim was placed behind a silvered glass, with the light balance on the glass such that the victim could be dimly perceived by the subject (Milgram, 1961).

Though essentially qualitative in treatment, these studies pointed to several significant features of the experimental situation. At first no vocal feedback was used from the victim. It was thought that the verbal and voltage designations on the control panel would create sufficient pressure to curtail the subject's obedience. However, this was not the case. In the absence of protests from the learner, virtually all subjects, once commanded, went blithely to the end of the board, seemingly indifferent to the verbal designations ("Extreme Shock" and "Danger: Severe Shock"). This deprived us of an adequate basis for scaling obedient tendencies. A force had to be introduced that would strengthen the subject's resistance to the experimenter's commands, and reveal individual differences in terms of a distribution of break-off points.

This force took the form of protests from the victim. Initially, mild protests were used, but proved inadequate. Subsequently, more vehement protests were inserted into the experimental procedure. To our consternation, even the strongest protests from the victim did not prevent all subjects from administering the harshest punishment ordered by the experimenter; but the protests did lower the mean maximum shock somewhat and created some spread in the subject's performance; therefore, the victim's cries were standardized

on tape and incorporated into the regular experimental procedure.

The situation did more than highlight the technical difficulties of finding a workable experimental procedure: it indicated that subjects would obey authority to a greater extent than we had supposed. It also pointed to the importance of feedback from the victim in controlling the subject's behavior.

One further aspect of the pilot study was that subjects frequently averted their eyes from the person they were shocking, often turning their heads in an awkward and conspicuous manner. One subject explained: "I didn't want to see the consequences of what I had done." Observers wrote:

> . . . subjects showed a reluctance to look at the victim, whom they could see through the glass in front of them. When this fact was brought to their attention they indicated that it caused them discomfort to see the victim in agony. We note, however, that although the subject refuses to look at the victim, he continues to administer shocks.

This suggested that the salience of the victim may have, in some degree, regulated the subject's performance. If, in obeying the experimenter, the subject found it necessary to avoid scrutiny of the victim, would the converse be true? If the victim were rendered increasingly more salient to the subject, would obedience diminish? The first set of regular experiments was designed to answer this question.

ℰ Immediacy of the Victim

This series consisted of four experimental conditions. In each condition the victim was brought "psychologically" closer to the subject giving him shocks.

In the first condition (Remote Feedback) the victim was placed in another room and could not be heard or seen by the subject, except that, at 300 volts, he pounded on the wall in protest. After 315 volts he no longer answered or was heard from.

The second condition (Voice Feedback) was identical to the first except that voice protests were introduced. As in the first condition the victim was placed in an adjacent room, but his complaints could be heard clearly through a door left slightly ajar, and through the walls of the laboratory.[6]

The third experimental condition (Proximity) was similar to the second, except that the victim was now placed in the same room as the subject, and 1 1/2 feet from him. Thus he was visible as well as audible, and voice cues were provided.

The fourth, and final, condition of this series (Touch-Proximity) was identical to the third, with this exception: the victim received a shock only when his hand rested on a shockplate. At the 150-volt level the victim again demanded to be let free and, in this condition, refused to place his hand on the shockplate. The experimenter ordered the naive subject to force the victim's hand onto the plate. Thus obedience in this condition required that the subject have physical contact with the victim in order to give him punishment beyond the 150-volt level.

Forty adult subjects were studied in each condition. The data revealed that obedience was significantly reduced as the victim was rendered more immediate to the subject. The mean maximum shock for the conditions is shown in Figure 1.

Expressed in terms of the proportion of obedient to defiant subjects, the findings are that 34% of the subjects defied the experimenter in the Remote condition, 37.5% in Voice Feedback, 60% in Proximity, and 70% in Touch-Proximity.

How are we to account for this effect? A first conjecture might be that as the victim was brought closer the subject became more aware of the intensity of his suffering and regulated his behavior accordingly. This makes sense, but our evidence does not support the interpretation. There are no consistent differences in the attributed level of pain across the four conditions (i.e. the amount of pain experienced by the victim as estimated by the subject and expressed on a 14-point scale). But it is easy to speculate about alternative mechanisms:

Empathic cues. In the Remote and to a lesser extent the Voice Feedback condition, the victim's suffering possesses an abstract, remote quality for the subject. He is aware, but only in a conceptual sense, that his actions cause pain to another person; the fact is apprehended, but not felt. The phenomenon is common enough. The bombardier can reasonably suppose that his weapons will inflict suffering and death, yet this knowledge is divested of affect, and does not move him to a felt, emotional response to the suffering resulting from his actions. Similar observations have been made in wartime.

Figure 1 *Mean Maxima in Proximity Series*

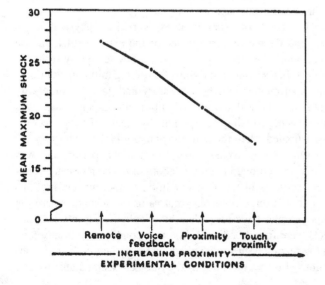

It is possible that the visual cues associated with the victim's suffering trigger empathic responses in the subject and provide him with a more complete grasp of the victim's experience. Or it is possible that the empathic responses are themselves unpleasant, possessing drive properties which cause the subject to terminate the arousal situation. Diminishing obedience, then, would be explained by the enrichment of empathic cues in the successive experimental conditions.

Denial and narrowing of the cognitive field. The Remote condition allows a narrowing of the cognitive field so that the victim is put out of mind. The subject no longer considers the act of depressing a lever relevant to moral judgement, for it is no longer associated with the victim's suffering. When the victim is close it is more difficult to exclude him phenomenologically. He necessarily intrudes on the subject's awareness since he is continuously visible. In the Remote conditions his existence and reactions are made known only after the shock has been administered. The auditory feedback is sporadic and discontinuous. In the Proximity conditions his inclusion in the immediate visual field renders him a continuously salient element for the subject. The mechanism of denial can no longer be brought into play. One subject in the Remote condition said: "It's funny how you really begin to forget that there's a guy out there, even though you can hear him. For a long time I just concentrated on pressing the switches and reading the words."

Reciprocal fields. If in the Proximity condition the subject is in an improved position to observe the victim, the reverse is also true. The actions of the subject now come under proximal scrutiny by the victim. Possibly, it is easier to harm a person when he is unable to observe our actions than when he can see what we are doing. His surveillance of the action directed against him may give rise to shame, or guilt, which may then serve to curtail the action. Many expressions of language refer to the discomfort or inhibitions that arise in face-to-face confrontation. It is often said that it is easier to criticize a man "behind his back" than to "attack him to his face." If we are in the process of lying to a person it is reputedly difficult to "stare him in the eye." We "turn away from others in shame" or in "embarrassment" and this action serves to reduce our discomfort. The manifest function of allowing the victim of a firing squad to be blindfolded is to make the occasion less stressful for him, but it may also serve a latent function of reducing the stress of the executioner. In short, in the Proximity conditions, the subject may sense that he has become more salient in the victim's field of awareness. Possibly he becomes more self-conscious, embarrassed, and inhibited in his punishment of the victim.

Phenomenal unity of act. In the Remote conditions it is more difficult for the subject to gain a sense of *relatedness* between his own actions and the consequences of these actions for the victim. There is a physical and spatial separation of the act and its consequences. The subject depresses a lever in one room, and protests and cries are heard from another. The two events are in correlation, yet they lack a compelling phenomenological unity. The structure of a meaningful act—*I am hurting a man*—breaks down because of the spatial arrangements, in a manner somewhat analogous to the disappearance of phi phenomena when the blinking lights are spaced too far apart. The unity is more fully achieved in the Proximity conditions as the victim is brought closer to the action that causes him pain. It is rendered complete in Touch-Proximity.

Incipient group formation. Placing the victim in another room not only takes him further from the subject, but the subject and the experimenter are drawn relatively closer. There is incipient group formation between the experimenter and the subject, from which the victim is excluded. The wall between the victim and the others deprives him of an intimacy which the experimenter and subject feel. In the Remote condition, the victim is truly an outsider, who stands alone, physically and psychologically.

When the victim is placed close to the subject, it becomes easier to form an alliance with him against the experimenter. Subjects no longer have to face the experimenter alone. They have an ally who is close at hand and eager to collaborate in a revolt against the experimenter. Thus, the changing set of spatial relations leads to a potentially shifting set of alliances over the several experimental conditions.

Acquired behavior dispositions. It is commonly observed that laboratory mice will rarely fight with their litter mates. Scott (1958) explains this in terms of passive inhibition. He writes: "By doing nothing under . . . circumstances [the animal] learns to do nothing, and this may be spoken of as passive inhibition . . . this principle has great importance in teaching an individual to be peaceful, for it means that he can learn not to fight simply by not fighting." Similarly, we may learn not to harm others simply by not harming them in everyday life. Yet this learning occurs in a context of proximal relations with others, and may not be generalized to that situation in which the person is physically removed from us. Or possibly, in the past, aggressive actions against others who were physically close resulted in retaliatory punishment which extinguished the original form of response. In contrast, aggression against others at a distance may have only sporadically led to retaliation. Thus the organism learns that it is safer to be aggressive toward others at a distance, and precarious to be so when the parties are within arm's reach. Through a pattern of rewards and punishments, he acquires a disposition to avoid aggression at close quarters, a disposition which does not extend to harming others at a distance. And this may account for experimental findings in the remote and proximal experiments.

Proximity as a variable in psychological research has received far less attention than it deserves. If men were sessile it would be easy to understand this neglect. But we move about; our spatial relations shift from one situation to the next, and the fact that we are near or remote may have a powerful effect on the psychological processes that mediate our behavior toward others. In the present situation, as the victim is brought closer to the man ordered to give him shocks, increasing numbers of subjects break off the experiment, refusing to obey. The concrete, visible, and proximal presence of the victim acts in an important way to counteract the experimenter's power and to generate disobedience.[7]

❧ CLOSENESS OF AUTHORITY

If the spatial relationship of the subject and victim is relevant to the degree of obedience, would not the relationship of subject to experimenter also play a part?

There are reasons to feel that, on arrival, the subject is oriented primarily to the experimenter rather than to the victim. He has come to the laboratory to fit into the structure that the experimenter—not the victim—would provide. He has come less to understand his behavior than to *reveal* that behavior to a competent scientist, and he is willing to display himself as the scientist's purposes require. Most subjects seem quite concerned about the appearance they are making before the experimenter, and one could argue that this preoccupation in a relatively new and strange setting makes the subject somewhat insensitive to the triadic nature of the social situation. In other words, the subject is so concerned about the show he is putting on for the experimenter that influences from other parts of the social field do not receive as much weight as they ordinarily would. This overdetermined orientation to the experimenter would account for the relative insensitivity of the subject to the victim, and would also lead us to believe that alterations in the relationship between subject and experimenter would have important consequences for obedience.

In a series of experiments we varied the physical closeness and degree of surveillance of the experimenter. In one condition the experimenter sat just a few feet away from the subject. In a second condition, after giving initial instructions, the experimenter left the laboratory and gave his orders by telephone; in still a third condition the experimenter was never seen, providing instructions by means of a tape recording activated when the subjects entered the laboratory.

Obedience dropped sharply as the experimenter was physically removed from the laboratory. The number of obedient subjects in the first condition (Experimenter Present) was almost three times as great as in the second, where the experimenter gave his orders by telephone. Twenty-six subjects were fully obedient in the first condition, and only nine in the second (Chi square obedient *vs.* defiant in the two conditions, 1 d.f. = 14.7; $p < .001$). Subjects seemed able to take a far stronger stand against the experimenter when they did not have to encounter him face to face, and the experimenter's power over the subject was severely curtailed.[8]

Moreover, when the experimenter was absent, subjects displayed an interesting form of behavior that had not occurred under his surveillance. Though continuing with the experiment, several subjects administered lower shocks than were required and never informed the experimenter of their deviation from the correct procedure. (Unknown to the subjects, shock levels were automatically recorded by an Esterline-Angus event recorder wired directly into the shock generator; the instrument provided us with an objective record of the subjects' performance.) Indeed, in telephone conversations some subjects specifically assured the experimenter that they were raising the shock level according to instruction, whereas in fact they were repeatedly using the lowest shock on the board. This form of behavior is particularly interesting: although these subjects acted in a way that clearly undermined the avowed purposes of the experiment, they found it easier to handle the conflict in this manner than to precipitate an open break with authority.

Other conditions were completed in which the experimenter was absent during the first segment of the experiment, but reappeared at the point that the subject definitely refused to give higher shocks when commanded by telephone. Although he had exhausted his power via telephone, the experimenter could frequently force further obedience when he reappeared in the laboratory.

Experiments in this series show that the physical *presence* of an authority is an important force contributing to the subject's obedience or defiance. Taken together with the first experimental series on the proximity of the victim, it would appear that something akin to fields of force, diminishing in effectiveness with increasing psychological distance from their source, have a controlling effect on the subject's performance. As the victim is brought closer, the subject finds it harder to administer shocks to him. When the victim's position is held constant relative to the subject, and the authority is made more remote, the subject finds it easier to break off the experiment. This effect is substantial in both cases, but manipulation of the experimenter's position yielded the more powerful results. Obedience to destructive commands is highly dependent on the proximal relations between authority and subject.

ᖇ Tensions

The description of final scores does not fully convey the character of the subjects' performance, and it would be useful to interrupt our reporting of quantitative relationships to remark on the subjects' general reaction to the situation.

One might suppose that a subject would simply break off or continue as his conscience and temperament dictated. Yet this is very far from what happened. There were powerful reactions of tension and emotional strain in a substantial pro-

portion of the participants. Persons were observed to sweat, tremble, stutter, bite their lips, and groan as they found themselves increasingly implicated in the experimental conflict. Some sense of the subjects' mood can be gotten from a transcript of their remarks at break-off point. Here are the remarks of two defiant subjects:

> Is he banging? . . . Is he hurt out there? Well, I don't want to be responsible for anything that happens to him. No, I can't go on with it. I don't know whether he's all right or not. I mean he may have a heart condition or something; I wouldn't feel right doing it. He's banging for help. He's evidently in trouble or he wouldn't bang . . . I don't see any sense to this—to knocking him out or something. I just can't see it. *(Subject refuses to administer shocks)* [S u b j e c t 0108]

> The man is banging. He wants to get out . . . I'm sorry. If the man wants to get out I'd just as soon stop . . . I don't want to administer any more [extremely excited] . . . 1 will gladly refund the check, but I will not harm this man . . . I'm sorry, I will not give him any more if he obviously wants to get out. There is no money in the world that will make me hurt another individual. *[Subject 010X]*

And here is a transcript from an obedient subject. He began the experiment calmly, but became increasingly tense as the experiment proceeded. After administering the 150-volt shock, he began to address the experimenter in agitated tones:

> *150 volts delivered.* You want me to keep going?

> *165 volts delivered.* That guy is hollering in there. There's a lot of them here. He's liable to have heart condition. You want me to go?

> *180 volts delivered.* He can't stand it! I'm not going to kill that man in there! You hear him hollering? He's hollering. He can't stand it. What if something happens to him? . . . I'm not going to get that man sick in there. He's hollering in there. You know what I mean? I mean I refuse to take responsibility. He's getting hurt in there. He's in there hollering. Too many left here. Geez, if he gets them wrong. There's too many of them left. I mean who is going to take responsibility if anything happens to that gentleman?

> *[The experimenter accepts responsibility.]* All right.

> *195 volts delivered.* You see he's hollering. Hear that. Gee, I don't know. *[The experimenter says: "The experiment requires that you go on."]*—I know it does, sir, but I mean—hugh—he don't know what he's in for. He's up to 195 volts.

210 volts delivered

225 volts delivered

240 volts delivered. Aw, no. You mean I've got to keep going up with the scale? No sir. I'm not going to kill that man! I'm not going to give him 450 volts! *[The experimenter says: "The experiment requires that you go on."]*—I know it does, but that man is hollering in there, sir . . .

Despite his numerous, agitated objections, which were constant accompaniments to his actions, the subject unfailingly obeyed the experimenter, proceeding to the highest shock level on the generator. He displayed a curious dissociation between word and action. Although at the verbal level he had resolved not to go on, his actions were fully in accord with the experimenter's commands. This subject did not want to shock the victim, and he found it an extremely disagreeable task, but he was unable to invent a response that would free him from *E*'s authority. Many subjects cannot find the specific verbal formula that would enable them to reject the role assigned to them by the experimenter. Perhaps our culture does not provide adequate models for disobedience.

One puzzling sign of tension was the regular occurrence of nervous laughing fits. In the first four conditions 71 of the 160 subjects showed definite signs of nervous laughter and smiling. The laughter seemed entirely out of place, even bizarre. Full-blown, uncontrollable seizures were observed for 15 of these subjects. On one occasion we observed a seizure so violently convulsive that it was necessary to call a halt to the experiment. In the post-experimental interviews subjects took pains to point out that they were not sadistic types and that the laughter did not mean they enjoyed shocking the victim.

In the interview following the experiment subjects were asked to indicate on a 14-point scale just how nervous or tense they felt at the point of maximum tension (Figure 2). The scale ranged from "Not at all tense and nervous" to "Extremely tense and nervous." Self-reports of this sort are of limited precision, and at best provide only a rough indication of the subject's emotional response. Still, taking the reports for what they are worth, it can be seen that the distribution of responses spans the entire range of the scale, with the majority of subjects concentrated at the center and upper extreme. A further breakdown showed that obedient subjects reported themselves as having been slightly more tense and nervous than the defiant subjects at the point of maximum tension.

How is the occurrence of tension to be interpreted? First, it points to the presence of conflict. If a tendency to comply with authority were the only psychological force operating in the situation, all subjects would have continued to the end and there would have been no tension. Tension, it is assumed, results from the simultaneous presence of two or more incompatible response tendencies (Miller, 1944). If sympathetic concern for the victim were the exclusive force, all subjects would have calmly defied the experimenter. Instead,

Figure 2 *Level of Tension and Nervousness*

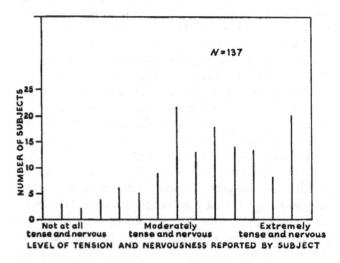

Figure 2 shows the self-reports on "tension and nervousness" for 137 subjects in the Proximity experiments. Subjects were given a scale with 14 values ranging from "Not at all tense and nervous" to "Extremely tense and nervous." They were instructed: "Thinking back to that point in the experiment when you felt the most tense and nervous, indicate just how you felt by placing an X at the appropriate point on the scale." The results are shown in terms of mid-point values.

there were both obedient and defiant outcomes, frequently accompanied by extreme tension. A conflict develops between the deeply ingrained disposition not to harm others and the equally compelling tendency to obey others who are in authority. The subject is quickly drawn into a dilemma of a deeply dynamic character, and the presence of high tension points to the considerable strength of each of the antagonistic vectors.

Moreover, tension defines the strength of the aversive state from which the subject is unable to escape through disobedience. When a person is uncomfortable, tense, or stressed, he tries to take some action that will allow him to terminate this unpleasant state. Thus tension may serve as a drive that leads to escape behavior. But in the present situation, even where tension is extreme, many subjects are unable to perform the response that will bring about relief. Therefore there must be a competing drive, tendency, or inhibition that precludes activation of the disobedient response. The strength of this inhibiting factor must be of greater magnitude than the stress experienced, else the terminating act would occur. Every evidence of extreme tension is at the same time an indication of the strength of the forces that keep the subject in the situation.

Finally, tension may be taken as evidence of the reality of the situations for the subjects. Normal subjects do not tremble and sweat unless they are implicated in a deep and genuinely felt predicament.

❧ Background Authority

In psychophysics, animal learning, and other branches of psychology, the fact that measures are obtained at one institution rather than another is irrelevant to the interpretation of the findings, so long as the technical facilities for measurement are adequate and the operations are carried out with competence.

But it cannot be assumed that this holds true for the present study. The effectiveness of the experimenter's commands may depend in an important way on the larger institutional context in which they are issued. The experiments described thus far were conducted at Yale University, an organization which most subjects regarded with respect and sometimes awe. In post-experimental interviews several participants remarked that the locale and sponsorship of the study gave them confidence in the integrity, competence, and benign purposes of the personnel; many indicated that they would not have shocked the learner if the experiments had been done elsewhere.

This issue of background authority seemed to us important for an interpretation of the results that had been obtained thus far; moreover it is highly relevant to any comprehensive theory of human obedience. Consider, for example, how closely our compliance with the imperatives of others is tied to particular institutions and locales in our day-to-day activities. On request, we expose our throats to a man with a razor blade in the barber shop, but would not do so in a shoe store; in the latter setting we willingly follow the clerk's request to stand in our stockinged feet, but resist the command in a bank. In the laboratory of a great university, subjects may comply with a set of commands that would be resisted if given elsewhere. *One must always question the relationship of obedience to a person's sense of the context in which he is operating.*

To explore the problem we moved our apparatus to an office building in industrial Bridgeport and replicated experimental conditions, without any visible tie to the university.

Bridgeport subjects were invited to the experiment through a mail circular similar to the one used in the Yale study, with appropriate changes in letterhead, etc. As in the earlier study, subjects were paid $4.50 for coming to the laboratory. The same age and occupational distributions used at Yale, and the identical personnel, were employed.

The purpose in relocating in Bridgeport was to assure a complete dissociation from Yale, and in this regard we were fully successful. On the surface, the study appeared to be conducted by RESEARCH ASSOCIATES OF BRIDGEPORT, an organization of unknown character (the title had been concocted exclusively for use in this study).

The experiments were conducted in a three-room office suite in a somewhat run-down commercial building located in the downtown shopping area. The laboratory was sparsely furnished, though clean, and marginally respectable in appearance. When subjects inquired about professional affiliations, they were informed only that we were a private firm conducting research for industry.

Some subjects displayed skepticism concerning the motives of the Bridgeport experimenter. One gentleman gave us a written account of the thoughts he experienced at the control board:

> . . . Should I quit this damn test? Maybe he passed out? What dopes we were not to check up on this deal. How do we know that these guys are legit? No furniture, bare walls, no telephone. We could of called the Police up or the Better Business Bureau. I learned a lesson tonight. How do I know that Mr. Williams [the experimenter] is telling the truth . . . I wish I knew how many volts a person could take before lapsing into unconsciousness . . .
>
> *[Subject 2414]*

Another subject stated:

> I questioned on my arrival my own judgment [about coming]. I had doubts as to the legitimacy of the operation and the consequences of participation. I felt it was a heartless way to conduct memory or learning processes on human beings and certainly dangerous without the presence of a medical doctor.
>
> *[Subject 2440 V]*

There was no noticeable reduction in tension for the Bridgeport subjects. And the subjects' estimation of the amount of pain felt by the victim was slightly, though not significantly, higher than in the Yale study.

A failure to obtain complete obedience in Bridgeport would indicate that the extreme compliance found in New Haven subjects was tied closely to the background authority of Yale University; if a large proportion of the subjects remained fully obedient, very different conclusions would be called for.

As it turned out, the level of obedience in Bridgeport, although somewhat reduced, was not significantly lower than that obtained at Yale. A large proportion of the Bridgeport subjects were fully obedient to the experimenter's commands (48% of the Bridgeport subjects delivered the maximum shock *vs.* 65% in the corresponding condition at Yale).

How are these findings to be interpreted? It is possible that if commands of a potentially harmful or destructive sort are to be perceived as legitimate they must occur within some sort of institutional structure. But it is clear from the study that it need not be a particularly reputable or distinguished institution. The Bridgeport experiments were conducted by an unimpressive firm lacking any credentials; the laboratory was set up in a respectable office building with title listed in the building directory. Beyond that, there was no evidence of benevolence or competence. It is possible that the *category* of institution, judged according to its professed function, rather than its qualitative position within that category, wins our compliance. Persons deposit money in elegant, but also in seedy-looking banks, without giving much thought to the differences in security they offer. Similarly, our subjects may consider one laboratory to be as competent as another, so long as it is a scientific laboratory.

It would be valuable to study the subjects' performance in other contexts which go even further than the Bridgeport study in denying institutional support to the experimenter. It is possible that, beyond a certain point, obedience disappears completely. But that point had not been reached in the Bridgeport office: almost half the subjects obeyed the experimenter fully.

✣ FURTHER EXPERIMENTS

We may mention briefly some additional experiments undertaken in the Yale series. A considerable amount of obedience and defiance in everyday life occurs in connection with groups. And we had reason to feel in the light of many group studies already done in psychology that group forces would have a profound effect on reactions to authority. A series of experiments was run to examine these effects. In all cases only one naïve subject was studied per hour, but he performed in the midst of actors who, unknown to him, were employed by the experimenter. In one experiment (Groups for Disobedience) two actors broke off in the middle of the experiment. When this happened 90% of the subjects followed suit and defied the experimenter. In another condition the actors followed the orders obediently; this strengthened the experimenter's power only slightly. In still a third experiment the job of pushing the switch to shock the learner was given to one of the actors, while the naive subject performed a subsidiary act. We wanted to see how the teacher would respond if he were involved in the situation but did not actually give the shocks. In this situation only three subjects out of 40 broke off. In a final group experiment the subjects themselves determined the shock level they were going to use. Two actors suggested higher and higher shock levels; some subjects insisted, despite group pressure, that the shock level be kept low; others, followed along with the group.

Further experiments were completed using women as subjects, as well as a set dealing with the effects of dual, unsanctioned, and conflicting authority. A final experiment concerned the personal relationship between victim and subject. These will have to be described elsewhere, lest the present report be extended to monographic length.

It goes without saying that future research can proceed in many different directions. What kinds of response from the victim are most effective in causing disobedience in the subject? Perhaps passive resistance is more effective than vehement protest. What conditions of entry into an authority system lead to greater or lesser obedience? What is the effect of anonymity and masking on the subject's behavior? What conditions lead to the subject's perception of responsibility for his own actions? Each of these could be a major research topic in itself, and can readily be incorporated into the general experimental procedure described here.

✣ LEVELS OF OBEDIENCE AND DEFIANCE

One general finding that merits attention is the high level of obedience manifested in the experimental situation. Subjects often expressed deep disapproval of shocking a man in the face of his objections, and others denounced it as senseless and stupid. Yet many subjects complied even while they protested. The proportion of obedient subjects greatly exceeded the expectations of the experimenter and his colleagues. At the outset, we had conjectured that subjects would not, in general, go above the level of "Strong Shock." In practice, many subjects were willing to administer the most extreme shocks available when commanded by the experimenter. For some subjects the experiment provides an occasion for aggressive release. And for others it demonstrates the extent to which obedient dispositions are deeply ingrained, and are engaged irrespective of their consequences for others. Yet this is not the whole story. Somehow, the subject becomes implicated in a situation from which he cannot disengage himself.

The departure of the experimental results from intelligent expectation, to some extent, has been formalized. The procedure was to describe the experimental situation in concrete detail to a group of competent persons, and to ask them to predict the performance of 100 hypothetical subjects. For purposes of indicating the distribution of break-off points judges were provided with a diagram of the shock generator, and recorded their predictions before being informed of the actual results. Judges typically underestimated the amount of obedience demonstrated by subjects.

In Figure 3, we compare the predictions of 40 psychiatrists at a leading medical school with the actual performance of subjects in the experiment. The psychiatrists predicted that most subjects would not go beyond the tenth shock level (150 volts; at this point the victim makes his first explicit demand to be freed). They further predicted that by the twentieth shock level (300 volts; the victim refuses to answer) 3.73% of the subjects would still be obedient; and that only a little over one-tenth of 1% of the subjects would administer the highest shock on the board. But, as the graph indicates, the obtained behavior was very different. Sixty-two percent of the subjects obeyed the experimenter's commands fully. Between expectation and occurrence there is a whopping discrepancy.

Why did the psychiatrists underestimate the level of obedience? Possibly, because their predictions were based on an inadequate conception of the determinants of human action, a conception that focuses on motives *in vacuo*. This orientation may be entirely adequate for the repair of bruised impulses as revealed on the psychiatrist's couch, but as soon as our interest turns to action in larger settings, attention must be paid to

Figure 3 *Predicted and Obtained Behavior in Voice Feedback*

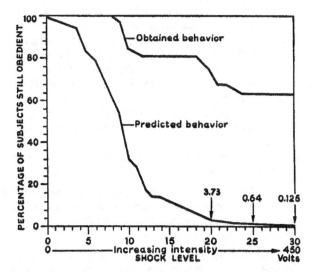

the situations in which motives are expressed. A situation exerts an important press on the individual. It exercises constraints and may provide push. In certain circumstances it is not so much the kind of person a man is, as the kind of situation in which he is placed, that determines his actions.

Many people, not knowing much about the experiment, claim that subjects who go to the end of the board are sadistic. Nothing could be more foolish as an overall characterization of these persons. It is like saying that a person thrown into a swift-flowing stream is necessarily a fast swimmer, or that he has great stamina because he moves so rapidly relative to the bank. The context of action must always be considered. The individual, upon entering the laboratory, becomes integrated into a situation that carries its own momentum. The subject's problem then is how to become disengaged from a situation which is moving in an altogether ugly direction.

The fact that disengagement is so difficult testifies to the potency of the forces that keep the subject at the control board. Are these forces to be conceptualized as individual motives and expressed in the language of personality dynamics, or are they to be seen as the effects of social structure and pressures arising from the situational field?

A full understanding of the subject's action will, I feel, require that both perspectives be adopted. The person brings to the laboratory enduring dispositions toward authority and aggression, and at the same time he becomes enmeshed in a social structure that is no less an objective fact of the case. From the standpoint of personality theory one may ask: What mechanisms of personality enable a person to transfer responsibility to authority? What are the motives underlying obedient and disobedient performance? Does orientation to authority lead to a short-circuiting of the shame-guilt system? What cognitive and emotional defenses are brought into play in the case of obedient and defiant subjects?

The present experiments are not, however, directed toward an exploration of the motives engaged when the subject obeys the experimenter's commands. Instead, they examine the situational variables responsible for the elicitation of obedience. Elsewhere, we have attempted to spell out some of the structural properties of the experimental situation that account for high obedience, and this analysis need not be repeated here (Milgram, 1963). The experimental variations themselves represent our attempt to probe that structure, by systematically changing it and noting the consequences for behavior. It is clear that some situations produce greater compliance with the experimenter's commands than others. However, this does not necessarily imply an increase or decrease in the strength of any single definable motive. Situations producing the greatest obedience could do so by triggering the most powerful, yet perhaps the most idiosyncratic, of motives in each subject confronted by the setting. Or they may simply recruit a greater number and variety of motives in their service. But whatever the motives involved—and it is far from certain that they can ever be known—action may be studied as a direct function of the situation in which it occurs. This has been the approach of the present study, where we sought to plot behavioral regularities against manipulated properties of the social field. Ultimately, social psychology would like to have a *compelling theory of situations* which will, first, present a language in terms of which situations can be defined; proceed to a typology of situations; and then point to the manner in which definable properties of situations are transformed into psychological forces in the individual.[9]

☙ POSTSCRIPT

Almost a thousand adults were individually studied in the obedience research, and there were many specific conclusions regarding the variables that control obedience and disobedience to authority. Some of these have been discussed briefly in the preceding sections, and more detailed reports will be released subsequently.

There are now some other generalizations I should like to make, which do not derive in any strictly logical fashion from the experiments as carried out, but which, I feel, ought to be made. They are formulations of an intuitive sort that have been forced on me by observation of many subjects responding to the pressures of authority. The assertions represent a painful alteration in my own thinking; and since they were acquired only under the repeated impact of direct observation, I have no illusion that they will be generally accepted by persons who have not had the same experience.

With numbing regularity good people were seen to knuckle under the demands of authority and perform actions that were callous and severe. Men who are in everyday life responsible and decent were seduced by the trappings of authority, by the control of their perceptions, and by the uncritical acceptance of the experimenter's definition of the situation, into performing harsh acts.

What is the limit of such obedience? At many points we attempted to establish a boundary. Cries from the victim were inserted; not good enough. The victim claimed heart trouble; subjects still shocked him on command. The victim pleaded that he be let free, and his answers no longer registered on the signal box; subjects continued to shock him. At the outset we had not conceived that such drastic procedures would be needed to generate disobedience, and each step was added only as the ineffectiveness of the earlier techniques became clear. The final effort to establish a limit was the Touch-Proximity condition. But the very first subject in this condition subdued the victim on command, and proceeded to the highest shock level. A quarter of the subjects in this condition performed similarly.

The results, as seen and felt in the laboratory, are to this author disturbing. They raise the possibility that human nature, or—more specifically—the kind of character produced in American democratic society, cannot be counted on to insulate its citizens from brutality and inhumane treatment at the direction of malevolent authority. A substantial proportion of people do what they are told to do, irrespective of the content of the act and without limitations of conscience, so long as they perceive that the command comes from a legitimate authority. If in this study an anonymous experimenter could successfully command adults to subdue a fifty-year-old man, and force on him painful electric shocks against his protests, one can only wonder what government, with its vastly greater authority and prestige, can command of its subjects. There is, of course, the extremely important question of whether malevolent political institutions could or would arise in American society. The present research contributes nothing to this issue.

In an article titled "The Dangers of Obedience," Harold J. Laski wrote:

"... civilization means, above all, an unwillingness to inflict unnecessary pain. Within the ambit of that definition, those of us who heedlessly accept the commands of authority cannot yet claim to be civilized men.

" .. Our business, if we desire to live a life, not utterly devoid of meaning and significance, is to accept nothing which contradicts our basic experience merely because it comes to us from tradition or convention or authority. It may well be that we shall be wrong; but our self-expression is thwarted at the root unless the certainties we are asked to accept coincide with the certainties we experience. That is why the condition of freedom in any state is always a widespread and consistent skepticism of the canons upon which power insists."

ENDNOTES

[1] This research was supported by two grants from the National Science Foundation: NSF G-17916 and NSF G-24152. Exploratory studies carried out in 1960 were financed by a grant from the Higgins Funds of Yale University. I am grateful to John T. Williams, James J. McDonough, and Emil Elges for the important part they played in the project. Thanks are due also to Alan Elms, James Miller, Taketo Murata, and Stephen Stier for their aid as graduate assistants. My wife, Sasha, performed many valuable services. Finally, I owe a profound debt to the many persons in New Haven and Bridgeport who served as subjects.

[2] Consider, for example, J. P. Scott's analysis of war in his monograph on aggression:

". . . while the actions of key individuals in a war may be explained in terms of direct stimulation to aggression, vast numbers of other people are involved simply by being part of an organized society.

". . . For example, at the beginning of World War I an Austrian archduke was assassinated in Sarajevo. A few days later soldiers from all over Europe were marching toward each other, not because they were stimulated by the archduke's misfortune, but because they had been trained to obey orders." (Slightly rearranged from Scott (1958), Aggression, p. 103.)

[3] It consisted of an extended discussion with the experimenter and, of equal importance, a friendly reconciliation with the victim. It is made clear that the victim did not receive painful electric shocks. After the completion of the experimental series, subjects were sent a detailed report of the results and full purposes of the experimental program. A formal assessment of this procedure points to its overall effectiveness. Of the subjects, 83.7% indicated that they were glad to have taken part in the study; 15.1% reported neutral feelings; and 1.3% stated that they were sorry to have participated. A large number of subjects spontaneously requested that they be used in further experimentation. Four-fifths of the subjects felt that more experiments of this sort should be carried out, and 74% indicated that they had learned something of personal importance as a result of being in the study. Furthermore, a university psychiatrist, experienced in outpatient treatment, interviewed a sample of experimental subjects with the aim of uncovering possible injurious effects resulting from participation. No such effects were in evidence. Indeed, subjects typically felt that their participation was instructive and enriching. A more detailed discussion of this question can be found in Milgram (1964).

[4] To obey and to disobey are not the only term one could use in describing the critical action of Y. One could say that Y is cooperating with X, or displays conformity with regard to X's commands. However, cooperation suggests that X agrees with Y's ends, and understands the relationship between his own behavior and the attainment of those ends. (But the experimental procedure, and, in particular, the experimenter's command that the subject shock the victim even in the absence of a response from the victim, preclude such understanding.) Moreover, cooperation implies status parity for the co-acting agents, and neglects the asymmetrical, dominance-subordination element prominent in the laboratory relationship between experimenter and subject. Conformity has been used in other important contexts in

social psychology, and most frequently refers to imitating the judgements or actions of others when no explicit requirement for imitation has been made. Furthermore, in the present study there are two sources of social pressure: pressure from the experimenter issuing the commands, and pressure from the victim to stop the punishment. It is the pitting of a common man (the victim) against an authority (the experimenter) that is the distinctive feature of the conflict. At a point in the experiment the victim demands that he be let free. The experimenter insists that the subject continue to administer shocks. Which act of the subject can be interpreted as conformity? The subject may conform to the wishes of his peer or to the wishes of the experimenter, and conformity in one direction means the absence of conformity in the other. Thus the word has no useful reference in this setting, for the dual and conflicting social pressures cancel out its meaning.

In the final analysis, the linguistic symbol representing the subject's action must take its meaning from the concrete context in which that action occurs; and there is probably no word in everyday language that covers the experimental situation exactly, without omissions or irrelevant connotations. It is partly for convenience, therefore, that the terms *obey* and *disobey* are used to describe the subject's actions. At the same time, our use of the words is highly congruent with dictionary meaning.

[5] A more detailed account of the laboratory procedure can be found in Milgram (1963). A similar and independently evolved experimental procedure, employing a shock generator, victim, and learning task, was reported by Buss (1961). Buss used the technique for studying aggression, not obedience, and did not make use of the fundamental measure employed in the present study: break-off points. His investigation promises to be a useful complement to the present research.

[6] It is difficult to convey on the printed page the full tenor of the victim's responses, for we have no adequate notation for vocal intensity, timing, and general qualities of delivery. Yet these features are crucial to producing the effect of an increasingly severe reaction to mounting voltage levels. (They can be communicated fully only by sending interested parties the recorded tapes.) In general terms, however, the victim indicates no discomfort until the 75-volt shock is administered, at which time there is a light grunt in response to the punishment. Similar reactions follow the 90- and 105-volt shocks, and at 120 volts the victim shouts to the experimenter that the shocks are becoming painful. Painful groans are heard on administration of the 135-volt shock, and at 150 volts the victim cries out, "Experimenter, get me out of here! I won't be in the experiment any more! I refuse to go on!" Cries of this type continue with generally rising intensity, so that at 180 volts the victim cries out, "I can't stand the pain," and by 270 volts his response to the shock is definitely an agonized scream. Throughout, he insists that he be let out of the experiment. At 300 volts the victim shouts in desperation that he will no longer provide answers to the memory test; and at 315 volts, after a violent scream, he reaffirms with vehemence that he is no longer a participant. From this point on, he provides no answers, but shrieks in agony whenever a shock is administered; this continues through 450 volts. Of course, many subjects will have broken off before this point.

A revised and stronger set of protests was used in all experiments outside the Proximity series. Naturally, new baseline measures were established for all comparisons using the new set of protests.

There is overwhelming evidence that the great majority of subjects, both obedient and defiant, accepted the victim's reactions as genuine. The evidence takes the form of: (a) tension created in the subjects (see discussion of tension); (b) scores on "estimated pain" scales filled out by subjects immediately after the experiment; (c) subjects' accounts of their feelings in post-experimental interviews; and (d) quantifiable responses to questionnaires distributed to subjects several months after their participation in the experiments. This matter will be treated fully in a forthcoming monograph.

(The procedure in all experimental conditions was to have the naïve subject announce the voltage level before administering each shock, so that—independently of the victim's responses—he was continually reminded of delivering punishment of ever-increasing severity.)

[7] Admittedly, the terms *proximity, immediacy, closeness,* and *salience-of-the-victim* are used in a loose sense, and the experiments themselves represent a very coarse treatment of the variable. Further experiments are needed to refine the notion and tease out such diverse factors as spatial distance, visibility, audibility, barrier interposition, etc.

The Proximity and Touch-Proximity experiments were the only conditions where we were unable to use taped feedback from the victim. Instead, the victim was trained to respond in these conditions as he had in Experiment 2 (which employed taped feedback). Some improvement is possible here, for it should be technically feasible to do a proximity series using taped feedback.

[8] The third condition also led to significantly lower obedience than this first situation, in which the experimenter was present, but it contains technical difficulties that require extensive discussion.

[9] My thanks to Professor Howard Leventhal of Yale for strengthening the writing in this paragraph.

REFERENCES

Buss, A. H. (1961). *The psychology of aggression.* New York and London: John Wiley.

Kierkegaard, S. (1843). *Fear and trembling.* English edition, Princeton: Princeton University Press, 1941.

Laski, H. J. (1929, June). The dangers of obedience. *Harper's Monthly Magazine, 159,* 1–10.

Milgram, S. (1961, January 25). *Dynamics of obedience: Experiments in social psychology.* Mimeographed report. *National Science Foundation.*

Milgram, S. (1963). Behavioral study of obedience. *Journal of Abnormal Social Psychology, 67,* 371–378.

Milgram, S. (1964). Issues in the study of obedience: A reply to Baumrind. *American Psychology, 19,* 848–52.

Miller, N. E. (1944). Experimental studies of conflict. In J. M. Hunt (Ed.), *Personality and the behavior disorders.* New York: Ronald Press.

Scott, J. P. (1958). *Aggression.* Chicago: University of Chicago Press.

Biographical Note

Stanley Milgram conducted cross-national experiments in the
Institute for Social Research, Oslo, and the Laboratoire de
Psychologie Sociale, Sorbonne, in 1957–59. He spent a year at
the Institute for Advanced Study, Princeton, and received a
Ph.D. in Social Psychology from Harvard University in 1960.
He completed the experiments described here while an assis-
tant professor of psychology at Yale University. Subsequently,
he joined the Department of Social Relations faculty at
Harvard, where he teaches experimental social psychology.

The present paper was awarded the Socio-Psychological Prize of the
American Association for the Advancement of Science in
1964.

❧ Questions

1. Why is the difference between "obedience" and "cooperation" important to Milgram?

2. What conflict did the participants face in this study? Why
   did Milgram present participants with this conflict? What
   are participants' options for dealing with this conflict?

3. Why were "no vocal feedback" and "mild protests" ineffective in getting participants to stop shocking the "victim"? Why were these conditions useless in an
   experimental study of obedience?

4. Did participants perceive the victim's responses as genuine, or did they realize that the responses were fake? What
   evidence is there to support your view?

5. What would be the correct "specific verbal formula" that
   would have freed participants from the experimenter's
   authority? Does our culture provide adequate models of
   disobedience? Why or why not?

6. What does the social context or the situation have to do
   with obedience?

7. Comment on Milgram's statement that "human nature,
   or—more specifically—the kind of character produced in
   American democratic society" cannot be counted on to
   resist authority. Do you agree or disagree? Why? Is the
   problem one of "character" or something else? Explain
   your reasoning.

8. Are there aspects about this study that you think were
   unethical or harmful to participants? Are there steps
   Milgram could have taken to minimize these problems? In
   your opinion, should Milgram have been allowed to conduct these studies? Could he have studied the question of
   how far people would go to obey an authority figure without raising ethical problems? Explain.

Chapter 13

Persuasion and Power

Automobile salesmen have honed stepwise selling into an artform. I not only took jobs selling cars during my research but studied many other dealerships. Some have converted to nonnegotiable, "no hassle" Saturn-type pricing. Most, however, have retained the classic methods of car sales to one degree or another.

I encountered vast differences in techniques. But I was struck by how many of the best salesmen employ the grammar of patient, step-wise sequences. In most dealerships, the staff is required to follow specific steps. I observed programs using everywhere from seven to twelve or more steps, all of which covered pretty much the same ground. Some agencies require sales staff to review the steps on a daily basis or at weekly meetings; that's because if they have to turn a customer over to colleague during the sales process, they can tell their colleague what step they're on. One of the most impressive salesmen I came across was Michael Gasio, who sold new cars for fifteen years. Gasio followed a ten-step procedure, which he explained to me.

The initial step, as in any sale, is getting a foot in the door. In the auto business, this means getting the customer on the showroom lot. Sometimes customers come on their own, other times the salesman needs to push in front of his competition. This may entail a bit of deception. There is, for example, a variation of the foot-in-the-door technique known in the trade as "throwing the lowball." "The lowball," Gasio says, "is when I give you a price that no one else can beat. I quote you a figure that's lower than invoice and tell you not to pay any more somewhere else. I know that no matter what price they give you at another place you're going to come to see me." (There's also what's called "throwing the highball," which is when the salesman offers an unreasonably high trade-in price for a customer's old car.)

From: John Levine, reprinted from *The Power of Persuasion: How We're Bought and Sold* (2003), by permission of John Wiley & Sons, Inc.

When I myself was selling cars I heard a lot about a related technique called the bait and switch. In this case, the salesman quotes a low price for the exact car the customer wants. When the customer comes to the lot, however, he learns that the advertised car is missing an important feature. The salesman then finds another car on the lot with that feature—but at a higher price.

The lowball and the bait and switch are often thrown at customers who are in the "just looking" stage, such as when they're phoning around for price comparisons. Gasio's response when he gets these phone inquiries is "I'm pretty sure I can get it for you at ———" and then names a sub-invoice price. He tells the customer to come in and ask for him by name when he or she is ready. "I've dug a hole I'll have to work to get out of," he observes, "but I know the customer will come back." The lowball is phrased to elicit the first small commitment from the customer, Gasio says. "The big question I ask is 'If I could, would you?' That's the key to a telephone call. Knowing that I can't do it, I still ask him, 'If I could, would you?'"

Most important, it gets the customer physically on the lot. The moment the customer comes and asks for him, the lowballing salesman becomes entitled to split half the commission should another colleague eventually make the sale. This split is recognition from the agency of how crucial it is to get that first foot in the door.

The lowballer knows his deception will eventually work against him, so he makes a fast exit. "I immediately 'turn' the customer to another salesman," Gasio says. "I'll have a phone call. I'll have an emergency. I'll need to go to the bathroom. I'll have some excuse to turn you over to another salesman." Later on, the new salesman explains that the lowballer made some mistake when he quoted such a low price. During my research, I heard a multitude of excuses: "He misunderstood which model you were asking about." "He forgot to figure in the options you wanted." The new salesman might distance himself from the lowballer: "He's had a lot of personal problems lately." "Frankly, we've been having terrible trouble with him." My favorite explanation came from Gasio himself: "Because there's a contest here and he wanted to get you in so he could win a prize."

Once the customer is on the lot, the salesman proceeds to steps two and three: selling himself and the dealership. This begins with the "meet and greet." "There's a five-minute window to decide whether or not the customer likes you," Gasio says. "If they don't like you, they'll use you for the information you have and they'll dump you. If I don't feel I'm in control after the first five minutes, I'll turn you to a new salesman." If the customer was lowballed into coming in, this means seeing a third salesman. During those first five minutes, however, a good salesman would have sized up the customer well enough to decide whom to turn him to. Usually it's someone who has things in common with the customer. The "turner" tells the new salesman what step he's on in the sales process and then disappears.

A cardinal rule in sales is to avoid questions that may result in the answer "No." This is particularly true in the early stages of the process. A dangerous meet-and-greet question, for example, is "May I help you?" The invariable response is "No, I'm just looking," which stops the salesman cold. (Every salesman I interviewed said the most common opening words they heard from customers were "I'm just looking.") Instead, one manager I worked for instructed, I was to hold out my hand and say, "I'm Bob Levine. And you are . . .?" Virtually every customer will return the handshake, and the vast majority will respond with at least their first name. Similarly, later on in the sales process, instead of asking the customer a question such as whether she liked a particular car, the salesman might ask, "Would you prefer the economy of the four-cylinder engine or the power of the six-cylinder?" Avoiding "No" answers discourages the chain of commitments from being broken.

The salesman then sells the dealership. "I want you to know you've made a wise choice in coming to my dealership," Gasio explains. "At the last place I worked, we'd tell you, 'The company has been here for twenty-seven years. The owner has a good name in the community. I may not be here when you need something, but he will.'" Another approach at this step is to bring up social proof. One dealer I studied would say, "I know your neighbors like us because we're growing twenty-five percent a year." Another dealership—one where I worked—made a point of letting the customer know that it was the biggest volume dealer in our city. The salesperson applauds the customer for choosing that dealership.

These early steps ask the customer for very small commitments—essentially to acknowledge the credibility of the agency. More important, however, they start the clock ticking. This is no small matter. One of the early goals is to slow the customer down. The passage of time, in fact, almost always works in favor of the salesman. For one thing, as we've seen earlier, the time spent with the salesman activates the reciprocity norm. We know that since the salesman is working on commission, the time he spends with us is, in a sense, costing him money. If he's established good rapport with us, we're left with a feeling of obligation (i.e., the reciprocity rule) to do something for him in return.

The passage of time also works against the customer in other ways. Since we live in a society where time is money, it means any time we spend at this dealership is an investment—a deposit of sorts. If nothing productive comes of the visit, we've wasted our time. We've blown our deposit. It's the sunk-cost trap.

"You have to stall them," Gasio observes. "The main thing in sales is you make it such a long process they don't want to go through it again." The customer is inclined to say, "Just tell me your best price. I'm in a hurry." But if the salesman does that, it rarely leads to a sale. "The salesman needs to cover all the steps in their precise sequence," Gasio observes. "Before we talk about price, I need time to get you to surface all your objections. As long as you're willing to express your reservations, I'll find a way to overcome them. Otherwise, I know you're not serious and I'm going to 'broom' you [sweep you off the lot]. The rule is 'If you don't have time to drive it, I'm not going to give you a price.'" You'll notice that many salesmen—Gasio included—don't wear a watch. Like casinos without clocks in Las Vegas, they want you to stay longer than you'd planned.

Now the salesman turns to the product. Step four is "the walk." "I'm going to take control now," Gasio says. "I'm going to have you follow me all around the lot. I show you every car. 'I don't want to look at trucks,' you might complain when we move in that direction. 'But I need to show you this Ranger,' I explain, 'because I want you to see the stereo since it's the same system I can get for you in the Maverick you want.'" The salesman gets you in deeper and deeper by "giving you" as much of his time as possible. Gasio points out that time also works for him in another way: "Maybe I waste so much of your time that the next dealership is closed."

"All the while, I'm establishing in you a mind-set of obedience to my authority. The walk begins when I say, 'Come with me.' I've given you an order. You can choose to follow it or reject it. But I can tell you from experience that almost every customer is going to come with me. I get you to follow me in as many ways like this as I can."

Some agencies teach salespeople to do the "turn and walk" whenever they start losing control. "If I see you fading off while I'm showing you a car," another salesperson told me, "I turn and walk toward a different car. Or toward my office. Ninety-nine percent trail right behind me. I walk. You follow."

Step five is the "walk around," sometimes known as the "seven-point walk around." You're getting closer to a car here. "I'm now going to find out if I'm still in control," Gasio says. "We start in the front of the car. I pop the hood and tell you to look under it. If you follow my instructions, I know everything's going fine. Then we go around to the passenger side. When I sold Volvos, for example, I'd emphasize the safety features, things like the childproof door locks. Eventually I work you over to the driver's side. I tell you to sit in the car and I show you the dashboard. During the walk around I explain everything I can think of about the car to you. Most people get bored by this, so I give you a reason to listen to me, maybe that 'Someday you'll have to know these things to resell the car.' I'm not selling you a car. I'm educating you. I'm your friend."

Step six, after the customer gets in the car, is the watershed commitment—the test-drive. When my student researchers and I went car shopping, we found that if we appeared the least bit reluctant at this point the test-drive might begin by surprise. Jenny Gutierrez, for example, was being led on the walk around when the salesman told her to get inside and see how it feels. "Next thing I knew, he sat himself in the driver's seat, closed the door, and off we went. He never asked if I wanted to go for a test-drive." Gasio confirmed the common use of this approach. "When I worked for Ford, the front seat made it easy. You'd set the customer in the driver's seat and then you'd scoot them over and we were gone, off the lot and on the demo drive." For some customers, Gasio uses a softer approach. "Sometimes I'll say, 'I know you may not be ready to buy this car, but I'll get ten points if you go with me on a test-drive.' (There are no such points, of course.) Once we start, I always drive far enough away so you'll have a nice long drive back when I put you behind the wheel."

The overriding goal of the test-drive is to build "mental ownership." One of my sales trainers taught me to refer to everything about the car as "yours" during the test-drive: "Let me show you how to adjust your mirrors." "How do you like your sound system?" "These are the controls for your air conditioner."

Used-car dealers sometimes take mental ownership a step further by following the test-drive with a technique called the "puppy dog close." The customer is encouraged take the car home for a while with the expectation that the car, like a puppy, will grow on you and everyone else at home. A saleswoman from the used-car sales division of a large rental company told me that her agency aggressively encourages potential buyers to borrow the car. "We try to generate attachment during the test-drive," she observed. "But if that doesn't work, we encourage them to take it home by themselves overnight, or even for the weekend. When they do, that usually makes the sale." If the attachment takes as planned, the idea of returning the car becomes as uninviting as returning your puppy to the pound.

But the test-drive itself is often attachment enough. "After the test-drive," Gasio says, "I do what we call 'the assumed close.' I'm assuming that one hundred percent of the people who have followed me to this stage are going to buy a car. Otherwise, you just wasted my time. So I'm assuming we now have an agreement to sell you a car." One agency I trained with taught us to test the assumed closed by stating/asking (auto salespeople are good at masking statements as questions), after the test-drive, "Looks like we found the right vehicle for you and your family?" If the customer doesn't immediately object, the salesperson becomes more assertive: "Bob, go ahead and park it in the sold line and I'll start the paperwork." "Bob, were you going to register this in just your name or did you want Vickie on the title, too?" "You folks are going to love your new van. Did you want us to install the roof rack today, or do you want to bring it back on Thursday?" The salesman may now do a turn and walk into his office.

Step seven is requesting a hypothetical commitment. "I ask you," Gasio says, "'how much would you be willing to pay for this car to buy it today? Give me an offer, even if it's ridiculous, to bring to my boss.' One of the rules in the automobile business is 'Don't come to the manager without a commitment.' Most of the time the customer's in a hurry and asks you to just go to your boss and ask the lowest price he'll take. If the salesman does that, he's lost control and isn't going to finish the sale. So I ask you again, 'What's it going to take today?' I want a commitment."

The customer usually responds with an impossible offer—say, $20,000 for a $25,000 car. The salesman doesn't challenge the offer. He explains that he's not authorized to change the marked price. Only the boss can do that. But if we work together, the salesman tells you, we can figure a way to convince the boss to agree to your proposal. "I turn to the trade-in now," Gasio explains. "'What if I can get you a good price for your old car?' I ask. I start very low. 'We took a car like yours in about a month ago. It wasn't quite as nice as yours'—we always say that, to give us flexibility later—'and I think they only gave him $500 for it.' I write the figure '$500' on the paperwork so you'll be aware of it the whole time we're negotiating." The customer is usually startled by the low price. The salesman calms him down and eases up in small increments. "You don't want to give the money away fast," Gasio says. "It's important to leave room for a lot of steps. Maybe I say, 'What if, instead of five hundred, I could go seven hundred and fifty?' I now put one line through '$500' on the paper—making sure you can still see the number—and write '$750' above it. 'No, no, I want $3,000,' the customer screams. In the corner of the paper, very small, I write '$3,000.' I say, 'Sir, if I can get the manager to go to $1,000, would that make us a deal?' The customer undoubtedly says no, again. But I've made some small steps here which set up my next move."

Now the salesman plunges aggressively for a commitment. "'You asked for a $5,000 discount on the new car. Is that correct?'" Gasio asks the customer. "I wait for them to answer 'Yes.' 'And you want $3,000 for the trade-in?' 'Yes,' they say. Then I ask, 'What if I can get you eight thousand for your old car? Will we have a deal today?' I proceed to negotiate the same way on the down payment and your monthly payments. I need to get a commitment about how much you can afford a month. I write the figure down. What I don't write down is the number of months of payments."

Eventually, the customer agrees to the proposal. The salesman, of course, hasn't committed to anything other than bringing the customer's offer to his boss. "Now we have the customer initial the page," Gasio says. But this round isn't over. "Since you've agreed to this offer," he tells the customer, "you shouldn't have any objection to filling out a credit application." The customer is made to fill out the application completely. If you don't have some required information about one of your references, the salesman may have you phone the person. (The dealer rarely has any need to call the references. When they do phone the references, it's sometimes to try to sell them a car by emphasizing the great deal their friend or relative just got.)

Some dealers squeeze you further during the credit check. For example, a finance manager may come out and ask how serious you are about buying the car. It costs money, he explains, to run a credit check. He might toss out a figure like $20 or $50 or whatever. You're getting in deeper and deeper.

Step eight—if you're trading in a car—is the appraisal process. Before turning your car over to the agency's appraiser, the salesperson may tell you that he needs to get some information about the automobile. He walks around the car taking down information like your license and vehicle numbers and the car's mileage and features. While doing this, he makes a point of touching, usually without making comments, every obvious flaw—scratches, stains, oil leaks. This is known as "trade devaluation." It's intended to lower your expectations for the trade-in price.

Other commitments occur during the appraisal process. "In order to appraise your car," Gasio says, "you're now going to give me two things you've probably given to no other salesman—the keys and registration to your car. Mentally, you're kissing that car good-bye. And if I'm successful, you'll never see these items again." Giving up your keys can also lead to other problems: if you decide to leave during negotiations, some devious agencies have been known to "misplace" the keys to hold you hostage while the salesman applies more sales pressure.

Some dealers use your old car to rub a contrast effect in your face. The buildings in most car lots have glass all around. The salesman takes advantage of this by parking the car you've just test-driven so you're looking right at it. When your old car comes back from the appraisal it gets parked next to the new one.

At step nine, the customer is asked to commit money. "You need to give me something to bring to my boss that shows him your offer is in good faith," Gasio tells them. "What can you give my boss to show you'll buy this car if he accepts your offer?" The salesman might suggest the customer write a check for $1,000. If the customer doesn't have a thousand, he's asked to come up with whatever he can. The dollar amount is less important than making some commitment. In dealer terminology, the salesman is now trying to "tie 'em in close." If the customer says he doesn't have his checkbook with him, the salesman might come up with some money himself under the assumption that just getting the customer to sign the form is a better commitment than nothing. (The salesman's money is removed from the order as soon as the customer leaves.) The salesman wants to "put the guy on paper." But it's most effective to have the customer commit his or her own money, no matter how little the amount.

The salesman now carries the offer to the manager. After an appropriate lapse of time, the salesman returns with the news, which you on some level expected, that your offer has been refused. The boss doesn't give a counteroffer. This sets the stage for step ten—the "bumps." The customer is asked if there's a way he or she can raise their earlier offer, perhaps by increasing the monthly payments or the down payment or accepting a lower trade-in price. "I don't set the size of the bump. You do," Gasio points out. "I ask you, 'What can you come up with?' And the size of your bump gives away something critical, because a big bump predicts another big bump." The sequence of bumps plays the rule of escalating commitments to the hilt: "As soon as I get a bump," Gasio says, "I write down the new figure, have you sign your initials, and I get up and leave. I'm not going to try for another bump right then. I'm only trying for one bump per round."

Other psychology may also be used here. The salesman may, for example, coerce you with limited-time, scarcity pressures. You might be offered limited-time-only rebates or told this price is *today only*. The salesman may emphasize that people who hesitate may lose their first choice. In an agency where I worked, there was a sign posted on the wall of every salesperson's office that read "The car you looked at today and want to think about till tomorrow may be the car someone looked at yesterday and will buy today." In another agency, one of my students, Amanda Morgan, was negotiating the price of a white '99 Ford Escort when a voice came over the loudspeaker announcing: "Congratulations to Mr. and Mrs. Marcus Smith on their purchase of a '99 white Escort." "The salesman's head jerked up," Morgan recalled. "'White '99 Escort? I hope that's not the one we were looking at!' He then punched in some numbers and breathed a sigh of relief as he assured us it wasn't the car we wanted."

Some salesmen exert more generalized time pressure. Tony Razzano, who works out of the Gold Coast of Long Island, is reputed to be the most successful salesman of used, ultraluxury cars (Jaguars, Rolls-Royces, Bentleys, etc.) in the country. ("I could sell ice to an Eskimo," he says about himself.) Razzano encourages reluctant customers with the carpe diem philosophy. In a world of anthrax and terrorists, he reminds them, "why would you wait for tomorrow to get what you want today, when tomorrow may never come?"

The salesman hopes that some of this motivates you to up your offer. If you do, he then brings the new offer to the manager. But, alas, he soon returns with the news that it, too, has been rejected. Again the customer is asked if he can raise his offer. If so, the salesman gets your initials and immediately leaves. This process is repeated over several rounds. If the customer refuses to bump up to an acceptable price, he's turned over to another salesman or manager or whatever for another try. Some agencies are known as T/O (turnover) houses, meaning that at some point in the process every customer gets turned over to a higher-up who presses for a new bump.

The bumps continue until the deal is closed, which is the final step. As salespeople say, "Closers are the winners."

For Gasio, this is the end of the process. "Buying and paying for the car are different stories," he observes. "I just want you to sign to buy it. Someone else can figure out how you'll pay for it later. That's the finance manager's problem. As soon as we get that sold sticker in the window, we're done. We could care less about you."

What advice does Gasio have for potential car shoppers? "Buyer beware, always," he says. "You need to recognize that your hormones become imbalanced in this process and that this can make a difference between having a clear head and making the wrong deal. Be patient. Never forget that if it's a good deal today, it's going to be a better deal tomorrow. And there's no such thing as an absolute best deal. You have to decide when you're comfortable. Is the car something you can afford and something you like? If not, there's absolutely no reason to finish the transaction without sleeping on it. You'll have a better perspective in the morning."

And beware of the illusion that you can outsmart the dealer. "People almost always think they're good at negotiating," Gasio observes. "It's worst when they're with close friends or lovers—then the macho and ego feed their illusion even more. As a salesman, I'll let you look like a big shot for a while. Until I go in for the kill. The salesman will joust with you all day. I'll let you think you're in control at first. But when the time comes, I'll knock you off your horse. Even if I don't, you're not going to win the match. You can't. Because it's always the manager who decides when it's over—either when he gets his price or decides to broom you."

There's also a postscript to Mike Gasio's story—and it's an encouraging one. Gasio quit the auto sales business a few years ago and began a new career. He's now a teacher and counselor to at-risk youths in an inner-city junior high school in Fresno, California. But although the content of his message has shifted, much of its form remains the same. Gasio applies the same process of escalating commitments to effect change in his students that he did to sell cars to his customers. He doesn't confront students with the value of achieving good grades or other long-term goals until they're ready to accept these challenges, no more so than he would have quoted a bottom-line price to a customer before the end of the selling process.

"With these kids," he observes, "the motivation has to be something other than a letter grade. The grade has no value to them as a reinforcer because an F doesn't hurt them. You've lost that power over the students as a teacher because the grade has no meaning or consequence." Instead, Gasio has developed a point system that begins with short-term goals and builds from there. The points are written on a chalkboard—much like the paper he used to put in front of car buyers to tally offers and counteroffers. Gasio sets the students up in teams. This develops camaraderie and cooperation while at the same time taking advantage of peer pressure. If their team succeeds, they immediately see the points on the board. Students trade the points in at the end of the week for longer-term reinforcers—soda, candy, bus tickets, or whatever else has value to them. Eventually points are saved for even longer-term rewards.

More than anything, what Gasio learned from car sales is the importance of getting the customer on the lot. He translates this to the school environment by offering students the most points for just showing up on time. Then, to begin their work. The points for accomplishments diminish as the day goes on.

The great Taoist Lao-tzu once observed, "The journey of a thousand miles begins with a single step." Or, as Mike Gasio might say, get a foot in the door and you're halfway home.

Some techniques bring a paradoxical approach to the escalation sequence by pushing a request to or beyond its acceptable limit and

Index